The 305th Field Artillery in the Great War

The 305th Field Artillery in the Great War

History of the 305th Field Artillery
Charles Wadsworth Camp

In France With Battery F 305th Field Artillery
Ben Jacobson

The 305th Field Artillery in the Great War

History of the 305th Field Artillery
by Charles Wadsworth Camp

I*n France With Battery F 305th Field Artillery*
by Ben Jacobson

Leonaur is an imprint of Oakpast Ltd

Material original to this edition and
presentation of text in this form
copyright © 2010 Oakpast Ltd

ISBN: 978-0-85706-381-6 (hardcover)
ISBN: 978-0-85706-382-3 (softcover)

http://www.leonaur.com

Publisher's Notes

The views expressed in this book are not necessarily
those of the publisher.

Contents

History of the 305th Field Artillery
Charles Wadsworth Camp
7

In France With Battery F 305th Field Artillery
Ben Jacobson
285

History of the 305th Field Artillery

Charles Wadsworth Camp

CHAPTER 1

The Regiment is Born

When it comes to beginnings, regiments are not unlike humans. They aren't pretty objects, or self-sufficient. They gaze upon the world with inquiring eyes. They address it with lusty and surprised lungs.

We were very much like that, and our first surprises came with our first days, when the men commissioned from the second battery at the first Plattsburg Reserve Officers' Training Camp reported at Camp Upton.

The adjutant's office was in an unpainted wooden barracks. A line stretched hour after hour, snake-like, half around it, its head investigating the sombre corridor where the adjutant's assistant sat making assignments. Nearby, those who had survived the ordeal stood in groups, ill-at-ease, wondering.

"What is a casual officer? Something to do with casualties?"

"They told me at Plattsburg," you might hear another say, "I was in the regimental quota. That fellow in there says no. I'm in a thing called Military Police, and when I told him I'd never swung a billy in my life he wanted to know what that had to do with it."

"I'm in the Depot Brigate," a third grinned sheepishly. "Good God! Do we have to run the trains?" A captain walked from the corridor and came up with a pleased smile.

"What did they hand you?" someone asked.

In his voice was pride, and a vague, new responsibility.

"I'm assigned to the 305th Field Artillery, National Army."

Several joined as in a chorus:

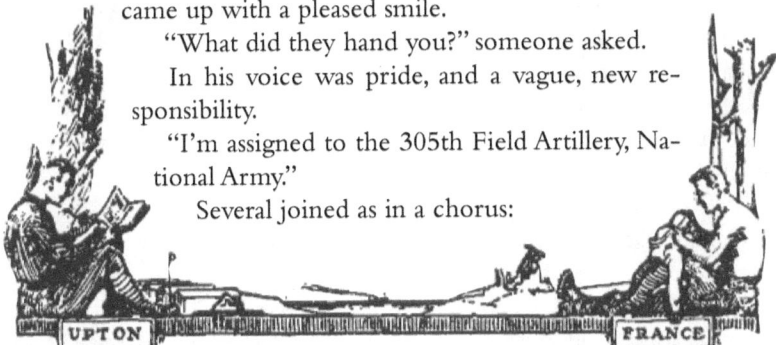

Drawn by Private Enroth, Battery D

"So are we. That's going to be the number of our regiment."

And the surprise and gloom deepened on the faces of those shifted thus unexpectedly to unforeseen branches of the service.

After that fashion the regiment was born and baptized, and we heard for the first time the significant number in which officers and men have, to an extent, merged their thoughts, their actions, and their individualities.

Colonel Fred Charles Doyle was the first to report. He came from the regular army, and received his assignment from Major-General Bell on August 28th, 1917. For ten days afterward the officers poured in and commenced to prepare for the men who would arrive in the course of the next few weeks.

Without the men, during those days of its beginnings, it wasn't, to be sure, much of a regiment, yet it possessed from the start ambition, pride of organization, and already—a noticeable factor—an instinct that ours was to be bigger, better, and more terrible to the enemy than any other regiment of Field Artillery.

Yet we went gropingly at first, asking earnest but absurd questions about equipment and rations, or demanding with concern where we could house even a single section. For the welcome Camp Upton gave us was not of arms outstretched and smiling hospitality. We had stepped from New York through a screen of dreary pine wilderness to an habitation, startling and impossible.

A division was to be trained here to fight the Hun, but to any observing person it appeared that if the war should last another decade Camp Upton could not become useful. It wore an air of having just been begun and of never wishing to be finished. A few white pine barracks stretched gaunt frames from the mud against a mournful sky. Towards the railroad two huge tents had an appearance of captive balloons, half-inflated.

For the rest there were heaps of lumber of odd shapes and sizes, and countless acres of mud, blackened by recent fires—half-cleared land across which was scattered a multitude of grotesque and tattered figures. These workmen went about their tasks with slow, indifferent gestures, their attitudes suggestive of a supreme faith in the eternity of their jobs.

Some of us gathered on Division Hill the night of our arrival. We gazed from the little that was done to the immensity that remained untouched.

"Where are they going to put the 305th?"

Captain Devereux had gathered some information. He pointed to the northwest.

"That's the area assigned to the regiment. We'll live and train there."

For a long time, with sceptical eyes, we continued to stare at that blackened desert. We strolled back to J22, our temporary quarters, depressed and doubtful. In the barn-like upper floor, where we had erected cots, we gathered about a candle lantern, and in low tones probed the doubtful future. Colonel Doyle, who was to be the regiment's commander from its birth to its final demobilization, was to us that night no more than a name. He lived somewhere on Long Island and would be in camp the next day. At least we had a colonel, but who would be our lieutenant colonel? We had one major, made at Plattsburg. What about the other we needed?

Lieutenant Derby pronounced the first of the regiment's innumerable rumours. It should be said, too, that it's about the only one that ever came true. He had heard in town that Henry L. Stimson, former Secretary of War would come to us as lieutenant colonel.

We gossiped about the unexpected shifting about of our friends. Many that we had expected to have with us had been quietly spirited away. Others, whom we had not hoped to see after Plattsburg, sat in our circle, assigned to the regiment. We had, at the start, found the army full of odd surprises. It gave us all, for the moment, a sense of instability. Our commissioned tables of organization, filled out painstakingly the last night at Plattsburg, would have radically to be revised. Nor was that the only unexpected task. We couldn't forget the black waste, seen from Division Hill. Before many days the men of the first draught would stream in. We would have to share in the miracles that would feed, clothe, and house them; that would give them that vital initial impression they were going to be taken care of in the army. Our doubts increased when we sought our own washing facilities that first night. Who will forget the scouting among piles of lumber, the stumbling over roots and stumps, the escapes from superbly imitated swamps, or the final, triumphant discovery of a single pipe and faucet, surrounded by a mob of violent temper? For more than a thousand officers had reported at that time, and of the twenty-five thousand workmen of the Thompson-Starret Company, some undoubtedly craved that which is next to Godliness. Even then there may have been other pipes at Upton, but for a time that one remained our only discovery; and it had a miserable habit of falling languidly over into the mud unless it was supported by a comrade who had the strength and the will to fight off an army.

Yet we shaved. Yet we contrived to look clean.

"Horrors of War, No. 1," we labelled our pipe.

So we struggled on, preparing ourselves as best we could for the day when the first enlisted men would arrive. We gazed at night with new interest at the multitude of fires that blazed, crimson, against the forest, surrounded by ragged groups of workmen, who sat for the most part in a sullen and unnatural quiet. For the miracles happened under our eyes. Day by day the wilderness receded, the mushroom city spread. This morning you might walk in a thicket. Tomorrow you would find it cleared land, untidy with the beginnings of buildings. A faith grew that the 305th would have a home.

Side by side with these, other and more intimate miracles developed. Colonel Doyle established a regimental headquarters on a mess table in the mess hall of Jl. Whatever stateliness it may have acquired later, headquarters went in those days, as one might say, on hands and knees. Colonel Doyle explained how things should be done, and we did our best to do them right. Already from the pots and pans of J1 Paper Work raised an evil head and sneered at us.

Before we'd got the table really untidy with baskets and typewriters and files and reports, other organizations came enviously in, and established headquarters on that table too. There was a machine gun battalion, the ammunition train, and maybe a bakery company or so. Things became rather too confused for an accurate count. We stole quietly to J20, to the upper floor of which we had already moved our sleeping quarters.

That same afternoon Major Wanvig appeared, bearing under each arm an oblong board sign. One he nailed at the entrance of the building. The other he fastened to a post by the road, so that no one passing could deny the presence he approached.

Each of these signs bore on a white background in striking black strokes: "Headquarters, 305th F. A. N. A."

We stood about staring.

"That's us—the 305th Field Artillery. Are we going to make it big and successful enough?"

There were at least no visible shirkers, and we had acquired already a belligerent disposition to stand fast for the rights of the regiment. That was as it should have been, since we were destined to be among the first of the combat organizations. There was, moreover, need of such a spirit.

Take J20, for example. Once you had got a bit of floor space there the whole world conspired to tear it from you, or, as more convenient, you from it. Regimental Headquarters had established itself modestly in a corner of the lower dormitory. Officers of high rank sought sleeping space, complaining that we were in their way. Brigade Headquarters sent messengers to measure us broad and long. Commanding officers and adjutants of various organizations, quartered in the same building cast in our direction threatening glances. Low-browed hirelings of the Thompson-Starret Company came, demanding the return of panels of Upson board and pieces of deformed lumber with which we had endeavoured to barricade ourselves against an eager and conscienceless world. In spite of everything Regimental Headquarters clung to its corner until, in late

October, it moved to its own building in the 305th area. Those few weeks in J20, moreover, witnessed our adolescence. When we tramped across the hill we were, indeed, a regiment.

September 6 was a day that must be recorded noticeably. It saw the first enlisted personnel of the 305th. His name was Frank Dunbaugh. He stood at attention before Colonel Doyle, saluting.

"Private Dunbaugh reports as directed."

And behold we were a regiment—officers and man!

We all, I think, felt a call to take out that pleasant young fellow and give him dismounted drill, simulated standing gun drill, physical exercise, semaphore, wig-wag, and buzzer; the beginnings of firing data, and scouting; with, perhaps, in his off moments, a little of grooming and horse-shoeing, and the theory, at least, of equitation.

But he was a little man, and Division Headquarters tore him from us before we could really annoy him. An order came down: "Private Frank Dunbaugh is relieved from duty with the 305th F.A. N.A., and is attached to Division Headquarters," and so forth.

Paper Work grinned.

For that matter he had plenty to chuckle over already. Headquarters was aware by now of his portly and increasing figure. General Orders, Special Orders, Memoranda, and Bulletins were suspended in neat wads from the wall. Captain Gammell, the regimental adjutant, threaded his way among them with haughty ease. At his suggestion, indeed, an officer brought from Division Headquarters a bundle the size of a small bale of cotton. We gathered around it, admiring the countless neat forms it contained, all labelled "A. G. O., No. so and so."

"What a system!" everybody gasped.

What a system, indeed! But we couldn't dream of all those delicate forms portended. Captain Gammell distributed them. Colonel Doyle explained how simple it was to handle them, and we turned again to the apparently more serious business of getting ready.

Shorn of their sole enlisted personnel the officers with grim determination pounced upon each other. There was no reasonable drill ground, but we took ourselves to the stumps and the logs of half cleared spaces. We drilled each other. We shouted at each other. We abused each other. How, we asked, would new officers and men take this or that?

"If you make a rookie laugh it's all off," an officer said after an exceptionally piercing cry of command.

"Or," another put in dryly, "If you give him the impression you're going to murder him he won't respond cheerfully enough."

We endeavoured, therefore, not to resemble fools or assassins. Sometimes it was difficult.

Each day now, for a time, Colonel Doyle rescued us from our harsh treatment of each other. He took us to the slope of Division Hill where we sat on charred logs and listened to him discourse at length on various methods of computing firing data, or interpret the Articles of War and Army Regulations, drawing on his long experience in the Regular Army.

The activity about us was frequently distracting, unreal, a trifle prophetic. In the rapping of countless hammers you could fancy the stutter of machine guns. The fall of heavy timbers was suggestive of the crash of rifles of our own calibre. At the base of the hill, to give a more realistic touch of war, lay the encampment of the coloured troops of the 15th New York National Guard.

It should be recalled in passing that these dusky doughboys were a very small oasis of soldiers in a thirsty desert of officers. In salutes and courtesies they received a maximum of practice.

Lieutenant Colonel Stimson came to us during one of these classes. That was on September 6, and by evening of the next day the last of the officers sent down from the First Plattsburg Training Camp had reported and been assigned or attached to the 305th. Since the majority of them led the regiment into its first battles a record should be made of their names in this chapter of beginnings. We commenced then with the following officers, most of whom had abandoned civil life only three months earlier:

Colonel Fred Charles Doyle, commanding the regiment; Lieutenant Colonel Stimson, temporarily assigned to the command of the First Battalion; Major Harry F. Wanvig, commanding the Second Battalion; Captain Arthur A. Gammell, regimental adjutant; 2nd Lt. Allen A. Klots, acting adjutant, First Battalion; Captain Douglas Delanoy, adjutant Second Battalion; Captain M. G. B. Whelpley, commanding the Headquarters Company; 1st Lt. Edward Payne, temporarily in command of the Supply Company; Captain Alvin Devereux, commanding Battery A; Captain

Drawn by Private Enroth, Battery D
Headquarters Hill, Camp Upton

Gaillard F. Ravenel, commanding Battery B; Captain Noel B. Fox, commanding Battery C; Captain Frederick L. Starbuck, commanding Battery D; Captain Robert T. P. Storer, commanding Battery E; Captain Cornelius Von E. Mitchell, commanding Battery F; First Lieutenants Sigourney B. Olney, George P. Montgomery, William M. Kane, Harvey Pike, Jr., Watson Washburn, James L. Derby, Edgar W. Savage, Frank Walters, and Drew McKenna; Second Lieutenants Sheldon E. Hoadley, Thornton C. Thayer, Norman Thirkield, George B. Brooks, Lydig Hoyt, Thomas M. Brassel, Lee D. Brown, Chester Burden, Charles W. Camp, Paul Jones, Oliver A. Church, Roby P. Littlefield, William H. M. Fenn, John R. Mitchell, Warren W. Nissley, Harold S. Willis, Frederick L. Beck, Danforth Montague, Melvin E. Sawin, George P. Schutt, Lloyd Stryker, Lawrence Washington, John A. Thayer, Karrick M. Castle, Harry G. Hotchkiss, George E. Ogilvie, William L. Wilcox, Lewis E. Bomeisler, Jr., Darley Randall, and Edward W. Sage.

Almost at once changes were made in this list of our charter members, as one might call them. Officers were assigned away from us, while strangers were brought into our midst. Thirty-five of the charter members accompanied the regiment to France. After the armistice there remained only nineteen.

The eternal changes of the army system were largely responsible for these losses, as they accounted also later for the passing of many enlisted men, but whenever we meet the old friends we think of them as belonging peculiarly to the 305th. Some we can't see again, because the Vesle, the Aisne, or the Argonne holds them forever away.

But it is a dreary business to anticipate. They were very much with us and very much loved at Upton.

So the first week ended, and we were, speaking sketchily, on our feet, if still unsteady.

CHAPTER 2

It Has Growing Pains

Going into the second week the colonel talked daily with his organization commanders. Such conferences revolved largely about the almost scented forms from the Adjutant General's Office. These, it developed, would, when the men arrived, have to be decorated with countless, neat statistics. Soldiers, as far as we knew, might go hungry or without equipment, but, as far as figures went, they would unquestionably be cared for tenderly. No one would have the slightest doubt as to their most intimate family history, the number of years it had taken them to dribble through public or private institutions of learning, or their degree of proficiency on mandolin, harmonica, or Jew's harp.

The officers at that period filled forms about themselves in odd moments. The most persistent and suggestive demanded the name of the relative one wished notified in case one should become a casualty. Whenever in America or France things got a little slack a request for that information would come around. It kept one, as it were, on one's toes. But we wondered why that bureau never got fed up with paper work.

Into these daily conferences, almost at once, crept a sense of imminence. Huge bulletins descended from Division Hill dealing now in dates. They described with an admirable detail how the first of the draught men would be received. To aid us in this task non-commissioned officers, it was promised, would be sent us from the Regular Army. They appeared one day—a score or so for our regiment.

We looked at them. We looked at their service records. Then we looked at each other. We swallowed our first lesson in how to send, on order, one's best men to some other organization. Certainly, in this case, few commanding officers had parted with their jewels. Some of these rough diamonds, we suspected from a comparison of dates, indeed, had been set in chevrons for our needs, There lay their records of battery punishments and courts martial. We pitied those distant, unknown commanders. If these were their best we shrank from picturing their days and nights with the worst. The audacity of the thing caught our imagination. There was, we felt, something to be had from it. They weren't all bad, by any means. Some became the most useful of soldiers.

Our medical department arrived about the same time, a worried-looking little group, that trudged through the dust, dodging piles of lumber. It was led by Lieutenant James B. Parramore, who later became captain, and for a time, regimental surgeon. Lieutenant Dennis J. Cronin was assigned as 1st Battalion Surgeon, and Lieutenant Marshall A. Moore as 2nd Battalion Surgeon.

That very day Dr. Parramore constructed a table in Regimental Headquarters. He placed upon it with proud gestures a tin of alcohol, a demijohn of castor oil, a few assorted pills, and gallons, literally, of iodine. He announced himself open for business.

Business, fortunately, was dull, so the adjutant reached out for Parramore's enlisted personnel, sat them on a bench in the hall, and—Behold!—for the first time Regimental Headquarters had orderlies. There was no doubt about it. We were growing.

On September 27th the arrival of our chaplain, John J. Sheridan, was another reminder; and two days later the long dreamed of moment arrived. Five hundred and thirty-five recruits were assigned to the regiment.

These men, of course, did not come directly to us from their local boards. We received them after two weeks' work of reception and assortment in which all the officers of the division shared. During that phase the once strange term "casual" became a by-word. For all the draught men arrived at Upton as casuals. Officers met the first train loads at Medford on September 15th.

There are, let it be granted, few days in the history of our country more impressive than that one which saw the triumph of universal service and the birth of our great national army.' But it is rather so from a distance, for in the minds of the officers and men who assisted there lingers beyond question, woven with the sublime, a palpable tracery of amazement and mirth.

The draught came in ancient railroad coaches whose sides were trimmed with placards suggestive of an abnormally swift and terrible march to Berlin, via Upton; and a number of penalties for the Kaiser, very ingeniously thought out.

Then there was the provocative personal adornment. There had been word in the papers that all civilian clothing worn to Upton would have to be cast away. So these young men took no chances. Tattered straw hats were thrust from the windows; crushed derbies, through which wisps of hair straggled; top hats, in a few cases, so venerable that it was a pity to see them out of their sepulchres. And Palm Beach suits of previous summers were there, and the dinner jacket, an affair of generations, and the suit that had been worn on Sundays long before the owner's maturity. It was an assortment that would have taxed the sanity of a Hester Street dealer.

You tried to sound the meaning of such a trip to these young citizens. You could only sense definitive separations from home and comfort and affection; a shrinking from our uniforms, which meant a discipline, terrifying and undesired; and, perhaps, a perplexed apprehension, somewhere just ahead, of violence and the close of experienced things.

No mind, however, could linger on that side. There were too many races, clamorously asserting themselves. There had been too much made of a number of departures. There still lingered too many souvenirs of feasts. Out of the shadows slipped an eager voice.

"Hay, Tony! Finish off that bottle before these officer guys can grab it."

And another, less concerned:

"Grabba da hell. My gal, she givva me a charm against da evil eye of officers."

And some had reached the point where speech ends.

A man in uniform grew disgusted.

"So," he grumbled, "that's what we've got to teach to fire a three inch gun!"

But we knew he was wrong. He had judged by the high lights. In the really fundamental background we saw a sober and determined spirit. We felt even then the presence of some of the best soldier material in the world.

After meeting a few of these erratic train loads the least confident of shavetails could forecast his ordered garrison tasks with ease of mind. For such recruits weren't simple to control.

When we gathered at night in J20 the gossip of every group revolved around the arriving casuals.

"How many souses did you have today, Bill?"

"Two. One wanted to weep on my shoulder, and the other wanted to give me an uppercut."

"What did you do about it?"

"Ordered the fighting one to take care of the weeper."

"Say! Did he?"

"You bet. Closed both eyes so the tears couldn't get out, and satisfied himself at the same time. I remember he shouted as he swung: 'Hay, Boss! It's a grand war!'"

Those already in uniform, none the less, felt a quick sympathy for the newcomers. Their individualities slipped away from them so easily! At the station they were labelled and assigned to barracks. They were herded and marched in long, uncouth lines, to the hospital for physi-

Drawn by Musician Boyle, Hq. Co.

cal examination. We formed squads and tried to instruct them in the school of the soldier. Rich and poor, Hebrew and Gentile, short and long, straw-hatted, felt-hatted, or without any hats at all, they faced us, eager, one knew, to learn.

"One, two, three, four. One, two, three, four. Squad halt. Right face. Left face. About face."

Those that couldn't speak English very well got the commands confused. Others had a curious lack of balance. All had a disposition to laugh at mistakes and accidents, and to discuss and argue about them while in ranks at attention.

At morning and evening roll-call argument was warmest. No linguist existed, sufficiently facile to scan that list intelligibly. Sprinkled among remembered English names were pitfalls of Italian, Russian, Spanish, Lithuanian, German, even Chinese.

"Krag—a—co—poul—o—wicz, G."

The officer, calling the roll, would look up, expecting the response his triumph deserved. A protest would come, as likely as not in fluent lower New York accents:

"Do yuh mean me? That ain't the way tuh say my name. Me own mother wouldn't recernize it."

"Silence! Simply answer, 'here.'"

In a tone of deep disgust:

"Then I ain't here. That's all. I ain't here."

An appreciative laugh would ripple down the ranks. Men learned to be officers and non-commissioned officers in those days.

Afterwards the citizen soldiers would get their mess kits, and, sitting on burned stumps or Thompson-Starret rubbish, would eat a palatable meal. For the food was coming from somewheres, and the gear to dispose of it.

We had noticed that Walters, Payne, and Savage were up to something. During long hours they sat in Regimental Headquarters studying documents. Then they filled out many forms, and sample clothing and equipment straggled into the barracks. This meant a new phase, and now, as we labelled, we equipped. We became tailors, hatters, booters. We would begin the night's work by choosing as comfortable a place as possible in the mess hall with a pile of pink qualification cards before us. The queue of awkward and pallid youths would form.

"Name?"

It would flow out in various accents. More frequently than not it would demand painstaking spelling.

Education, occupation, average wages, capacity for leadership, ability to entertain, previous military experience—it all went down. There was one question in which we took a special interest.

"For what branch of the service do you wish to express a preference?"

Some had weighed the matter carefully. They believed themselves born to the Quartermaster's Corps, but the majority had not foreseen that interrogation, nor, if they had, it is likely that the meat of their answer would have had a different texture. Its sincerity was sometimes naive.

"Oh, hell! I don't care, just so I lick the Choimans."

We concentrated on the finest. Shamelessly we proselytized, out of this impromptu mission came some of the regiment's best.

Those hours of dreary, yawning statistics, moreover, had their relieving moments. Here comes a slender young man in the familiar suit of remote beginnings. The officer asks him formally the formal question.

"Wages in your last job?"

"$50,000 a year."

That officer, one recalls, rose to the occasion, for the young man was not boasting.

"And I understand you wish to express a preference for the Field Artillery?"

Wasn't it Hoadley who faced a youth just the reverse of this last—that is, flashily tailored?

"What can you furnish in the way of entertainment?"

"Me?" the flashy young man replied. "I could steer the village miser into a poker game, and, believe me, bo, I can make a deck of cards lay down and roll over. What's the idea? What d'ye mean? I got to split with you?"

When he declared for the Cooks and Bakers his choice went down without argument.

Afterwards we would line our charges up again and desert qualification cards for sample shoes and hats and clothing. Sizes were limited, and we hadn't suspected before nature's infinite variety in modelling the human form. We made an axiom at the start. The more peculiar the shape, the more particular the owner.

"For the lova Mike, mister, I can't wear that coat. Makes me look as if I'd broke me breast bone." Or: "You got to melt me to get me into this."

Everybody worked with patience and a desire to be fair, but, just the same, you had to make both ends meet and as the hours flew by you may have hurried a little.

It was during these sessions that a rotund and good-natured officer gave us a stirring example and prophesied his own future.

"You're in luck. That's a wonderful fit," you'd hear him say to a man with a 38 chest lost in a 36 blouse. "You're a perfect 36. Might have been cut for you."

The man would gather a fistful of the excess cloth, stretching it towards the officer.

"Cut for an elephant."

"The tailor will alter it so it won't look like the same blouse."

"I'm not saying anything about its looks. All I'm saying is maybe it isn't quite big enough for a good-sized elephant."

The officer's buttons would stretch.

"If you want to get along in the army, young man, you'll do as you're told. I wouldn't mind wearing that blouse myself."

"But," an officer would whisper to him. "You're not quite as big as a good-sized elephant."

The officer would grin and continue to show us how to make the best of the material in hand.

"That hat isn't too big for you," he would call out in his cheery voice. "Gives your hair a chance to grow."

So we struggled on through the days and nights until the first quota was classified and at least partially equipped. And out of that quota came for us, as related, five hundred and thirty-five recruits—not far from half a regiment.

"The men we're to live and fight and die with," someone said.

It wasn't to turn out quite like that. We didn't foresee the wholesale transfers, the all-night conferences when officers and non-coms tried to do the fair thing without destroying their organizations. Still those dark days of transfers fall more reasonably in another chapter. For the present we were a trifle hypnotized by our growth and our power. We looked along the lines, guessing at the good and the bad for, like all regiments, we had both.

The faces we saw were pretty white, and the frames not, as a rule, powerful. For we were a part of the Metropolitan Division. Most of our men came from the crowded places of New York. Out of city dwellings, offices, subways, and sweatshops they poured into the wind-swept reaches of Upton. They knew none of the tricks a boy picks up in the country that fits him, after a fashion, for such fighting as we were destined for in the Vosges, on the Vesle and Aisne, in the Argonne, and on the Meuse.

"Will soldiers grow from such material?" visitors asked.

From the start officers and men knew the answer as affirmative. Day by day beneath the bland autumn sun faces bronzed, chests seemed to expand and shoulders to broaden before the tonic of physical labour. For it wasn't all drill. The miracles continued, but there weren't enough civilian workmen available to construct the city, to clear vast spaces for drilling, and to arrange artillery and small-arms ranges. So orders came for the draught men to pitch in and help. Thus commenced the cheerful game of stump pulling.

Of our original quota there are very few that couldn't qualify as expert destroyers of wildernesses. The famous skinned diamond exists as a monument to our skill. The target range is a document written in the passionate sweat of our brows.

During this education the first effects of discipline were apparent. Faces might darken with rage or whiten from weariness, but in the realized presence of a superior work went on without too painful comment. Occasionally, if hidden through chance by a screen of bushes, you might hear burning opinions of army life in general and stump snatching in particular. At school we had been taught that the average man's vocabulary is scarcely more than five hundred words. The understatement is obvious. Any soldier of the 305th who couldn't apply as many adjectives as that to the common noun "stump" was frowned upon as mentally deficient or as one affecting an ultra religious pose.

Such tasks were, in a sense, a digging of a pitfall for one's own feet. As the skinned diamond expanded our drills waxed proportionately ambitious. But the entire process was performing another miracle. Where formerly had slouched slovenly ranks appeared now straight lines of soldierly figures, heads up and shoulders squared, exuding a joy in things military.

"What's all this guff about West Point?" you'd hear. "Watch my outfit drill any day."

And the veterans of a week or so exposed a most amusing tolerance for newer recruits. The difference between a uniform and civilian clothing created an extensive gulf. In a few days it would be bridged. The awkward squad of the day before would face the awkward squad of today with expressions of veteran contempt. For the recruits poured in during

October. On the first we received one hundred and thirteen, on the ninth one hundred and eighty-three, on the tenth two hundred and fifty-four, on the twelfth, two hundred and eight. So that by the end of that month we had forty-one officers assigned, eighteen attached, and one thousand three hundred and thirteen enlisted men. The 305th was a regiment. All we needed were horses and guns to realize that we were, indeed, artillery, designed to throw projectiles at the Huns.

How you felt the first time the Medical Officer, used your arm for a Pin Cushion

Drawn by Musician Boyle, Hq. Co.

To give variety to our stump-pulling sport Colonel Doyle called our attention to certain long, low and harmless-appearing buildings across Fifth Avenue. Still living in the J section, remote from these constructions, the men hadn't suspected in them any further spur to their vocabularies. Now, it seemed, they were to be our stables. The civilian workmen's responsibility had ceased when they had put up sides and roofs. The rest we must do. We had many fences to build around them, and more land to clear for riding rings and paddocks. We were encouraged to enormous efforts on October 18th when the government presented us with eight mules. They were led to the most comfortable stable. They were treated as honoured guests.

Quite fittingly, our first veterinarian, Lieutenant North, arrived soon after.

The problem of our missing field officer was solved on October 14th when Major Thomas J. Johnson reported. No one had an opportunity just then to know him very well or to judge him competently. It wasn't until we had reached Prance that we were to realize our good fortune.

For on October 26th he was detailed to the School of Fire at Fort Sill. Major Wanvig left for the same destination on November 7th.

Without formal battalion commanders the work of the regiment continued, in view of the lack of equipment, amazingly well. Reserve officers of only a few months' training displayed exceptional qualities of leadership. New soldiers wanted to learn. An artilleryman must be able to do more than use a sight, work a breach, or pull the lanyard. The chances of the draught had given the 305th a number of highly-educated specialists for the more complicated work of conduct of fire, and the delicate details of scouting and communication. To that important extent the regiment was already better off than some of the older organizations. By day the officers instructed and drilled the men, and by night the officers went to school themselves to Colonel Doyle and Lieutenant Colonel Stimson, who did the best they could with the slight material at hand to keep us abreast of artillery developments in the war zone. When finally we got to France we were overwhelmed to realize all we had to learn.

****

When now we glanced from the slope of Division Hill at the bleak landscape which only a few weeks before had aroused our scepticism we saw barracks, quarters, and department buildings rising from the ashes of the forest.

Piecemeal, during October, the regiment moved from the J section to its own area. The change was complete on October 24th. As we had policed J and its vicinity so we made our surroundings in M neat and military. Officers and men received a fortunate impression of permanence. As long as we remained in Upton we would have our own home. Things, we felt in our ignorance, were going well. Even a band had been collected, and could play one or two pieces in public with comparative safety.

During the latter part of October and the first part of November the officers were brought a little closer to their mission. They were conducted by twos and threes to Sandy Hook to watch the practical working of projectiles and fuses; and forty attended a six-day artillery course in New Haven under the experienced instruction of Captain Dupont, of the French Army, and Captains Bland and Massey, of the Canadian artillery.

It was on these trips that most of the officers saw for the first time the famous *soixante-quinze*. They admired it as a piece of artillery perfection without being able to guess that it would be their companion for many months, a thing nearly as animate as the men who served it.

What we actually got at Upton at this time was a single battery of venerable three-inch guns, relics of the 51st Field Artillery Brigade, New England National Guard. Lieutenant Colonel Stimson snared this for us, together with much other useful equipment which aroused the envy of less fortunate organizations who didn't have a former secretary of war. Certainly one battery among six was better than none.

When the guns arrived on November 10th the regiment gathered around them, patted them fondly, examined their mechanism, peered down their throats.

Pride leaped.

"God help Jerry when we show him these!"

But Jerry never saw them. Perhaps one day in the dust of some ordnance museum they may be observed by all the world—precious relics of the extended battle of the 305th at Camp Upton.

Chapter 3

And Becomes Acquainted With Paper Work

Paper Work had now become our perpetual companion. Neither by night nor by day did he leave us lonely. He strutted at mess. He paraded across the drill ground. He sat by one's cot through the troubled watches of the night. It becomes, therefore, necessary to study the creature's habits.

Let us take a fanciful case that everyone can understand, since even in those early days Corn Willy was omnipresent. Let us suppose that a mess officer desires some information about this old friend. His impulse might be to dash off a note like this:

Capt. Blank
Dear Sir:
Having heard that you've made a life study of the subject, it's occurred to me that you might tell me how it is possible to make Corn Willy palatable.

If one didn't care to bother the colonel about details of paper work, Captain Gammell was always glad to put one right.

"Not at all, my dear young mess officer. Not at all. You must send it through channels."

"I don't think his office is far away. I might just run up and see him."

"What nonsense, my poor ignorant young mess officer! In that case what record would exist of this matter?"

So picture the mess officer in question studying in "Army Paper Work" all about going through channels. As a result he might turn out something like the following:

Camp Upton
N.Y.
October—,1917
From: 2nd Lt. Blank

To: C. O.
Dep't of Household Enemies
Subject: Corn Willy
I. Information is desired as to any known method of making corn willy palatable.
(sig) *John Blank*
2nd Lt., 305th F.A.

That would occupy some two inches on a sheet of foolscap. A few months later Lt. Blank, probably in charge of stables now, might receive a breathless messenger, bearing a huge envelope with his original sheet of foolscap pinned to reams of endorsements. These would run something like this:

1st Ind. From C. O., Bat'ry Blank, To C. O., 305th F.A.

1. Forwarded.

2. Approved.

2nd Ind. From C. O., 305th F.A. to Com. Gen. 152nd F.A. Brigade, with, perhaps, a paragraph or two.

3rd Ind., From Com. Gen. 152nd F.A. Brigade, to Com. Gen. 77th Division, with, perhaps, several paragraphs, scarcely ever more than a word in length.

4th Ind., From Com. Gen., 77th Div., to Adjutant General of the Army.

1. For investigation of record of Private C. Willy.

5th Ind., From Adjutant General of the Army to Com. Gen., 77th Div.

1. Received.

2. Contents noted.

3. No record.

4. Should be forwarded to Quartermaster General of the Army.

6th Ind. Prom Com. Gen. 77th Div. to Quartermaster General of the Army.

7th Ind. Prom Quartermaster General of the Army, to C. O. Subsistence Division.

8th Ind. C. O. Subsistence Division, to Chief Q. M., Dep't of East.

9th Ind. Chief Q. M., Dep't of East to C. O. Eastern Subdivision Department of Household Enemies.

10th Ind., From C. O. Eastern Subdivision of Household Enemies to Lt. Blank. (Through Channels)

1. Received.

2. Contents noted.

3. No method Known.

"What shall I do with it now that I've got it?" asks Lt. Blank.

"What would you suppose?" is the tolerant answer of the expert. "It has become a matter of official record. Consequently it must be preserved for ever, or nearly so. File it away."

"There isn't much room left in our barracks," says Blank hopelessly.

But the expert, you may be sure, doesn't let him brood over that very long.

"Your morning report was in a shocking state today, Blank."

"But I sat up all night, making out individual horse records."

"No excuse. How many horses *have* you got, anyway?"

Blank gulps.

"In the stables, or on paper?"

He retreats with visions of facing charges.

****

That matter of preparing charges, by the way, sprinkled with grey the temples of organization commanders, and the scanning of charge sheets made many an enlisted man fancy his last hour had arrived. Every "Whereas," and "In that he did", must be in its proper place; and, no matter how accurately the sheet might set forth the vivid language usually employed by the accused, unless "or words to that effect" capped the quotation the whole business was sent back to the drawer with caustic comment.

In those days men learned to be expert witnesses, and officers became judge advocates, counsels for the defence, and judges with supreme power. But most of the cases brought before the regimental courts martial were not vicious ones. There really were surprisingly few of any sort. It was inevitable we should have one type of case, for home was very near Camp Upton, and passes were not plentiful. A handful of men, when they did get home, found it strangely simple to miss the proper trains back. When they missed too many, battery punishment wouldn't cover the crime, and they had to stand trial.

Tuesday was the worst day. Then such little dramas as this were not infrequent:

Scene: The orderly room. Battery Commander at his desk, outwardly tyrannous and uncompromising; at heart, fighting a very human sympathy (Some battery commanders have been known to wish that they, too, might have stayed an extra twenty-four hours with their families). Opposite: Culprit stands, shame-faced, pulling at his hat. B. C.—Stop pulling at your hat. Stand at attention. (Culprit snaps his heels together)

B. C.—Now, Doe, what possible excuse have you for overstaying your pass twenty-four hours? The time was written down. The other men got back. You know what it means, Doe, to be A. W. O. L.

(That sequence of four letters has a sound suggestive of blank walls and firing squads.)

Culprit, (Head drooping, voice thin and tremulous) Well, sir, you see me mother-in-law was down already with the rheumatiz. She was that bad that——

B. C, (Impatiently) Go on. Go on.

Culprit, (less confident)—and me wife was took Sunday night with the same terrible disease. I was just leaving for the train, too, and I couldn't get a doctor, and—

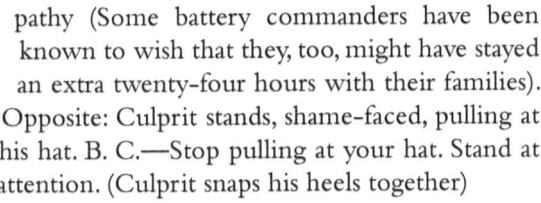

Drawn by *Muncian* Boyle, Hq. Co.
Reflections on Liberty were alike a Upton and in France

B. C. (In an arctic voice) That's enough, Doe. Those excuses were old when Noah overstayed his leave from the ark.

Culprit—(A gleam of disappointed tears in his eyes) I told 'em I wouldn't get away with it, but, hones' to Gawd, Captain, they was the best lies we could think of, and me mother-in-law said the last thing: "Stick to it, Tim, no matter what your cocky officer says."

****

In an army, plentifully sprinkled with men of German or Austrian descent, it was, of course, necessary to be cautious. "When is an enemy alien not an enemy alien?" became for a time the pet riddle of the paper workers. From month to month the successful answer appeared to alter, yet, except from the point of view of paper work, it troubled us little.

There were, however, conscientious objectors—not many, just enough to irritate soldiers who couldn't express their displeasure in a natural, fistic fashion without infringing the law. Were the most of these creatures nervous or sincere, men asked? Their days and nights in barracks, I fancy, weren't to be coveted. For a conscientious objector, whose sincerity you couldn't question, you might conceive a certain admiration, but with such a war facing a nation the burden of proof, unfortunately, rests on the objector.

Worst of all, conscientious objectors complicated paper work. From many sources came orders and suggestions as to their treatment; and when they flagrantly refused to obey commands, as they had a nasty habit of doing, they had to be court-martialled, and they usually picked the most inconvenient times for their performances, arguing, perhaps, that salvation lay there. We desired to see the last of them. But how? Providence reaches its ends in devious ways.

This is really not straying to another topic. Just then one of our castles tumbled. We weren't going to live, fight, and die together as we had started at Upton. Specific orders commenced to arrive, demanding large numbers of men. Up to the end of November we had lost by transfer two assigned officers, two attached officers, and 346 men. We got in return First Lieutenant Frederick H. Brophy, of the dental corps, on October 16th; Second Lieutenants George H. Hodenpyl, Karl R. McNair, and William A. Walsh, on November 12th; Second Lieutenant H. Stanley Wanzer, on November *22nd;* and some straggling enlisted replacements.

It is impossible to say where those friends of a few weeks went. They left, more often than not as casuals, bound for some remote division in the South or West. We didn't see them again.

This abrupt snapping of barrack ties painted for us more colourfully the serious nature of our new profession. With a sober comprehension we watched the small bands of casuals, bent beneath blue barrack bags, go lurching down Fourth Avenue to the station—away from Upton, away from us who had more often than not learned to like them, away from the land of passes home.

The philosophy of the average soldier is direct and competent. It was after such an exodus that one explained to his companions during mess:

"What's the use of grouching? That's what war is—saying goodbye. Just saying goodbye, fellows. Might's well get used to it now."

These partings, nevertheless, weren't all sentiment. Let us value them at one-third regret and two-thirds paper work. The orders demanding them frequently slipped into the regimental area during the quiet hours before the dawn. Anything that awakened you was known as a Trick Order. Trick Orders seldom came singly. For several nights running they would glide in, lights would gleam from orderly rooms until shamed by the sun, and all those concerned would display at reveille acute symptoms of insomnia. There was no evasion when trick orders rustled through the camp. If a battery commander sought a way by preparing a list against unexpected transfers, Paper Work merely sneered, thinking of the devices he had up his sleeve. At three a. m., it might be, a red-eyed battery clerk would appear at a captain's cot.

"Sorry to disturb you, sir."

A groan.

"Barracks on fire?"

"No, sir. An order's just come to transfer five men."

The captain cries out, sitting up.

"Don't you know this is the first sleep I've had for three nights? Didn't I give you a list just so I could get some sleep?"

"Yes, sir," replies the battery clerk gently, "but this is a very tricky trick order. The men are to be reported at the station fully equipped, at 5:30 this a. m. They'll be equipped, even though the supply sergeant does lead a hunted life for a while. Meantime I've brought the service records for the captain to initial."

The battery commander surrenders, convinced that, no matter how artfully you may dodge, paper work will always tag you around the corner.

The preparation of these lists for transfers was a delicate matter. That's why the subject wasn't changed when we slipped away from conscientious objectors a moment ago.

Some soldiers, clearly, could be better spared than others. A few, officers and men desired enormously to get rid of. But we couldn't picture running along at all without the greater part. It had been impressed upon us that by *men* was meant men of the first quality. At conferences on the subject developed a touching and sublime faith in human nature, an out-and-out belief that in the very worst of artillerymen resides a mine of extraordinary virtue only requiring the delving of the receiving officer. And, one might add, even in the very most conscientious of conscientious objectors. . . .

The battery commander glances up from his roster.

"Could we," he asks, "spare this man Richard Roe?"

"It would be like amputating a limb," a lieutenant answers, "but it might be managed."

The battery commander grunts.

"Didn't realize he was as bad as that. What the deuce is the matter with him? Isn't he strong and handy? Doesn't he look like a soldier?"

"If you look hard the other way."

The first sergeant says in a small voice.

"He's a conscientious objector, sir."

"Goodness gracious! I'd quite forgot that."

"Do we sit in judgment on a man's religion?" someone asks gruffly.

"My dear boy! It isn't a religion at all. It's a state of nerves."

"I don't care what any one says," the lieutenant puts in, "he's got *the* makings of a good soldier—if properly handled"

The battery commander's indignation is arresting.

"Who's been mishandling him here? It's clear someone has, and I'll look into that later. I'm bound every man shall get a fair show. It's clear that Doe isn't getting his here, No matter whose fault now. I'm going to give him his show—send him where hell get all that's coming to him. Put his name on the list for transfer."

One day the trickiest of trick orders came down. No more conscientious objectors would be transferred. An attempt would be met by the return of the objector and the prompt trial of the offending officer. The 305th read the thing complacently, glancing down the sturdy brown lines. It had no significance for us then. Had we ever had a conscientious objector? No one seemed able to recall. At any rate there was none then. There was none when we sailed for France.

****

Now and then the trick orders contained troublesome particulars. Perhaps an organization would be called on to furnish a man equipped to become a battery or company clerk. Then the committee on transfers would really get down to work, for good battery clerks were as rare as good first sergeants. You can see the members anxiously scanning again and again the well-worn qualification cards. You can picture the shaking of heads, the helpless frowns. Then, perhaps, you can remember one speaking up victoriously.

"Here's the very bird."

"Read the chief particulars of his qualification card," the chairman demands.

The other holds the card to the light, declaiming in a singsong voice:

"Ivan Stroffowaki. Born in Russia. Occupation: push cart peddler. Education: None. Neither read nor writes English."

The members of the committee glance at each other. A tentative whisper filters through the room. It isn't one whisper. It is a sibilant chorus.

"Ivan! Thou art the man!"

****

Aside from Trick Orders and routine paper work, there were family allotments, insurance allotments, and liberty loan allotments. And it mustn't be forgotten here that, up to October 28th the regiment had gone into its pocket and subscribed $70,300 to the second liberty loan. All of these records figured on the pay-rolls, at the making up of which Paper Work had some of his cheeriest moments. Pay-rolls, too, gave the men rather more than their share of paper work. Everybody recalls that spirited lyric, set to the tune of *John Brown's Body*.

All we do is sign the pay-roll.
All we do is sign the pay-roll.
All we do is sign the pay-roll.
And we never get a blank, blank cent.

Like much poetry, this was a trifle exaggerated, for on pay day, when the long lines formed, there was always some real money on the orderly room table. Nevertheless, on pay day night groups could be heard intoning such another lyric of the war as this:

The U. S. pays us thirty per,
Or so the papers say;
But if you get a dollar ten,
It's a heluva big pay day.

Yet consider the soldier who gets nothing—the replacement, perhaps, who was entrusted with his own service record and who has lost it.

"Do you know what this means?" the captain snaps at him. "Do you realize your entire record is gone—punishments and rewards, clothing, allotments, everything? Do you understand that without your service record you can't be paid?"

The replacement glances at the paper work suspended from the walls, cluttering the table, overflowing to the floor. His lip trembles.

"I don't know much, sir, since I got inteh the army."

And, as the captain glances at the paper work, too, there flashes through his mind:

"How much this man and I have in common!"

Chapter 4

On the Range

We learned things, in spite of that curse of efficiency, Simulation.. Cold weather found us well along in standing gun drill. One battery would get the pieces one hour, another the next, and so on. Caissons simulated pieces, and limbers, caisson. But we got the mechanics of laying, loading, and firing, and the specialists learned enough to make panoramic sketches of the dreary Upton landscape and to lay telephone lines in suicidal fashion. Stirring in every mind, moreover, was the desire to hear the crack of a rifle and the rush of its projectile.

That wouldn't be long now, for the target range was progressing. Large signs at neighbouring crossroads warned the countryside of danger. When, we asked, were we going to justify such violent displays?

The range outlined to many of us for the first time our mission. It is one thing to call out at drill a range of 5,000. It is quite another to walk from a projected gun position to a target 5,000 yards away.

Drawn by Private Enroth, Battery D
A quiet game in a mess hall at Upton

The range impressed us as enormous. Without reaching its boundaries you could walk across it for hours. Its broad stretches of woodland and brush appeared scarcely scarred by the months of our labour. It hadn't been intended, for that matter, that they should be. The plan had been to have the range masquerade as an actual battle terrain. About the target areas, however, many acres had been cleared, and with a few thrills. The conflagration happened on a sharp December afternoon. Considering the labour, the hunger, the investigations that accompanied and followed it, it would be an affectation of conservatism to speak of the thing as a mere fire.

Brushwood mysteriously caught at the far end, sprang to the woods, and, a spreading column of flames and smoke before a half gale, swept towards our mushroom city. Practically the entire regiment worked the latter part of the afternoon and half the night getting the flames under control and some toiled for an indefinite period trying to fix the blame. That was never done, but for months shadows hung over suspected spots, and Colonel Doyle's lips were often severe.

Yet the accident wasn't without benefit. Those who surveyed the charred areas pronounced the range about cleared for action.

Horses still lacked. The range was some miles from camp. To get our guns there with a shadow of dignity or comfort we would need horses. While we lacked such vital transport, indeed, we could not look upon ourselves as a real Field Artillery regiment.

There had been rumours. There always are about everything, but early in December an amazingly real order came to send details to the remount depot. On December 10th eighty-seven horses were brought up and quartered in our stables.

They didn't appeal to us as at all what we would have chosen for our own stalls. They fell into two classes—cavalry and artillery, that is, individual mounts and draught animals. They were shaggy and unkempt. Some seemed overburdened by the cares of life. Others endeavoured to express through vivacious gestures a desire to get at the greener officers and men who hitherto had been mounted only in the tables of organization.

Often, while struggling with the curious replacements we received in France, did we look back wistfully to these our first and best animals.

From this moment Paper Work clutched at Department B officers and stable sergeants.

The horses arrived just in time for our first target practice, which was scheduled for December 12th.

Each of four batteries had the pleasure of harnessing, with make-shift harness, a team of the new, untried animals to a piece and drawing it from the park to the range.

That day, everyone will recall, was the first bitter one of an uncommonly severe winter. It distilled in those horses a vaunting ambition. It nearly, in consequence, upset one carriage, and it delayed the rest because of cold hands and stiff equipment.

Cannoneers and spare drivers stood in line along Fourth Avenue, between Fifteenth and Seventeenth Streets. The scarlet battery guidons fluttered before a frozen wind. Yet, as the first carriage appeared at the top of the grade, there was a satisfied warmth in all our hearts. At least a share of all the trappings was ours. We could grin and shout *"Finis"* to that inefficient monster, Simulation.

The carriages rumbled down the slope, swaying from side to side. The drivers didn't look happy. More often than not the near horses were out of hand. Some animals pulled; others ambled, enjoying the prospect. But the carriages did advance. It was these city-bred men, abruptly informed that they were artillery drivers, who controlled untrained stock to that extent.

They got past the difficult turn into Seventeenth Street. Later they swung with more confidence into the Middle Island Road. They drew the guns into position. They trotted off with the limbers in really dashing fashion.

The dismounted men marched out. They were stationed near the guns so that they might see exactly what happens when the lanyard of a three inch rifle is pulled with a shell in the breach.

Later we may have fired as many as 8,000 rounds in an evening, while today we were to expend only 19. But many soldiers were to hear for the first time the sharp crack of the piece, and the swishing, rocket-like flight of the projectile; were to watch that pleasing white ball of smoke, like a pretty cloud appearing without warning, that is a shrapnel burst.

In order that all this might be appreciated the target was in clear view from the vicinity of the guns, although indirect laying was to be used.

News of the event had spread. Officers of the 304th and 306th came to admire. Several officers of marines walked up the road. Where they had come from no one knew, and there was too much else on hand to bother about finding out.

Lieutenant-Colonel Stimson was to fire the first problem. He walked with Colonel Doyle and a knot of officers to the observatory a few hundred yards ahead. Everything seemed to be ready. Lieutenant Hoyt, in charge of the range party, was said to be down near the target. As soon as he announced that the range was clear——

Crews from each battery were to fire in turn. The battery commander and his executive ran here and there, giving final words of advice to the gun squads, examining the sights, inspecting for one last time the bores. The telephone officers and their details struggled with the primitive system of communication. There were no switchboards. All lines were party lines. There would have been no wire if a friend of Colonel Stimson's hadn't presented the regiment with sixty miles or so of heavy twisted pair. Yet we were quite proud of that net. We had done our best according to the sacred precepts of Volume III. One shudders trying to conceive what it would have done to us at the front. Anyway it worked most of that afternoon in the winter peace of Long Island. We limited our faith, however. On nearby crests lonely figures etched against a sullen sky the broad strokes of the semaphore code. We had even erected two wireless stations, using Lieutenant Church's homemade set. They didn't work particularly, but they looked exactly as well as if they had. It took an expert to know one way or the other.

The men, standing waist-deep in the underbrush, shaking from the cold, and, probably, a little, too, from the excitement, craned their necks in the direction of the target, 2,000 yards away.

The white flag on the hill continued to flutter, advertising that there was no firing and that the range was safe. We knew, until white was replaced by red, nothing of interest to us would happen. The grey afternoon waned. Cannoneers blew impatiently on their hands. The ranks in the underbrush stamped their feet and waved their arms, setting up a crackling like the advance of a vast army. Little groups ran up and down the road to keep warm. Whispers lost their stealth, became audible, burst into an impatient chorus.

"Why don't they shoot and let us go home?" Through the mysterious army channels of rumour drifted down a fact.

"Somebody was seen on the range nearly an hour ago, and they haven't been able to find him."

"Where's Hoyt? Why doesn't Hoyt get him off?"

"Hoyt's on the range, seeking the cheerful villain."

The executive strode to a man stretched beneath a shelter tent with the receiver of a service buzzer at his ear.

"Get me the observatory."

(Or didn't we call it B. C. station in those ignorant days?)

After a time the operator passed him the receiver and transmitter.

"It isn't altogether clear, sir."

"Observatory?"

A pause.

"Hello! Hello! Hello! Observatory? Hello! Hello! Hello! (Very low.) My God! (Very high.) Hello!—Hello!—Hello!"

The telephone officer stood by, watching. He made a gesture of disgust.

"Don't say 'Hello!'" he offered. "It's meaningless. It only wastes time. It never gets you anywheres."

If a telephone officer has ever talked to you like that when you held a dead instrument and big things were afoot, you need precisely no analysis of the executive's emotions.

The executive sprang up, casting the offending parts from him. He glanced dangerously at the telephone officer. He, as they say, collected himself.

"I've said 'hello!' all my life," he muttered, "and I'll admit it's never got me less than it has this afternoon."

"Oh, don't get sore," the telephone officer said breezily.

The executive confided quite in private.

"If you do as well as this at the front the Huns will court martial the first man that hurts you."

"Buzz it," the telephone officer said indifferently.

The executive chained his wrath.

"I'd rather give it to you straight. Want any more?"

"No, no," said the telephone officer pityingly. "I mean your message. The buzzer often goes through when the voice won't."

"Oh!"

The executive turned to the operator.

"Tell them it's nearly dark, and what the deuce is the delay?"

A whining buzz came from the shelter tent. It lacked conviction.

"Your man up there got the Saint Vitus dance?" the executive wanted to know.

On the nearest crest one of the lone figures was now etching with eager and excited strokes.

"Says," the private in observation read off, "Colonel... Doyle... wants. . . to. . . know. . . why. . . wire. . . communication. . . has. . . ceased. . . func. . . tion. . . ing."

"Test your instrument," the telephone officer called to the man in the tent, "and you," he ordered another, "get out on the line."

A stooped figure threaded the underbrush, letting the wire run through his fingers. In a few minutes he was back, saluting.

"Line was cut, sir, not fifty yards out there."

"Probably one of your cannoneers," the telephone officer complained to the executive. "They must learn that wires are sacred. Court-martial offense—carelessness with wires."

"Speaking of courts martial," the executive whispered. "Remember that the Hun that hurts you'll be tried by some bigger Hun."

"Got you the first time," the telephone officer grinned.

****

Behold! The white flag fluttering down! The red flag streaming up!

"Lieutenant Hoyt is back," came over the wire. "The range is clear."

The chief actors became rigid and expectant.

"Cannoneers posts!"

The men sprang to the pieces like a football formation jumping into play. From the shelter tent the operator commenced to shout out the firing data that drifted over the repaired wire from the observatory.

"Aiming point that bare pine tree five mils to the left of the left hand edge of target. Deflection, six-three hundred and fifty. On second piece open ten. Site three hundred. Korrector thirty. Battery right. Two thousand."

The sights and the tubes responded to the febrile motions of our amateurs. The executive repeated the commands one by one. You fancied that through the taut atmosphere came their echoes from the far target.

A captain ran along the line, verifying the laying. There was no longer any stirring in the underbrush, nor any movement on the road. A branch snapped. Lt. Norman Thirkield, the recording officer, balanced in a tree, precariously raised his glasses.

The brown cloth of the shelter tent bulged. The voice of the operator ran with awed vibrations across the tight silence.

"Fire when ready!"

The executive raised his hand. He brought it down with a sharp motion, bawling out:

"Fire!"

The section chief of the first piece repeated the gesture and the command. The silence was destroyed. It seemed to fall away before the snapping concussion of the discharge, and the departure, invisible but fairly sensed, of the projectile.

The operator cried:

"On the way!"

The first shot fired by the 305th sailed majestically over Long Island.

In succession the other pieces followed, and far off, in the general direction of the target, one by one, appeared after several seconds the white smoke balls.

The stirrings in the brushwood recommenced. A great sigh went up. It resembled an exclamation of childish wonder.

A relaxation took place. It was as if with that first shot we had altered from an inert, incoherent thing into a body abounding with an ordered and flexible purpose. We sensed it as we swung back through the sharp, early dusk. The rumbling of the carriages behind us expressed it. Ahead the lights of camp twinkled at us with a new appreciation. We had made a crossing.

****

We said goodbye that night for a long period to Lieutenant-Colonel Stimson. He had been ordered to report to the port of embarkation at Hoboken for transportation to France. That firing of the first problem was his last duty with the 305th until he rejoined us nearly six months later when we were training in the south of France. After that, until a few days before we sailed, Colonel Doyle was the only field officer with the regiment.

On the thirteenth we took our *materiel* to the range again and fired ten rounds at the same target, Captain Gammell conducting.

Glancing back from our veteran viewpoint, it may require a difficult focus to see those pitifully few rounds in their just perspective. Each one might have been a priceless jewel released by some patriotic collector. It took the better part of two afternoons to sprinkle their contents on the target, or near it. They were responsible for hours of discussion in preparation, and evenings of the same in retrospect. Every burst became the subject of orations. Each was recorded on special forms, and the War Department in general and the ordnance people in particular were told all about it. Temporarily one of the shell cases was mislaid. The dark eye of suspicion rested on possible souvenir hunters. Those in any way responsible were frowned upon as unique criminals, because that was in the days before the Regular Army got over its ritual attitude towards ammunition. Only when the case had been found did the atmosphere clear.

We had trained for more than three months before firing the precious twenty-nine, and we were to wait more than three months before firing another; but—for one must focus—they taught us what a rifle would do if rationally treated. Each gun squad had had a chance. Incredulity as to sights and scales and instruments of precision had been demolished by the men's own labour. To that measure they had already become artillerymen.

It was of even greater advantage that those nineteen rounds had let us measure the results of our training. We could judge ourselves and each other; could see that, on the whole, we were good. The various details had had practical experience. Operators had actually transmitted over lines laid by their own hands words of the highest importance.

Twenty-nine rounds at twenty-five dollars a round! They did more to make our regiment find itself than millions of dollars spent in other ways.

Chapter 5

Holidays and Rumours

During these thrilling days the powers of administration had not by any means neglected us. They caused to descend upon the regiment on December 15th twenty-five officers from the Second Officers' Training Camps. The proportion of first lieutenants made at the second camps was greater than at the first. A number of our young second lieutenants had been recommended for promotion some time before, but when their commissions finally came through they were dated later than all the commissions given at the second camps. They, in other words, who had set their hands first to the tasks, had struggled with raw beginnings, had moulded regiments, were outranked by these youngsters fresh from three months at school. The amazing fact is mentioned in passing because it created a situation a trifle delicate and not without humour.

It is simple to say: Here are captains and first lieutenants. Give them the authority and responsibility that goes with their rank. It is quite another to project instantaneously into their brains the necessary practical experience our officers, junior to them, had acquired during four hard months.

The problem was solved by detailing temporarily these superiors as assistants to their veteran juniors.

"Please do this and that, Captain," a second lieutenant would have to say.

Or at retreat—to which the new ones, thirsty for things military, always turned out—a second lieutenant would make his assignments, wondering what was wrong with the world.

"Please take the first platoon, Captain."

And he would distribute the other platoons in a dreamy way among the group of first lieutenants.

"At ease!" or "Attention!" the shavetail would roar, and the silver-decorated shoulders would droop or straighten obediently, but in the eyes above would appear inevitably a light of something out of the way.

These were excess officers, so a rearrangement of quarters was necessary. No longer could every one have that little rough sanctuary so essential to concentrated study. The juniors were doubled up to give the new superiors each a room to himself.

The majority of these officers were merely attached, and remained with the regiment, receiving valuable experience, only until its departure for France.

During this period, however, we received a number of officers who did become a part of the organization. Second Lieutenant Ellsworth O. Strong came to us on December 10th. First lieutenants Wilfred K. Dodworth and Paul G. Pennoyer reported on the 17th. Second lieutenant Edward F. Graham was assigned on the 20th, and First Lieutenant Albert R. Gurney on the 27th.

Just before the Christmas holidays Captains Anderson Dana and Alvin Untermeyer were attached to the regiment. They had trained with the Second Battery at the First Plattsburg Camp, and had been held as instructors for the Second Camp.

Except for a brief period Captain Dana remained with the regiment during the remainder of its history. He came, of course, as an old friend, since he had known and trained with most of the officers during their novitiate. A few days after his arrival the powers transferred him to the 306th F.A., but when Captain Devereux was promoted and transferred to the 304th Captain Dana came back, definitely assigned to the command of Battery A. That change was made officially on February 4th.

Until just before we sailed for France Captain Untermeyer remained attached to the regiment as adjutant and acting commander of the First Battalion.

Drawn by Musician Boyle, Hq. Co.

****

After target practice our minds turned to the holidays. They were heralded by a series of lectures from British officers who had survived some of the bitterest fighting of the war. We heard at first hand of tanks, and machine guns, and gas, and discipline. We gathered from these few intimate talks more knowledge than a library of books and months of reading could have given us. They reminded us of what lay just ahead. They told us of the nasty effects of phosgene and mustard gas, with which we were to have too close an acquaintance later on. From Colonel Appen's stirring talk on discipline we carried away an un-bendable belief that in discipline resided a defence almost as powerful as ordnance. We resolved to equip ourselves with that weapon.

In spite of such grim reflections, the holiday spirit captured us excessively. Or was it because of them? There was a strengthened pleasure, a trifle pathetic, in the holly wreaths and mistletoe and tinselled evergreens, of home. That classic tinkle, *For Christmas Comes But Once a Year*, was in our minds. What changes would pass before another year should bring its unique feast? It was, roughly speaking, twelve months later that the regiment held its first memorial service in a sodden meadow of the Haut Marne.

****

Paper Work was so chained that every officer and man, except just victims of discipline, could have either at Christmas or New Year, the period between Saturday morning and Tuesday night at home. Some fortunate ones got both holidays.

The crazy specials pulled out of the terminal with eager youths overflowing to the platforms; and always fresh columns marched up, were inspected, and passed through the gates. At the Pennsylvania Station a civilian was a sombre piece of driftwood in a restless, muddy sea. We gave all New York a brown tinge that Christmas. In clubs, hotels, on the streets, and in nearly everybody's home khaki was a perpetual reminder of war and of approaching departures.

When we returned we found that the few left behind had not gone cheerless. There had been turkey and mince pies, and the mess halls were still green and red from brave and abundant decorations.

The return from New York New Year's night we put down without dissent as Horrors of War No. 2. They had had us out at fire drill Saturday morning and a few frozen ears and fingers had warned us that the Frost King was after new honours. The journey up, through a lazy snow storm had been suffered patiently because of its warm destination. But the mercury continued its ambitious ways, and it was always colder at night than by day. Towards midnight of New Year's, to any one standing on the platform at Jamaica, it was obvious that records had been broken.

When the train finally came along, we crowded eagerly to get in. Then strong soldiers shrank from the open door. Hoarse voices called on regions of perpetual warmth. But the strongest and the hoarsest had no antidote for steel coaches, fresh from the yards, unheated, unlighted, save for a single candle in each, burning high, suggestive of a votive light in some Eskimo tomb.

Compared with the atmosphere in these coaches we recalled the outside air as warm. We had to remain where we were, crouched on seats or in the aisle, our feet on suitcases or on each other, while the train crawled, while we counted the minutes, while the air froze tighter.

Gems of advice slipped from one to another.

"Don't go to sleep, Edward. They says they never wake up."

"Better try it. Be a dashed sight warmer where you'd go, Benny."

"Move your legs, boy. Keep 'em moving. If you freezed in that position they couldn't get you out of the car till the spring thaws."

"I heard that if you thought anything hard enough it would be so. I'm going to think I'm warm."

"Tell that to the Baptists, George. I'm a Shaker."

And that night because of these things, the railroad, too, suffered a little. In some cars the metal floor was discovered to be an excellent bed for a fire, and the wicker seats passable as fuel. The combination resulted in discussion between Headquarters and the railroad barons.

****

Home from that moment receded. The bitter weather lasted, and there was a famine of coal in the land. These facts, added, probably, to our improvised heating arrangements, caused special trains practically to become extinct, and passes nearly so.

The first warm weather brought a new complication. At best it had taken delicate handling to get an automobile, without prematurely aging it, in or out of Camp Upton.

Spring altered rock-like dirt roads into unnavigable morasses. For a time the railroad was our only practical means of communication with the outside world. Fortunately the coal situation had improved then, and our erratic fires been forgiven. Specials ran again. The days of generous passes were revived.

While the cold weather had cut into drill there had been plenty to busy us. More horses had arrived, and we had get another veterinarian, First Lieutenant John J. Essex, assigned on the 14th of January. Grooming occupied a lot of time, and care of harness and carriages a lot more. The liaison schools worked so hard with theory and practice during the cold days that a regular army inspector was lost in admiration to the point of saying:

"Regular Army, National Army, or National Guard, I've never inspected details as well instructed as these."

No matter how cold it was, unless snow or fog made the visibility bad, Colonel Doyle took the officers and portions of the details to the hill above the infantry practice trenches, where he instructed them in the Fort Riley method of conduct of fire. We fired problem after problem from imaginary guns, while Lieutenant Hoyt, at the targets a mile or more away with erratic smoke bombs, made us feel how bad we were.

In February Dame Rumour stole from her winter quarters. One day we were going to France on a moment's notice. The next, we would be lucky if we ever got there. The third, our boat was in the harbour, and we'd have to hustle to get off.

Some of the saner-minded weighed the matter.

We couldn't fight the Huns with our one battery, our few horses, our insufficient harness, our incomplete instrument equipment. Moreover, a number of our battery commanders were at Fort Sill for instruction. Others were scheduled to go. If proposed departures should be cancelled, and the absent captains recalled we would begin to put our affairs in order, for it was clear we couldn't go on marking time perpetually at Camp Upton.

Washington's Birthday, in some measure, cleared the air. It fell on a Friday. We commenced to speculate when we were informed that on the holiday there would be a parade, and that night a monster Division ball in the armoury of the Seventh Regiment, and that as many of us as possible would be given passes between Thursday evening and the following Monday's reveille.

"Looks like a farewell show, and a last chance for a good visit home," sums up the commoner interpretation.

This was strengthened when, as we struggled to town Thursday night, word passed through the train that the absent battery commanders had been recalled.

The parade was solemn. It had an exotic touch. American soldiers had never looked quite like that before. The men wore their new winter caps instead of the familiar campaign hats. A blankety snow fell and became, apparently, a part of the uniform. The spectators gazed with a sort of wonder at city youths, broadened and ruddy and clear-eyed, and in a setting that placed them all at once, as it were, in a different world.

It was almost entirely an infantry affair. In spite of the highly technical nature of our branch, our lack of equipment even at this late date, barred most of the artillery brigade from the column. Among the entire three regiments there were still only our four venerable rifles. The honour of parading these fell to Battery A, in command of Captain Dana. He was the first officer of the brigade to have a chance at entraining and detraining a battery. It spoiled his holiday, but it was good experience.

The crowd cheered that single battery as it crunched through the snow past the reviewing stand, little Wing, the Chinaman, on one of the lead houses, pointing with unconscious pride the democratic, the universal power of our army.

At the Division ball that night, sombre with brown figures, and gay with the evening best of mothers, wives, sisters, and sweethearts, stalked an oppressive succession of hazards. What did it all mean to these cheerful brown figures and these smiling women who danced away the night together?

****

Two days later, in the Cohan and Harris theatre, Lieutenants Sage and Roesch staged a monster benefit for the regiment. Our own talent was supplemented by a glittering array of Broadway stars. The show made enough money to pay off the debts owed by the regiment to members who had gone into their own pockets to buy where the powers had failed to provide.

On our return to camp we waited for the verifying word. It came on Tuesday morning. The acting division commander, an infantry brigadier, desired the presence of every officer that could possibly be spared from duty, in the Y. M. C. A. hall on Upton Boulevard.

The non-commissioned officers ruled the regiment during that pregnant hour.

A huge theatrical success wouldn't have filled the hall more uncomfortably. Infantry, artillery, machine gunners, medicos, the trains, they were all there. And this was not like previous gatherings for advice, or reproof. Suspicious individuals stood at each entrance, scanning the arriving officers. Certainly we were going to hear secrets. The usual laughter, gossip, and calls to distant friends were replaced by a dreary and unnatural silence. It was as if we had aged unexpectedly. Curling towards the rafters was more than the customary smoke.

The brigadier entered and faced us with countenance and attitude sterner than the ordinary.

"Are there any enlisted men present?"

Verily we were to hear secrets!

After we had heard everything we questioned if the enlisted men didn't know nearly, or quite as much, and we wondered why they shouldn't. For the discourse developed the fact that while we were sailing soon no definite date had been set. All we could do was to equip and train the new men we were going to get. In order that the enlisted men might be kept in African ignorance of these things, we were to tell them carefully there were rumours we might leave.

The officers filed out, and wandered back to the regimental area chatting softly. In those first hours it seemed inevitable we should go almost at once.

When organization commanders faced their men, they gathered that the men knew where they had gone, and why. A recital of the rumours seemed superfluous. For in the faces of the men, too, there was a solemn sense of imminence.

CHAPTER 6

The Ages of Getting Ready

We failed to sail within a fortnight, or within several fortnights. Perhaps it was as well that transportation lacked, for there was much more preparation necessary than we had suspected. Lieutenant Walters left us, and Lieutenant McKenna came into his own. That is, he was assigned to the command of the Supply Company. Before many days his promotion to the rank of captain arrived. From constitutionally reluctant quartermasters he tore supplies with the same cheerful energy he had displayed in the days of recruit fitting. Yet the more we got the more we appeared to need, and lack of artillery harness was from the first like a too high hurdle between us and the docks.

While McKenna hustled we entered two new phases, One might be labelled The Age of Gas, and the other The Age of Equipment Checking. Of the two in memory the second looms larger.

"A complete check of personal property will be made before retreat."

Day after day that order faced us on the threshold of the afternoon. It meant the laying out on bunks of all issued equipment, according to an intricate pattern. It meant a review of every piece, checked against an official list of equipment C. Some day a Regular Army quartermaster may divulge to us the structural secrets of those lists. For our part, we never quite understood the logic of reversing, sometimes mutilating, the descriptions of familiar and intimate articles of clothing.

"Bags, barrack," it began.

Why, in the name of abused commas, wouldn't "Barrack bags" have done as well?

"Breeches, O. D.," "Socks, winter," "Gloves, riding," "Poles, tent," "Razors, safety," "Tags, identification."

It ran something like that, and so far we followed, if reservedly. We revolted only at:

"Shirts, under," "Drawers, under."

Perhaps an obsessed clerk, typing the copies, was responsible for that.

****

This is how one spent one's time in the age of equipment checking:

In the somnolent barracks you arranged your equipment according to the intricate pattern. Everybody had a different idea as to some of the more esoteric details of the pattern, and you compared notes until you didn't know whether you would be passed, arrested for distortion, or praised for acute originality. Then you endeavoured to keep awake. If you were an officer, you took your lists, tried to get the cunning pattern through your head yourself, and wished to heaven you could smoke on the job.

A non-commissioned officer slams into the sleepy room, singing out: "Attention!"

The officer walks in. It probably isn't severity that gives his face that peculiar expression, you decide. It's more likely a stifled yawn.

"Rest!" he croons. "All except this first man."

He checks the articles on the cot.

"Where," he demands, "is your fifth pair of socks?"

The warrior blushes.

"On me pusson, sir."

The officer reflects. This time his frown isn't wholly concealed. The orders were absolute. Everything must be seen before being checked.

The soldier stoops obediently, removing his legging, and probably murmuring in his mind:

"I'm not trying to put anything over on you, and I'd wear them in the army whether it was my habit or not, because your issue shoes aren't exactly plush."

"Where's your other O. D. shirt?"

The officer catches himself.

"I mean, Shirt, O. D."

Again the soldier displays emotion.

"In the laundry, sir."

Once more the officer reflects. It seems expensive, unjustifiable, and meat in the mouth of Paper Work to issue this man, and all the other cleanly men, masses of equipment to be turned back on the arrival of their laundry. On that point there should be something definite. He seeks the captain for a ruling. The responsibility is great. So the captain seeks the battalion adjutant. The battalion adjutant seeks the regimental adjutant. The regimental adjutant seeks the Colonel, and beyond that the chain is vague, but in a few days a ruling comes down that for the present equipment in the laundry may be considered as present and accounted for.

The checking officer, meantime, makes out a painstaking little list for each soldier.

"Private Doe has in laundry——"

The list is long. Those who hear it decide that Doe is effete.

The conversation in the room, from tentative whispers following the officer's "Rest!", has developed into comments, exclamations, and arguments, centring about the flow of well-known raconteurs. The officer hears all this, grows at times a trifle absent-minded, has to make alterations in his neat lists.

"I pasted him in the jaw, honest to Gawd I did, and he didn't have no come-back. You saw the bout, Jim. If I hadn't caught my shoulder in the ropes, he'd never have knocked me out. Ain't it the truth, Jim?"

"If you ask me," Jim replies evenly, "I think you had horseshoes hung all over you to last as long as you did."

Or, from a group of three serious-faced young men, two of whom have just returned from the third R. O. T. C.:

"Germany's financial structure is as restless and insecure as a house built on sand."

"That's logic, but logic and the truth are often bad friends."

"Oh, Lord," groans the officer inwardly, making another mistake with his lists.

And, to cap the climax and spoil an entire sheet:

"Billy told me about it. If the Y. M. C. A. could have seen him then! Nellie had him up to tea Sunday. Least he thought he was drinking tea. Looked like it. You know a Martini and tea are the same colour. They put cocktails in his cup instead of tea, and he smacked his lips and drank four cups, and all the time the poor simp thought he was drinking tea."

A deep voice cuts the air, snorting and booming:

"The hell he did!"

The sergeant tries not to grin. The officer swings passionately.

"Attention! Sergeant, if another man speaks put his name down, and I'll take care of him later. At Ease!"

He turns back to his checking, aware that what he had wanted to say was: "Men! This job has got to be done. It hurts me more than it does you."

****

Sometimes we checked and were checked at night, too. Whose fault was it, this ceaseless repetition that carried us each time only a trifling distance forward? In some measure, it must be admitted, the blame was our own. There were a number of men whom you could check at two o'clock and find, with the exception of allowable deficiencies, up to the mark. At three you might check them again, and learn they had lost within the hour such prominent objects as tent poles and shelter halves. One little bandsman was suspected of an appetite for tent pins, his disappeared so rapidly and regularly. But we weren't to blame for that futile effort after the complete check that could only be made with every soldier in his place and each piece of equipment in view.

At one time the stable sergeants and the grooming and feeding details would be at the stables. Check or no check, the horses had to be cared for. At another the cooks were scattered on various duties. Naturally the men couldn't be checked at the price of starvation. And every day at headquarters and in the orderly rooms soldiers of clerical ability bent before the sacred shrine of Paper Work, and couldn't be torn away.

So the Age of Checking was prolonged through March and April, and even up to the day we sailed.

****

The *Age of Gas*, while less irksome at that time, was rather more unpleasant. Lieutenant Mitchell had taken a course from a Scotch non-commissioned officer. He was looked upon as an expert now, and we were content to pin our faith to him. But one night we were summoned to hear Mitchell lecture. He sprinkled bright little stories among statistics, depressing, and, we fancied, a trifle exaggerated for our good. We drank in extended figures of casualties caused through carelessness or ignorance; of casualties, on the other hand, scarcely to have been avoided. He had his house at his feet. In a fashion he beat the English lecturers at their own game. He'd found out about some new gases that shrivelled you up all at once or got you with a delayed and terrible kick long after exposure, and instead of a cheerful Christmas time just ahead, there was actually—gas.

He asked us to listen to him again the next night, and when we obeyed we found a table piled with masks. He showed us how to put them on and take them off. We gasped in the strange, uncomfortable, stinking contrivances. We laughed—not uproariously, you understand—at our own appearance, abruptly converted into something monstrous.

Gas non-commissioned officers were appointed. The men spent a definite period at gas drill each day. They held competitions. They ran courses. They looked like types of a new race, born of some dreadful catastrophe.

We were introduced to the gas house—a wooden shack near the machine-gun range. The Scotch sergeant was heard to say:

"We got to ha' a wee bit o' luck this afternoon. We carried out thu-ree corpses this marnin', and they only allow me fower for a full day."

"Laugh," Mitchell prompted in a stage whisper, "or you'll hurt his feelings."

So we laughed, *"Ha, ha, ha,"* at his joke. It was more like a cry for help.

A captain of the Medical Corps explained the procedure, for that was before the powers gave gas to the Engineers.

"I'm going to loose a killing mixture of chlorine," he ended, "so it would be as well to inspect masks carefully."

We hoped he was trying to impress us, but the ranks, one noticed, took a long time over the inspection of face pieces and canisters.

We were ready finally. The medico then put on his own mask, entered the shack, and sealed it. Through the single window we saw him turn the escape valve of a cylinder tank. He opened the door, stepped out, and removed his mask.

"Come close," he said, "so you can smell the stuff. Then you'll know I'm not putting anything over on you."

When we had obeyed our lungs refused to breathe the sickly air. We donned our masks and filed in. The door clanged shut behind us. We were imprisoned for ten minutes, half expectant of catastrophes. Through our goggles the air had a bluish appearance, but in our lungs it was pure.

We escaped at last, relieved to be able to breathe naturally again and to know that the masks were really good. Afterwards we were treated to a lachrymatory mixture which hurt our eyes. After that we were permitted to march away, cracking gruesome jokes for the benefit of those whose ordeal still waited.

We took gas in the stride of our work of preparation. That continued with slow sureness. Day after day Captain McKenna opened the regimental storehouse on newly-collected treasures, and each organization sent details to bring home its share. Then followed hours of fitting and issuing and checking again, until we realized that the regiment was nearly equipped.

Each officer and man was given twenty-four hours at home to attend to his personal affairs. That brought it so much nearer. On March 18th a review and a dance of the Brigade was held in the 69th Regiment armoury. It offered us from Saturday until Tuesday morning at home.

"And this time it's surely so long, Mary," one heard going up on the train.

There was, indeed, an atmosphere of climax about that affair. For March the weather was warm. Lexington Avenue and the side streets, as we came up, were nearly blocked by restless spectators. They lacked the air of a crowd at a parade. Their brief cheers touched formality. They were restrained. They vibrated with a quality a little choked. Suddenly one realized that the men and women, unrecognizable in the night, were those that loved us.

Automatically one recalled stories of the departures of regiments from

New York for the Civil War. Always such pictures were set in sunshine, with a ring of quaint costumes and a brave show of flags and music. We had looked forward to something of the sort.

There was music, all the more brassily insolent because its source was unseen; and, lost in the shadows, we knew our flags shook in the tepid air. The rest was wholly contrast. The columns, swinging up through the dark, pushed back the restless shapes. The door of the armoury opened, and the shapes slipped through. They had to traverse a broad band of light; and, as we looked, I think it came to all of us quite abruptly, that it was simpler to be of the offering than among those who tended the altar.

****

On our return to Upton we entered the age of packing—a most complicated and laborious epoch. Every day and until far in the night the mess halls resounded to a new activity. Battery carpenters hammered on packing cases. Painting details striped them with maroon and white, the division colours. Packing details filled them with instruments, and ordnance, quartermaster, signal, and engineer property—and paper work. From duplicate lists clerks checked everything in. Typewriters clattered on the tables. In one corner two men bent over, tap-tap-tapping numbers and names on identification disks like a new race of Nibelungs. In another an exchange had been established, and brisk bargaining over odd sizes of equipment imposed on the general pandemonium a shrill note of wheedling or invective. Such harness as we had was draped from uprights; and, depending from the ceiling beams, were rows of blue barrack bags, still wet and splashed with white and red from the division markings.

There followed black days of unpacking and repacking to meet some new trick order, while the checks continued.

One Saturday a check of the harness disclosed the fact that two sets were missing from the regiment. The men were the more fortunate that time. The columns of pass holders marched down Fourth Avenue as usual. But an edict came from the Colonel that no officer, whatever his remoteness from harness, should leave Upton until the missing sets, or a reasonable explanation, had been found.

By night the amateur detectives—and everyone had joined the quest—saw their last theories crumble. Every inch of the area, they swore, had been searched. No one had escaped a bitter third degree. The harness, to all appearances, had dissolved. We were released, but the shadow of the mystery long hung over us; and through the shadow, after a time, gossip stole. You may accept it or reject it, but it might be well to picture a couple of officers and a few men gathered in an orderly room. There's no point trying to identify that. Studying their faces, you might decide they gaze with horror on the result of some red and impulsive work their hands have just accomplished. That, or that the souvenir of some murderous indiscretion, has unexpectedly risen from the past to challenge their content. For their faces are not without horror—a helpless, desperate horror, and one does gasp:

"Great Caesar's ghost!"

But there's really no ghost, or any crimson relic—nothing exceptional at all in the plain little room except one perfectly good set of artillery harness.

An officer flings his hands above his head in a gesture of despair.

"Surveyed! Finished with! Bunches of paper work on its grave! Where in the name of kind heaven did you find it?"

"In the stables, sir, covered up by accident in a manger—"

The desperate hands go higher. They now express also supplication.

"It can't be found! My God! It can't be found!"

"You're right," one agrees, "because according to Army Regulations it has ceased to exist. To try to bring it to life again might take years of investigations, valuations, boards, I guess it would stop the war."

"Probably," says another, "it would put G. P., meaning general prisoner, on the backs of most of us."

"Drather find nitro-glycerine."

A murmur crystallizes the thoughts of all.

"If it were done away with quietly, dispassionately, without cruelty?"

You can't depend on this idle gossip, for the set was never heard of, at least publicly. One of the conspirators was seen in friendly converse with an officer of the Supply Company. Perhaps a stratagem was found. Maybe there's something in the story after all.

****

Days of doubt descended. For some time, each week end at home had been treasured as our last, but we didn't move.

"An order has come from General Pershing," McKenna informed us, "that no artillery units are to sail without their full equipment of harness."

But a word might alter that. If we could go without guns or caissons or horses—for gradually it had become clear our animals would be left behind—why all this fuss about harness?

And the division was moving.

Headquarters stole out of camp one early April night.

Not long after we were awakened by the shouts of many men and the wanton splintering of barrack window glass. The sky reflected many bonfires. Next morning the area of one of the infantry regiments was empty. Machine-gun battalions followed. Another infantry regiment. Each day we expected our orders. During this period of suspense several changes occurred. A special order from the War Department arrived giving Captain Untermyer an extended leave of absence. In his place arrived Captain Henry Reed. He had received his commission at the First Niagara Training Camp, had instructed at the Second Camp, and during the winter and early spring had been just across the hill instructing at the Third Camp. He was assigned to the regiment as adjutant of the first battalion. Major Wanvig returned from Fort Sill. Lt. John W. Schelpert of the Dental Corps came to us on March 24th, and remained with the regiment until August 19th when he was transferred to the Ammunition Train.

Then the blow fell. A very high officer indeed was heard to say with a laugh at the Officer's House:

"The artillery? They won't get to France before apples are ripe."

And on top of that came the order that seemed to confirm him. An infantry regiment that was moving at once was short of men. The artillery brigade would fill it up.

By that time we had developed that organization spirit that is just as essential as it is delicate to breed. To take fifty or sixty men from each battery seemed a destruction of the greater part of all that we had worked to achieve. Men who had trained during seven months in the ways of artillery as a rule resented being transplanted all at once into a branch of the service to which they were strangers. Nor did their officers care to see them go.

"Good men! Good men!" was the cry.

By that time, we believed, there weren't many that didn't fall in that class. But somehow the lists were made up, the victims equipped, the dazed exiles marched away to a new formula, to strange companions.

It happened once more just before the last infantry regiment departed. As the result of those two orders, within a few days of our sailing for France as a combat regiment we had torn from us 698 men. The Headquarters Company lost 50, the Supply Company, 27; Battery A, 93; Battery B, 119; Battery C, 113; Battery D, 95; Battery E, 116; Battery F, 82; the Medical Detachment, 2; and the Veterinary unit, 1.

At Upton the artillery alone remained, and we stared with a sense of threading the mazes of an unpleasant dream at half filled mess halls and skeleton ranks. Troops began to pour in from the south. Upton, we heard, was to become an embarkation camp. Our area, however, would remain sacred to us.

The vast German offensive of the spring of 1918 was dangerously under way. We could understand a stern need of infantry; yet, we argued, infantry in such a war isn't very valuable without supporting artillery. How could Europe furnish enough of that?

"We won't move before July," was the general cry.

Studying our shattered regiment, that was easy of belief.

The changes—the incredible changes of army life!

Coming back from town on the night of April 14th you heard October as the most likely date of our departure, yet, as it turned out, that was to be our last Sunday home before sailing.

On Monday morning the October guess continued good. A new smoke-bomb range had been designed and miles of wire laid. We were instructed to unpack a great deal of equipment. Elaborate schools were planned for the warm, favourable weather.

On Tuesday whispers slipped apparently from nothing. On Wednesday the Supply Company awakened to a new activity. From it escaped the significant news that we would get harness at once. Nothing more was to be unpacked. All that we had taken out was to be put back again in the cases.

"But," we objected, trying to stick to logic, "they wouldn't have stripped us this way. We can't go without men, and you can't take green men and train them on an ocean voyage."

Can't you, though? We were to find out about that. For on Thursday the officer in charge of arriving casuals conferred with us. From him we learned that trainloads of men from the West had been gathered at Camp Devens, and would come to us at once. We grasped at every comfort. If these replacements were from the West they'd probably know something about horses.

Selected officers and non-commissioned officers were awakened at 2 o'clock on the morning of the 19th. The trains were about to arrive.

There was a chill in the air. A mist, pearl-coloured about the lamps, veiled the dreary similarity of the barracks.

The trains crawled in with a stealth harmonious with the secrecy of all these movements. The throbbing of the locomotives was discreet as if the mist sought to muffle it.

Out of the cars they poured, sleepy-eyed, struggling ineptly with barrack bags, not at all voluble as soldiers in groups usually are. Our old men lined them up with a gentleness designed to destroy their attitude of strangers, bashful and apprehensive. We counted them again and again to be sure we were getting all we were entitled to. We marched them off in groups through the fog. The fog seemed friendly to them, for at that time they were without personality to us—just so many things, counted and recounted, to fill the ranks of a regiment about to go to war.

Taking up the march again, after a rest in which two groups had got a trifle mixed, an officer counted his objects and found one missing. He and his non-commissioned aides ran up and down through the mist.

"I'm shy a man. Have you got an extra man? Count up."

"What's he look like? Know his name?"

"How the deuce could I? Doesn't make any difference. All I want's a man. Anything'll do."

After many counts he was supplied, and the nameless things, taking up their barrack bags, stumbled on through the mist.

****

It was four o'clock when we reached the area, but lights burned in the mess halls, and mess sergeants and battery clerks were about their tasks. The odour of coffee was prophetic.

Each barrack swallowed its quota. The old men neglected the sleepy, half-frightened expressions of the recruits to stare at the amazing variety of hat cords. Only on a very few hats did the red of the artillery show. On the rest were the colours of the infantry, the signal corps, even the medical corps. With sinking hearts we remembered how our artillery-men had gone to fill the ranks of the infantry. By what curious chances during those days did a man find himself here or there? By what devious contrivances was such a circle drawn?

With so many men in them the mess halls were curiously silent. The drone of voices, reading service records or questioning, increased an atmosphere of somnolence. There was the familiar variety of names and accents and countenances. Most of these men were, in fact, from the West and many of them had had experience with horses. That would help.

The mess sergeant placed steaming cans of coffee and tins of corn bread on the counter. His voice sang out cheerily: "Come and get it!"

The inert and drowsy groups aroused themselves. A rough line was formed and passed stolidly by, each man taking his share without words.

As they munched they stared at the bare walls and the pine tables and the windows beyond which the indifferent dawn illuminated a little through the mist the unfamiliar wastes of Upton.

A sergeant cried with rough good humour:

"We're not going to bite you. What's the matter? Talk up! Haven't you got a song?"

On some of the sleepy, grimy faces a grin struggled. There was no song, but sporadic conversations sprang up here and there and died away.

One man's head rested on his arms which were stretched across a table. A snore disturbed the silence. Others followed with unequal effect. There was a laugh or two.

In a corner a little fellow, bronzed from the western sun, sat before his untasted bread and coffee. He didn't laugh with the others. His expression altered. There grew about his mouth an uncontrollable twitching. For a moment we thought he was going to laugh, too. He began silently and with difficulty to cry.

CHAPTER 7

Goodbyes and the Submarine Zone

In retrospect those who got home may wonder at the quiet force of the regret that crowded those farewell hours. As that philosopher of ours had said, "War is saying goodbye." And goodbyes are seldom easy.

Since most of the regiment couldn't go to town, families came down; and wives, mothers, sweethearts don't speed their nearest on to battle with dry eyes.

These final farewells were given as far as practicable a just proportion of the last rushed days. From morning to night the hostess houses were filled with women, soberly clothed, who knitted, and, for the most part, sat silently, glancing up each time a brown clad figure hurried in.

Towards the end they learned the way to the barracks, and sat in noisy, cluttered mess halls. At each opportunity their men would sit with them. One marvelled at the lack of words. There seemed nothing left to say except goodbye.

At night in the dusk of the station this unnatural repression would be momentarily destroyed; shattered, as it were, by an unavoidable release of emotion too long subdued.

Always the long trains filled slowly, for the passengers, as a rule, waited until the last minute, huddled in the pen-like enclosure beyond which soldiers might not pass. From it arose a perpetual monotone, like a wind in heavy pines—the last effort at repression, the farewells of those who only dared whisper.

Guards and railroad officials urged the unwilling civilians.

"See here, you've only got a minute! Want to miss. the train?"

Then almost always as the dark mass would begin to move, fighting back upon itself, the monotone would rise, as the wind in pine trees rises; and like a knife in the heart of the whispering stillness would flash a cry:

"My boy, my boy! Oh, my boy!"

****

The last goodbyes weren't said until a few hours before our departure.

On April 22nd Lieut. Arthur A. Robinson was assigned to the regiment from the Depot Brigade. He had been with us for a few days in December, coming down from the second Plattsburg Officers' Training Camp. The powers had taken him away almost at once, but there had lingered an impression of an exceptionally pleasant and efficient personality. When the regiment found itself a second lieutenant short at the very last, therefore, it got Robinson, and gave him for the time to the Headquarters Company. Lieutenant Robinson's career was unique in a number of ways. He was, as you shall see, the only officer in the brigade to be awarded the Distinguished Service Cross. He served with more organizations of the regiment than any other officer. As soon as we got to France he went from the Headquarters Company to Battery E. After a few weeks Battery B got him. In the Lorraine sector Battery C was short and had to have a competent officer, so Robinson was shifted, and fought through the war as executive. McKenna got him for the Supply Company in the piping days after the armistice. Everybody wanted Robinson, and when he left us so tragically on the journey to the embarkation centre there was a gap that couldn't possibly be filled.

Colonel Doyle and Captains Dana and Starbuck went to Hoboken on Tuesday, April 23rd. Major Johnson returned from Fort Sill that day, and, in the colonel's absence, took command of the regiment. Under his friendly and easy guidance the task of getting off seemed simple.

We were to leave at 2 o'clock on the morning of April 25th. On Wednesday morning immediately after reveille the straw from the bed sacks was dumped in huge piles in the area and burned. The flames rose high above the buildings. Men, waving their empty white bed sacks, danced around the fires. The picture had a ceremonial air. Before long only ashes remained.

We policed barracks and quarters. They were ready for the next to come, as empty as when we had first invaded them. We wandered about bare places, all at once unfamiliar to us. We were homeless. We had only to count the minutes while we reviewed details. At midnight we had a supper of sandwiches, cakes, and coffee.

Paper Work alone enjoyed himself, altering not at all his ways. In Regimental Headquarters the clerks still toiled.

The organizations were formed on the parade ground, and each man placed his pack in his place, so that when the command to fall in for departure should come we could be off in a minute. The imaginative busied themselves with the manufacture of placards which they nailed to the barrack doors.

"This house to rent. Owners spending the warm season in France."

"Goodbye, Upton! Hello, Berlin!"

"Wipe your feet. We're off to kiss the Kaiser, and can't do it for you."

Out on the parade ground Pullen's bugle blared. The lights in Regimental Headquarters expired. Paper Work went to sleep for the night.

****

"Fall in! Hustle it up there! Squads right! March!" We moved off through the darkness, and turned to the left on Fourth Avenue. It was past belief. We were walking away from Upton. Feet shuffled as if trying to dissipate a dream. It was real. We were actually marching, and our destination was the front.

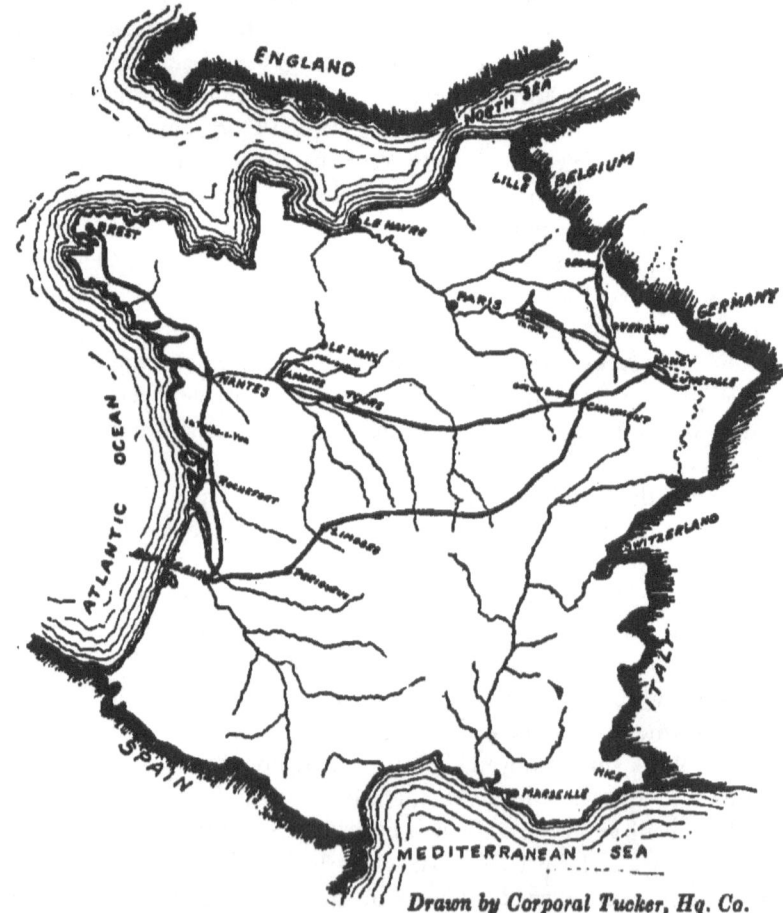

Drawn by Corporal Tucker, Hq. Co.

This map illustrates the travels of the regiment from its landing at Brest to its final billets at Malicorne

There was a precision about that movement that augured well. We found our trains waiting at the railroad station. The column was divided and the proper number of men placed in each car without delay or confusion. Scarcely were we packed in when the trains started.

Through the dawn we approached Long Island City. The first green flashed from trees and bushes. We wondered what the spring would be like in France.

We were under strict orders not to open windows, not to call to people on the roads or at the stations, not to sing. Early passengers watched with a dumb curiosity these trainloads of soldiers silently gliding by.

At Long Island City we crowded our way on ferry boats which took us around the battery to Hoboken. The city was scarcely awake. Only here and there did a man wave his hand carelessly from a park or a wharf. There was nothing glorious about it. We were only interested in what boat we would get. Wallowing up the North River we saw that a number of big ones were in harbour. We nosed towards Hoboken where the *Northern Pacific* and the *Von Steuben*, the old *Kronprinz Wilhelm* lay. The first battalion was destined for the one, and the second for the other.

We poured off and formed in the odorous dusk of the pier. The place was crowded with a feverish activity. It was reminiscent of a factory—a huge factory, greedy for material, which it belched forth, after a moment, ready for the front.

Red Cross men and women trundled little carts along the lines, offering us hot coffee, buns, and cigarettes. We ate greedily but we couldn't smoke, because it was forbidden in the factory.

While we munched, Paper Work awakened. But we had him well in hand. Our passenger lists were right, and so were our accommodation lists, our service records, and our inoculation cards. We were permitted to embark. We went up the gang plank in single file. We were counted off. We were assigned to space. And then they stopped bothering us for awhile.

We examined our temporary home. Our hearts sank a bit. The bunks were in three tiers crowded close to-together. There was an odour of disinfectants, of departed meals. The top bunks seemed safer on the whole.

But we were fortunate. The *Northern Pacific* and *Von Steuben* were better than a good many other transports. And they were fast. Anyway there wasn't much grumbling. Whatever came it was a part of the game. Yet that day and the next were hard—more difficult than storms at sea or the conscious dodging of submarines. For during that period we lay at the pier, seeing the ferryboats go by, answering the fluttering handkerchiefs or the few cheers, and all the time, forbidden to step from the transport. We watched the smoke curling above our homes.

We took refuge in our only antidote. We wrote letters, and signed safe arrival cards. These bore on the back the printed legend, which we were ordered not to alter: *I have arrived safely in Europe.*

Yet when those cards came through to be censored there were few that didn't carry something else—about love. It didn't do any harm. Probably the final censors thought so.

Naval officers seemed to have lost their voices. We had no idea when we would cast off. And there was a strain about this waiting, chained within sight of home. At five o'clock on the afternoon of April 26th the strain broke. The fuel barges moved away. Men hauled in the gangplanks. They commenced to cast off the moorings. The boat slipped into the river with only a discreet blowing of its whistle.

Everyone was ordered below decks. No uniform showed visible except the blue of the navigators on the bridge, and the brown of the officer of the day dashing importantly here and there.

And the world outside seemed oddly indifferent. We crowded to portholes and windows, hungry for a last look.

At dusk the companionways were opened, and we climbed to the decks. We were through the narrows. Ahead lay the grey, empty sea. Behind us, far in the distance, resembling details of a mirage, the towers of New York penetrated the haze, then were lost.

****

The following seven days shared a drab, uncomfortable similarity. Aside from a half hour's sketchy physical exercise and abandon ship drills there was no effort towards concerted work. The limitations of shipboard decreed that.

Abandon ship drill was our most serious occupation. It began on Saturday. Everybody had a blue life jacket. We grew so accustomed to life jackets that they seemed a part of the uniform. They were light, and not uncomfortable. That was as well, for after the first four days, when we reached the danger zone, we wore them at all times. We were no longer, in fact, permitted to remove our clothing at night. We slept in boots and breeches and blouses, with the blue life jacket over all.

At first the drills fell at anticipated hours. We would get our belts and be ready when the bugle blustered. We received at once assignments to boats and rafts. There weren't very many boats, but there were a lot of rafts, so that the great majority of us examined the floats and the open lathe work between, and speculated on methods of launching, wishing we had been lucky enough to get boats. For the rafts would simply be flung overboard, and we would go down rope ladders and get on them as best we could. It looked hazardous, but we believed it could be done if we had a system. So we developed one and tried to account for everything.

We resented the advice of a fortunate individual assigned to a boat; and it wasn't merely a boat. It was the captain's gig.

"It's well enough for you to talk," we said, "you're in a boat. You're lucky."

Our hearts were full of envy.

"I thought I was at first," he admitted, "but I'll swap with any of you. Somebody's reminded me of a thing I'd forgotten, and I'm trying to duck that boat."

"What is it?" we asked. "You're crazy."

"Oh, no. Not at all. You see the captain's the last man to leave the ship."

****

No matter where you were, even at your appointed place, when the bugle cried for abandon ship drill you had to rush to your bunk and wait there in the dusky, close hold of the ship until the gong sent the long lines worming at double time up the companionways and to the deck. It was a good deal to ask a man to leave the air and the sun, in an emergency, and to fight his way through narrow, insufficient passages to the stifling hold; but we could see it was the most efficient way.

As the days passed the drills became more ambitious. They came at unexpected moments—often in the middle of the night.

"Shake it up there! Get to your place! Don't block that passage! Hay, Brown, where did you get the molasses on your shoes?"

And we were never quite sure whether it was a drill or a dangerous actuality.

It was forbidden to talk at abandon ship drill. That was difficult, for sometimes it was nearly an hour before the recall blew. So men talked, and when they did strange punishments were invented. You might see a forlorn individual standing in ranks with a placard hung about his neck, informing all the world: *I talked at abandon ship drill.*

Or another at the head of the companionway, singing out to the running lines: *"I got to learn to hush up when it's orders."* Over and over again, like a man reciting some frantic litany.

The necessity of such precautions, and this severity, were clear to the dullest of us. Because of their speed the *Northern Pacific* and the *Von Steuben* had no convoy. They crossed side by side—two little specks in an endless waste of water. But there were places in that waste where it was necessary for us to go, and there submarines lurked. We would be picked up by destroyers only a day or so out of Brest.

Sometimes the boats were so close together that with glasses we could recognize friends of the other battalion. One was tempted to shout across. And through this narrow lane one night, with the whole sea to accommodate him, a tramp blundered. There was something of the miraculous about that escape. We conducted abandon ship drill more earnestly.

The crossing wasn't all abandon ship drill. The weather occupied us quite a little. After the first two days the sea rose, and the boats showed us how they could roll. Familiar faces disappeared. By Tuesday there was a really high sea running, and preparation for morning inspection of quarters became an ordeal. Instructions were to get every man on deck unless he was literally too ill to be moved.

"What's the matter with this man?" an officer asks the first sergeant, peering into a clearly occupied bunk.

"Says he isn't sea sick," the sergeant answers with a cruel sneer.

"Not seasick, Blank?" the officer interrogates.

Very weak but firm from the bunk:

"No, sir, not a bit."

"Then what's the matter with you?"

"I think I got the—the—the grippe."

"Up then, and get where the air is fresh. It's what we're prescribing this morning for grippe."

Thus caught, the invalid does get out, but not without leaving awful souvenirs of his prevarication.

There were some, heaven knows, that didn't lie.

"And why is this man still in bed?"

"We can't move him, sir," the first sergeant says.

"Feel better if he'd get up. Now what's the matter with you, Doe?"

"Oh! Oh! Oh! Oh!"

"Answer up. What's the matter with you?"

"Oh, my God! Oh, my God!"

"That's nonsense. Do you good to get on deck. Seasickness is all imagination."

The officer looks around him quickly. His own words fail to comfort him. A lurch of the ship throws him against the bunk of pain. If he doesn't come up for air pretty soon himself his end is clear.

"All imagination," he insists weakly. "Get out of here."

With the aid of the first sergeant he gets Doe out. Doe sways, clutching at the air:

"If," he moans, "I ever live to get to France, I'm going to stay there and become a frog."

"Excuse me, Sergeant," says the officer vaguely, "Be right back. I've got to report——"

"All imagination, did I understand the lieutenant to say?" grins the sergeant.

But the officer hears, as he staggers up the ladder, the complaining voice of the invalid.

"Honest, Sergeant, they wouldn't treat a dog so."

"What you kicking about, Doe? Didn't you see the officer had all he could stand?"

And last of all the invalid's voice, suddenly strengthened:

"You ain't foolin'? Honest, Sergeant? *Ha, ha, ha!* Damfi don't feel better."

****

Tuesday was our day of greatest casualties, and wicked was the wit of the survivors. If the quarters were bad the mess hall made them seem very pleasant by comparison. Men, as long as they could manage it, went there, because, except for a few crackers and such things at the commissary, it was the only place on the boat where they could get anything to eat. And somebody had started the abominable lie that eating is the best cure for seasickness. The food was good, too. Let that be put down.

The mess hall was the old first class dining saloon. It was so far down that with any sea running at all no port holes could be opened. Here and there survived traces of its former luxurious decorations, but in place of mahogany one gazed on deal mess tables, crowding each other. An ancient square piano was lashed to the end wall. By the main entrance were the tubs and cans of the cleaning detail. It is no wonder that the grease of one meal couldn't be cleaned from the mess kits for the next. For meals nearly overlapped each other. Organizations had to be fed in turn. In the corridors were processions of men, wondering if they could last until they got in, or if they could manage to get through if they did. And the odorous ghosts of many vanished meals pointed the transient nature of the one in progress.

For one on the edge, the atmosphere inside was nearly unbreathable. The floor was awash with greasy, coffee-coloured water. Kitchen police in those days should have got citations.

On that wildest night the old piano broke its lashings and went drunkenly fraternizing with the tables. It lost a leg and then permitted itself to be led back and tied up again. It furnished a humorous interlude that helped some men. They asked that it be allowed to perform every night.

The guard and the soldier lookouts had to do their jobs, seasick or not. The Captain of the ship had offered a prize to any soldier who spotted a periscope. It kept the lookouts wide awake and it didn't do any harm to the flotsam and jetsam that were reported as periscopes. There were rumours every night that submarines had seen us.

On Thursday evening, when we knew we were well within the danger zone the bugle called us to abandon ship drill. There was an element of strain present. The naval officers had looked glum all day. It was whispered that submarines had been reported near us, that we weren't far from the French coast, that our escort of torpedo boats ought to have picked us up that afternoon, and that the skipper was crowding the air with demands to know where they were. So a feeling grew that this wasn't a drill at all. Yet we all came tumbling down to the close hold, which was lighted only by an occasional blue globe. We stood attentively at the bunks. When the gong rang, we jumped up the stairs with no more than the prescribed hurry. While the last light faded over the water we waited patiently for whatever might follow.

Both boats, one could see, were taking a zigzag course. It strengthened the belief that there were submarines about. The minutes slipped by. The recall didn't come. The presence of submarines was accepted. One strained his ears for an explosion. From the bridges of the two ships signals flashed out. After a long time, when it was quite dark, the recall blew. The men gathered about the decks in whispering groups. No one regretted the experience. It had shown that the crowded boats were at the pitch to behave just so if the thing should happen.

That night, or early the next morning, a story went on the lips of the most conservative, that we had, towards midnight, actually run into a submarine nest, and that two torpedoes had been fired at the *Northern Pacific,* and one at the *Von Steuben.* Judging from the letters home it was accepted generally as a fact.

We knew we should be in by Saturday, and everyone was glad. It was growing irksome to sleep with one's clothes on, to carry everywhere the blue life jacket, to stumble about at night in the insufficient green light, unable to read or play cards.

Friday morning when we went on deck we saw five destroyers, low in the water, their sterns piled with depth bombs, their hulls and superstructures curiously camouflaged. They chased about us as if in pursuit of each other, tearing along our sides, doubling about and dashing perilously beneath our bows or stern. They cheered everyone. The sun was unclouded. The sea had gone down. We commenced to pack.

Early the next morning thick fog shrouded us. We were summoned to abandon ship drill—another business like call, and when we glanced at our compasses we saw that the boat had turned around, and that we were headed west. Was it a flight? We were not released from the stuffy hold until nearly noon, when the white pall thinned and we got back on our course.

Because of this delay we didn't pick up land until after luncheon.

There was no dramatic abruptness about our first glimpse. In the beginning there was just a shadow on the sea far in the south-east. Little by little it deepened and lifted itself above the water.

Nearly without words we crowded the rails and watched the thing grow.

Out of the sombre, low cloud protruded details. Above it wavered a suggestion of green. It spread along the water, ceased to be nebulous, defined itself for us as a bold headland of Finisterre.

France, we thought, where it's happened for four years, and flames now, waiting for us!

That was the reason for the nearly motionless silence along the decks, for the eyes fixed on each detail which seemed a little sacred.

The outlines of trees and houses traced themselves before us. We had left America just struggling from the sober cloak of winter. Spring had done all it would for France. The coast appeared abnormally green and gay.

Aeroplanes whirred overhead. A dirigible, catching the sun like a placid planet, came to meet us, swung about, and escorted us in. The white and brown cliffs closed around us, like a welcoming embrace from the land. We felt ourselves drawn to a smiling serenity, a drowsy and remote content. Yet all the time we knew it was nature's masquerade. It changed nothing for us. We were in France, which for nearly four years had submitted to the scarlet and voluble shock of a perpetual disaster.

CHAPTER 8

Brest, Pontanezin and the Chemin de Fer

Down in the throat of the harbour the houses of Brest detached themselves from the hillside. Small boats bore French officials and men in our own uniform to us.

The *Von Steuben* anchored in the inner harbour. The *Northern Pacific* was warped against a stone pier. A few soldiers waved their hands at us. Here and there a French civilian stared, saluted, and passed on. We had come when the world waited in suspense between two phases of the great German offensive. It did not seem odd that we were welcomed as we had greeted France, with sensations that unconsciously avoided expression.

Colonel Doyle had caused so much to be read to the regiment, under orders from G. H. Q., of precautions of one sort and another that many men expected to be invited ashore at once and introduced to all the gaieties of the city. Now it was announced that, except for the baggage details, no one would be allowed ashore. Glancing back, the prisoners seem to have had something the better of it.

The details, with packs, left the ship at dusk and marched through the railroad yards to an unpainted enclosure, crowded with long, low sheds. Our baggage would be brought from the ships in scows to the enclosure. We would sort it there and carry it to the sheds reserved for the 305th. We were told what to expect.

"No man will be permitted to leave the yard. There's nothing to do until the lighters begin dumping the baggage. Make yourselves comfortable."

A friendly fellow who had been through the mill gave us a word of advice.

"Sleep while you can."

But where? How? We set watches and stretched out on the ground. There was nothing else to do, and it seemed particularly unpleasant and soiled ground. But at midnight the lighters commenced to dump their freight, and we didn't have to worry about getting to sleep after that.

From then until the next night the details worked, sorting, checking, and wrangling with ambitious people from strange organizations. We got our barrack bags, trunks, bedding-rolls, and boxes of equipment piled in the sheds. Then the details were marched out of the dusty yard and back to the boats in time for supper and a bath.

The rest of the regiment, meantime, had stretched its legs for two hours, doing a sort of Cook's tour of the town and its neighbourhood. They had come close to the French and had been able to judge how much of young France was at war. They had set eyes for the first time on Hun prisoners marching under guard through the streets.

We became aware at once of a distressing habit of French children. Three English words they all knew: *cigarette, penny,* and—*goodbye.* We never could understand why, when they probably meant *hello* they always gave us a farewell. Or after so much war had even the children become fatalistic and a trifle cynical? It was not, we realized later, a local habit. Marching into some places it was a most depressing one.

Cigarettes and pennies we gave them until the demand threatened our own supplies. At the close of that second night in Brest we were convinced, in spite of its nearly voiceless welcome, that France was deeply grateful we had come.

No one seemed to know exactly what the immediate future held for us. After our seven months' training at Upton we realized we were far from fit for the line. It seemed certain that we would go to some training camp for a few weeks' instruction in the real things. We understood that men were needed and that we would be sent up, as soon as possible.

We were told that night that we would march the next morning to a camp four or five miles from Brest at a place called Pontanezin Barracks. It was, we were informed, known as a rest camp. That sounded enticing, and we were up early, and trooped off the boats, and marched up the long hill and into the open country.

According to the information gathered by the soldiers nearly everything in France was built either by Caesar or Napoleon. Pontanezin went on Napoleon's score card. From a distance it was entirely picturesque. More intimately it developed white-washed buildings, like barns within, and arid, dusty courtyards. We congratulated ourselves when we learned the barracks were full, and that we would be quartered in tents in a pleasant grove to one side.

The grove had the appearance, in fact, of a rest camp. As it turned out, the name was as perverted as "shirt, under."

What with getting settled, posting guard, drawing rations, setting up kitchens, preparing to police on the morrow, accepting the omnipresent casual, and returning the same, it was dark before the regiment had time to breathe. Still the night loomed restfully. Then the night descended and brought new demands. Orders came. Battery A would break camp at 4:30 a. m., because it was to travel with the 304th Field Artillery, and the brigade was moving at once. The rest of us would march back to Brest at 10:30 in the morning. Then we did have a destination! Some located it on the Swiss border. Others in something they called the forward training area. A third group spoke of the vicinity of Bordeaux. It carried off the laurels. We were bound for the Champ de Tir de Souge.

Weary-eyed we turned our backs on our sylvan rest camp, and tramped to the Brest railroad station. It was here that most of the regiment saw for the first time the now familiar Hommes and Chevaux palace cars. The regiment that pulled out ahead of us had them. Our train was composed of third class carriages, and we laughed at the other fellows while we munched our luncheon of bread and corn willy in the railroad yards.

"Those bullies are travelling like a lot of cattle," one heard. "We can sit up and play cards and look out of the window——"

Perfectly true, but after one experience you should hear how eagerly we would ask on the eve of another journey if we weren't going to have Hommes and Chevaux.

"Sardine boxes are all right for sardines," was the verdict on third class carriages, loaded to capacity, after that first ride, "But they didn't give us any oil."

It was seldom necessary to fill goods vans uncomfortably, and you could stretch out and go to sleep. In the third class carriages there were nearly always broken windows. In the goods van, if it got cold, you simply shut the door.

That first trip, however, we piled in thankfully, and had our first doubt when we realized how little room there was for stowing equipment.

A number of small boys from the summit of a neighbouring wall watched us entrain. Proudly they chanted for us that haphazard Marseillaise of the American soldier.

"Hail! Hail! The gang's all here."

And when the train started a little after two they followed us with the inevitable "goodbye" which rose to a supplicating shriek.

The placid and picturesque landscape of Finisterre and Brittany was a little unreal. Many of the regiment were seeing it for the first time. After the cramped voyage and the thorough rest at Pontanezin such a journey seemed like a holiday. We had been afraid of starvation, and had bought here and there. We found, therefore, that we had more than we really needed to eat, and at every station there were carts and stands loaded with fruit and cakes. We always descended to exercise what French we had or to acquire some. In return for cigarettes we get the beginnings of a vocabulary.

France, clearly, wasn't starving, nor was it going thirsty. Wine was forbidden on the train. A guard was set at each stop with instructions to see that no one carried bottles aboard. He couldn't have eyes in the back of his head, however, and the French thought it very funny to help fool him. There was plenty of opportunity, for water was allowed, and the faucets marked *Eau Potable* were often at some distance from the train. There were usually vendors of stronger stuff about these places. Coming back, men's coats bulged oddly. As the train rolled on the shattering of glass now and then on the right of way was at least suggestive.

If the stuff got aboard it didn't seem to do any damage. There was no disorder. The customary songs didn't increase in volume or expressiveness.

We enjoyed the scenery, commenting on the quaint and calm costume of the Breton peasant, forgetting almost that we were at war, until just at dark a peculiar and riotous alarm recalled us.

Confused cries ran along the train, indistinguishable at first, but carrying a note of excessive tragedy. They rose. A pistol shot rang out. Another. A salvo. A bugle blared.

We sprang to our feet and stared from the windows. The train bowled through a cutting. Heads leaned from every window. Nothing more unusual was visible. The racket continued, and out of it slipped words that could be grasped.

"Stop the train! Stop the train!"

The plausible explanation sprang at everyone. Someone had fallen out. Back on the line must lie a still form. But a calmer mind reasoned. In time of war, its logic ran, troop trains, squeezed into schedules with difficulty, don't stop and block things for the carelessness of a single man. Such a catastrophe would be treated by sending back word from the next station. No, the calm reasoning went on, it must be something far more serious than that. We believed it when word came along that The Great wanted the train stopped. We could hit on only one explanation. The train must have broken in two. An express thundered behind us. We were, we learned later, to get out of its way at the next stop, a few miles ahead. The fate of that motionless string of cars, packed with, perhaps, half our companions, was terrible to contemplate. So an officer and several men, crawled forward over a string of goods vans to the locomotive. The execution to their clothing was appalling. But they persuaded the driver to stop the train, although he seemed in danger of a fit before he yielded, shouting things about the express that our amateur interpreters had difficulty with. They gestured rather more than he did and got their way.

The train stopped. The engine driver animated himself volubly. He saw that the train had not broken in two. He sprang to the throttle, threw it open, dashed us into the station on a side track, and pointed to the express which roared in a little after us.

Colonel Doyle, Majors Johnson and Wanvig, and the train interpreter hurried to the engine, while we waited to learn the truth. But there came the answer himself across the tracks—a wobbly soldier just descended from the express and supported by a medical orderly.

There is, after all, a great deal of anti-climax about war. The present case failed to give us the thrill we had anticipated. It boiled down to indigestion, rather severe, still vulgarly gastric. It had struck the wobbly soldier at the previous station. Captain Parramore had instructed one of the medical orderlies to take him from the train and care for him. The train had departed sooner than anyone had expected, leaving the sick man and his attendant. They hadn't worried because they were told they could catch us by the express. Captain Parramore had told the Colonel they had been left. After our premonitions we didn't miss a more dramatic *denouement*.

Such incidents break the monotony of a journey. A different sort spelled variety the next morning. We rolled into Nantes about seven o'clock after a cramped night. We weren't surprised to learn we would be there until eight, for Nantes is a large city. A warm breakfast beckoned. Some of us snatched it in nearby cafes, and hurried back to the train which left without any particular warning at 7:50. Men scurried from every direction and scrambled through the open doors of the compartments. We made a hurried check.

Everything was all right except that neither battalion had a commander or an adjutant. Majors Johnson and Wanvig and Captains Reed and Delanoy had breakfasted not wisely but too well. What the colonel thought about it we never heard. There was, this time, no effort made to hold the train for the missing, although their misfortune, too was vulgarly gastric.

So we crossed the Loire and turned to the south through Les Roches Sur Yonne, La Rochelle, and Rochefort, where our missing officers rejoined us, grateful to the French for a travel order and convenient express trains. They looked so well shaved and comfortably fed that we gathered they wouldn't make any trouble for the railroad company about leaving them.

At Saintes on the Charente, where we stopped at dusk, the war seemed to come closer. We all piled from the train and had half an hour's brisk march through the picturesque little city. But it was the railroad station that impressed us most. *Permissionaires* swarmed there

THE COOLIES HARD AT WORK, AT CAMP DE SOUGE.
Drawn by Musician Boyle, Hq. Co.

in faded blue uniforms and battered helmets. Some were smiling and happy, talking with vivacity and wide gestures to civilians. Evidently they had just arrived. The soil of the front line still stained their clothing. Others, far neater and encumbered with equipment, did not have much to say. Clearly enough their holiday was over. They were going back to the thing that waited for us.

We tried to visualize ourselves within a few weeks at one with these men whose faces were bronzed and sadly wise. We tried to approximate their emotions. Our next train journey, we remembered, would be in their direction. There was a fascination in standing close to them and wondering.

After another cramped night the spires of Bordeaux greeted us across the vineyards of the Gironde, and at seven o'clock the train halted with a definite jerk at the railhead of Bonneau.

Lt. Klots, who had come as our advance agent, met us and guided the tired column, bent beneath its packs, down a road that entered a pine wood.

"It looks like Upton," we said.

But these evergreens were larger, the sand was deeper, and at a crossroads was an *estaminet* with tables and chairs set on the edge of the road.

It was only two miles to an arched gateway, surmounted by the republican cock and the legend: *Champ de Tir de Souge*.

Within we found endless rows of French barracks, painted brown. As we marched along the main avenue we noticed inscribed panels above the doors, reciting the valorous death of some officer or non-commissioned officer who had trained there.

By noon assignments were made. Barrack bags and baggage had arrived. Except for the sand, we gathered, Souge would not be uncomfortable. We were vastly amused at hordes of French coolies, parading around beneath umbrellas against the sun, or languidly making a pretence at work.

CHAPTER 9

Souge and First Casualties

The coolies, we soon realized, would be an irritation, for we wouldn't be allowed to loaf here. We were to be put at once into the way of fulfilling our destiny. We were equipped first of all like the artillery regiment we were. Six batteries of *soixante-quinzes* were delivered to us in the spacious gun park. Sleek and lithe with an iron grace, they stuck their noses from their painted shields. They looked terribly competent, a little snobbish, too. They seemed to remind us that they weren't three inch guns, and that we had a lot to learn before we would really be fit to handle them.

Limbers and caissons were of an unfamiliar pattern. We gathered about the grey *fourgons*—a cross between a gypsy van and a prairie schooner. They looked sturdy and faithful, and they turned out so.

Telephones, switchboards, wire, wireless sets, *goniometers*, scissors—they all came streaming in. Except for horses we were fully equipped within the first few days, and the horses commenced to arrive and breed dissension almost at once.

We didn't have much time to admire all this. We were put to work to learn something about it before we tried it on the Bosche. The course was announced as eight weeks long. After the first day we glanced at each other hopelessly. What had they done with us at Upton for seven months? How could we absorb all this strange, fascinating, and fundamental knowledge in a few days?

At first officers and men went to standing gun drill. The officers followed with terrain board work, the men with specialist instruction. The officers spent the rest of the day at general lectures on conduct of fire, orientation, communication, materiel. We were given elaborate range tables. We heard of stripping ranges and transport of fire, and D v zero, and K zero. Heads buzzed.

"If I have to figure all these things before I shoot at the Bosche," someone said, "the war will be over before I get my first shell off."

The sun grew hot and the sand more clinging, reminding us we were in the south, as we trudged to classes or walked many kilometres with plane tables and instruments for orientation exercises.

During this period of education the regiment more or less ran itself. Officers and men went to different classes. The hours didn't coincide. Often for drill there would be no officer present. Yet the work didn't slump. Discipline maintained its old standard.

We were the first national army division in France, so our instructors had been drawn from the few Regular Army and National Guard Divisions that had preceded us. They had had some little experience in what might be called parlour trench fighting. We grasped at it. It was invaluable to us. We tried to emulate their easy command of the finer points of French artillery specialization.

Frequently we got to Bordeaux for a week end relaxation. The neighbouring villages of Martignas and St. Jean d'Illac offered a smiling hospitality. For less adventurous spirits there was a collection of booths just outside the gate, where one could sample French cookery and wines. Then during the second week measles appeared, and for a time all passes were stopped.

We had solved the mechanical puzzles of the *soixante-quinze*, and something of the mysteries of orientation and modern conduct of fire. On May 27th we went to the range to shoot. There were just enough horses at that time to draw one battery out, and the second battalion got them for E battery, which had won the gun drill competition and had been selected to fire with C the first shots on the range.

C battery tried trucks. They got the pieces and caissons as far as the macadamized road went. There remained, perhaps a mile and a half of sand. The trucks wouldn't touch it. The cannoneers looked at the deep ruts and the heavy pieces.

"We have been honoured with this first job to fire," they said to each other.

They put their shoulders to the wheels. They kept talking about that honour. They wondered why they had ever gone into the artillery to be so appreciatively singled out. They managed, however, a little limp themselves, to get the carriages to the position in front of observatory 3, where others had dug emplacements and sunk trail logs. The details located the guns, got the aiming sticks up, and ran wires to the observatory and into the range telephone system.

Captain Roger D. Swaim, of the New England National Guard was the First Battalion's firing instructor, and Capt. Kelly, of the same organization, the Second's. They met us at the observatories at 7:30 Monday morning, and we started.

We had so much ammunition that we forgot to gaze at each shell as if it were a precious pearl being cast before swine.

The projectiles went away in quick salvos, and after the first few we knew that while we weren't perfect we could bracket a target and get real effect on it. Then the instructors criticized, the colonel did the same, and the majors usually had their say. Those who hadn't fired looked at the man conducting smugly. Yet always sooner or later they got, as one phrases it, theirs.

That was the beginning of endless hours in the observatories. We averaged four hours firing and eight hundred rounds a day.

Our first day on the range, it will be recalled, saw the opening of the great German offensive across the Chemin des Dames, through Château Thierry, and nearly to the gates of Paris. After the thrust at Amiens and about Ypres the Bosche had lain quiescent, and his startling initial successes carried a vivid shock to us in the midst of our schooling. We guessed our plans would be altered, for more artillery was needed. A cry went up for every available man. Yet the change when it came was no less of a shock than the great battle. The schedule was published at the end of the week. We would start on the range at 7 o'clock. We would get back in time for a hurried bite of luncheon. From then until 5 o'clock we would have terrain board and specialist instruction, and gas would have to be worked in now. It went between 5 o'clock and supper. From supper time until nine o'clock we would listen to lectures on ammunition, fuses, and various subjects. Then, if we liked, we could attend to our routine organization work, and study. Then, if there was any time, we could go to sleep.

The emergency was, indeed, grave. We even heard rumours that the government had moved from Paris to Bordeaux a second time, and we went into town that week end apprehensive of too many figures in frock coats and silk hats.

After a few days the news was better, but it didn't affect our schedule. During the afternoon classes, after nights of insufficient rest and mornings of intricate calculations and eye strain on the range, we struggled against sleep.

Lieutenant-Colonel Stimson returned to the regiment during this phase. He had visited several fronts and had taken the course at the staff college at Langres.

Lieutenant Mitchell, in spite of his experience, was not named regimental gas officer. That position went to Lieutenant Gilbert Thirkield. Our gas drill consisted in exercises in speed, and walks or runs, wearing the masks. We tried to accustom ourselves to goggles that always clouded, to mouthpieces that left us a trifle choked, to head bands that exerted a painful and increasing pressure.

Into the midst of this earnest endeavour the horses came, and time had to be found to take cape of them and to wrangle over them. They weren't very good horses, but they served to arouse that passionate gypsy instinct that informs all lovers of animals. There was sharp trading and devious scheming to get the best of each lot.

A new batch would arrive from the remount depot. It couldn't be assigned to one organization without giving the others a fair chance for its best. An order would come around that organization commanders might exchange the choice of their individual mounts for anything that caught their fancy in the new lot. The horse fair would begin.

This fair was usually held in the deep sand by the stables. Officers and men would form a ring about a row of shaggy beasts held by self-conscious orderlies. Critical eyes would run down the line, taking in the badly used thoroughbred, a thing of possibilities; the narrow-chested over breed; the useful animal of poor but honest ancestry; the pitiful crocks. Arguments would spring up as to the virtues of some particular beast. You invariably weighed the reverse of an expressed opinion. Faces would grow red, and voices hoarse from reiterated convictions.

"I'll swap for this one," a captain says.

"All right," from the officer in charge of the fair. "Bring on your best mount."

The captain strides away. After a time the circle parts to admit him and his prize—a spring-kneed, mangy cob from the hospital. It takes two orderlies to support it.

"*Whoa!*" cries the captain, and pats him gently as if to persuade him not to cut up.

He points to the new horse he has chosen, and instructs his orderly.

"Lead that fellow out. I think I'm getting stung, but I agreed to swap, and I will."

The orderly leaves the invalid, glancing back as if to make sure he hasn't toppled over. The other side of the exchange raises his voice.

"like the deuce you'll swap. What did you bring that hat-rack here for?"

The captain's expression is of innocent surprise.

"To trade with you as the order directed."

The other sneers.

"Thought you'd made a mistake and believed I was running a soap factory, or maybe you want to borrow a detail to dig his grave."

"Very funny! Very funny! That's one of the best horses in the regiment."

The orderly puts in gravely:

"It's a real hardship to see him go, sir. He's just a little sick."

"My interpretation of the order," the objector says, "is that you can trade your best individual mount. If that's it, your battery will walk."

The captain gestures.

"Orders are orders. You've got to trade."

A very superior officer intervenes.

"Gentlemen!—Or maybe I ought to say gypsies—We can't do business this way. We'll get an interpretation that will give everyone a square deal. Meantime, put the horses up."

And the red disappears from the faces of the wranglers, and they go away arm in arm, good friends until the next fair day.

****

Sharp trading was necessary. Not only were many of the horses bad, but they died in large numbers, and replacements weren't simple to get.

Major Johnson was largely instrumental in holding casualties down and in conditioning the survivors. He was also a bulwark between us and the gypsy desires of other organizations. For the horse trade fever swept the entire brigade.

"I thought they might court martial me today," he would say after an hour or two at the stables or brigade headquarters with higher ranking officers than himself, "but I've held them off our horses."

The remount men watched the bargaining and smiled. They had their own axe to grind, and they liked to see a favourite animal well placed. They were capable of diplomacy when officers of higher rank than the one chosen threatened to interfere.

"Sure. A beautiful horse, sir," the remount man might say to the very high ranking officer. Few better in looks have come out of the depot. You *might* go farther and fare worse."

He winks at the junior officer for whom that horse is destined. The senior glances up.

"What do you mean? What's the matter with him?"

"Matter! Who said anything was the matter? Of course, sir, all horses have their little foibles."

"I thought so. Talk up. What's the matter with this one?"

The remount man gazes at him admiringly.

"No fooling you, sir! But I don't go back on what I said. A beautiful animal, and he might give you good service if you took chances and had a little luck. I go on the principle that no horse is hopeless, but this one is a genuine bad actor."

Exit high ranking officer.

****

We had practical uses for our horses now. Some of the gun positions and observatories were five kilometres or so from our quarters. It often took hard riding to snare a bite of luncheon before the first of the afternoon classes.

Lieutenants Hoyt, Montague, Gurney, and Church, who had been delayed in America to bring over casuals, joined us early in June. Shortly afterwards Lieutenants Hoyt and Norman Thirkield were sent to balloon school, and Lieutenants Jones, Montague, and Gurney to aviation instruction. Lieutenant Hoyt soon after was ordered by G. H. Q. to the liaison service, and the regiment said goodbye to him regretfully.

We had got into lateral and bi-lateral observation by this time. Often the guns were several miles from the officer conducting fire, but communication was always open, and the result of these exercises plainly told us that we were nearly ready for the Hun. Before this war it would have been considered an absurdity to try to train an artilleryman even in the old fashioned methods during so brief a period. But here we were—good. The regiment felt it. A little later, the Hun felt it, too.

Our first casualties came to us on the range at Souge. It was on June 20—We were registering for an intensive barrage that would mark the close of the course.

The two battalions had established command posts at some distance from each other. Each had put in elaborate schemes of communication, practically independent of the range system. Major Johnson had received permission to locate the pieces of the first battalion according to the technique of actual warfare. He got camouflage nets which, with the natural cover, hid the positions so successfully that an aeroplane photograph, taken for our instruction, was innocent of warlike indications.

The first platoon of Battery B was scarcely more than fifty metres from Major Johnson's command post, Observatory 1. The pieces were echeloned, each under its own camouflage net.

The registration progressed, as registrations do, to a precise and dreary measure. Without warning and with no unusual noise Battery B's number 2 piece was shattered by a premature burst. For a moment a cloud of smoke obscured it. As it drifted away we saw that the camouflage net had disappeared, that the caisson was blackened and smouldering, that the breech of the piece had gone. The crew, from an ordered group, had become a thing, scattered and incomplete. Men stumbled oddly as they ran out of the cloud. There were not enough of them.

"Cease firing!" Major Johnson ordered. "Where's the sturgeon?"

The operator passed the word over the telephone. Flames sprang from the smouldering caisson. Shells there were evidently bursting. Major Johnson ordered everyone from the observatory, and, followed by his adjutant, Captain Reed, and Captain Ravenel walked forward and threw sand at the caisson. Unasked, volunteers sprang from the ranks into the danger zone. In a few minutes the fire was extinguished. Those on the outskirts questioned.

Early and Imperfect Days on the Range at Souge

"How much damage? Anybody hurt?"

And from the group about the smashed piece came back the quiet answer: "The gunner and No. 1 killed."

Everyone had guessed that would be so. Sitting on either side of the breech there had never been much chance for them.

The director of the school came. A board was appointed and the evidence taken. We had learned to fear long fuses, but the damage had been done by a white fused shell, and No. 2 had looked through the bore, so that the blanket verdict of faulty ammunition went down.

An ambulance dashed up and backed towards the group. Two covered forms were lifted into it, then it clanged a swift-way towards camp.

"Brace up!" an officer called with kind brutality. "You'll see plenty of other men killed before you get through with this war. Get on the job now. Firing will be resumed."

The men responded, shaking themselves rather as dogs do after an unexpected immersion. That afternoon there was a new piece firing from the destroyed gun's platform. The gunner and No 1 did not flinch. The day's work went on with a noisy rapidity.

"Yet," as someone wisely remarked, "it can't be like seeing men killed in battle."

Privates Jeremiah S. Lynch and Harry J. Posner were buried the next day. Chaplain Sheridan conducted the services, and Mrs. Gariessen, of the Y. M. C. A., who had a short time before lost her own son in action, tried as best she could to take the place of the mothers. Lynch and Posner received full military honours. Men from every organization attended the funeral and saw more distinctly in the bland southern sunlight the vicious and amazing shadow that is war.

Chapter 10

Hustled to the Front

The regiment went about its business with its former eagerness. We were told that our first rolling barrage was worthy of veteran troops. It certainly made enough noise and black smoke. The next, with the guns of the two light regiments in a long row, was as good. We admired the dust clouds half obscuring the quickly sliding tubes, and the changing black curtain drawn across the range.

"No one," we told ourselves, "could get through that."

Our instructors admitted that there didn't seem to be any holes.

Such perfection wasn't reached without delays and adventures. The weather had grown steadily warmer. There had been scarcely any rain. Consequently the range was abnormally dry. When the 306th got its 155 howitzers and opened fire with practice shells these factors produced worse conflagrations than we had had at Upton. They stopped our work. They sent us to warm and uncongenial labour. Towards the climax of a delicate adjustment it was distracting to hear someone say to the instructor:

"Isn't that smoke over there sir? I think it's a fire on the range."

The instructor always looked through the binoculars, and nearly always in a tone of helpless disgust, called to the operator.

"Cease firing! Fire on the range."

The battle roar would die before a threatening silence.

We never learned. We always hoped until the last minute that the flames would burn themselves out. But always the small smoke ball with its red centre would grow, and spring into a black fan with a flame fringe, sweeping before the wind which always blew in that place.

Then the colonel, or the brigade commander, if he was there, would call for trucks and men until the greater part of the brigade and the ammunition train was on the range, starting counter fires, or with picks and shovels clearing ground before the flames.

It usually meant an afternoon's hot work at the expense of specialist instruction. That had about run its course anyway. The days had slipped

Drawn by Corporal Roos, Battery D
"The Battle Roar Would Die Before a Threatening Silence"

into weeks, and towards the end of June we knew we were as nearly ready as Souge would make us. Our departure waited only on transportation. We speculated as to where we would go. Our infantry had trained with the British in Flanders. For a long time we thought we would fight there.

Tours wanted to know which regiment would volunteer to hold itself ready to move at a moment's notice. The 305th offered itself. We entered a new age of packing. We had more equipment, but we also had more experience, and we got ready with little of the neurasthenic hurry of Upton.

Here at the last, our carefully studied organization was shattered. Other artillery brigades were coming to France, and they would have to be instructed. Under orders from the Chief of Artillery the Souge instructors chose from the brigade a certain number of officers who, they considered, had shown aptitude. They would either remain behind now, or be called on later to teach artillery.

We felt our regiment had been unduly complimented. Captains Reed, Delanoy, and Ravenel were to leave us at once. Lieutenants Camp, Church, and Fenn might be called from their organizations at any time.

Lieutenant-Colonel Stimson went to G.H.Q. hoping to accomplish the release of the three captains.

Lieutenant Camp was made acting adjutant of the First Battalion, and Lieutenant Fenn of the Second. Lieutenant Montgomery took command of Battery B. Captain Fox had some time before been made personnel adjutant, so Lieutenant Kane was the commanding officer of Battery C. With these radical changes made we were ready to go into action.

****

From day to day we waited for word from Tours that our transportation was ready. The Fourth of July was near. The general commanding the base section wished the brigade, if it had not moved by the holiday, to take part in a monster parade in Bordeaux. That ceremony kept us on the anxious seat for a number of days. In the morning the parade would be a certainty. After luncheon there wasn't a chance that we would make it. The next morning there was no question. We would make it. It wasn't until July 3rd that we knew, and then we were told that we would leave, mounted, immediately after luncheon, camp at a race course outside Bordeaux, march in the next morning, parade, and come all the way back before night. On July 5th the regiment would start entraining.

It looked like a difficult programme. Our drivers had had very little road work. The regiment had never before been mounted as a whole. We were afraid of our horses. Could they do it? Was it wise to make them do it, when they would have to stand immediately afterwards for three days in box cars?

Just before we left, Major Johnson's promotion to the rank of lieutenant-colonel came through. It cast another shadow, because we knew the powers wouldn't let us have two lieutenant-colonels.

After luncheon the regiment gathered in the gun park. The teams were brought from the stables, protesting at the unusual exercise. The drivers reproved them with harsh voices. A fog of dust arose and settled over the place. Through it you caught glimpses of prancing horses, struggling men, yellow harness. Out of it came a chorus of commands, entreaties, threats. Guidons flashed red, like a gleam of sunlight through the rolling mist. The sunlight grew. The mists rolled away. Wheels, swings, and leads stood in their places. Behind them the yellow and black carriages rested expectant.

"Prepare to Mount! Mount!"

Drivers sprang to their saddles. The leading battery moved out. The others followed. Leaving camp, the column may have twisted a little, and wheels may have slipped into the sand on either side of the avenue, but the column kept growing, until from the park it stretched into a string incredibly long and business like and military.

Road discipline came to us, as it were, instinctively. There were no stragglers. Drivers mounted and dismounted precisely at every halt, We took a narrow country road, and on a curving hill—as difficult a place as you could choose—met a supply train coming up. We got our carriages into the ditches. We wormed by. Nothing upset. On the jammed roads at the front we found nothing much more puzzling. We commenced right there to take a pride in the regiment mounted. Self-satisfied we listened to the heavy rumbling of the carriages. We glanced back from every turn at the struggling horses, the sleek pieces, the caissons, low and awkward. The whole had an appearance of grotesque beauty.

The Stad Bordelaix was green and trimmed, like a huge formal garden. We camped by the steeple chase course. We parked, and pitched tents, then for the first time faced the problem of watering on the march. We found the familiar lack of facilities, the accustomed waste of time in going long distances with a few horses. But it was experience that we needed, and we saw it was a good thing we should have come.

A few fortunate ones got passes for Bordeaux. The rest, after mess, lay about in fresh-cut hay, and tried to realize it was their last experience in the S. O. S.

The next morning our apprehension vanished. The First Battalion took one road to town the Second another.

"We'll rendezvous all right," the commanders said confidently.

They did, moreover, in spite of the apparent confusion in the city. Every element fell into its own place in the column. The parade started.

Bordeaux gave us a gracious welcome. Masses of citizens threw flowers and confetti from bunting-hung buildings. They liked the looks of the American artillery, equipped with their own *soixante-quinzes*. They were glad to see the Americans. Turning into the Place de la Comediae the band blared out the *Sambre et Meuse*. The closely packed mass of the French burst into cheers, flung hats into the air, madly waved banners.

A tribune had been erected in the Grande Place. Local celebrities stood there, and French and American generals. Opposite was a line of veterans, some with missing limbs. They held flags, decorated with the names of breathless battles. These they dipped, and our bright new colours bobbed back. It did us good. It painted our work for the first time with sentiment. It was our first touch of the spectacular side of things military. That has the thrill that war lacks.

We paid a small price. Only one piece was put out by unmanageable horses. Only one man on that piece was hurt. Only one was thrown from his horse, and that was Dr. Parramore, tearing back to attend the victim of the accident. The crowd was interested.

Regimental Headquarters and organization commanders hurried by automobile back to Souge immediately after the parade to prepare for the movement to the front.

The regiment, in command of Lieutenant Colonel Johnson, returned to the Stad Bordelaix, watered, fed, and messed, and afterwards made the long march back to camp.

We had one lesson that impressed on us the necessity of close liaison even in the smallest column. At a crossroads another regiment cut our line of march, and the Second Battalion followed in its wake. There was a good deal of time and energy lost in finding the three batteries, turning them around, and getting them back in line.

We pulled into Souge at dusk, tired, dirty, and with a lot of grooming and rubbing before us, but on the whole triumphant.

The next day the movement commenced. The Headquarters Company left the railhead at Bonneau, where less than two months before we had detrained, uninstructed and unequipped.

Nearly everyone, it might be said, thought that we would be billeted behind the lines for several weeks of the road work we so much needed. That took a little of the seriousness from the journey.

Regimental Headquarters and the Supply Company left the afternoon of the sixth, and First Battalion Headquarters and Battery A that same evening. During the next three days the other batteries pulled out, while the 304th and 306th waited their turn.

We said goodbye to Captains Reed, Ravenel, and Delanoy without knowing when we would see them again.

Entraining a battery mounted was a new experience for all our captains except Dana. The entire regiment had arrived in one train. Now each organization had a train to itself, and was forced to crowd a little to get everything on.

These artillery trains were all of a pattern. There were the *hommes* and *chevaux* for animals and men, a combination first and second class coach for officers, and a string of flats for the carriages.

At Bonneau there was a loading platform. In some places we found none, and used instead clumsy moveable ramps. Yet methods varied little. With practice we got some of the skill of circus men. The different tasks proceeded simultaneously. An incoherence seemed to prevail. Then all at once the groups would scatter, and you would see that the job had been done, that the train was either loaded or unloaded.

None of our organizations needed the three hours allowed them for entraining at Bonneau. The carriages were little trouble. Squads ran them from the platform to the flat cars across heavy planks, fitted them into the constricted space allotted, and lashed them there with cleats.

The drivers struggled with the horses. The horses never got to like the *hommes* and *chevaux*. They rose on their haunches, at times crying out their disapproval. The men tugged at their halters, and persuaded them from the rear. A horse already in the narrow, shadowy car would look out and shake his head. It was often quite difficult to combat such friendly advice.

The stallions were a problem. If you put them together they gossiped about old scandals and ended by fighting jealously. If you placed them with lesser beasts they expressed their contempt with tooth and hoof.

"Get 'em in so tight they can't fight," crystallized the advice of most of the men, and it worked fairly well.

We got to know after a time which horses liked to travel together, and that simplified matters.

From the moment the train was loaded until it was unloaded one lived in a racket like the beating of countless bass drums. Noiselessness on the part of a horse was a symptom of extreme illness.

Sick horses were, in fact, a problem. Unless an animal was practically in *rigor mortis* we took him along. Sometimes one died *en route* then we had to telegraph ahead and make arrangements to evacuate him. Sometimes the sick survived the journey and died on the picket line afterwards. Infrequently they got well. It was the best we could do with animals as scarce as they were.

When a battery had finished loading it looked a good deal like a circus train. The heads of horses appeared through the open doors of some box cars. Men sat, dangling their legs, in others. The *fourgon* always appeared gigantic on its flat, and behind it stretched the sleek inquisitive noses of the pieces and the stubby bulk of caissons and limbers. Usually the water cart and the rolling kitchen were on a flat next to the men's cars. Brown figures were busy about the kitchen, and a promising smoke belched from its chimney.

It was on that first journey that we learned to know and love the clumsy, sooty rolling-kitchen. On the road it was incredibly noisy, and it had a habit of shedding its parts; yet it stood frequently between us and hunger and cold. It was our best friend against evil weather and too much physical labour. On these train journeys it gave us hot food, and it made us independent of the very unsatisfactory coffee stops.

There were certain stations that were announced to us by that name. The train paused at them usually at inconvenient hours, long enough for the men to line up with mess cups which were filled with a black liquid from unappetizing pails. They were supposed to be a convenience, but they seemed to possess also a routine element. An interpreter would rush up to the officers' car sometime before reaching one of these places.

"Coffee stop in an hour. You will want coffee there."

Drawn by Corporal Roos and Private Enroth

The horses never got to like the Hommes and Chevaux

Not a question. A command.

The train commander would shake his head, pointing to the black cloud rising from the rolling kitchen. He could grin at the surprise and disapproval of the interpreter.

Corn willy, too, it ought not to be forgotten, loses much of its agony when warmed and disguised with some less dreadful substance such as canned tomatoes or stewed carrots.

Eating from the rolling kitchen introduced a sporting element into our travels. The mess sergeant gambled on having his meal ready for a suitable stop. The train commander hazarded leaving many men behind when he ordered them to descend from their cars and form a line by the kitchen. For you couldn't tell much about the length of halts anywhere except at coffee or watering stops.

The train would pull up, let us say at noon. The mess sergeant would announce himself ready. The train commander would confer with the *chef de gare*. Sometimes the train commander would know French. More often he wouldn't.

"*Ici!*" he would say. "*Combien de temps?*"

The *chef de gare* would look at him, puzzled. Then a gleam of pleased intelligence would light his face.

"*Oui. 'Fait beaux temps—tres sec.*"

The train commander would look at him doubtfully. Did that mean much or little? *Sec* had a brief sound. One had to make sure. He would point, therefore, to the train. He would then with his hand indicate motion. He would display his wrist watch. He would wheedle:

"*Ici! Beaucoup or petit?*"

The *chef de gare* would smile in friendly fashion.

"*Oui, Mon Capitaine. Beaucoup des Americans. Les Boches seront malade.*"

The captain's face would usually express an emotion bordering on tears—an eloquent emotion, which usually interpreted everything for the official. His face would brighten. He would look at his own watch. Realizing the futility of further words, he would carefully indicate two points on the dial.

"*Quarante—minutes,*" the captain would say. "Get them out with mess kits," he would call to his aides.

Tumbling from their cars the men would come and form a feverish line. Details would carry pails of food forward to the drivers. The captain would watch with a smile.

"You know I'm picking up a lot of this lingo," he would boast contentedly.

Then the locomotive whistle would blow.

"That can't be for us!"

But the *chef de gare* would think otherwise. He would come running, waving his arms.

"*En voiture! Vite! Le train partira.*"

That's always easy enough to understand.

"*Quarante minutes. Vous—dit.*"

The *chef de gare* would be through with argument. The engine driver, never having wasted words on the subject, would simply start the train, out of the kindness of his soul holding the pace down at first. The men would tumble back into the cars with their half-finished dinners. The details would come scurrying back with their pails. From all directions soldiers who had gone in search of water would tear back, their clusters of canteens tinkling pleasantly.

Usually everybody got aboard. Word would come back to the captain that the men had been checked. Then everyone would comment pleasantly on the customs of the country.

But as a rule we got fed, and it was good, very, very good.

When we could we planned meals for the long halts allowed us for watering the horses. But the schedule for a troop train is not a constant thing, and these halts often came at bad times. They were not troublesome affairs as a rule. Beside our siding were usually a number of taps, so that the job seldom occupied much time. Sometimes we could wheedle hay from the American officials. Sometimes we couldn't. Yet on the whole those summer changes of stations were not unpleasant or too troublesome. The weather was fine. The men were not crowded. They sang. That's the best indication you can have that things are going well.

Up through Bordeaux, Perigueux, Limoges, Château-roux, and Auxerre we journeyed towards the front. We expected our definite orders at Is-Sur-Til, but at noon on the 8th when we paused at Nuits Sous-Raviere we received a telegram which

Drawn by Capt. Starbuck F and S.

A group of gaunt walls suggested a devastating fire

changed our route, and promised us orders at Chaumont. We got them there in the evening. We would detrain the next morning at Baccarat.

It rained that night. It was in depressing and grey weather that most of the regiment reached its destination.

Exactly as the entraining of one battery is much the same as another, just so the arrival of each organization at Baccarat differed only in the hour.

Escaping from sleep, we glanced from the cars at a strange France. The change was due to more than the dull sky, the drifting rain, and the deserted appearance of the little station.

Opposite stretched a row of depressing stone barracks, oddly scarred as if they had been for a long time neglected. Nearby a group of gaunt walls suggested a devastating fire. A large sign depended from the front of the station: *Shelter for forty men.*

There existed about that place an air of stealth and imminence. One responded to a feeling of the proximity of the Bosche. A man set down there unexpectedly would have taken one look and known himself in the war zone.

We asked the officer in charge of the yard if we could have breakfast before unloading. He looked at us as if he suspected our sanity. He glanced about with nervous eyes.

"Get this battery out of here," he said in a low tone, "as quickly as you can. Bosche planes come over all the time. You don't want to get caught, do you, with your whole outfit in this yard?"

We went to work without argument. It seldom took a battery, under those circumstances, more than an hour to desert its train.

The horses were hustled down the runways. The carriages were lowered along ready planks. The teams were harnessed and the battery stood ready for the road.

We glanced often at the dull sky, our ears alert for the whir of aeroplane engines, or the crash of bombs. The air remained free of menace, but the sense of imminence persisted, and we were glad when a French guide appeared and told Colonel Johnson he was to conduct us to our bivouac. The column started. Colonel Johnson paused to confer with the colonel commanding the French artillery brigade which our brigade was to relieve. For three days later, the colonel said, a *coup de main* was planned. Colonel Johnson determined then to win permission for some of our artillery to take part in the preliminary bombardment, and he dashed ahead to Neuf Maisons where infantry brigade headquarters had been established.

The column, meantime, left Baccarat. The order was for a fifty metre interval between carriages so that if Bosche bombing planes appeared they would do a minimum of damage.

There were a number of ruined buildings along the road, souvenirs of bombardments and bombing attacks. We turned into a woods road that breasted a hill, and rested at the top behind a heavy screen of evergreens. The first sounds of actual warfare reached us there. To everyone it seemed that we were too near the front for road training. The men fell silent. Faces were serious.

A good deal of that firing was undoubtedly from infantry grenade and small arms ranges, but we couldn't know that. We didn't even suspect it then. Our minds absorbed the bark of cannon, and the hateful stutter of machine guns as special menaces for us. We visualized ourselves as just behind the front line.

We reached finally a thick forest on the slope of a hill. Scattered among the trees were Adrian barracks and huts constructed of small logs and trees, of a pattern we had all seen in pictures of fighting in the Vosges.

This was the Bois de Grammont on the main road from Bertrichamps to Neuf Maisons. The Headquarters and Supply companies, we learned were in the woods by Bertrichamps. The Second Battalion would bivouac near them. Both these woods were too peaceful for wartime. In their shelter even the firing we had heard fell away.

"A bad place for gas," Colonel Johnson decided.

'We're as close as that?" someone asked.

"Rather near for a bivouac."

Colonel Johnson smiled, and whispered: "Not a bivouac. It's our echelon."

Such a place didn't meet with one's preconceived notion. An echelon, station of extra carriages, animals, men, and supplies just behind the lines, surely could not be as peaceful as this— peaceful and attractive even on a grey day.

Drawn by Capt. Dana, Battery A
The picket line

"The first platoon of Battery A," the colonel said to Captain Dana, "will go into position tomorrow night."

It brought it very close, but those who got that first word received also the impression that the movement would be a temporary one, and that the battery would come out again after the coup de main, and that we would somehow get some road work. The colonel shook his head. The batteries would go into position as soon as possible after their arrival. The French would remain for a while to show us the ropes, but the task of supporting our infantry was now to be our own. How would the men accept such news in its naked unexpectedness?

The National Army was a good deal of an experiment. It contained every type, race, and temperament. Had its brief training fused these uncongenial elements into a serviceable whole? Each battery commander asked himself this when he made his abrupt announcement immediately after his arrival, before his men had had an opportunity to forget the fatigue of their three days' journey. One such scene answers for the whole.

The day was about done. In the chilly shadow of the woods the battery stood in line. Shelter halves were draped from the men's arms. They waited for the order to take interval and pitch tents.

Except for a pleasant rustling of wind in the tree tops the forest was silent when the captain faced his command.

"At ease!" he called.

There may have been something unfamiliar in his tone. The dead leaves of the forest carpet rustled with the restless movement of many feet. Serious, expectant eyes answered the battery commander's stern regard.

"Men," he began," I have an announcement to make. I know you have looked forward to a period of road training before going into action. My announcement is that you won't have it. You're going into the line. The first platoon of this battery will go in tomorrow night. The second platoon will follow the night after. That's all. Battery attention! Count off!" Heels clicked together.

"One, two three, four. One, two, three, four." The numbers ran crisply down the line. You've heard any quantity of organizations count off, but it's doubtful if you've ever heard anything like that outside of the National Army in France. The serious expressions didn't alter particularly, but the heads snapped around with a rare precision. The voices were big and hoarse with a sort of helpless effort. It was as if these oddly assorted men were all trying to tell their captain the same thing, and, because they wanted to tell him so hard, couldn't quite get it out.

Chapter 11
Making the Hun Dance

That same evening the expected blow fell—rather sooner than anyone had anticipated. Major General Duncan, commanding the 77th Division, sent for Colonel Johnson, took him away from the regiment, and assigned him to G. I. at division headquarters. That loss is hard to estimate. The regiment missed his understanding and the inspiration of his ambition. He never lost his interest in the 305th, but his influence came from afar off. He was no longer a part of us.

For the difficult moment Captain Dana became acting battalion commander. Early on the morning of the 10th he took his acting adjutant and his battery reconnaissance officer and set out to reconnoitre the position Battery A would take up.

There are all sorts of reconnaissances, and we experienced most of them between Lorraine and the Meuse. Some are pleasant and not particularly hazardous. Some are dangerous in the extreme. Some are not fit to write about, because of their labour, their anxieties, and their lack of result. This was one of the first kind. It was always more or less pleasant relieving the French. And both battalion commanders can tell you the same story of a kindness, helpfulness, and hospitality utterly at variance with one's notions of life at the front. We never ceased to marvel at the easy and efficient control the French had of their work. Things that seemed most dreadfully complicated and difficult to us at first, they took with a smile and a careless gesture. They impressed you as having assumed a habit of war that obliterated all the past, that assumed until the end of the world a continuation of disagreeable and morbid events that must be made the best of.

You trotted towards them through a succession of bivouacs of troops either resting or waiting to go up. We came, of course, on those Lorraine reconnaissances to our first shell screens—rows of dead cedar branches or dirty sacking, stretched between poles. At frequent intervals overhead hung lines from which branches were suspended. These shielded the road from aerial observation.

Regimental Headquarters had been established in Neuf Maisons, a village of perhaps a hundred houses nestling in a fold of the hills. The French for the present were standing by and rather teaching the child to walk. They gave us our destination, the group headquarters in Pexonne, a mile and a half nearer the enemy. The road beyond Neuf Maisons was more carefully screened. Ahead at last lay a village, which, even at that distance, had the appearance of something dead and corrupt. There wasn't a house which hadn't suffered from shell fire. Many were heaps of rubble. Here a facade would be gone. You could see into the intimacies of that house—clothes hung against a wall, a row of bottles in an open cupboard, a tumbled bed. In the choir of the church yawned a hole large enough to take a column of squads.

There were doughboys in the streets, keeping close to the walls with furtive movements, as if they expected someone to catch them at an indiscretion. Engineers suggested the presence of nearby dumps. Guards were posted. One stopped us near the church. He seemed to think we had lost our way. He wouldn't let us pass until he had learned our mission and had scanned our identity books.

Just beyond we found the French group headquarters in a large dwelling reinforced with splinter screens constructed of logs and sand bags, and comparatively unhurt.

We had been told to ask for Captain Nicoll, the acting group commander. It must have been after seven o'clock by that time. We knew the captain had been warned the night before of our coming. Our minds were full of ourselves, and the serious nature of our errand. The war might have depended on what we where doing that morning. War for us was a matter of perpetual wakefulness, of extended hurry and effort, whether useful or not.

There was no stir about the headquarters. We knocked. We pulled at a broken bell handle. We glanced, amazed, at each other.

Drawn by Private Enroth, Battery D
"Something dead and corrupt"

"Is it possible," we asked in our innocence of amateurs, "that they are still in bed?"

It was possible. After an interval a shuffling step within became audible. The door opened. A sleepy soldier, half-dressed, might have been gazing at a collection of unexpected specimens. Yet he overcame his astonishment and led us into a dining-room, tastefully panelled in dark wood. From there we heard reluctant stirrings upstairs, and before long three lieutenants appeared. Their astonishment, perhaps their disapproval, was smothered behind greetings and an undreamed of hospitality.

The captain, they explained, had been occupied until very late the night before, but our affair was quite simple. One produced from a cupboard in the dark panelling a cobwebbed bottle.

"It is forty years old," he said, pouring a white liquid into glasses.

Coffee appeared. These officers were in no hurry to discuss our affair. We experienced a sense of guilt while we waited for them to come to business. Our restlessness grew. We wanted to be doing something.

At first that was the attitude of the average American soldier towards his job. Experience taught him eventually to take the day's work a trifle more sanely. But on the whole he was in a hurry. In quiet sectors he was up and at work earlier than the French. He took about one-fifth as much time for meals as they did. He went to bed a good deal later and seemed seldom to have had enough sleep; yet, until he learned something of the tricks of war, he was always surprised at the end of a day to find that the French, while apparently loafing, had accomplished a good deal more than he had done.

When the coffee was finished our Frenchmen were inclined to smoke and chat. Since we were in their hands we could only hint our anxiety.

They pointed out the panelling of the room.

"The house belongs to a rich man. Your soldiers call him the Count of Pexonne."

One picked up the dusty bottle.

"He had a taste for such things. You haven't seen his cellar. You know in French a cellar is a cave, and a cave has come to mean a shelter from bombardment. When we saw the Count's cave we decided never had war led us to such a shelter, and we didn't care how long the Bosches kept us there. It was filled with such bottles as these. They're about gone now, for the town is to be abandoned, and since there is very little transportation for the civilians the Count has sold his treasures to the French and Americans for a nothing."

We were astonished to learn the town was to be abandoned.

"Yes, as you can see, it is under constant shell fire, but the principal thing is the gas. They can fill it full of gas in a moment. You will notice that all the civilians carry gas masks, for the gas comes in frequently. In a few days the village will be deserted."

We moved at last. We descended first to the famous cave, the heart of the group's system of communication. We stood in a damp, vaulted cellar. A telephone operator crouched before three four-direction switchboards against the front wall. A number of wires came through an opening. They meshed like an untidy spider's web across the ceiling.

"You can communicate with the whole army system from here," one of the lieutenants explained. "That will make a little difficulty for you at the start, because, since the village is to be abandoned, you will have a new command post. You will have to arrange a new telephone central there."

Another of the officers got his horse, and we mounted and rode from the village at last. We hadn't expected to be able to continue our reconnaissance mounted, but most of the road, our guide explained, was defiladed, and on such a dull day the Bosche wasn't likely to be troublesome.

We left the dying village by a country road which brought us after a few hundred metres to the first of the battery positions. The pieces were placed in casemates constructed in the high bank of the road. The whole was extremely well camouflaged, and impressed us at first as a perfect position. The road did away with the danger of fresh tracks. It simplified the bringing up of ammunition. Then we noticed on both sides of it, and close to the guns, many shell holes.

"Yes," our guide said, "the Bosches have located this position. It would be well for you to leave this camouflage up and locate your guns somewheres else."

We examined casually a number of possible positions, but that morning we were chiefly concerned with the location of Battery A's guns which were to fire in the proposed coup de main. The French had decided on their approximate position near one of the French batteries in the thick woods of La Haie Labarre.

Drawn by Capt. Dana, Battery A
The water cart

As we climbed a hill the sun appeared from behind the clouds. We were captured by the beauty and apparent peace of this rolling wooded country of the foothills of the Vosoges. Between groves of birch and hemlock the fields were yellow with ripe wheat. From the yellow, like elaborately set jewels, flashed the turquoise blue of corn flowers, and the vivid scarlet of poppies. What firing there was that morning was far off and troubled us not at all. Except for our mission there was really nothing to remind us we were at the front, well within range, likely to be opened on at any moment.

We rode down a slope along a narrow path that overhanging branches nearly obliterated. Here and there among the trees appeared French artillerymen. One took our horses. The forest was full of a quiet, intense activity. Some figures lifted with difficulty stones and great blocks of cement. Others moved among the trees, bearing iron beams and logs, heavy and unwieldy. Many stooped and rose rhythmically. Accompanying their motions came the crunching of spades in earth and the thud of dirt on the dead leaves.

Our guide took all this in with a sweeping gesture.

"We have already got the new battalion command post well started here. You have only to install yourselves and complete it as you go along."

Nearby we found the battery under the tutelage of which our Battery A would be placed until the final relief. Captain DesVignes, the officer commanding, took us over the position. We marvelled at the neat and efficient arrangement of the positions and the ammunition dumps. We had never imagined such trail logs as the French had here.

The captain showed us, not four hundred metres to the right, the temporary position suggested for Battery A. There was plenty of natural cover. Just to the rear sloped a steep wooded hillside, perfect for the construction of dugouts. At the edge of the forest was a rough road which men and carriages could track safely. Captain Dana was satisfied and returned to the echelon to arrange for getting the first platoon up that night.

It was understood that morning that the French group would remain with us for a week or more. On their departure we would leave the temporary positions for the ones they occupied now. All that was altered the next day, and, except for the first platoon of Battery A, the guns of the regiment went directly to the French emplacements.

It was noon. The French habit obtruded itself. Why, the captain wanted to know, shouldn't we lunch? Captain DesVignes' one officer appeared, Lieutenant Riveau, executive, reconnaissance officer, telephone officer, department B man, and *popotte*, as the French call their mess officer. In front of a round, white tent a table had been laid beneath the pine trees with cloth napkins and china. It wasn't war. It was a picnic. A copy of the *Mercure de France* lay nearby. We didn't talk of war. The only reminder was the mutter of guns, distant and undisturbing.

The Americans tried to wheedle the chatter back to the things that obsessed them.

"Do you French always run an orienting line?"

"Always," Riveau answered languidly, "in theory; never in practice."

He steered quickly away.

"I have been reading some of your American books———"

The captain sipped his *pinard*—the French issue wine—as thoughtfully as if it had been a rare vintage. With a ceremonial air at the end of the meal he produced from the tent a nearly priceless bottle of liqueur. But the minds of the Americans were on orienting lines and gun positions. Riveau surrendered at last, and accompanied us to a jog in the woods of La Haie Labarre.

We had a plane table. Riveau set it up. We removed our helmets so as not to disturb the needle, while Riveau oriented his board with a declinator compass. We shot a line across the map from our location through the registration point. We drove a stake on the continuation of that line in the wheat field. We drove another stake beneath the plane table.

A rocket went up. We scarcely noticed. It had suddenly come to us that we were locating the first piece of the National Army at the front. Lieutenant Riveau, of the French Artillery had his hand in that with Lieutenant Camp, acting adjutant, and Lieutenant Brassell, Battery A's reconnaissance officer.

That was the climax of the afternoon. Everything was ready for the guns. We returned to the echelon. We were met with the news that the change necessitated by Colonel Johnson's departure had been made. Lieutenant-Colonel Stimson had been given command of the first battalion. He brought with him from Regimental Headquarters his old Upton adjutant, Lieutenant Klots.

Battery B had arrived during the morning reconnaissance, and Battery C came in that afternoon.

The movement commenced that night according to schedule. It was not a relief. That started the next night after it had been announced that the French would depart, leaving us to work out our own salvation.

During the afternoon Captain Dana had sent a detail of men to La Haie Labarre to prepare the emplacements. At eleven o'clock the horses were harnessed to the carriages, the drivers mounted, and the platoon moved out of the black woods and down the road. There was no nervous accompaniment. These men went about the job with the efficiency of veterans. It would have been impossible to suspect that they faced the enemy for the first time. There was only one thing. Everyone was unnaturally quiet, as if the Hun might hear. The rumbling of wheels on the hard road surface was disquieting if you didn't stop to compute how far away the enemy actually was. It was a dull night. Except for some firing on the left and an occasional star shell there was nothing to startle.

Neuf Maisons had gone to bed. From the country road above it the star shells were plainer, but the woods were peaceful—and black.

We were to learn to use such darkness as cats do, but that night was the regiment's first experience. Anyone that flashes a light at a battery position is either a spy or a fool. The discipline is pretty nearly the same in either case. Delicate tasks must be performed by the sense of touch, by a special instinct that an artilleryman has to develop. The pieces must be accurately placed. The trail must be nicely fitted into the trail log. You have to pile ammunition according to the law. Your camouflage must be perfectly arranged so that the first gleam of daylight will find everything covered. The only lights that are ever allowed at a battery position are the shrouded bulbs at the sights, the tiny slits of the aiming stick lamps, and the hidden gleam of a candle in a dugout, perhaps, where the battery commander or the executive figures new targets. These, if properly arranged, give away nothing.

The green men of the 305th accomplished their tasks in the brief time they had. No. 1 piece was set directly over the stake the reconnaissance party had driven that afternoon. No. 2 piece was twenty paces to its left. The platoon was ready to fire before daylight.

With the departure of the French announced, a more extended reconnaissance was made the morning of the 11th. Colonel Stimson went ahead to Pexonne in the side car. The commanding officers of Batteries B and C had their first touch of the front that day. Our little party was welcomed. As we rode into Pexonne eight shells fell in the town, and were followed by a noisy and thick barrage from anti-aircraft guns. We glanced overhead and saw among the white bursts directly over the ruins eight Hun planes, flashing white in the sun.

We dismounted hurriedly at the command post. Our guide of the day before came running from behind the splinter screen by the door.

"Get in here quick!" he warned.

The officers responded. The orderlies trotted the horses off to a comparatively safe stone stable.

We waited inside while the anti-aircraft barrage drove the planes higher and higher and finally back to their base. Then we settled down to the business of arranging the relief. It was complicated. It required a delightful luncheon, moistened with some survivals of the Count's cellar. It irritated the Americans who felt they were wasting time. As a matter of fact there was far more to be got from that luncheon than appeared on the surface. In spite of our impatience we absorbed sector gossip that would scarcely have come to us from a study of plans of employment or the terrain itself.

Our infantry, we gathered, was having greater losses than we had expected from the normal activity of that portion of the front. One battalion had been caught during a relief and had had many casualties. A few nights before the Huns had placed a box barrage around a platoon, had come in with gas and a new type of grenade, and had practically wiped out the command. An officer from our infantry battalion headquarters dropped in for coffee and told us a story of the affair.

"Blank who was in command of the platoon, you know, got hurt—lost his foot, in fact. That's tough luck—in a way. Looking at it in another way he'll go home, and maybe be decorated.

"By the way, he had a little Italian in his outfit. I remember the fellow well. Utterly worthless. That's what we all thought. Couldn't speak English. Rotten soldier. On kitchen police most of the time. Blank had tried to transfer him, but nobody would stand for it. So the *dago* was in the trenches with the platoon when the show started. The barrage Jerry treated 'em to plastered the whole works. Then he threw in gas. Shrivelled some of 'em up. Then he came himself with these new-fangled grenades, and mopped things up. Blank, as I say, was hurt, He lay on the floor of the trench. A Jerry officer and two or three Jerries were around him, going through his pockets. Blank heard something and glanced up. There at the turning of the trench stood the *dago* who couldn't speak English, who was just about perpetual kitchen police, that Blank had tried all along to shake. His gas mask was off. His face looked different. It expressed a decided disapproval of the whole proceeding. The little fellow's lips set. His rifle, bayonet fixed, rose slowly to the charge. He leaned forward. Blank saw, and called to him.

"'Get back, you idiot! For God's sake, get back!'

"But the *dago*, single-handed, ran to the rescue of his officer. He charged the lot of them."

The narrator paused, as if all was finished.

"Well?" someone asked.

"Oh! What do you suppose? One of the Jerries tossed a hand grenade and blew the little *dago* to pieces."

The story interpreted something for us.

At that luncheon, too, we heard of the various barrages we were supposed to fire under a variety of conditions, and why some positions in the sector were better for the work than others. Capt. Nicoll, it developed, had an exceptionally complete dossier. It contained plans of the telephone, wireless, and optical liaisons. There were careful maps showing the barrages and the O. C. Ps. There was an extended plan of employment and infinite orientation data. It made us rather dizzy. It seemed incredible that any human mind could digest the voluminous contents of that folder.

We examined the positions recommended by the French. Battery A would move into the French emplacements occupied at present by

Captain DesVignes' battery. Battery B would go to a fresh position in a wheat field a kilometre and a half to the south west of Pexonne. Battery C would take over an old French position on the edge of Ker Arvor woods. Its platoons would be separated by a hundred metres. To balance this inconvenience there was an elaborate system of dugouts, and a quarry offering dead space close to the back wall. Lieutenant Kane at first established himself here, but the menace from gas was great, so he moved to a dugout on the hill.

Lieutenant Montgomery chose for command post a tumbledown farm house near his guns. Dugouts were well under way at the Battery A position and the new battalion command post.

We would not, we learned that day, have perfect observation. The battalion observatory in a fringe of birch and hemlock between two fields of standing wheat offered a good view of the left of the sector, but nothing of the right. It was called Nenette and the command post went by the name of Rintintin. It was our first introduction to this interesting pair.

During our stay in Lorraine we were always reconnoitring for a more satisfactory observatory. We became convinced that it didn't exist. Most of our barrages, then, would have to be fired, as it were, blind. Rockets from the right of the reference point, the ruined church tower in Badonviller, would have to be relayed, always a dangerous and uncertain expedient.

Battery C had an eventual barrage in front of the left of another army. There was an observatory at a place called Pierre Perceé from which Lieutenant Kane could register his guns for this mission. The dossier recorded a forward observatory. When it was examined it was found to be well in front of the normal position of our front line platoons—that is, in No-Man's Land. The French advised against making use of it, for it is a serious thing to place artillerymen in danger of capture needlessly. They know too much.

The situation in the Baccarat sector was unusual. The front was so thinly held that one was always apprehensive of a surprise attack. There was a line of resistance. Forward of that everything was provisional. Patrols moved cautiously through a maze of abandoned trenches. Cossack posts at night crouched in shell holes or at trench corners. Often Americans glided inside the Hun outposts. The reverse, of course, was inevitable. There were desperate little combats in the dark. It was troublesome to get the wounded back. Such conditions moulded too expectant an attitude.

In case of an attack in force these outposts were to fall back on the line of resistance where the real stand would be made. That necessitated an extreme care in the system of rocket calls for barrages. How it worked out you will see later. It made us all the more dissatisfied with our observatories. Yet we only established one new one which was in no way superior to Nenette. We built a platform in the tops of several birch trees on the edge of a wood. It gave us something to fall back on in case we were shelled out of Nenette.

About three o'clock that afternoon of July 11th Captain Dana, Lieutenant Brassell, and Lieutenant Camp were at Nenette, locating points in the sector from the battle map. Lieutenant-Colonel Stimson appeared. Captain Dana wanted to register. Lieutenant Colonel Stimson was anxious to avoid stirring the enemy up. But the platoon was in. The guns were ready. The effect on the men of a few rounds was worth considering. So Lieutenant-Colonel Stimson consented, and Captain Dana telephoned the data down to the battery. The registration point was a corner of a Hun trench at a range of 5,500 metres.

"Fire when ready!"

The *crack* of the gun reached us. We heard the projectile rushing over our heads towards Germany. The first shot of the National Army artillery was on its way.

That shell was normal charge, high explosive. Considering the range and the nature of the terrain it was quite reasonable it should not be observed. The captain called for high burst shrapnel, and not long after we heard its swishing flight we saw appear near the corner of the trench a pretty white ball of smoke. There was an error of only three mils in deflection, and less than a hundred metres in range.

Drawn by Private Everts, Battery E
An observatory

Corporal Andrew Ancelowitz laid the piece. Sergeant Fred Wallace gave the command to fire. Private George Elsnick pulled the lanyard for the shot that put the National Army artillery in the war.

"Guess," said someone drily, "they heard that shot in Berlin."

Certainly it was the first note of the music to which the Hun danced back to the Rhine and defeat.

CHAPTER 12

Consolidating in Lorraine

The second battalion followed close on the heels of the first. Major Wanvig and his staff arrived in Baccarat with Battery D at midnight July 10th. Battery E came in on the morning of the 11th, and Battery F that afternoon. Major Wanvig established his echelon near the Supply and Headquarters Companies in the woods above Bertrichamps.

The major with Lieutenant Fenn, his acting adjutant, Lieutenant Church, acting telephone officer, and Captains Starbuck, Storer, and Mitchell, commanding the three batteries, made his reconnaissance on July 12th.

These reconnaissances for the relief of the French, as has been said, all shared the same surprises and the same hospitality. The conditions the Second Battalion found, however, differed in some ways from those met by the First. To begin with the French group had only two batteries in position. It was decided to place Batteries D and E in their emplacements. A new position was chosen for Battery F to the right of the Neuf Maisons-Vacquerville road.

The group command post was in Vacquerville, a pleasant little village which shell fire had spared. Major Wanvig moved into the Frenchmen's quarters and offices. Scotland was the inherited name of the command post and Godfrin of the battalion observatory.

Here, too, the question of observation offered no perfect answer. Godfrin was not better than Nenette, nor had it as good natural cover. It was an overgrown hole in the ground, covered with a sheet of elephant iron. It was in front of the woods. Because of its vulnerability it was used only for observation of the sector. For conduct of fire each battery had an observatory of its own, but no one of them approached perfection.

At the start an unexpected task faced the Second Battalion. There was a battery in their portion of the front of two ninety millimetre and two ninety-five millimetre howitzers, sector property. Lieutenant Pike of Battery D was given these guns with nine men from each battery of the

Drawn by Corporal Tucker, Hq. Co.
The regiment's home in Lorraine

regiment, and told to find out how they worked, to register them, and to fire them on demand. He and his makeshift crew solved the mechanical and theoretical mysteries of the strange guns. They fired with the rest of the regiment.

The relief, meantime, was well under way. The second platoon of Battery A, and the first platoons of batteries B and C went in on the night of July 11th-12th. The remainder of B and C followed the next night. Two guns each from D, E, and F moved up on the night of the 13th-14th. The rest of the second battalion completed the relief, the night of the 14th-15th. We escaped a single casualty. Either the Huns hadn't got wind of the change, or else they had guessed the wrong roads.

It is, nevertheless, always a nervous business going into position over main highways which you know the enemy has registered, and when you are well aware that his intelligence department is performing miracles to learn the exact hour of your relief. All you can do is to leave wide distances between your carriages, and often the roads are too crowded for that. The whir of every aeroplane is a warning to take cover, and, of course, you can't leave the road.

The chief danger lurks at the position itself. The pieces to be relieved must remain in their emplacements ready to fire on call until the relieving guns are at hand. Consequently the guns are jammed in a small space. Many men and horses are crowded in and about the pits, working in the dark. It is at such a moment that a shell gets the maximum confusion and the greatest number of casualties. In the Baccarat sector the Huns shelled and dropped bombs at the wrong moments. We could laugh at him. We were in position, and fairly well protected. We were ready to back up our own infantry.

Now we faced for the first time the problem of organizing a position. That is an irritating and endless process for a green outfit. During the three weeks we spent in Lorraine we learned more than months of school could have taught us.

The Second Battalion, with the plant it had inherited from the French, settled itself with less trouble than the First.

Colonel Stimson moved at once from Pexonne to the new command post in Haie Labarre woods, and, with details drawn from the batteries, hurried the work on the dugouts the French had started. Until some of these dugouts should be completed the headquarters would be quite unprotected. And that was only one task. A new system of communication was necessary. Both battalions had to organize their observatories and arrange their liaisons with the infantry.

We had realized all along we were short of officers, but we had felt we were plentifully supplied with men. This abrupt concentration of work, even in a quiet sector, taught us that the artillery tables of organization, made in America, had not foreseen all the demands of this type of warfare.

At the front the Headquarters Company could no longer be treated as a unit. Regimental headquarters, the two battalion headquarters, and the echelons were separated from each other by several kilometres. At the start, then, the three details were divorced for tactical and administrative purposes. That raised new problems of subsistence and transportation. Each detail, moreover, was subdivided. Men had to be at the echelon to care for the animals, and to draw and transport rations. When we had got the specialists to the command posts we found it necessary to supplement them by draughts from the batteries. The batteries complained that that left them short-handed. The telephone details were woefully small. We shifted scout and instrument men into communication. We tortured the dignified tables of organization until they were unrecognizable, but the result was something that could wage war.

At the start let us review what we did with communication, for that was the first problem we had to solve. A regiment at the front without practical means of communication might just as well be in America. It is out of action. Telephone officers and men, therefore, must lay and maintain wires, no matter how heavy the shelling; must keep every portion of the organization in touch with the others, and the whole in talking radius with neighbouring units.

In that sector the 305th had something like a hundred kilometres of wire to lay or maintain. We took over many lines from the French, but a good deal of their wire might have been a souvenir of the first battle of the Marne. For no apparent reason beyond senility it would go dead, and that type of trouble is difficult and hungry of time to locate. A great deal of the new wire issued us had insulation that cracked easily, and, because of colour and texture shielded its faults jealously. We had to lay it, consequently, with an extreme care.

The weather helped. It rained very little, so, with the heavy twisted pair given the regiment in America, we supplemented our poorer stuff and kept communication always going.

The cellar in the Second Battalion command post at Vacquerville made an ideal central, and the few new lines necessary for the command were quickly nm.

The First Battalion completed a small dugout the first two days in, and set up its switchboards there. It made use of what French lines ran to Captain DesVignes old position, but for the most part it had to run new ones to its various units.

Two men were on duty in the centrals for shifts of twenty-four hours. One man sat at the switchboard, and the other could sleep or read or write letters. They could change about as they pleased. It wasn't as simple as it seems. At times those boards were busier than the busiest central in the stock exchange, and often there was mote necessity for speed than in the commercial world, and high ranking officers as a rule are less patient than the tired business man.

Then there were unforeseen complications.

We all knew that code names were used at the front. That was natural. It was impossible to shout names and organizations over wires when the enemy was almost certainly listening in. But we hadn't suspected how quickly such customs of secrecy cast a net of fascination about even mature men. In Lorraine nearly every officer devised a code name for himself, and until higher authority interfered, guarded it jealously. It produced a clenching of hands and a tearing of hair among earnest operators.

Colonel Doyle was "Hub." His adjutant went to the tinkling sound of "Mess-kit." Lieutenant-Colonel Stimson was "Night gun." His adjutant, with perfectly straight hair, was "Pompadour." Major Wanvig was "West", and his adjutant, "Kansas," which suggested at least an origin.

The operators took it seriously enough. They had to. Their mispronunciations were due to phonetic idiosyncrasies rather than any humorous intention. Rintintin, for example, got to a *staccato* Ra-ta-tin and Nenette often was Nanny-et. So one might hear: "Pump a door's busy Mess skit." Or: "I can't get Night gown."

****

Such stealth had its more critical side for the telephone men. The infantry had listeners in, who spent their days and nights trying to catch operators talking in the clear—that is using the numbers of organizations or the names of places or well known individuals.

One day a terrifying document reached the regiment. One of our operators had been heard using the names of places. The infantry brigade commander, we were informed, was extremely angry about it. There must be no more talking in the clear. Word went around, to meet the situation, that the operators were to put no one through unless he asked for organizations and persons by their code names. That same evening the irritated general wished to speak to one of the command posts. His adjutant got the switchboard.

"Any officer will do," he said.

The youthful operator, faithful to his job, not being able to guess that the infantry didn't know the local trick names of the artillery, replied:

"Can't put you through unless you ask for the officer you want to talk to by his code name."

Drama!

Persistent diplomacy alone spared a breach between the two branches of the service. But the operators couldn't get it straight,

"If you talk in the clear," they said, "you get the deuce, and if you refuse to talk in the clear you get the devil."

But generals as well as men learn from practical experience with such inevitable inconsistencies. And Division Headquarters stepped in. It published a list of those officers who ranked code names. No others would be authorized or tolerated. But such habits aren't broken easily, and often over the wire sighed the eccentric nicknames of the lowly.

The operators did a good job, and, even in that sector, a hard one. Lines go out from shell fire, from weather conditions, from traffic, from bad wire. The panels were tested every hour. The operator would plug in. If he got a response from the other end, he simply said:

"O.K."

Which meant he was testing and was satisfied.

If he got nothing, or ground noises, he reported to his telephone officer that the line was out, and two men were sent to find the break and repair it. They went in pairs, so that if a man should be hit in a lonely place help could be got to him.

The hauls were long in Lorraine. You had to carry a telephone for testing. You would go along for a few hundred metres, scrape the insulation from the wire, hook your telephone in, and call central. When you failed to get a response you knew the break lay between you and your last testing point, and you examined that section of wire until you had spotted the trouble.

There were alternative talking routes to all stations. When the operator found a line dead, he got the other end through a different line and warned the operator there to send men out. The other fellow didn't always do it, and one pair of men might have to walk five or six miles to find the trouble—it really happened a number of times—in the other fellow's switchboard. That didn't make for the best of feeling among the details, but such irritations were temporary.

Then there were always curious things happening to lines. We had a grounded circuit to Pierre Percée. There was a French

central there. The fact that the line had a ground return indicated that it was not much used. It was, in fact, only important in an emergency. Still, in view of that emergency, it had to be kept working, and it was perpetually going out. One day Corporal Caen and an operator went through the lonely, wooded country that separated the two centrals. About half way they came upon a party of French telephone men who were stringing a wire that looked suspiciously like a remnant of our Peirre Perceé line. A gap nearly a kilometre long existed in that. Corporal Caen spoke French. He could gesture, too, like a Frenchman, and he knew some of the most powerful French phrases. But the party shrugged its shoulders.

"You could be shot for this."

"*Ah, oui,*" said the Frenchmen indifferently.

They finally consented to explain.

"Our officer told us to run a line to the infantry, *coute que coute*. We didn't have enough wire. It's only cost a kilometre or two of yours. What are you scolding about? Don't we, like you, have to obey orders?"

The corporal didn't crave international complications, so he trudged back, got more wire, and bridged the gap. But there was a curse on that line. Another day he found a party of Americans from a neighbouring unit playing the same salvage trick, and those fellows he had on their knees, begging him not to court martial them or have them shot at dawn.

For tampering with a line in the field is a very serious offence. It is likely to do incalculable damage.

There was one line that some of the men thought bewitched. It played its tricks on a very rainy night. Coheleach was on the switchboard. When he tested about ten o'clock, instead of calling his customary "O. K." he looked puzzled, and said something rapidly in French.

"There are frogs on this line," he announced.

"Impossible, because that line runs to Battery B."

"Sure, and I can hear the B operator talking across the frogs."

It looked like a cross. The French line had probably been blown from its supports and had fallen over ours. The wet weather and faulty insulation would account for the rest. Only one man left from one end. In half an hour a small voice came over the wire, reporting. Through his uncertain words we could hear French flowing. The conversation had an astral quality. We could not interrupt it. The groping demands of our man somewhere on that line in the wet, dark night, failed to dam it.

"The line," we distinguished above the queer conversation, "has been tied into close to the road."

It seemed impossible. We asked the startled linesman if he had traced the wire.

"Ye—ye—yes."

"Where does it go?"

"That's just it, sir. It isn't natural. It goes to a dark dugout."

"Maybe Huns with a listening in set."

But even the puzzled linesman didn't believe that, for over the wire came a weaving of French phrases which meant that it was a bitter night for those who fought, a bad night to die.

Our man wasn't afraid of Huns with a listening in set. That meant a fair fight, but he didn't like that dark dugout with such a conversation slipping from it over a wire. He hadn't followed the wire in. He disapproved of attempting it. A direct command was necessary.

He was so long reporting after that that we became uneasy. Perhaps there had been something he couldn't control—too many Huns talking French.

The B drop fell at last, and he was on the wire. His voice was conversational again—rather more agreeable than usual.

"Spooks? Quit your kiddin'. Who said anything about spooks. Frogs. Line looked as if it was tied in, but it wasn't. A cross. One of these frogs was *couchayed*. Other got lonely and was chinnin' with some central. He had *beaucoup mangay*, and after we chowed he came out with me and helped fix the line. O. K. now. Goodnight."

We had always that fear of Germans tapping our lines. There were spies about. Conditions favoured them. In Lorraine most of the inhabitants speak German, and there are many German names. The mingling of Americans and French helped. A Hun in American uniform among the French, or one in French uniform among the Americans was likely to go unquestioned.

A line to one of our advanced positions was interfered with several times. Switchboard operators were called by men whose voices they failed to recognize. These men asked carefully formed questions designed to draw military information. Investigation would disclose tiny breaks in the insulation such as a listening in set might make. We placed patrols on that line. One day, close to the infantry, they caught a fellow fumbling with the wire. He couldn't give a clear account of himself, so he was turned over to higher authority. What became of him we never heard. But that form of annoyance on that line ceased.

We were particularly anxious about our wires to the infantry. In order that the artillery may properly support the in-

Drawn by Capt. Dana, Battery A
The rolling kitchen

fantry it must know the doughboys' needs, where his front line is, where his advanced patrols are. In Lorraine we kept telephonic communication open fairly easily. In other sectors it was, as you will see, a more difficult problem. But you must have something besides that. Artillery officers must live with the infantry commanders, explaining the possibilities and limitations of artillery fire, acting as go-betweens, as it were. Regimental headquarters kept personally in touch with infantry brigade headquarters. An officer was usually sent to infantry regimental headquarters. Always a lieutenant went from each artillery battalion to the infantry battalion commander in the front line.

Lieutenant Edward F. Graham went from the First Battalion to the infantry; Lieutenant Karl McNair from the Second. Each took with him half a dozen enlisted men to act as runners and forward agents.

The first day down some of these men were taken on a tour of inspection forward of battalion headquarters. In the smashed village of Fenneviller they were caught by Bosche harassing fire. They dropped into a ditch by the side of the road, but they saw a medical captain and a doughboy seriously injured, and another doughboy killed. They found the ditch comfortable until the Bosche had had enough.

When they reported at headquarters that afternoon with a message from the infantry their attitude was prophetic. They had flung off the shadow of the disaster they had witnessed. They were elated because they had received their baptism of fire. Little Michel of the First Battalion came up grinning. He called to his friends.

"Say, boys. This chicken's been under fire. Gee! It was great."

A spirit of frivolity coloured the triumph of the little party. A soldier removed his tin hat, pointing to a deep dent in the side.

"Pretty close one that!"

A snort of disgust from one of his companions.

"Saw him myself. He took an axe to it."

CHAPTER 13

Barrages and Raids

In Lorraine, however, liaison with the infantry was never the bugbear we had feared. One had to be diplomatic. The gravest danger lay in a slip there.

We had, as a matter of fact, forward guns nearer the Hun than infantry battalion headquarters. We were ordered to place these as soon as we were in position. They were called pirate guns. Their code name was, appropriately, the goat. Their mission was to deliver harassing fire, to snipe at fleeting targets, to safeguard the battery positions from sound and flash ranging by making it necessary to fire only barrages from them. In other words the pirate gun went into action with its eyes open. The Hun could spot it by sound or flash ranging. The Hun did. Those guns were always shelled more or less.

Battery A sent in the first pirate gun for the First Battalion under command of Lieutenant Ellsworth Strong. The emplacement was an excellent one in the cellar of a ruined house in Fenneviller. It was heavily casemated. To guard against emergencies it was necessary to keep the limber and teams at hand in a stone stable.

The Second Battalion pushed its gun forward to a French emplacement in a piece of woods. Lieutenant Watson Washburn took it up.

We wanted to keep an officer with each of these pieces. We had too few. It was necessary to put them in charge of non-commissioned officers. It was a good thing. The results increased the confidence of the officers in their enlisted assistants.

Both of these positions were shelled. Fenneviller got it nearly every day. It was the custom when the music started to take the men off to a flank and keep them there until the concert was over.

Later the Second Battalion put out a piece from Battery F.

Another phase of organization concerned the observatories. To be serviceable they had to run according to a perfect system. Conduct of fire was only a short side of their usefulness. Rocket signals from the infantry were relayed through them. Scouts sat at the instruments all day watching for signs of enemy activity and for fleeting targets. Minute watchfulness will often locate enemy positions and observatories; will indicate to a certain extent his immediate intentions.

There was always an officer at each battalion observatory, and at the regimental one, far back behind Neuf Maisons. Battle maps were carefully marked. Dead space and visibility maps were made, and elaborate panoramic sketches. Anything observed on the terrain could be reported by its coordinates.

Our organization was good, but the question of rocket signals disturbed it always. It seemed simple enough in the beginning. Heaven knows why it wasn't always. We placed at each observatory a circle on which the limits of our sector were fixed. When a rocket went up an indicator was turned so that it pointed to the burst. That showed us at once whether or not the rocket was intended for us. The rocket guard was always on duty.

There were very few rocket signals—one for each of the various barrages, one for short firing, another for gas, but among the higher officers there seemed to be a diversity of opinion as to which signal should indicate what. It gave the men in the front line lots of fun guessing what signal to use in an emergency, and the men in the observatories an equal pleasure gambling on what was wanted when a rocket appeared.

The system was altered frequently. That's where the confusion lay. One morning during a reconnaissance of the front line a captain of infantry asked our advice. He ran through a batch of orders and memoranda. He flung up his hands.

"If I should need a normal barrage tonight," he said, "I honestly don't know what I ought to send up. Anyone of three rockets might be right—or wrong."

Such a situation could not be tolerated. Our officers in liaison with the infantry did what they could. Both branches were equally anxious. There's enough danger in a rocket signal anyway, and that is no reflection on the doughboy. An inexperienced non-commissioned officer with a small squad in an exposed and lonely place, when he becomes aware of danger or fancies it, wants help in a hurry. He may in his anxiety send up the first thing that comes to hand, or everything he's got. Or in the dark he may easily mistake a rocket. The artillery must sense such mistakes. When signals are changed too frequently it requires a clairvoyant.

A new order came down, settling the matter. There would be a rehearsal of the new signals that night.

The telephone officers had arranged a system of barrage calls by projector with the infantry. While the rehearsal was in progress that and the telephone were the only means open to the infantry to cry for help. The Hun didn't catch on and attack. The rehearsal proceeded peacefully. It was like a pleasantly conservative display of fireworks. The telephone system was given every conceivable test. Runners were sent breathlessly from organization to organization, and to and from the infantry. Bicycle messengers tore along the dark roads. Everything worked. Towards midnight we talked it all over and went to bed with a sense of security that had hitherto lacked.

That's the way things go in war. Within an hour we were awakened by our first real emergency. And there was plenty of confusion that the night's display had not accounted for.

Lieutenant-Colonel Stimson's telephone buzzed. The officer at the First Battalion observatory was on the line. A red rocket, he said, had just gone up from the infantry. He had repeated it to the batteries. A red rocket under the new system called for a barrage on the line of resistance. It was not, therefore, to be fired without confirmation by telephone. Yet those at the observatories were certainly under the impression that they had been told to pass red rockets directly on to the batteries. Our line of resistance was full of men, happily asleep.

It was one of those times when the switchboard is busier than one on the stock exchange during a panic. Colonel Stimson got to work. He put in calls for all three batteries at once. He wanted infantry battalion headquarters, too, to find out what the emergency was, for certainly there had been a mistake in the rocket. Our officer with the infantry wanted him. The battery commanders had judgment. They wanted him too, to find out why the red rocket had been relayed to them. Regimental headquarters wanted the battalion commanders. The regimental observatory was in the same case. It was necessary to report to three outside stations that a barrage was to be fired.

Meantime, while waiting for the battery commanders to respond we listened, apprehensive, for the sound of our own guns, firing that short and murderous barrage.

As has been said, the battery commanders had judgment. They didn't respond to the signal. Our operators were good enough for. the stock exchange on a panic day. They got the calls through. They put the battery commanders on Colonel Stimson's wire as they came in until he was talking to all three at once. That situation was saved. But what the deuce did the infantry mean, firing a red rocket? They wanted something, and they wanted it in a hurry. It might mean anything from a small trench raid to the attack in force we always felt was a possibility in that thinly held sector.

A captain back in pleasant Neuf Maisons evidently sprang at the worst.

We had no time for him. Lieutenant Graham was on the telephone, calling from infantry battalion headquarters. They hadn't been able to get anything from their front line. Infantry brigade took a hand.

As far as we could get any satisfaction the infantry seemed to want the Negre barrage, a barrage similar to our so-called normal, but to the right.

The battery commanders had the receivers at their ears. Lieutenant Colonel Stimson called the single word "Negre." The guns spat. The rapidity of their fire filled the night woods with an evil, staccato crashing. And although it has taken moments in the telling, that response came in an amazingly swift period after the red rocket had awakened us.

Infantry brigade headquarters took a hand again. They had had enough of the Negre. They wanted the normal. Two batteries were about through and finished before shifting. Another, a trifle behind, shifted nonchalantly in the midst of its firing.

The Second Battalion was in much the same case. Its central boiled, too. Neuf Maisons informed it that the Huns were breaking through the centre, and cried for the Chamois barrage. One battery was ready to respond to the red rocket, but was stopped in time. Another fired the Grand Bois, and then shifted to the Chamois.

"By gad!" the infantry said afterwards, "it was bully to hear those shells ripping over. Sounded efficient and safe somehow."

We smiled in a superior fashion. Why had they sent up their red rocket anyway? No one ever found out. As far as we could learn it spoiled the evening for everyone except the Germans. They seemed particularly peaceful that night.

While the firing continued, the details were armed with the few rifles available, and runner relays were got out. But most of the men agreed with the infantry. It was worth staying awake to hear such a superior noise.

When quiet descended upon the woods, except for some distant firing, a call came through from Battery C for an ambulance and the surgeon. Three men had been struck by shell splinters.

****

That was our only material damage. But the night's work disturbed us. There was a vagueness about the whole proceeding. It intimated that the infantry was not in that close liaison with us that we conceived as necessary to success. And other sectors would offer nastier problems.

Only one unpleasant incident followed this affair, a charge of short firing against one of our batteries. It was not pressed, because of the strain under which our under-officered brigade was working.

In view of the generally peaceful nature of the sector sleep was surprisingly scarce in Lorraine. We tried to do everything at once. We felt

Drawn by Capt. Dana, Battery A
The mess line

that a multiplicity of endless conferences was necessary. A man needs a clear head, especially when he is new at the game, to figure complicated corrections for modern artillery.

Nor should it be forgotten that Paper Work had taken a new interest in us. We had foolishly imagined he would be left behind when it came to killing Huns. Absurd dream! He stalked into our midst with a new confidence. He destroyed friendships. He threatened reputations.

The morning report and the sick book were complicated by the fact that each organization had men in two or three places. The firing battery, for instance was at the position. The drivers and extra cannoneers were at the echelon several miles away. Communication between the two was seldom good. A few men would be at the observatory, at a pirate piece, with the infantry, or on detail at battalion headquarters. Yet reports on these men must be consolidated and at regimental headquarters at the usual hour.

There were reams of extra paper work. The war diary became a bogey. If, the men asked, they had to have anything of the sort, why not do away with all the other reports. For the war diary brought everything together, positions, men, animals, casualties, rations, forage, ammunition. At the front where we had less time than we had ever had repetition haunted us. The information on that little war diary blank had to be collected from many sources, and the batteries had to have their figures together by five in the morning, for battalion headquarters wanted them by six, and regimental headquarters insisted on receiving them by seven. That meant somebody had to sit up nights, and usually it was the battery commander.

The figures didn't always come through on time. They couldn't understand that in Neuf Maisons. One makes no excuse for these delays. Those at the front were engaged in the biggest and most dangerous war in history. It is incredible, perhaps, that they should have been more interested in hurting the Hun and sparing their own men than in compiling innumerable neat figures that scarcely changed from day to day. It took some harsh words from Neuf Maisons to bring them to their senses. Paper work had to be fed, for regimental headquarters had many people whose only duty was to look after the thing. And Brigade was voracious, and Division was unappeasable.

Then there was an observatory report in code to go down at 5:30 a.m.; a munitions report at 6.; another at 11; a third during the afternoon. There were firing reports, and supplementary observatory reports.

In spite of all this, we did manage to annoy the Hun at times, and after a while we got enough system to run the thing after a fashion.

Another ideal was shattered in Lorraine. At Souge they had told us that while supplies might be difficult to get there, we would need at the front only to telephone the echelon to have anything we needed brought up the same night. Our instructors had been at the front during a period of stabilized warfare with only a handful of Americans on whom our entire service of supplies had been concentrated. Conditions had altered when we got in. There were more Americans, and warfare was no longer stabilized. Echelons were further back, and roads were not so well protected as they had been. Actually the material didn't exist to satisfy everybody. Yet we were absolutely dependent on equipment. We learned, therefore, to be economical, to improvise, to salvage.

Camouflage was one of our chief needs. We got enough flat tops to take care of the batteries, but we needed protection for ammunition dumps, wireless stations, the observatories, the entrances to command posts and positions. We made a careful study of camouflage in Lorraine, and the experience we had there was invaluable in Champagne and the Argonne.

When we were left in complete possession we found a number of fresh tracks that had to be covered up. The springs were danger points. Water is heavy, and men want to carry it by the shortest route. We covered such places with fresh cut foliage, and established penalties that kept us all in the desired ways. For larger work, such as entrances to positions, we used small trees to supplement our insufficient nets.

The engineers helped all they could, but they had many organizations to look after. They gave us what material they had for our dugouts, which progressed day by day. We needed gas proof curtains, and got them somehow. A sly spirit developed here and there. A man who got much needed material usually went around with an expression that connoted:

"Ask me no questions, and I'll tell you no lies."

And one watched carefully what one had got.

While all this work of organization continued we paid some attention to our more strictly military affairs. One does not recall the number of supporting barrages we figured for one purpose or another, and never fired. It was splendid practice, but the futility of it depressed us. Things didn't always come off as one planned in Lorraine. The show for which Battery A had been rushed into the line had never got beyond paper. That wasn't the only case.

No one in the regiment is likely to forget Sunday, July 28th. We figured a box barrage for a raid that day. We were a good deal concerned about it, for we had been told it would be a daylight raid whose object was the bringing back of prisoners. Capt. Barrett of the infantry would be in command of fifty men. It seemed a hazardous undertaking to us. We knew that the most accurate fire would be necessary. That noon we were informed that we would not fire. Yet the raid would go on.

Between two and three o'clock we heard machine guns, and the popping of grenades. The rest is history.

Eighteen men, we were told, came back, just two of them unhurt. Capt. Barrett and the rest were killed or made prisoners. Evidently the secrecy which had eliminated the artillery, had failed to mystify the Huns.

Many other raids were projected and died. There was, too, the usual crop of rumours. You would hear after nightfall that the Huns were going to attack before dawn, and to hold yourself in readiness. You sat up all night, waiting for the first guns, and as a rule, nothing happened. Sometimes, as you waited, sleepless, you almost wished for the real thing. Our officers in liaison with the infantry were lavish with these rumours. It is inevitable that the infantry should get its wind up, and one must take its fancies as seriously as its facts.

False gas alarms were more annoying than anything else. You can't fool with a gas alarm, for discipline's sake, even though your judgment tells you the presence of gas at a given place at a given time is impossible.

You would hear far in the distance towards the front line three rifle shots in quick succession. They would be repeated nearer. Steadily they would drift back, exigent, uncompromising, accompanied usually by the jarring screech of gas horns. Weary men would turn over and groan. Our own alarm would belch, and you would struggle into your stifling respirator, and give up all idea of sleep until you got the all clear.

It may as well be said now that where gas was infinitely more plentiful we weren't so conscientious. We had too much work to do, and we formed the habit of trusting our own noses.

After one of these alarms the whole world would seem to lie awake and ask for trouble. A screech owl would set a dozen alarms going. A runner would tear in from the infantry, gasping in his mask. He'd got a whiff of something on the road, and the wind was blowing in our direction.

The men at the echelon usually wore their masks in the alert position when they came up. That was proper, and they had to put up with it for only a few hours at a time. They had become strangers to us. Often we envied the more comfortable conditions under which they lived. They appeared at the front only by night when they brought up rations and ammunition.

No one coveted that side of their job. Registered roads don't make for contented travel.

The drivers announced their approach by shouts and a cracking of whips. The details rushed to the entrance to the position. The contents of the G. S. carts or the *fourgons* were unloaded and carried away with anxious haste. The drivers would chat with the cannoneers for awhile. Now and then a nearby battery would cut in, and the horses would grow restless. Then the drivers would mount and rattle off again to the remote and desirable woods they inhabited.

That's the way our rations came to us. Food, too, brought its new problems at the front.

A book might be written in praise of the army cook. His name, as everyone knows, is no stranger to the casualty lists. His devotion to his work was nearly fanatic. Others might falter or straggle by the road. The cook clung to his rolling kitchen or his field range with pathetic devotion. And always, quite naturally, I dare say, he craved to build fires. Flame became to him a sort of god, and its resultant smoke was incense from an altar. The rest of us couldn't look at it that way. Smoke was as dangerous as the flash of our guns. For the enemy it was a banner, advertising our positions.

As long as wood was dry we could manage to keep the cooks at their devotions, not without benefit to ourselves; but in damp, chilly weather the wet wood was too much for our experimental smoke screens. It was frequently necessary to scatter and extinguish fires while the cooks stood by with an air of witnessing a sacrilege.

Fortunately it didn't rain much in Lorraine, and we were sufficiently far back to make fires practicable most of the time. We weren't destined to fare so well again until the close of the war.

Nor did we dream we would be left in Lorraine for long. The fighting was taking a new turn, that destined to be its final phase. We had been rushed into the line. So, it developed presently, would we be rushed into the hottest battle of the war at the war's supreme strategic point. As the truth faced us more and more frankly we reviewed our slight training, our mistakes on this front, and we asked ourselves if we were ready.

The powers were in no mood to consider such things meticulously. We were a regiment, and we could shoot, and so we were needed.

We had erected our wireless station on the hill above battalion headquarters, and from it the communiqués slipped down to the command post, unofficially but vividly. Newspapers, a trifle stale, came up at night from the echelon. So, after a fashion, we kept in touch with the vast workshop of the western front. We could see there roughly the modelling of our immediate future.

We read of the Hun's last great offensive on the side of the Château Thierry salient. We shrank from a repetition of the anxious days at Souge when Paris had been menaced. That menace seemed to exist again, uglier than ever. But all at once the spirit of the news altered. Foch's brilliant counter attack was under way. And as green American troops had stood with smiling ease and confidence on the defensive against those vicious thrusts of May and July, so now they were tearing forward with the French, laughing and singing as they went, killing Huns and dying themselves with a courage superb and indifferent.

Château Thierry came back to France, and many smaller towns. The Huns were going out of the salient like water from a pressed bulb. Fére-en-Tardennois, their base of supplies, was threatened, had been entered by American troops. The allies stood in front of Fismes, were in the city. Except for a few outposts the enemy was between the Vesle and the Aisne.

Rumours thickened into fact. We were to move almost at once. No one shirked the fact that we would probably be thrust into that vast, sanguinary, and decisive battle.

Battery B offered a complication. On July 15th Corporal Samuel W. Telling was sent to the field hospital in Baccarat, and back to us drifted the dread word typhus. The battery would be quarantined and the most minute sanitary precautions would be taken throughout the rest of the regiment. Except for its officers, Battery B was passed through the delousing station, and placed in shelter tents in the woods near Baccarat. Yet the battery could not conceivably abandon its share in the missions assigned to the regiment. A detail of cannoneers, drivers and telephone men were sent from each battery to Lieutenant Montgomery, and in his stride, as you might say, he welded them together so that his work suffered no interruption.

At the echelon, however, things didn't go so well. The officers there were very few. This influx of green drivers added much weight to their already great burden. When the regiment finally pulled out some property was left, paper work was involved, the colonel was annoyed, and there was a good deal of harsh language about. From a broader point of view, however, the meeting of this emergency by Battery B was an extraordinary accomplishment.

The situation was a little relieved about this time by the arrival of two officers, fresh from Saumur. Second Lieutenant Charles F. Wemcken was assigned to us by order of July 10th and was sent to Battery C. Second Lieutenant Charles F. Perry was assigned by order of July 20th and was sent to Battery B, while Lieutenant Robinson was shifted from B to C with which organization he fought with pronounced success until the armistice.

Another encouragement came in a telegram for Lieutenant-Colonel Stimson. An extraordinary exception had been made in response to his plea. We would soon have Captains Reed, Ravenel, and Delanoy back. On the other side We lost definitely First Lieutenant Watson Washburn who was transferred to a staff job at Corps headquarters; and First Lieutenant Paul Pennoyer, who, while on a temporary mission from Souge, had been given a corps staff job, too.

The Hun probably had got some of our rumours. At least he was extremely attentive during our last days in Lorraine. Nearly every night now we got some kind of an alarm from the infantry, and we retaliated by planning many *coups de main*, ordered by infantry brigade headquarters, few of which materialized.

One morning towards the end we were awakened by a heavy bombardment. Shells were bursting close to the First Battalion command post. Either the Hun was registering to transport directly on us, or he was after Nenette.

Lieutenant Brassell was at Nenette with Corporals Tucker and Goldberg, and Private Braun. Lieutenant Brassell telephoned down while we snatched a bite of breakfast, and, to all appearances, dismissed our uncertainty.

"I think they're bracketing Nenette, sir." We settled our tin hats on our heads and climbed the hill. The arriving swish of the shells and the noisy bursts were not comfortable. With each burst, close at hand, little volcanoes of jet black smoke sprang out of the pretty wheat field.

Thirty odd projectiles fell over and short of Nenette and to either side. There the show ended. Nenette had not been touched. We tried to assure ourselves that all we had got were overs intended for an

Drawn by Corporal Roos and Private Enroth

A three-cornered fight

123

anti-aircraft battery near the Pexonne road. Yet Nenette was always an anxious place after that, and we held ourselves ready at the first alarm to shift to the alternative observatory among the birch tops. And we endeavoured again to find other points suitable for observatories near the front line.

During one of these reconnaissances Colonel Stimson came upon an observatory unique in conception and treatment. It is doubtful if the war produced anything of the sort more admirable.

We were on a defiladed road immediately behind the infantry front line. To the right was a hill, thick with tall pine trees. A fundamental protection of the place was its patent antagonism to terrestrial observation. You can't observe through pine trunks and heavy foliage. But the French had got around that. They had gone above the foliage and without using the common expedient, which sooner or later gives itself away, of building a platform in the trees. They had constructed a huge new tree. They had a tower raised from similar trunks, and covered with the same foliage. You could stand within a few feet of it and remain unsuspicious of its existence. You climbed many ladders to the observatory at the very top. There you had a sense of Peter Pan come true. You swayed in the breeze. And you looked almost directly down into the Hun lines.

The infantry was in possession and we went back to Nenette and our poor makeshift.

On July 30th French officers appeared at the command posts and informed us they were going to take over, beginning the next night. These men had just come out of the great battle. We, who suspected an immediate entrance into that which they had left, listened breathlessly to their talk of unheard of artillery concentrations, of long casualty lists, and of a supreme exhaustion.

"Formidable!" was their favourite word.

"You've never dreamed of the noise and the effect of their barrages," they said. *"Formidable!"*

One glanced about our pleasant woods. He sighed contentedly.

"It is tranquil here. A sector for *un pere defamille*."

In spite of ourselves there was a little envy in our hearts.

Certainly the Bosche guessed something was going on. We had known all along that he had control of the air in Lorraine. His planes were constantly overhead, and the bell like note of the archies was with us much of the day and night, and there were nearly always white clouds in the air undetermined by the weather. Still Jerry had not been very aggressive. French planes had been up and given us one or two *reglages* undisturbed. The night of July 30th, however, the Huns came over in force loaded with bombs. Unquestionably they fancied the relief was under way that night.

A huge ash can dropped beside the Battery F position. The force of the detonation knocked Lieutenant Derby down, and spattered a dozen men with dirt and twigs. By an incomprehensible good fortune the hot, ugly pieces of metal touched no one.

Another big one landed in the field back of Nenette, and sprinkled fragments all about the observatory. That was near enough to the command post to make it advisable to get the men in the dugouts. Then the planes turned and went back to Germany, sprinkling their foul droppings as they went. We escaped, but there were casualties close by in Ker Arvor woods.

The next day our formal orders arrived Two pieces. from each battery, except B, whose position would not be taken over by the French, would be relieved that night. The whole of B and the remaining guns of the other batteries would go out on the night of August 1st-2nd.

The first guns out would go to the echelon and wait there until the next night when they would join the last guns which would proceed without stopping at the echelon to the division regrouping area two marches away. The Huns were evidently satisfied with what they had done a night too soon. The relief was undisturbed.

Battery B again presented a special problem. Since its position was not to be taken over by the French it was necessary that its plant be kept intact until the last moment. Yet it could not delay to the point of losing its place in the column. There were miles of wire to salvage and much equipment to be packed at the very last. Lieutenant Montgomery managed it, and pulled out on time.

Lieutenants Camp and Fenn remained behind with the two French groups for twenty-four hours to induct them into the mysteries of the sector. The French weren't exigent. Half a morning served to organize them completely. Again one was forced to admire the way they achieved the completest results with a minimum of effort.

The first night of the relief Lieutenant-Colonel Stimson left the regiment never to return to it. A telegraphic order had reached him that afternoon, instructing him to report to America for duty with the Field Artillery there. We watched him drive away that night with a sense of grave loss. Afterwards we heard that he had been made a full colonel and given command of a new regiment in training at home. The armistice came before that regiment could sail.

CHAPTER 14

The Fires Beyond Château Thierry

Our movement from the Baccarat positions was not as simple as we had expected. The road for its entire length was perfectly visible to Hun airmen, so it was advisable to march at night. The column was late starting, and it crawled, as such columns do, on traffic laden roads. Our schedule called for a bivouac at Magnieres during the day of August 2nd. But it was long after daylight when the regiment arrived, anxiously glancing aloft; and by the time horses and men were settled the hour of departure was at hand.

Again the roads were packed, and progress was snail like. It was nearly noon of the 3rd before the column, dusty and tired, entered its regrouping area on the Moselle. We hadn't imagined the movement of a single division could be so complicated and tedious.

That march, however, was not without its valuable impressions. For the most part it lay through the district of Lorraine, destroyed by the Germans during their retreat after the battle of the Couronne de Nancy, the eastern phase of the battle of the Marne. The smashed villages were now sketchily inhabited, and the fields were under cultivation again, but about this resurrection still clung an appearance and an odour of death.

Our own area was just beyond high tide of the Huns. To us after that journey it was impressively undisturbed and peaceful. We felt that our ugly carriages parked in fields along the Moselle were out of place in such a landscape.

Regimental headquarters and the Second Battalion were at Bainville. The First Battalion was at Mangonville, two kilometres to the south. The Headquarters and Supply Companies were in and about the charming *château* of Menil Mitry, three kilometres to the east of Bainville.

Significant changes were announced here. Among them was the transfer of General Rees, who had commanded the brigade, to other duties, and the appointment of Colonel Manus McClosky, soon to be made a brigadier general, to replace him. For a few days Colonel Doyle, as senior colonel remaining with the brigade, was in command. There was a feeling in the air that the changes wouldn't stop there.

Captain Dana, of course, was again in temporary command of the First Battalion. Captain Reed reported back from Souge on the first day and took over his duties of battalion adjutant while Lieutenant Klots went back to the Headquarters Company. These two officers set to work with a will to get the battalion ready for the serious work just ahead.

Captain Mitchell was transferred from Battery F to the Field and Staff as adjutant of the Second Battalion. Lieutenant Derby took command of Battery F.

We had expected two days in this regrouping area. They stretched into four, and no one was sorry for the delay. It was pleasant there, and we had a great deal to do. We settled down to straightening out the tangled paper work situation. We made more complete than before the divorce of the three details from the Headquarters Company. Men, animals, and equipment were reported to regimental and battalion headquarters, and were assigned to organizations for travel and rations. The Battery B men, released at last from quarantine, reported back.

We were ready when the order came to march on the mornings of August 6th and 7th.

Regimental Headquarters, the remnant of the Headquarters Company, and the Second Battalion proceeded to Charmes on the 6th, where they entrained. The First Battalion and the Supply Company entrained at Einvaux on the 7th.

This movement was unlike the one from Souge. There a brigade had had a week to entrain. Now from a small section an entire division was going out practically in a single day. While there were a number of points of departure the congestion at each was such that a careful schedule had to be made and followed.

Each battery broke park and took the road at a stated moment. It arrived at its entraining point at a given time. It fed and watered according to the clock. We passed large parties of our doughboys manoeuvring in the fields while they waited their turn at the trains. They interested us. We intrigued them. Their glances followed the long, overladen column from which the sleek snouts of the pieces, escaping from burdens of forage and equipment, peered at them encouragingly.

The Supply Company was off first. Battery A commenced entraining at 2 o'clock and was completely loaded at 3:30. Before the tram had pulled out the head of Battery B was on the ramp. Before B had gone C appeared and was ready to load.

At Charmes there was a similar precision of movement.

We were surprised to learn how much we had profited by our one previous experience. The drivers made short work of refractory animals. The carriages seemed to roll into their places on the flats automatically.

These days were warm, and such speed makes men thirsty. There was a little Y, M. C. A. hut on the ramp. When the job was complete the men were allowed to line up for a glass of raspberry syrup and water, and a limited quantity of chocolate, cakes, and tobacco.

Not until the trains had left did any one know the projected destination of the regiment. That is, we had moved under sealed orders. Before the departure of his train each battery commander had received an envelope with a typewritten command that it was not to be opened until he had passed a certain station. Inside each envelope was a rough engineers' map of the district North of Paris—a map covered with significant names—and a small typewritten slip of paper which said: *You will detrain at Nanteuil-le-Houdin.*

We spotted it eagerly on our maps. Its location indicated to us that we might either go in with the British, or swing more to the east through Soissons. There was another possibility. Were we going to lie in reserve behind the lines? Didn't the powers think us good enough for the big show, except in an emergency? Whatever the original intention it was altered the next day, as everyone remembers.

Except for the customary struggles with a few unruly animals the trip was tame enough, but there were plenty of reminders the next morning that we were close behind the busiest portion of the front. We saw many spreading nets of tracks, crowded with flat cars on which reposed battle-scarred cannon, camouflaged tanks, trucks, automobiles. On everything the deep wounds of shell fire could be seen. We passed huge gun parks, ammunition dumps, airdromes, dreary and interminable hospitals.

We gazed at such sights with a depressed interest, and wondered if we would crawl through the outskirts of Paris. Then the trains halted shortly after noon at a small station, and an officer climbed aboard each one, presenting the commander with a new envelope. Everyone guessed as soon as he saw it that our destination had been altered.

There was a map inside—a 1:80,000, marked Meaux. And there was an order, brief and to the point. The division would detrain at Coulommiers and nearby stations, and on August 10th would commence a movement forward into the zone occupied by the First United States Army Corps. The infantry would be moved by motor busses to be furnished by the French. The artillery would go on its own wheels and legs. Within half an hour after receiving that order the batteries were detraining.

Battery A detrained in the yards at Coulommiers; Batteries B, C, and F at Chailly Boissy; Batteries D and E, and the Headquarters and Supply Companies at St. Simeon.

There were huge evacuation hospitals at Coulommiers through which thousands of Americans, gassed or wounded in the Château Thierry salient, were passing at that time. We listened, fascinated, to the gossip of hospital orderlies about the effects of big shell fire and concentrated phosgene and mustard gas.

The sky was full of aeroplanes. Constantly they circled overhead. We tried to impress on each other that, although, they were our own planes, discipline must be maintained as if we were at the front. The bugle, consequently, blared alarm after alarm, and our work was retarded. Still we were willing that it should be, for in our ignorance we believed this great flock of airmen behind Château Thierry meant that we had control of the air, that, therefore, our offensive and defensive dispositions would be made simpler and safer on this nasty front.

Battery A was billeted for that night and the next at the comfortable little village of St. Germain-sous-Doue. Battery B went to La Loge Farm, Battery C to Epieds. Regimental Headquarters, the Headquarters and Supply Companies, and the Second Battalion were at the comparatively large town of Doue.

Things had been fairly hectic on the Moselle, but that wasn't exceptional. Going into billets for a battery is always much the same problem, much the same mad struggle for a solution. And, when it's reached, the solution is always about the same. Yet invariably out of the confusion emerges a sort of order and comfort. Eventually we became more than ever like a great travelling circus whose discipline automatically repairs the mistakes of a poor advance man. And that isn't intended as any reflection on our billeting officers and non-commissioned officers. They, as a rule, had too much to do, and they were restricted to too small an area by the advance agents of the division.

Some towns had a better welcome for infantry than for artillery, but that fact didn't seem always to be appreciated. Besides billets for officers and men, the artillery needed ground suitable for extensive picket lines and gun parks, and no matter how suitable; the ground you couldn't establish either near the front without overhead cover.

Organizations, whether they arrived in the afternoon or during the dark hours, ran into much the same conditions in those billets north of Coulommiers. The billeting officers couldn't be all over the district, so the non-commissioned aides, as a rule faced the battery commanders alone.

One always experienced a quick sympathy for these unfortunates. Invariably they glowed with a naive pride. They always produced careful lists, showing the billets available, and the number of men that could be housed in each. A battery commander going into billets, however, is only interested at first in two things.

"The picket line and the gun park!" he cries as he meets his man.

Perhaps the glowing advance agent has let the Battery slip past these vital points, and it may be necessary to turn the entire column around by sections in a narrow street. Battery commanders never take to that kindly, nor do tired drivers. It is seldom that the places chosen for the picket line and the park please. The ground is swampy, or there isn't enough room, or the tree trunks are too small,

The most indifferent commander can find something lacking in the most perfect park or line.

The advance agent, of course, isn't to blame for these shortcomings. The town major, as a rule, has given him no choice.

"That's it," he has said. "Take it or leave it."

But a battery commander doesn't analyze causes when he is displeased by effects. He decides darkly to make the best of things. He considers his disappointed advance man.

"All right," he says. "The thing's impossible. You ought to have done better than this, Smith, but it's getting dark. We'll make it do. Undoubtedly you've arranged to billet the drivers in a group close to the picket line, and the cannoneers by the park. Explain your distribution to the first sergeant."

If the advance agent is a man of parts he salutes, seeks the first sergeant, curses, and with him arranges some kind of a compromise. If, on the other hand, he flushes and stammers forward with facts about some of the billets being large and some small, and everything scattered through the town and the surrounding country, he usually tries the battery commander's patience too far. Then he sees himself as others see him.

As soon as the animals are arranged for, and he is certain his men will have some kind of a lodging, the battery commander turns his attention to the kitchen. The site of this, too, has been more often than not an arbitrary selection of the town major's. It is nearly always in a farmyard, redolent and wet with manure, and thronged by an assortment of unclean animals.

It is at this point that the billeting non-commissioned officer generally goes back to his section a sadder and a wiser man. He mutters over his lists and his wrongs. He tells everybody that he has done just what he was told to do by those above him in rank. He has, probably. But no one is sympathetic. The customary response of his friends is:

"Can it, will yeh? It's a heluva billet yeh gave me."

****

That detail became more unpopular than kitchen police. It reduced corporals to the ranks. It made officers lose faith in their men, and men

A Train Bivouaced

in themselves. You see, you usually billet at the close of an exhausting day. Everything about you is strange. Often black night covers the world. And, more than the rest, the whole battery is hungry.

No meal tastes so good as the first one in billets. You sit around on the grass or a stone wall, eating with the comfortable assurance that for a few hours no violent effort will be demanded of you, that in a little while you will probably be able to go to sleep. Or, if it is in colder weather, maybe you carry your dinner or your supper to your new home where a hospitable housewife gives you a corner by the fire and maybe crowns Corn Willy with fried potatoes or a piece of cake.

Afterwards, except for the guard, and the few necessary details, everybody seeks his bed. You climb a ladder into the loft of a house or a barn, centuries old. You find straw there, sometimes clean, sometimes not, but always soft. You drop off to sleep with a healthy and abrupt unconcern scarcely known to civilian life.

There was enough in the Coulommiers area to keep any but the weary awake. As we strolled to bed that first night we watched in the sky to the north vivid and endless flashes spreading and contracting with a variety of intensities.

Somebody chuckled self-consciously.

"Reckon the world has never seen such northern lights before/'

Judged by our experience of flashes in Lorraine it was clear that highest battle, even according to the standard of this war, raged up there. In a very few days we would be among the flashes.

As you watched that pallid, violent display you strained your ears for appropriate sounds. But the night was silent, except for a distant and amorous song and the rhythmical music of a breeze across the foliage.

The song vibrated away, and the breeze fell. All night long before that distorted sky the silence was ironical.

Chapter 15

Across the Marne to Nesles Woods

More detailed orders reached us the next day. We would take the road Saturday, the 10th, and march thirty odd kilometres before the next morning to Chezy-sur-Marne. The next night we would cover approximately twenty kilometres to a point to be chosen near Courpoil. The third night we would complete our journey to Nesles Woods, which had recently been cleared of the enemy.

We pored over our maps. The march would be a forced one. It would carry us through the heart of the salient. Chezy was only a few miles from Château Thierry. Courpoil probably smoked from the fierce fighting it had witnessed. Nesles Woods lay between Fere-en-Tardenois and Fismes.

We spent Friday getting ready. In our spare moments we wrote letters home. That afternoon we were summoned to brigade headquarters in Doue to meet the new brigade commander. He intimated the serious nature of our next step. Afterwards Colonel Doyle gave the organization commanders an extended talk about aiming points and the identification of targets.

Since it was understood we couldn't safely start our march before four o'clock the next afternoon, everyone hoped for a good sleep Friday night. The men needed it, but they didn't get it. About 9 o'clock regimental headquarters stirred itself and began sending orders to the battalions by bicycle messengers. The first was to the effect that we would be prepared to take the road by eight o'clock the next morning. That meant reveille around four o'clock. Other orders came to send teams and G. S. carts to various points to change and move equipment. It wasn't until 2 o'clock Saturday morning that the excitement subsided. Bicycle Messenger Montgomery came around then with a verbal order that we wouldn't move until the time we had been given originally, four o'clock in the afternoon. We took advantage then of what remained of the mutilated night.

The regiment was to rendezvous at Doue. It would take its place in the brigade column on the national highway beyond. So at four o'clock each organization mounted and pulled out of its comfortable billets.

August smiled its best that afternoon. The cheerful countryside seemed reluctant to let us go. Natives watched us with emotionless faces. In their eyes we saw dull souvenirs of four years of departures.

In the old days of pitched battles men walked from their bivouac directly into the obliterating shock of a fight whose duration was a matter of hours. Maybe that was simpler than to move as we did for three nights into a battle apparently without end, with sights and sound of a new and peculiar brutality crowding each moment closer about us.

We did get tired.

During our wait at the rendezvous we drank hot coffee, and munched cold rations. When we turned into the straight national highway, flanked by huge lime trees, we could see the entire brigade stretching before and behind us. French and American trucks snorted past without end.

The pleasant, warm sun sank lower. By twilight, on the outskirts of a town, we watched youths of the French 1920 class, freshened after their day's training, walking in groups, and watching our dusty column out of curious eyes. Here and there one strolled by the side of a pretty girl, shyly silent because of this undesired publicity.

They waved hesitant farewells. In the village little children shrieked after us:

"Good, by! Good, by! Goodbye!"

****

The sun slipped away altogether. Night closed about us. By the last light we twisted through Epieds. The people gave us feeble cheers. But we paid little attention. We were already footsore. Even the mounted men, to save the animals, walked alternate hours. Our halts because of the length of the column, had become extremely sketchy. Sometimes you missed them altogether, closing up a gap. And there were innumerable unexpected stops when you dismounted and were up and off again almost before your feet had touched the ground.

Our feet weren't up to much. During the past month we had been either in the line or changing station. We were soft. But songs brightened our worm-like progress along the dark country roads.

The night brought the flashes back to the sky ahead of us. They were not quite so pallid. They spread farther. They soared higher. They were streaked by ominous lines of ruddier flame.

Always the traffic of supply ground past us, forcing us to the side of the road, struggling desperately forward to feed the fires.

A cheery voice flashed bravely back at the burning sky.

"Gonna be some little fight, boys!"

Another voice rose with a quavering, melancholy quality. Its song was something about a girl waiting at home, waiting patiently and unselfishly for a man to come back out of the fires——

The ranks fell silent. The voice died away.

Somewheres ahead a rolling kitchen commenced to drop a trail of sparks. It wound, as the road twisted, like an unbelievably long and phosphorescent serpent.

It kept pace with us. After a time the odour of coffee floated back along the trail. Between midnight and the dawn we would know there was a jewel of a cook up there. But was it safe, this red, serpentine trail? Are cooks ever safe near the front? Everybody saw the sparks. And everybody caught the aroma. The fires were still distant. Nobody disturbed the cook. The red serpent persisted until it was certain the coffee in the containers was hot and would stay so.

We drank it between one and two o'clock, when we were halted for some time on a high ridge. The flames seemed nearer and brighter than they had been. Or perhaps it was because the night was so dark up there. Then for the first time we distinguished star shells. They separated themselves from the flashes so slowly and disappeared so reluctantly that you couldn't be sure at first they weren't born of your imagination and your smarting eyes. You thought the first one, perhaps, was the Pleiades, less distinct than usual. They all looked exactly like that, tiny constellations, blurred by the shifting glow ahead. But they were everywhere so you knew what they were.

As we munched a sandwich or a cracker and sipped the hot, fragrant coffee everything impressed us as abnormally still. We missed the rumbling of the wheels, just silenced, and the rap of the horses' shoes on the road. In the beginning there was only the slow shuffling of feet in the dirt as the forms, detached a trifle from the night, by the flickering in the sky, formed a line by the rolling kitchen—that, and occasional dull clashing of mess cups. Then a man spoke, and after a time another. It was usually only some banal remark, drowned and forgotten at once in this flickering stillness.

"You're spilling it on my wrist."

"God bless you for the chow, sergeant."

Or from the sergeant:

"Move on! Do you want to delouse yourself in it?"

Such aimless accents of the silence were forgotten at once.

Out of the subsequent, pallid calm stole the voice of battle.

Men shifted their feet uneasily. It was the first of the cannon mutter to reach us from the flames. A quick activity thrust it back again.

"Prepare to mount!"

"Mount!"

"Forward yo-o-o-o———"

The orders came down the line, growing apparently out of nothing as the cannon mutter had done, reaching a climax in one's own mouth, dying away on the long drawn vowel of the last command.

We were moving forward again, drawing an odd and comfortable companionship from our rumbling, rapping progress.

At the scarcely perceptible birth of dawn we were winding sleepily on the shoulder of another ridge which looked down on what might have been a long lake or a deep and gigantic river flowing between the hills. It was possible to guess, and here and there a man raised his head and stared. Someone spoke in a harsh whisper.

"That's the valley of the Marne."

He whispered because we were somnolent and unalert. The name possessed no dynamic power for us then. One fellow did manage:

"Didn't know it was so blamed wide."

The other offered to instruct him.

"Oh, that's the mist."

"You don't say? Goodnight!"

Shoulders drooped again.

"Ha-a-a-lt!"

The command sang down the line like a savage chant. The regiment dismounted. One by one men dropped over against the bank, and drifted into sleep, keeping a listless hand on bridles. The horses, weary too, for the most part stood with drooped heads, not even troubling to nibble the lush grass. Now and then one would wander indifferently from the feebly restraining grasp of his master. An officer would rebuke sleepily, consigning the careless one to walk the rest of that stage. At such a time the world seemed drunk with sleep.

A dim headlight pushed through the mist below—guiding one of the first trains, we guessed, to carry troops along the reopened Château Thierry line. The dawn strengthened. It grasped the fringes of the mist and lifted it slowly from the valley. A stream, like a ribbon, narrow and decorative, was strung across the fields.

Tired eyes opened to gaze with an expression of discovery at the pleasant little river that twice had been wider than the ocean to Germany.

Drawn by Capt. Dana, Battery A

On the march

We resumed our crawling. There was no longer any reason in mounting and dismounting. We would go ahead for a few paces, then stop again. An anxiety grasped the command to get somewheres beneath green trees before the light should grow much stronger. Then we saw the head of the column moving to the left to be swallowed by a large grove of trees. A sigh went up. We were nearly there. Each halt seemed longer than it was. We glanced upwards. We listened for aeroplanes.

We, too, reached the fork. We turned and entered beneath the friendly shrubbery. The chill of the night had disappeared before the mounting sun.

As we parked an officer from headquarters ran about.

"Keep everything covered up, and don't let anybody stand in open places. The Huns are watching these woods for bivouacs."

Where carriages were parked in thinly roofed places we draped them with cut shrubbery. We started the animals down a path behind a guide who knew where water was to be had. We got our paper work out of the way. We hurried the war diary to regimental headquarters which had been established in the deserted town of Chezy.

The rolling kitchens smoked. Men forgot their weariness to form eager lines before them. Groups ate greedily among the trees. The forest was noisy with talk called from group to group. The Colonel arrived and approached a party of officers on a tarpaulin, making a stupendous breakfast in celebration of having brought men, animals, and carriages through a stage that had worried everyone.

"Keep your seats, gentlemen," the Colonel said. "I want to congratulate you on the way you handled your paper work this morning.,,

The group returned to its breakfast refreshed. A word of praise after such effort is a tonic.

The illusion of a picnic, however, was never very convincing. The sunlight searched the woods, exposing souvenirs of the recent fighting. Half hidden by the underbrush were stained and eloquent garments. Here lay a Hun helmet, a neat round hole through the front. There was the stock of a rifle.

Men picked such objects up curiously. They gathered them in little heaps, convenient for transportation. They prepared for sleep. The sun seemed to laugh.

That is the curse of night marches. You can't get a satisfactory sleep by day. There is a great deal to be done, that robs many men even of the opportunity to sleep. Guards must be posted. Kitchens must go as hard as ever. Animals must be more carefully cared for than when in billets or at an echelon. Equipment must be cleaned, and the damage of the previous night's march repaired.

All these operations manufacture a noise that disturbs those who do get a chance to rest. But it is the sun that irritates the weary more than anything else. No matter how shady the place you choose, the sun will find it out sooner and later, will grin in your eyes, will inform you that it is no time to be sleeping.

Maybe you move. Then a man shakes your shoulder, demanding information which he foolishly imagines you alone can furnish.

If on such a march you can average three hours' sleep out of the twenty-four you are lucky and insensitive.

In Chezy woods there were other disturbing factors. The men's feet had suffered. It was necessary to treat them. You stood in line for long periods waiting to get to the doctor. When you had been treated it was probably dinner time.

After dinner nearly everyone that wasn't on duty strolled down the hill, through the grounds of a modern *château*, and so to the bank of the Marne. The water was dirty, and, if one stopped to think, sinister. The afternoon, on the other hand, was warm, and we didn't forecast many more opportunities in the near future to bathe. We filled the murky water with active, noisy bodies. On the shore mature men reproduced the antics of schoolboys. From across the Marne frowned a landscape stifled beneath the pestilential haze of war—a condition scarcely palpable, reminiscent of a land whose inhabitants have been swept down by some black plague. For there weren't so many ruins. There pervaded everything, fields, farm houses, villages, only this sense of desertion and a morbid un-health. It was like a picture from an artist whose melancholy and diseased brain has retained of the visible world no more than a sense of form.

All afternoon the activity about the banks mocked this oppressive landscape. From time to time strings of animals were led down and watered. The antics of the bathers continued until dusk.

A few of our horses did not respond that day. We were under horsed anyway. A new fair started. Organizations swopped animals about so that no carriage should be left. That took time. Supper was a shadowy affair. We policed the bivouac. We lashed equipment to the carriages again. Souvenir hunters gazed at their stacks of trophies, shook their heads, and scattered the stuff about the woods.

One man picked up a Hun helmet and beat with it thoughtfully against a tree. "Seems tough enough," he mused—"too darned tough."

He flung it on the ground, thrust his hands in his pockets, and leaned against a tree. His attitude was, roughly, typical of everyone else's. The teams were harnessed. Everything was ready. We waited for the word to move out.

The dusk had forced into the woods an unwelcome alteration. Instead of patches of sunlight, the grim souvenirs of battle scattered about determined the values of the picture. There was a chill in the air, too. One's sense of sleeplessness returned with the night. And the increasing darkness meant the resumption of those breathless pyrotechnics in the north.

A little fellow, crouched on a stump, his hands clasped about his knees, gazed straight ahead. His face was immobile. You didn't like to look at it, because it seemed an expression of many more carefully guarded minds. You moved about, trying to throw the feeling off, this difficult conviction that the forest was crowded with homesickness.

A man strolled up and put his arm about the little fellow's shoulders. His voice came with understanding.

"What's the matter, buddy?"

The little fellow sprang upright as an animal is startled by the appearance of a hunter. He answered fiercely:

"Matter! Nothing the matter."

He burst into odd oaths, as if they might justify him. The other gave him a cigarette.

****

Word came around that we were to be careful where we sat down tonight, for there would be always the danger of mustard gas. Other messengers appeared. We would cross the Marne on pontoon bridges at Château Thierry. Carriages would cross on one bridge with intervals of fifty metres. Individually mounted men would use another, dismounted men a third. An apprehension of shelling at the crossing from long range guns saturated these orders.

The word to mount came with the last light. Whips cracked and horses strained forward. The carriages reeled drunkenly over roots and depressions. There were swaying escapes while men shouted warnings, put their shoulders to the wheels, and struck at the horses. Where the woods trail turned into the main road an officer sat his horse, repeating over and over again, like one reciting a piece.

"Men may smoke, but must use automatic lighters. No matches will be struck tonight."

Brakes set, we slid down a long, curving hill into the valley. The column moved faster this evening. A soft moonlight gave an air of mystery to the few empty farmhouses we passed. Several groups of these suggested that we were on the outskirts of Château Thierry. But the road was longer than we thought. It was nearly midnight when we entered the city at last. Through a dark silence we became aware of a multiple activity. The streets were full of half seen figures that passed us without words. The place might have been a rendezvous of criminals, furtively intent on avoiding discovery. There were no lights. We could scarcely distinguish the jagged remains of walls, and here and there in the building line a fissure that we knew was the grave of a home.

At the railroad the column was cut by the passing of a train, and the over-anxiety of the military police, which closed the gates too soon. Beyond, teams tore through the dark to catch up, and men rode back and forth keeping in touch with divided units.

In a narrow street close to the river more military police were stationed. Their suppressed voices were scarcely audible above the rumbling of the wheels on cobble stones as they repeated our instructions for crossing. Certainly the Hun wasn't so near!

We entered a wide place through the centre of which the Marne flowed. More military police stood on each bridge nervously hurrying the crossing. But no shells fell. Our own progress on the planking drowned the sound of guns and the hill ahead was a curtain against the northern sky.

We were over, but when we had climbed the hill above the town the voice and the gestures of battle became eloquent again. The passage of the river seemed to have brought us much, much closer. The sky was a wavering sheet of flame, no longer wan. It spread and contracted with a yellow intensity. Star shells stood out against it clearly enough now. As the rumblings increased and diminished one could almost guess the calibre of the guns engaged. An enormous mass of artillery was concentrated up there. It was folly to try to sing against that greater song. The column forged stolidly ahead.

We were in the heart of the salient now. Even by night the country was haggard. The Hun's departure had been a matter of a few days, and he had not neglected his reputation in leaving.

We rode silently through village after village. They all shared a dreadful similarity. They were clusters of homes, roofless and with gashed walls. They were filled with an odour which made the air reluctant in one's lungs. It was compounded of stale gas, of lime, of ancient plaster and woodwork, suddenly crumbled. It forced on one an impression of death, still warm. It suggested the proximity of departing souls. There seemed to be a connection between this sense and the ghastly light that flickered over everything.

****

Between these dead villages the open country stank, too.

****

At times we were sheltered by shell screens, raised by the Hun for his own safety.

Towards morning we munched sandwiches and crackers, but there was no hot coffee. The fires in all rolling kitchens had been ordered drawn.

Shortly after this meal we turned to the right at Courpoil, another slaughtered, empty, stinking town, and on a rough road ascended a long hill. The halts, as always before the long halt, became numerous and irritating. The road seemed interminable. In spite of the brief stage, and our earlier speed, daylight would probably catch us again, and the risk was greater here. Yet a little daylight might be a safeguard against this road which degenerated with each metre. *Fourgons* and escort wagons lurched dangerously. Why the deuce were we struggling so far from the main road anyway? We'd have to come back by dark again over this risky trail. And our horses were tired. The only excuse that occurred to us was that we were going to a particularly safe and convenient bivouac.

As the east grew ruddy the flashes faded. We saw a *fourgon* on its side by the road. The horses stood by, gazing at it with rather a pleased air. Tired soldiers made unavailing efforts to get it up.

"No sleep for those guys," we said pityingly. "They'll have to unpack everything, jack her up, and pack again."

"Say, that must be a peach of a bivouac we're going to."

It wasn't.

Just ahead two large masses of forest barely detached themselves from the slow dawn. There was an open field between. Some of the batteries were already strung out along the edge of the woods. The rest of the column halted. A group of officers and men stood in the field, talking and gesticulating. One heard:

"Who made the reconnaissance for this blasted thing?"

There had been a reconnaissance the previous day, but something certainly had gone wrong. We asked eager questions. The woods in spite of their size were for the most part choked with underbrush, and the remainder was rough and honey-combed with infantry trenches. There wasn't room for the regiment under cover, and Hun planes might appear at any moment.

"And those woods," you heard, "are full of dead things."

Without calling attention to it we had all noticed the thickening of the nauseating odour of wholesale animal decay.

"It's bad for the men."

"The men have got to get used to it."

"But it's better to see those things in the heat of action."

That, however, wasn't the point. We had to get covered up before the light grew stronger.

The Headquarters Company, and Regimental Headquarters got sketchily concealed in one piece of woods. The larger part of the Second Battalion got in the other. The First parked its pieces on the edge and cut

"Fourgons Lurched Dangerously".

Drawn by Corporal Schmidt, Hq. Co.

foliage with which it covered everything. Opposite, the Supply Company employed the same makeshift.

The picket lines had to be placed inside.

Those who entered the forest to locate these lines went softly. It was still night in there. You didn't want to stumble over unseen obstacles. You fancied that the woods were still inhabited by an army, which for the moment slept. The trenches made angular scars between the trees—shallow, makeshift defences of the retreating Hun. Their floors were littered with grey blouses, helmets, round Hun caps, Mausers, grenades, belts of cartridges. Scattered between them were artillery ammunition dumps, the shells in wicker containers, like wine baskets, or else in elaborate and expensive metal frames. As the light strengthened we saw quantities of rations which had been thrown away, gasoline tanks, pioneer tools. If there wasn't an army in the woods there was the equipment for one. That day if we wanted anything—gasoline, for example, for an automobile or a sidecar,—we went through no formalities.

"Go in the woods and get it," we said.

And the seeker obeyed and got what he wanted.

But in there the odour was poisonous. Everyone was warned not to prowl in the underbrush.

As soon as the picket lines were established we went out, clinging to the edge of the woods, and almost at once the first Hun planes came over, but we were pretty well concealed, and they didn't trouble us.

The question of water obtruded itself. By taking the water carts all the way down the hill water for the men could be drawn from a well in Courpoil. For the animals the best that was offered was a pond a mile away. Its banks were steep, so that the animals were watered individually from buckets. The process was tedious. Instead of watering three times that day we were lucky to struggle into the mud and out again twice.

The lake wasn't any pleasanter than the woods. Scattered equipment littered its banks. Some of our men tried it for bathing. One or two of them cried out, and they all waded to shore, talking among themselves. When we asked what was the matter they looked sheepish.

"The lake is full of dead Bosche," they said.

There was a large farm house a few yards away. It had evidently been used for some kind of a headquarters. The garden had been trampled, and the fences broken down. In a corner was a new cemetery with rows of wooden crosses, made, we guessed, from packing cases. They marked American graves. We were glad they were so few.

One man said brutally:

"There are a lot of things they *didn't* bury around here."

We practiced making our lungs do with a minimum of air.

On the higher ground, among the deeper shell holes were many small and shallow ones. We knew they had been made by gas shells. Now and then you saw one whose bottom was yellow with the spewed mustard gas that had failed to volatilize.

Everywhere was telephone wire, laid on the ground from position to position. There had been no time to salvage it.

As we ate our late breakfast we noticed that the flies were worse than they had been anywhere else, even at Souge. And there was a strange variety—a big, blue nosed sort that fought to get at your food and, defeated, flew greedily back to the secrets of the underbrush.

We ate, 'though, and we managed to sleep even in that woods. We failed to find in Courpoil forest, however, even the relaxation Chezy had offered. There was more to be done. The animals required more attention. There were more aeroplane alarms, and there was more danger of men being caught in the open and not standing still.

That afternoon Captains Ravenel and Delanoy rejoined. They had left Souge some time before, but had been unable to locate the regiment. Captain Ravenel, because he was senior, took command of the First battalion in place of Captain Dana. Captain Delanoy assumed command of Battery F.

We had with us two lame men who had failed to respond to treatment. A passing ambulance picked them up and carried them back to Château Thierry. The surgeon in charge gave us some cheerful gossip.

"Some of your infantry went in yesterday," he said in an off-hand way, "and last night they sent out a lot of casualties. You won't want anything much hotter than you'll get up there."

We thanked him, but we didn't press him to stay for supper. His gossip gave the persistent grumbling in the north a sharper threat. Yet, whatever the next day might hold, I don't think anyone regretted escaping from Courpoil woods.

We didn't dare budge until the dusk was thick. Then we tore our improvised camouflage from the carriages and formed in the shell-ploughed field for the final stage of our march into the Oise-Aisne battle.

The last sunset glow fought for a time against the violent and unnatural dawn in the north.

As always the fighting intensified with the night. The gun chorus reached thicker, heavier notes. Once a sheet of violet flame, supernatural in its vast luminosity, sprang from the earth, and, while we watched, speechless, unbelieving, mounted to the very zenith and spread half the immeasurable circle of the horizon. During the several seconds it lasted details of the landscape leered at us through a mauve daylight.

The end of the world might come like that. You mocked your savage instinct to fall prostrate before a power greater than the power of man.

"Some flares those Huns have!" you said to your neighbour, but you weren't quite sure it was an ordinary flare. Was it some new device?

The violet sheet fell from the sky like a wind-swept curtain. The lesser fires resumed their flickering. Rockets and flares streaked always upwards, so that we lived in a chameleon twilight. It was as if a gigantic and undreamed of catastrophe had happened, could not be controlled, and threatened to sweep Europe. That men fought in its heart that we would fight there, too, was a fantastic imagining.

"Organizations ready?"

Everyone reported ready. So forward then into the midst of this mad disaster!

****

The moment had obliterating demands. Our carriages were overloaded. The *fourgons* were top heavy. Horse covers, packs, and various paraphernalia were lashed to the tops. Inside were our instruments of precision and communication. A picket line, perhaps, and heavy tools were slung from the axles in an attempt to lower the centre of gravity. Sometimes a hand reel cart flopped drunkenly along behind. A sensitive child would have wept at sight of us. Of the attributes of vagabonds we lacked only one thing—a fortune teller.

That long, rough road down the hill was damned as perfectly as once in our remote youth stumps had been.

Horses were damned by drivers. Drivers were damned by non-commissioned officers. Non-commissioned officers were damned by officers, officers were damned by other officers in order of rank from bottom to top. That is in a fashion of speaking. Probably the language was quite polite, and it was only the intention that swore. At any rate it got us on. We reached the foot of the hill at last and turned into the main road amidst the ruins of Courpoil.

We halted at once in the shelter of broken walls. There was a block ahead. Pretty soon motor lorries detached themselves from it and stormed petulantly past. Others wormed a way from the other direction. These were heavily loaded. They demanded the right of way. Some of the trucks, we saw, belonged to our division ammunition train.

"What outfit, Buddy?" a chauffeur yelled at us.

"305th Field Artillery," a man answered thoughtlessly.

Angry voices rebuked his indiscretion. It was a spirit that had grown on us steadily. At the front no one knows what ears are about. The chauffeurs, however, recognizing us as of the same division, bandied words.

Drawn by Private Enroth
"The shelter of broken walls"

"Believe me, you're going to some summer resort."

"Where there's a will there's a way, but don't forget your will."

"Hey! you look as if you were moving from the Bronx to Brooklyn."

We didn't have much repartee. We were too anxious for the obstructing lorries to get by. An hour must have slipped away before the jam was broken. As we lurched ahead a message came down the column, repeated from mouth to mouth.

"Follow the carriage in front closely to avoid shell holes."

That meant that the shells were falling on this road too fast for the pioneers. To dodge such holes, in spite of the advice, moreover, seemed an impossibility. We couldn't snake along from side to side in all that traffic. We couldn't stop until there was a chance to get past a hole. So we assigned dismounted men to walk ahead of the precious *fourgons*. We threatened dire penalties if they didn't give plenty of warning.

The forest of La Fère closed about us, shutting out the flames ahead and the wan light of the moon. We could see nothing. The man riding beside you was blurred by the heavy pall. You glanced to right and left, trying to imagine the form of the forest and the things it hid. Your only clear sensation was of the intolerable stench of death.

We halted. Would we never go on again?

A double column of foot soldiers shuffled past. They, too, halted. We couldn't make out what service they belonged to, but it became clear something was wrong with them. They didn't seem to know where they were. They had an idea they had got on the wrong road, but they weren't sure. They stood there beside us for a long time, growing more and more impatient.

So there we were hopelessly blocked, a rare target for a shell or an air bomb.

One of the scarcely seen men lamented.

"Ah'd rather take my chawnces in the line than be walked ta death."

"Not me," another objected. "Ah can heah ol' Mistah shell a singin' now. He says: 'gonta getcha, gonta getcha, gonta getcha. *Bam!* Done gotcha.'"

What appeared to be a huge light flashed out ahead, and was immediately extinguished. It showed us that the foot soldiers near us were from a southern engineer outfit. Their lungs were good. They burst into a huge and angry chorus.

"Put that blank, blank match out."

Expressions of pity and disgust followed.

"Say, Bo! Put yo'sel on a plate an' hand yo'sel with a knife and fo'k to Mistah Jerry. But don't use me fo' the gravy."

"Hey, Captain, take me away from these city fellahs that strike matches in the dark."

We all shared the shame of that one culprit. We tried to spot him to teach him a lesson. But the thing had been too quick, and the night was too friendly a protection. We *were* from the city. Perhaps the game of concealment came harder to us than to some others, but we thought we had learned it better. We had, as we found out later. That particular crime wasn't repeated.

By this time the engineers had decided that they'd better try another road, so, without saying anything, they calmly countermarched, blocking the road more completely than before, and holding us up for another half hour, dividing our column at the same time.

We got out of the ruck at last, and upon a clear road. We made fast progress, urged by the necessity of reaching Nesles Woods before daylight. The dead towns echoed to our hurrying hoofs and wheels. And the walls shook to the reverberations of heavy guns just ahead.

We entered the outskirts of Fère-en-Tardennois, still under shell fire. We slipped through unmolested. Scarcely anything remained of the town—the largest in the district. It was a heap of rubble with a few walls, like torn masks. It might have been the site of a prehistoric capital about which an archaeologist has commenced to excavate.

Nearby batteries pounded away. Our horses, weary as they were, grew nervous. They moved restlessly about at halts. The men, on the other hand, forgetting their surroundings, the warnings against gas, everything except their great weariness, sank on the banks of ditches and slept fitfully.

Daylight caught us again as we wound through the town of Nesles. It seemed impossible we should ever reach a bivouac at the time scheduled. Nesles was in ruins except for its storied mediaeval tower, which shells had only scarred.

Beyond the town was a steep road, recently laid by the pioneers, which climbed to the forest.

Even from there the forest was haggard and shell torn. The sloping fields between us and it were strewn with graves, dug where their occupants had fallen. Most of them had rough crosses, from which German helmets hung.

The horses were unequal to the hill. We manned the wheels, and forced our way up. We entered between the broken trees.

We felt we had arrived too late. There had been aeroplanes in the distant sky. We had no doubt that the Hun knew there would be that night an artillery bivouac in Nesles Forest.

The place had been policed after a fashion. The stench of death was less here than it had been at Courpoil. A regiment of pioneers was already in possession. They had removed such refuse of battle as they had been able to. Everywhere about the forest floor were coffin-shaped holes. We guessed they were individual shelters from shell and bomb fragments. We learned to call them "funk holes," a term we later applied to far more ambitious refuges. Anti-air guns opened all around us.

Tsching! Tsching!

Two shell cases whistled down in our woods.

We put on our tin hats, but we knew they were no protection against shell cases.

We recalled all the aeroplanes that had bothered us at Doue. We asked the pioneers with a perfect confidence if we didn't have the control of the air up here. We felt that if the American air service was concentrated anywheres it would be on this front.

The pioneers looked at us with pity.

"The Huns," they answered, "own the air here and have a mortgage on the ether."

Usually they followed with accounts of American balloons brought down by Hun planes, and unrestricted bombing attacks. Our hearts sank. We knew we had been seen coming in that morning. Yet we felt the pioneers must be wrong. The money spent, the men enlisted in the air service, and all those fellows flying about Coulommiers!

Before many days we accused the pioneers of uttering conservative statements.

A messenger found Captain Ravenel and took him to the Colonel. The Colonel introduced him to an officer who had just reported as assigned to the regiment. His name was Major George W. Easterday. He would take command of the First Battalion. Captain Ravenel would return to the command of his battery.

Major Easterday, we learned, had come originally from the regular army coast artillery. He had entered the service from civil life. He had been removed by a telegram from a few days' dalliance in Paris after a lively share in the advance north from Château Thierry, and shot back into the show as a member of the 305th. He was destined to remain with the regiment until it sailed from France.

So the forced march ended, and we were in the woods which after disastrous experiments in other localities, was to become the regimental echelon. We breakfasted, unstrapped our packs, and stretched out to sleep. We were awakened almost immediately by the news that there would be a preliminary reconnaissance that afternoon. We studied our maps in preparation. The little party rode from the woods, and in an hour's time returned. There had been a blunder somewheres, for the rendezvous had not been made clear, and the various portions of the reconnaissance hadn't got together. So a real reconnaissance was set for early the next morning.

We dined to the mounting accompaniment of gun fire, and crawled gratefully into our shelter tents, believing that no amount of noise could keep us awake.

The old metaphor of the orchestra of the guns is justified. Batteries and individual guns seem to have their own tones. When a great many are firing perpetually, as on this front, the tones blend into crashing chords. We fell asleep to this gargantuan lullaby.

After a few minutes the hideous screech of the gas alarm had us up and snapping our respirators on. The screeching died away. After a time the gas officers went around singing out:

"Masks may be removed."

We went to sleep again. Again we were awakened by that unholy screeching. It happened three times. We told ourselves that the horns wouldn't awake us again, gas or no gas.

On the heels of the last alarm something else aroused us. We heard the throbbing whir of Hun aeroplanes. There were plenty of targets on the Vesle, heaven knows, but we remembered our fear that we had been seen coming into the bivouac that morning. And the throbbing grew.

Ba-room—ba-room—ba-room——

As if the engines missed fire rhythmically.

Then above the artillery we got the crunching detonations of large air bombs. Those aeroplanes were coming nearer. There was a squadron out, and if it wasn't after us it would pass very close.

Ba-room—ba-room—ba-room—Always nearer, and the detonations were louder now, and they came in salvos of four, each burst half drowned by the next.

Nearly overhead we heard the petulant rattle of a machine gun.

"That's the scout signalling to the bombers," someone said.

"Why," we asked irritably, "are our aeroplanes back in cheerful places while these fellows give us their droppings undisturbed?"

We thought of the other bivouacs, crowded with American soldiers, with the Hun birds merrily hopping from one to another.

The bombers responded to the scout, and their bombs fell on the edge of our woods with roars that made the artillery seem like childish fireworks. And you smiled grimly as you thought of those fellows making us blow our bugles all day long back near Coulommiers.

The Huns dropped several salvos, and throbbed away to other pastures.

Men were killed in Nesles Woods that night, but our check showed us that the 305th had escaped, and we crawled back to bed, and went to sleep, and didn't answer any more alarms until reveille dragged us out.

That was the first of many experiences on the Vesle with Hun aeroplanes, working nearly undisturbed. Most men will agree there is no form of attack less pleasant. You approximate the sensations of an insect above which a giant foot wavers, waiting to descend obliteratingly.

CHAPTER 16

Reconnoitring in Front of Fismes

The reconnaissance we made in the Fismes sector on August 14th was about as much like our Lorraine ones as a pleasant day is like a period of violent storm. Nor was it as agreeable as a reconnaissance made during an advance, for here we faced a semi-stabilized battle. The Huns could see our little party, and they had registered everything. Still all reconnaissances have one feature in common. They never work out exactly as one plans. They fail invariably to follow the pretty rules laid down by the books. At the front you mould technique to the demands of the moment, and to the necessity for quick results.

It is a matter of interest to preserve the field order that sent us into this, our costliest battle. The reconnaissance was made in pursuance to its provisions. It follows:

Headquarters 77th Division,
American E. F.
14 August, 1918.

FIELD ORDER NO. 23.
MAPS: FERE-en-TARDENOIS } 1:20,000
FISMES

1. The 4th Field Artillery Brigade will be relieved by the 152nd Field Artillery Brigade on the nights of August 15-16 and 16-17, 1918, in compliance with G-3 order no. 31, 3rd Army Corps, 14 August, 1918.

2. The 305th Field Artillery will relieve the 16th Field Artillery, the 304th Field Artillery will relieve the 77th Field Artillery, the 306th Field Artillery will relieve the 13th Field Artillery, assuming missions of organizations relieved. Necessary reconnaissances on 14th and 15th August as previously directed.

3. Relief will be completed as follows:

1st Night: (15-16) (a) ½ battery to be relieved in each position. ½ battery 152nd Brigade will be accompanied by an officer who will remain at the position. One chief of section of each ½ battery will remain at the position.

     (b) Telephone operators, linemen, and observors of the 152nd Brigade will report to their posts and will remain in observation only.

 2nd Night: (16-17) (a) Remaining ½ of each battery relieved. One officer and 2 chiefs of section to remain at position until following noon.

     (b) All specialists relieved, excepting one telephone operator and one observer of 4th Field Artillery Brigade in each post, will remain in place until noon following.

     (c) Ammunition dumps will be turned over to 152nd Brigade.

     (d) Battery combat train and other elements will stand relieved at 21:00 o'clock.

     (e) Ammunition train will stand relieved at 21:00 o'clock.

 4. Arrangements for exchange of wire, camouflage nets, etc. will be made between commanders concerned.

 5. Elements of 16th Field Artillery, as relieved, will proceed to position in FORET de FERE by roads to south through NESLES. Other elements will use main road through FERE-en-TARDENNOIS. Elements of the 152nd Field Artillery Brigade will use the roads running north from the FORET de NESLES.

 6. The 302nd Trench Mortar Battery will remain for the present in the location where it is bivouaced. Reconnaissances will be made to select suitable positions for this battery so that it may be put in position in the near future.

 7. Command will pass to battery, battalion, and regimental Commanders of 152nd Brigade, as the relief of each unit is reported complete.

 8. Command of the artillery of the sector will pass to Commanding Officer 152nd Brigade at 8 A. M. August 17, 1918; P. C. 152nd Field Artillery Brigade will open at FERE CHATEAU at the same time, same date.

      By command of Major General Duncan,
           J. R. R. HANNAY
            Chief of Staff.

 So we set out to study the ground. The regimental, battalion, and battery parties left Nesles Woods together, and trotted down the hill to Mareuil where the 4th Field Artillery Brigade had its headquarters. It was a warm, brilliant day. Therefore, we knew we would see and be seen. We dashed past parties of pioneers repairing roads that had been damaged by shell fire the previous night. In the stricken village ambulances stood outside a distributing station, and on the ground were many stretchers, bearing forms, some still, some restless, each covered with a secretive issue blanket on which the wounded man's tin hat and gas mask rested. Ether and iodine cut the pervading chlorine odour.

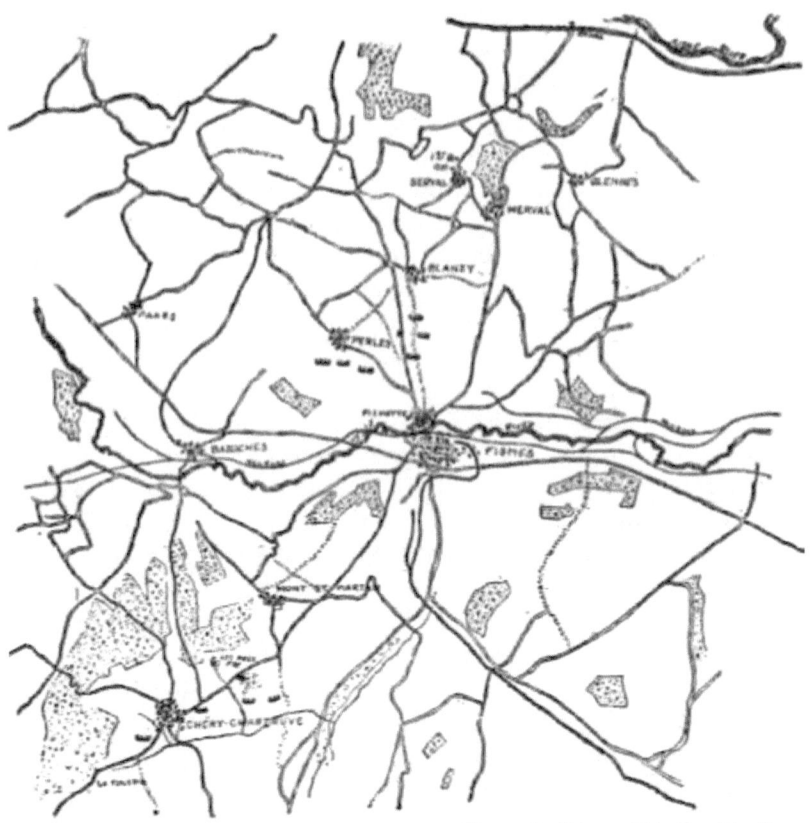

Drawn by Corporal Tucker, Hq. Co.
The Vesle and Aisne campaigns

Brigade Headquarters was a one story building, originally a cafe or a rural hostelry. It was dilapidated. The dusty square in front of it was white with chloride sprinklings. Opposite, an arched gateway admitted to a large courtyard surrounded by stables and dwellings. Our party was herded in here and commanded to keep out of sight, because Hun planes were constantly passing overhead, expressing an impudent curiosity. So we got as many horses as we could in the sheds, and kept the rest close to the walls. Then officers and enlisted men made themselves inconspicuous and awaited the result of the conference of field officers which continued in the reformed cafe across the street.

Every soldier, I think, has noticed that daylight acquires false qualities from one's own perceptions. To all of us there was an unnatural tone to that brilliant sun, streaked occasionally by enemy planes. Perhaps another planet might have light like that. You heard men commenting about it with little laughs.

Restlessness grew upon us. Would the conference *never* end? A group of field officers came from headquarters. Their faces were serious. They glanced about uneasily. Some of them appeared a trifle undecided. They paused, forming little groups, to which representatives from our party attached themselves. Gossip drifted into the hot, restless courtyard. One of the batteries which the 305th was going to relieve, we heard, had had forty casualties during a burst of harassing fire the afternoon before. There was always harassing fire it seemed, where we were going. We would have to take up new positions, we said confidently. Back from the gossiping groups slipped the depressing word that there were no positions much better than the ones already occupied.

The colonel came in. He said at first we would have to go forward from that point on foot. Those of us who had studied the maps groaned, for the road went diagonally toward the front line. By it our positions were many miles away. The colonel reconsidered. He talked again to some of the officers of the 4th. Doubtfully he decided we might ride as far as regimental headquarters with an interval of 200 metres between pairs.

No officer or man that took that ride cared much for it. We curved up the hill past the half destroyed Romanesque church, and turned into a main road on the crest. There were, of course, no shell screens, and, to the left, we could look all the way to Jerry's temporary home. One of the men expressed the general emotion.

"I feel all undressed up here," he grinned.

Everywheres along that road were nice fresh signs left by the enemy, pointing the way to dressing stations, to ration and ammunition dumps, to short cuts for the various villages. And there were newer French signs, regulating traffic, repeatedly calling attention to the exposed nature of the highway.

In the vicinity of a small group of buildings ahead large high explosive shells were vomiting blackly. We guessed that the group was Chartreuve Farm, the regimental headquarters of the 16th Field Artillery.

We waited in a lane, behind the shelter of a wall until the rest of the party had come up, then hurried across a courtyard into the farm. Two or three habitable rooms down stairs were packed. The colonel and the majors conferred behind a closed door with the field officers of the 16th. Less important but quite intelligent young men gave us the sector gossip while the Hun continually reminded us he knew where we were.

The sector gossip was simple. It was a rotten place we were going to and there wasn't much we could do about it. Jerry had a big concentration of artillery opposite and he was using it with an admirable and murderous skill. We listened mutely to recitations of casualties. We sensed some joy on the part of these young men that they were going out; a brotherly sympathy that we were going in.

"We Curved up the Hill Past the Half Destroyed Romanesque Church"

This conference, too, ended at last, and the 16th gave us a bite from their field kitchen set beneath great trees in the pretty grounds of the place.

The colonel and his party went no farther just then. The two battalion parties continued on foot, out of the friendly trees, across stripped fields, and into the ravaged village of Chèry Chartreuve.

Even on that busy day the 305th rendered even more bibulous the name of this dissipated appearing town. It was known ever after among us as "Sherry Chartreuse."

A military policeman stood between wrecked buildings at the first corner. He reminded the more careless of us to carry our gas masks in the alert position. Another, a hundred metres beyond, advised:

"Walk farther apart, sirs. They're giving the road hally-lool-yah right now."

They were. The louder whistling of shells preceded explosions close at hand. A bank on the side of the road towards the enemy was pitted with funk holes gouged out by infantrymen. Into these we ducked when the whistling warned us of a dangerously close explosion. We must have resembled animals of absurd habit that hopped aimlessly from place to place.

This erratic progress brought us to our first view of Les Près Farm—place of unbeloved memories.

A huge hangar rose where a country road crossed the main highway. The number of shell holes testified to the enemy's interest in that crossroads. The country road climbed a bare slope to a cluster of buildings, a third of a mile from the hangar. Your first impression was of a large and dignified stone dwelling house with half a dozen outpost trees, and wings of sheds and stables reaching behind it around a large courtyard. To the right were two small stone dwellings, with a horse shed and one or two outhouses just below them. The bare slope stretched upward for another half mile beyond the farm, blatantly broken by three battery positions, whose only protection was flat tops. Where ever you glanced you saw the mortal and redolent remains of horses in grotesque attitudes.

Jerry saluted us. He commenced raking those exposed battery positions. From beneath the flat tops soldiers scurried like an indignant party of ants whose hill has been disturbed. As we climbed the slope we couldn't help admiring the nicety of the Hun fire. Their volleys walked through the positions then walked back again until there was so much jetty smoke you couldn't be quite sure where the shells were falling.

"Hundred and fifties," we muttered.

"Battery positions!" Someone sneered. "Targets! That's all!"

The farm at first appeared deserted. Then we saw a red headed soldier peering at us curiously from a funk hole dug close to the wall of one of the smaller buildings.

This one, nearest the enemy, we had been told would be the First Battalion command post. The other would be used for a similar purpose by the second battalion. The large farmhouse and the courtyard were occupied by the infantry for a dressing station and a reserve position; and the 306th, it was understood, would establish a battalion command post there. The farm, it was clear, was already crowded. From its exposed position it was obvious it would give Jerry plenty of practice.

The two battalion parties went each into its little future home.

Walls decorated with coarse cartoons by the Huns, very recently departed; logs piled in the rooms above the cellars in an insufficient effort to hurry the burst of a direct hit; bedding rolls tumbled about; a greasy deal table with, strewn across its top, the remains of a meal and a few gay copies of *La Vie Parisienne*, incredibly out of place—these are the less animate things that greeted us. The others were some men with sleeves rolled up and a tendency to scratch, and flies innumerable—on the walls, on the men, obliterating the neglected food.

The men welcomed us. When, they wanted to know, did they get out?

We examined the cellars. There was one under each building—stuffy, fly-choked places with rough bunks improvised, and, inevitably, the switch-boards in the places of honour.

Gossip was unnecessary here. The place spoke for itself. Still they did tell us some things. This was the 16th's first trip to the front. They hadn't expected to stay here long.

"We used," a major said, "the observatory for a bleachers. I'm not joking."

Decidedly he wasn't. There were casualties in that observatory. We had to move it. As long as we stayed there the ridge was raked periodically by high explosives, gas, and air bombs.

We fought the flies away from a map and studied the dispositions. It was proposed to place batteries D, E, and F in the three positions the Huns were harassing on the hillside. From a rear window we could see a grove of trees just across the road, a few hundred metres from the farm. Battery C would go there—on a forward slope. We would have to walk some distance to inspect the possibilities for the other two batteries.

We set out after waiting for what we thought was a quiet moment. It might as well be said now that there were no quiet moments in or near Les Près Farm until the Hun moved back to the Aisne early in September. There was never a time you could go about your work there with a feeling of comparative security. Always shells were bursting near you or whistling unpleasantly close. To give the devil his due, it was great artillery work, and it was devilishly uncomfortable. We learned afterwards that we had made Jerry dodge rather more than he had us.

Now he opened up as we walked across the fields to the southeast, but we managed to reach the battery A and B positions and express a decided disapproval. We stood on the edge of a deep valley where B seemed fairly well off with a little natural foliage to break the angles of its camouflage. A was a hundred metres forward in the open with only its flat tops to make a futile attempt to deceive the Hun airmen.

The valley—the map called it the Fond de Mezieres; the soldiers a little later renamed it Death Valley—was full of artillerymen and infantry, bathing in a narrow stream, washing clothes, playing ball, or dreamily watching their horses as they grazed.

"It's doomed," we said to each other.

It was. A night or two later the Huns filled it with gas and high explosive, collecting a heavy toll. We decided at the first glance to have nothing to do with it even for our kitchens or first aid stations.

We learned a lot that afternoon about the radius of Hun shell fragments. They seemed to follow us wherever we went. They disturbed our consultations, and they hurried our walks. Even so it was nearly six o'clock before we got through and took the road home, dodging along the line of funk holes to Chèry Chartreuve.

We noticed, as we walked, hot, dusty, and tired, through the town, a Y. M. C. A. canteen in a half ruined building. That place was to impress us less pleasantly later on, but now we greeted it with joy. Chalked across the door by some German was the legend:

"*Hier wasser.*"

A big, cool looking pump stood inside, and the next room held a counter with chocolate, cakes, cigars, and cigarettes.

We wandered on, refreshed, to Chartreuve Farm where our horses waited for us.

Regimental headquarters, we learned, would not remain there. There was a farm house a mile or so farther back—considerably safer to all appearances—named La Tuillerie.

Nesles Woods impressed us as exceedingly peaceful and remote from danger when we trotted in just before dusk. We smiled. Clearly the lesson of the previous night had not been wasted on those who had stayed in the woods that day. Let the Hun airmen come! The floor of the forest was fairly honey-combed with elaborate funk holes. Some were even covered with sheets of elephant iron.

The 305th learned early the wisdom of taking every precaution possible, and undoubtedly, it is due to that habit that our casualty list is no greater.

We faced that night the Les Près Farm facts. We had to go there, and it was clear that, because of the amount of artillery already in and the nature of the terrain, there were no really good positions to be had. Those on

Colonel, Afterwards Brigadier General, Manus McCloskey, the Brigade Commander

the slope above the farm, however, probably could be improved on, and it was decided not to use more than two of them, and that only temporarily. A, B, and C, however, would start, at least, in the 16th emplacements. The communication experts were-as troubled as battery commanders. It was going to be a job to keep those lines working, and lack of equipment would have to be com-batted as well as shell fire.

"We've got to take our losses," everyone admitted, "but we can try to hold them down."

Those who had made the reconnaissance had brought back to Nesles Woods some stirring descriptions. In our bivouac no illusions remained, and each man went about the work of preparation with an extreme care, with a thorough understanding.

That day Major Miller replaced Captain Parramore, who had been invalided to a hospital, as regimental surgeon.

At dusk of the 15th the two pieces prescribed from each battery were ready to start. We had hoped by leaving early to dodge some of the night congestion on the roads. For those roads would be shelled.

"Keep your platoons moving," officers said with an effect of prayer.

Whips cracked, the horses strained forward. Our sections jolted out of the friendly and haggard forest.

Chapter 17

Les Près Farm and Much Shell Fire

Early as we were, the roads were crowded from the first. The two other regiments of the brigade had had the same idea of an early start. Quads, bearing ammunition, and ration trucks, bumped along, their drivers sarcastic and anxious. There was a great deal of infantry out—some *fantassins,* and very many of our own doughboys. A lot of heavy firing made the dusk noisy. The darkness came down nearly impenetrable and ominous. Frequently now the column halted.

There's plenty of chance in war. B's platoon had its captain. A's was in command of a lieutenant. During one of these halts B slipped past A, and a little later got what might have been A's share.

But it was all rather confusing, and conditions got worse on the main road above Mareuil. Shells came perpetually like unseen fingers tearing the black pall of night. One knew that they wouldn't all fall over or short. The halts were continual, and, because of the congestion, you couldn't keep your carriages separated.

E got it first. Shrapnel popped overhead, but nobody bothered much about that. Then a high explosive shell burst on the road in the midst of the platoon, and horses reared and tried to pull free, making queerly human sounds. It was impossible to tell at first how much damage had been done. Officers and non-commissioned officers rode up and down the line, shouting and exhorting, but they might as well have saved their breath. There was no panic among the men. Nor, miraculously, had a man been hit. Two horses had been killed, and their team mates were dangerously active.

"Cut 'em out," came the quick command. "Haul 'em over to the ditch, if you can. But let's go on."

The flashes from bursting shells helped the drivers. The dead animals were cut out and drawn to one side. The platoon moved ahead.

****

It wasn't all shrapnel and high explosive. As the column approached Chartreuve Farm gas shells came over in a dangerous concentration. Reluctantly men put on their respirators, shutting out what little light there was. They struggled with frightened horses and got the awkward masks over their muzzles. They went on through a suffocating blackness. The few commands were choked, and had to be mumbled from mouth to mouth.

It was under these uncomfortable circumstances that B suffered. The column was blocked again near Chartreuve crossroads. B was just short of the junction, clearly a registered point, consequently a dangerous one. Yet there was nothing to do about it. Some outfit has to be caught at or near crossroads in these blocks. You can ride ahead if you like, and try your hand at straightening out the tangle, but in the majority of cases you come back with nothing accomplished, and you stand still, or sit your horse, and pray for the movement of the units ahead of you.

The Hun came down on the crossroads, and some of the shells fell among the waiting cannoneers and drivers of B. Even in the blinding respirators it was easy to see that men and horses were down. The horses screamed, and there came a whimpering cry from some hurt fellow for his mother.

Nor was there any panic here. An amateur of the National Army cried out cheerily:

"It would be a hell of a war, boys, if nobody got killed."

"Where's the captain?"

The captain's horse stood riderless near the head of the platoon. Lieutenant Montgomery found his orderly, and that anxiety was removed. The captain had gone ahead on foot to try to break the jam. Lieutenant Montgomery sent a messenger to report what had happened, and with his own hands attended as best he could to the wounded.

There was nothing to be done for Private John W. Whetstone. He had been instantly killed. Private Harry E. Kronfield, it was clear, hadn't long to live. An ambulance, by rare good luck, was struggling through the jam at this point. It picked Kronfield up and hurried him to a first aid station, but he died before morning. This ambulance also took Private Douglas Tredendall, so severely hurt that he was evacuated and never returned to the regiment, and Private Joseph Horowitz. His injury was particularly unfortunate as he was the medical orderly with the platoon. His task of mercy was very brief. With one arm blown away he was evacuated and we didn't see him again. First Class Private George A. Thomas was wounded less seriously.

By the time these men had been cared for and the horses cut out the jam broke, and the column pounded on towards Les Près Farm.

D battery had no casualties on the way up. Its first platoon went, as did E's temporarily on to the hill above the farm. There was a lot of gas there and several bursts of heavy shelling. By choosing quieter moments, however, Captain Starbuck got his guns in and his limbers and caissons started for home.

Corporal Connie F. Geer was in charge of the second piece caisson. Going back the traffic had thinned out a good deal so that the column moved rapidly. Corporal Geer had been particularly cheery and helpful during the trying moments when the caissons had dumped their ammunition at the position. On the return journey he was at the rear of the column. He went back often to make sure there was no straggling. The train must have been half way home when one of his men reported Geer missing. A search of the road was unsuccessful. The shelling was still heavy, and it was necessary to get men, horses, and carriages back to the echelon. There a report was made, and Lieutenant Hoadley set out with a party. They found Corporal Geer's body at the lip of a fresh crater close to the side of the road. His death had probably been instantaneous. He was buried that day in a quiet corner of Nesles Woods.

****

Even at the echelon the night didn't wear itself away very comfortably. Regimental Headquarters had moved to La Tuillerie Farm that afternoon. At midnight a messenger arrived with a note from Colonel Doyle for the battalion commanders, explaining the arrangements for going in. This impressed some as altering a few of the dispositions. There were excited conferences. One, some of us will recall was held in a *fourgon*, heavily blanketed with horse covers. Even so, the light of the single candle within escaped wanly here and there. Outraged cries roared through the forest.

"Put out that light, you—fool!"

"If you want to croak go and do it by yourself." It was impossible to heed these compliments. If important dispatches arrive they must be read. What to do about the present one was a problem. The solution gave Captain Henry Reed a pleasant automobile ride through quarrelsome firing to headquarters. He found out there that the document hadn't been intended to change anything, so we went ahead on the basis we had agreed upon the day before.

The details went up on the morning of the 16th.

The movement of a detail was never a very dignified proceeding. Details went in for efficiency rather than appearance. The surrey was always an absurdity on a shell-torn road. There was never anything less military. But it carried a lot of stuff.

Doughboys used to grin at the group of very military appearing horsemen followed by a couple rambling cobs which drew this vehicle with its fringes flapping from a bent top. Underneath were piled switchboards, telephones, instruments of precision, and spare wire.

Everybody got to the farm, and pitched in. Officers and men of the battalion details, in spite of the fire, got an idea of where the lines ran, and how they were laid. They also appraised the task that lay ahead. These lines were continually shelled out. Some improvement could be made by relaying here and there, but at best it was going to be nasty work. For the Huns had so much artillery and ammunition that they didn't hesitate to snipe with 77s or Austrian 88s at a single man at work in the barren fields.

The detail men in such warfare have rather the worst of it. They work, as a rule, in pairs on the lines, or in an exposed observatory, or on the edge of woods, doing the careful work of a surveyor under the most distracting conditions. And it is always simpler to be brave in a crowd.

The yellow intelligence sheet for that day, too, informed us that the enemy was taking an increasing interest in Les Près and its neighbouring positions. Things were noisy while we settled ourselves. The B position, which we had thought the best of the lot, got a pounding during the morning. The B men escaped, but the 16th had a number of casualties. Captain Ravenel reconnoitred a fresh position, and Major Easterday decided that he should move his first platoon there that night, and bring his second into action alongside of it.

Major Wanvig had put F directly into a new position near the Les Près crossroads, and he settled on positions for D and E on the slope of the valley beyond Chèry Chartreuve, so that none of the sections took many chances with the emplacements on the hill.

The observatories looked nastier than their reputation, but we had to use the ridge above the farm. The regimental and the two battalion observatories were there, so close together that they were really one. Besides, the ridge was sprinkled with the observatories of other organizations, with division and corps stations; and the infantry had a reserve line near. All this activity added to the discomforts of that exposed place. Lieutenant Thornton Thayer had spent the previous night there and had got the lay of the land. We sent our observers and operators up, and, although an officer of the 16th remained for several hours afterwards, practically took over at noon.

Lieutenants MacNair and Graham were already down with the infantry, and we sent sight enlisted men to them to act as runners. It was found advisable at the start to alternate this work between the two battalions, so that after the first day only one officer and one group of men were with the infantry at one time. Such liaison was particularly dangerous in this sector.

A Neighbor at Work in Gas Masks

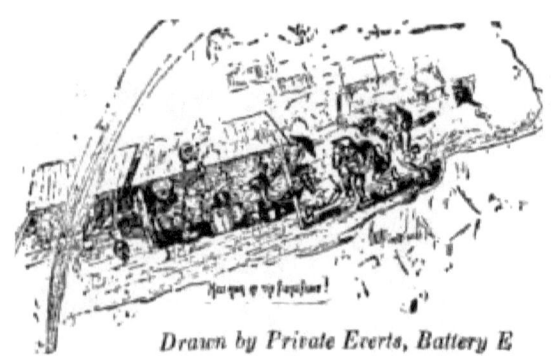

Drawn by Private Everts, Battery E

The infantry received a lot of high explosive, and, because of the low ground near the Vesle, suffered from gas more than the artillery. Yet it was really the only liaison we had, beyond rocket signals. It had been found difficult to maintain a telephone line between infantry and artillery battalion headquarters in spite of the division liaison order which gave to the infantry the task of laying and maintaining such a line. We put a wire through to a forward observatory at Mount St. Martin, very close to the front line, but because of the constant movement of battalion headquarters and the shortage of men, the infantry never hooked up with it. We connected with the infantry net through one of their switchboards, and when they had wire communication with their front line troops we did too. But in such a type of warfare runners furnish the only dependable communication, and our men were on the road day and night.

The sun set hot and red that first night in, and with his going Jerry awakened to a new interest in us. There were no dugouts. Men not on duty crawled into such funk holes as existed or into the stifling cellars at battalion headquarters.

Privates Shackman and Silber had already been sent to the observatory to act as operators. Lieutenant Thayer left the shelter of the cellar and with Corporal Tucker dodged up the hill to relieve the officer and the men of the 16th.

At Boston, as the observatory was called, there was, at that time, for protection only two narrow trenches, five or six yards apart, one for the operators, the other for the observers. They were less than six feet deep. They had no overhead cover.

A few minutes after the arrival of our party a thick curtain of high explosives descended on the ridge. The ugly little volcanoes bracketed Boston while our men crouched in the trenches. The curtain lifted. Perhaps it was just an evening hymn of hate, and the rest of the night would pass without music.

In five minutes the curtain was down again. The bracket narrowed. Fragments of shell shrieked over the trenches. Sand stung the faces of the little party.

Drawn by Corporal Roos, Battery D

"O.K.—O.K."

Lieutenant Thayer and the 16th officer decided to take their men to a flank until the show should end.

"Jump out and run for it after the next shell," they directed.

One burst closer than before. The little party clambered from the trenches. Some were quicker than others. A following shell hit directly on the lip of the smaller trench. The 16th officer fell back, his rain coat drilled full of jagged holes. Private Martin W. Silber slipped in on top of him, and the rest turned back without hesitation to see what could be done. They lifted Silber out. He was dead. The 16th officer had not been injured.

So those that remained dashed to the left and fell in shell holes where they waited for the curtain to lift again. But gas came in for a time with the high explosive, and they put on their respirators and worked from shell hole to shell hole until they were out of range.

In the command posts at the farm everyone knew the ridge and the crossroads were getting it. Our men were in the observatory and our platoons before long would have to pass the crossroads.

A drop on the switchboard fell.

"Silber's dead," the operator commented.

He commenced to test.

"O. K.—O. K."

He paused. He whirred the magneto of his home telephone.

"Red line out, sir."

A moment later he reported two other lines out. That's the way they went at Les Près.

Linesmen left through the noisy darkness with coils of wire and testing telephones over their shoulders.

In the First Battalion cellar the operator called to Major Easterday.

"Second Battalion wants you, sir."

The major lifted the hand set.

"Tucker. Which one is he?" he asked.

You see he had only been with the regiment a few days then.

"What's the matter with Tucker?" Reed asked.

"First battalion says they've just heard he's been killed."

There were close personal friends of Tucker's among the detail in that cellar. They swore softly as they went about their jobs.

As the major replaced the telephone hand set on the table the blanket which hung as a curtain at the cellar entrance waved. A hand drew it aside and in stepped Corporal Tucker. Our men didn't believe in ghosts. They grasped his hand and a laugh burst out.

Tucker denied the Second Battalion's story, and made his report. Thayer had sent word by him that he was going to establish a new observatory.

We had gone over the ground with a fine tooth comb. The change in the location of the observatory would only be a matter of a few yards. A digging detail was ordered up to him with a guide. Lieutenant Klots, with a number of bandsmen, bearing picks and shovels, arrived about the same time, and started to dig in a regimental observatory. Corporal Caen ran up to stand by the telephone in the old observatory until the change could be made to the new ones. And all night the Hun remembered the ridge with high explosive and gas, while stray aeroplanes swooped low there, to let fall a bomb or two. The curtain in the cellar swung in again.

"For the Lord's sake keep that curtain down," somebody grumbled. "If an aeroplane sees this candle we'll be bombed out in a jiffy."

But it was a battery commander who had halted his platoon at the crossroads. He took off his helmet. The perspiration poured from his hair. What, he asked the major, should he do about his platoon? He didn't want to lose his men or his pieces if he could help it, and the shelling down there was particularly vicious. Nor was there any way around.

"Watch your chance and take them through one at a time," the major said shortly.

The battery commander nodded, replaced his helmet, and backed cautiously out.

"Somebody on the line for the major of the 16th," the switchboard man called.

The 16th officers had sat there for some time, waiting only to hear that the relief was complete before striking out for quieter parts. The 16th major answered the call and looked annoyed. We gathered that an ammunition dump at the C position had been hit and was burning. His officer in command there evidently wanted to know what he should do.

"Go in and put it out," the 16th major said, and lowered the hand set.

Almost at once, it seemed to those in the cellar, the same drop rattled again, and the operator asked for the same officer. The 16th major picked up the hand set with a frown. Then his expression altered, and when he spoke his voice had changed, too.

"Wolff is dead," he said to Major Easterday, and everyone knew he spoke of the officer in command of the C position whom he had just ordered into the burning dump.

"Wolff is dead," he repeated, "and Dean, the only other officer I have there, is wounded. You don't take over until the relief is complete. I'll have to get one of the 16th's officers. Who is Robinson?"

"One of our battery C officers," Major Easterday answered.

No one asked for a moment, because it seemed certain that Robinson had been struck, also. The 16th major shook his head when at last the question had been asked.

"No, he's taken command, he seems to know what he is about."

Robinsonn did. It was for that affair that he and Corporal Johnson were awarded the Distinguished Service Cross. Wolff and he had been sitting together in a funk hole, and Wolff had just said to him, expecting to leave with the last of his battery in a few moments:

"You know, Robinson, I'm not so sure I'm going to get out of this place alive after all."

He had laughed a little, and just then the shell had tumbled into the dump, and he had telephoned battalion headquarters and had asked what he should do about it. He, and his assistant Dean and Robinson had all gone in, carrying dirt which they had thrown on the popping shells.

Robinson had just gone out for more dirt, and Deane was starting when the explosion occurred. There had been shrapnel there. While it was still bursting Robinson had dashed in. Corporal Johnson, without any command, without any request, had followed him, and they had dragged out Wolff's body, and the wounded lieutenant. It was then that Robinson had reported.

The major of the 16th looked very tired. At last he shrugged his shoulders, and called up his colonel.

"Wolff's dead. Dean's hurt. Burning dump. What? One officer of the 305th, but I'm getting an officer over to stay until the relief's complete."

It seemed at times as if that formality would never be accomplished. We got reports from A, and, at last from C. But B hadn't reported its second platoon in yet, or its command post moved to the new position. So we sat and waited.

We had had a number of gas alarms during the evening. Time after time our gas guard had wound his klaxon, and time after time we had struggled into respirators, and the switchboard operators had learned how difficult it was to talk intelligibly through a mask. But we had suspected nothing worse than mustard gas. While we sat impatiently there an officer of the 16th stumbled down the cellar steps and through the curtain. He seemed to be in a hurry, and his face was white. From a corner a quiet voice spoke:

"There's phosgene in this cellar."

The penetrating, sickly odour, was apparent to everyone. Masks went on with a rush. The newcomer, however, didn't disturb his. He waved his hand deprecatingly. It trembled a trifle.

"Don't bother. I think I've brought it in on my clothes. Those shells are all over the hillside. Good Lord! I tell you one of them fell at my feet. Don't know why the rotten thing didn't hit me. When are we getting out, Major?"

The major shook his head. Nobody knew. It was B that held us up,

Drawn by Corporal Roos, Battery D

A Kitchen near a Battery Position

and we tried them again. This time there was no answer to our call. We tried them through A and C. They were out of touch with the world.

Over there on the edge of Death Valley the B signal men worked frantically with a coil of twisted pair that had been snarled half a mile from the new battery position. We established runners from that point to the battery so that the relief could be reported and communication of a sort maintained until daylight when the battalion detail ran a new line in.

At midnight, then, the 16th was through, and it went out of Les Près Farm, leaving us our own masters.

We gazed upon our new kingdom. In the stifling cellars such men as were not on duty tried to sleep. They lay sprawled on the dirt floor, endeavouring in their restlessness to keep out of each other's way. Their respirators were conveniently at hand.

At the positions men crouched in funk holes, sleeping by turn. There lay one moaning softly with a bad touch of shell shock. Now and then a soldier paused and spoke to him sympathetically; for the hardiest realized that this was illness, not cowardice. You had only to feel his weak and rapid pulse. The surgeon was on his way.

Details struggled with the flat tops, softening angles against the daylight. Nearly motionless the rocket guards gazed in the direction of Boston. Nestling against the lip of the hill was a wan patch, like a dying bit of fox fire. It was a shelter tent, blanketed, and with flaps down where two officers worked over the intricate figures of new barrages.

Even in that unrevealing starlight each man you saw projected an expression of extreme weariness. And already many were ill with the dysentery that got us all sooner or later. And there was no prospect ahead of real sleep as long as we should stay in that place.

There seemed no diminution in the fire even when the stars paled. The details took advantage of the first light and went over the lines while Hun aeroplanes loafed about the ridge and the positions.

Instead of the brisk freshness of early morning we breathed the warning odour of animal decay.

The last officer of the 16th walked through Les Près Farm, asking about his horse, reminiscing disjointedly about his escapes. We watched him go without saying anything, wondering when we would follow him and how.

CHAPTER 18

The Cost of Battle

Somebody said they called our observatory at the Mont Saint Martin crossroads, Pittsburg, because it was so smoky. We inherited the name from the 16th, but there's probably something in it. Yet it is extremely doubtful if the Huns ever knew we had an observatory there. The instruments were behind a ruined garden wall, with a little foliage to protect them from airmen. The personnel was always limited and was taught to keep itself out of sight when aeroplanes appeared overhead. Against the heavier firing they sought refuge in an old wine cellar.

It was that crossroads that gave Pittsburg so much shelling. Our ambulances used the main road through Mont Saint Martin, tearing past Pittsburg and through the dismantled village. Always the Huns let them have it at the crossroads and through the town. That's really the reason the town was destroyed, for one fails to recall a definite bombardment of any of the buildings. After a time they tried carrying the wounded through on stretchers, but these seemed to draw as much fire as the ambulances.

The first aid station at the farm was a busy place. The ambulances would scurry up the road into the courtyard, unload, and hurry back again. Others would arrive empty and load up with men for the evacuation hospitals. Then we had a good many cases on the spot. For, as has been said, the shelling didn't let up until the enemy had retreated to the Aisne. The courtyard, perhaps because it was the centre of the farm and the Hun, consequently, tried to put his centre of impact there, received a large proportion of the hits. Certainly an average of five or six men a day must have been killed at the farm itself while our division was in on the Vesle.

The Second Battalion had established its first aid station under Dr. Moore in its command post. The First had located Dr. Cronin in a draw between A and B batteries, planning to use Dr. Moore for its command post and C Battery casualties.

The Second Battalion, however, decided on the second day to leave Les Près Farm and move back to Chèry Chartreuve which seemed less

Drawn by Corporal Roos and Private Enroth, Battery D
A Battery D piece at Chèry

exposed, and less attractive to the Hun gunners, so the First arranged with the infantry to use its first aid station for local casualties.

Gas cases came in large numbers. The infantry sent out hundreds of men daily from the Vesle bottom. When Lieutenant Graham was relieved on the 17th his eyes were seriously inflamed from mustard gas, and he was sent back to the echelon for two days. If he had asked he might have been evacuated and so have escaped his fate of a few days later. But Graham knew how short of officers the regiment was, and he insisted on carrying on with his duty in spite of his painful condition.

Consolidation here differed radically from similar tasks in Lorraine. We were so busy that we straightened things out as we went along, and we were often surprised to learn how efficient our makeshifts were. For it must be remembered we were fighting under new conditions. There had, until this time, been very little of this semi-stabilized warfare. The 305th faced new problems, solved them, and gave instructors and secret pamphlet writers something to pass back to newer outfits.

Always the digging on the ridge went on until Lieutenant Thayer was comparatively comfortable.

The firing, meantime, increased. On August 18th, the day selected by Major Wavig for the removal of his command post from the farm, Jerry commenced to take the most flattering care with us.

A number of the Second Battalion telephone men, under Sergeant Point, were salvaging wire, preparatory to the move. Point, I recall, was spinning a reel, calling out good-natured encouragement to his workers. A group of the First Battalion men stood behind the farm wall, commenting on what appeared to be a relief from the heavy fire.

The rising shriek of a shell made itself heard. For a moment we gauged the sound. That shell was going to fall mighty close. The shriek was right on us. Then it ceased. No explosion followed.

"Guess I'm getting jumpy," a man said. "Heaven knows where that bird burst."

"A dud," another warned. "Watch out for the next one."

Still one doesn't worry enough about the shell that doesn't burst. We went about our business. Within two minutes a shell exploded outside the window of the First Battalion command post, filling the room with smoke and knocking the adjutant, the telephone officer, and the sergeant-major across the room. Outside Point and his men had dropped. A fragment flew across to a shed against the farm wall, killing one of our horses.

Everyone picked himself up, grinning, and sought shelter. The prospect was uncomfortably clear. That was the commencement of precision fire on the farm. It was no time to salvage wire.

Point, with Lieutenant Fenn and Sergeant-Major Applegate, stood close to the wall of the Second Battalion command post, apparently safe from the burst of any projectile coming over the building. We hadn't learned to appreciate then the sharp angle of fall of some of the German howitzers. That cost Point his life. A shell whistled over the building and burst in the garden a few feet in front of the wall. The three fell to the ground, but a fragment, flying towards the house, caught Point in the back. He got first aid and was hurried away, optimistic as ever, and talking of a quick return to the detail. But Dr. Moore was doubtful, because a lung had been torn. In a few days word came back that the sergeant was dead, and the Second Battalion had had a loss difficult to repair.

The Second Battalion left Les Près Farm that afternoon just as an order came down that each battalion should put forward four pirate pieces. Major Wanvig decided his Battery F, near the crossroads, accounted for his four. A and B were designated each to send out two pieces, and Captains Dana and Ravenel made their reconnaissances and chose the best positions available at some distance from each other in a draw to the west of Saint Gilles. They were on a forward slope. It was necessary to lay lines to them approximately three kilometres long. There was always difficulty getting ammunition up, and it is probable that the pieces would have been more valuable in their battery emplacements. But as has been suggested, the higher command as well as the lower was often experimenting, and the move at the time seemed useful. It proved a decidedly uncomfortable one.

That night the limbers were brought from Nesles Woods. Details were already at work on the emplacements and the lines when Lieutenant Brassell started up with the A guns, and Lieutenant Montgomery with the B. One of the telephone men met the party with the cheerful news that the Huns had been strafing the positions all evening. With the usual optimism of the American soldier, the cannoneers grunted and said that in that case things would probably be quiet for awhile. So they sent the limbers away and manhandled the pieces into their emplacements. Shell by shell they carried the ammunition in and piled it in the least exposed spots. Then they started funk holes, for they saw they would need good ones. By midnight the Hun shells were dropping again, and the men drew off to a flank until the show seemed over. As soon as they had returned to their digging Jerry popped at them again, appearing to follow them with an uncanny malice as they scurried for safety. It was always more or less like that in those pirate positions. There were two regular programs that the men could foresee and guard against—one at 12:30 p.m., the other at 6 p.m. But in between came impromptu concerts that couldn't always be avoided.

A and B both got plenty of attention. Both had the same difficulty bringing up ammunition, and both suffered from a similar lack of officers and men. Sergeant Buchbinder was put in charge of the A pieces, and Sergeant Martin got Bs. There were no extra cannoneers. That meant that from ten soldiers at each position men had to be found to serve the guns, to post guard, to dig shelters, to carry cooked rations from the kitchens three kilometres away, to lug in ammunition, scrape, and polish it, and to attend to odd jobs of sanitation and getting back the wounded. It must be remembered, too, that at this time nearly everybody was suffering from the weakening dysentery. No one knows how he gets through such labour without sufficient sleep and with unsatisfactory food. Still, after a heavy shelling, even the digging went with a strong rapidity.

The second night in the Bosche took a particular dislike to the B positions. Sergeant Martin ordered his men to the flank, but one of the early shells killed Private George J. Lucking, and wounded Private Fred Scheuner.

Two men volunteered to carry the wounded man three miles to the First Aid Station. He was heavy. They had to rest. They paused in a dug out. While one of them remained with Scheuner the other hurried to the battery position and got a detail with a stretcher. Corporal Kelsey and Privates Terry and Elliot went back. The little party put Scheuner on the stretcher and started in. The Hun seemed to have a special sense for such missions. He opened up with gas. While the shells fell around them the stretcher bearers put on their respirators remarking:

"At that, gas is a darned sight better than H. E."

****

Drn by Corporal Roos and Private Enroth, Battery D

Carrying in ammunition

On the 20th Sergeant Bernhardt's section relieved Sergeant Martin's.

That same night a sergeant, who was an extremely good churchman, went up with two G. S. carts and an escort, bearing ammunition. The uncomfortable main road was his only practical route, and Jerry showed him that he had a better trick than high explosive for ammunition escorts. An aeroplane swooped low against the moonlight and began pumping machine gun bullets at the sergeant and his horses. There seemed a necessity both for divine intervention and more speed. A combination of the two might avail. So the sergeant, thorough in all things, prayed devoutly.

"Lord God, help us now!"

And to the horses with a different sort of fervour.

"Get up, you ——s."

The entire party lived to tell the story.

****

The difficult and disturbed routine of the pirate positions continued. Sergeant Buchbinder was carried out, wounded, on the 24th, and the affair ended when, the next day, the Bosche informed B that it had the pieces bracketed to a metre.

The early morning had been particularly quiet. The crews sat comfortably about one of the pieces, smoking after an early luncheon of cold chow and coffee.

Not a bad looking place, they agreed, when Jerry let it alone. Evidently Jerry had had enough of them, and what an afternoon it would be to make up sleep!

Whiz!

The racket started with no more warning than that. An avalanche of metal descended. At the first whistle each man scurried for his funk hole.

These little shelters had grown during the week. They looked like deep graves. Each cannoneer crouched in his, listening to the angry shrieks of the fragments, to the splintering of trees, fancying always that he was the sole survivor of the party. It was fire for destruction of the most intense sort.

At the end each crawled out and looked for the mangled bodies of his comrades. All that digging hadn't been wasted. The entire group stood there, half-dazed, but unhurt.

The position, however, was in ruins. The trees lay in a twisted mass. Sergeant Bernhardt's gun was out of action. A huge fragment had passed through the recoil mechanism. The telephone lines had been torn to pieces.

That was the end of those pirate positions. Orders came to salvage what was left. The limbers appeared that night and drew the guns out. Two G. S. carts arrived and loaded the ammunition.

Out on the open road one of the carts broke down. There was a good deal of shelling, and another aeroplane took a hand, dropping a bomb very close to the party. The limbers had gone on. The guide was evidently with them. The drivers of the carts had never been on the road before. They were at a loss. Private Margid, who had been at the position from the first day, volunteered to stay behind until the cart was fixed when he would guide both in. After another breakdown he got them to the position, and once more the firing batteries of A and B were united.

****

During these days the men at the regular positions hadn't had any too pleasant a time.

Private George L. Forman was killed on August 16th while walking from the Battery A position to the edge of Death Valley.

On the 18th Captain Douglas Delanoy was wounded at an improvised observatory near Boston. He had an old German dugout for protection, and at the first shell started to slide into this. A small fragment caught him on the knee, making apparently a trivial wound. His leg stiffened, however, and he was evacuated and did not return to the regiment until the last of October. This left Lieutenant Derby in command of Battery F.

On August 21st, while firing a normal barrage, Battery D's number 2 piece was destroyed by a premature burst, as B's had been on the range at Souge. Fortunately the full gun crew was not in the pit. Private Walter Rubino was killed. Gunner Corporal Arthur Roos—probably because he was for the moment adding the duties of number 2 to his own, and was not on his seat when the lanyard was pulled—escaped with a bad fracture of the skull. He was in hospital for more than two months, but was eventually returned to his battery. Sergeant Jacob Metzger and Private Joseph Cohen were seriously wounded and evacuated to America.

On the next day, the 22nd, the regiment lost its first officer at the front.

Lieutenant Graham had returned to duty, although still suffering from his gassing of a few days before, and had relieved Lieutenant MacNair at the infantry battalion command post.

On this evening he walked with Captain Belvedere Brooks of the 308th Infantry to a shelter near Ville Savoie, known as Cemenocal Cave. The Huns had not, apparently, fired on this point before. A number of other infantry officers stood near, and a large group of enlisted men. This congregation seemed unsafe, and Lieutenant Graham spoke of it.

A shell came over and fell near the party, a dud.

Captain, afterwards Major, Breckenridge, cried: "Lookout!"

There was a rush for the entrance of the cave. Graham and Brooks with the other infantry officers stood back to let the men in first. A second shell burst in the midst of the little group. Graham, Brooks, and a second infantry officer were killed. Lieutenant Bruce Brooks, Captain Brooks' brother, was at that time assigned to our regiment. Captain Breckenridge got word to him, and telephoned Major Easterday of Lieutenant Graham's death.

Lieutenant MacNair happened to be in the Second Battalion's command post. He was hurried down to the infantry, while Lieutenant Ellsworth O. Strong was summoned from the echelon to replace Lieutenant Graham.

Corporals Hickey and Rice and Privates Golden and Aasgard, who were on duty with the infantry, carried Lieutenant Graham's body to Les Près Farm over heavily shelled roads. Chaplain Sheridan was summoned and the lieutenant was buried in the little cemetery on the Chartreuve Road where so many of our men lie.

Three days later Lieutenant Strong, who had relieved Lieutenant

Barbed Wire

A Tank

MacNair, was killed with a number of infantrymen near the same spot while going about his work with that quiet and confident ability that characterized everything he did.

After that Lieutenants Klots and Brassel alternated on liaison. Lieutenant Klots was touched by a machine gun bullet in the arm, but fortunately the wound was not serious, and he was back at work within a few days. For the question of officers was growing daily more serious. An order came through requiring the regiment to send one captain, three first lieutenants, and five second lieutenants to America to serve with new organizations. The Colonel chose the following: Captain Fox; First Lieutenants Brooks, Dodworth, and Stryker; and Second Lieutenants Beck, Sawin, Schutt, Walsh, and Wemken. These officers left Nesles Woods on August 26th.

It was about this time, too, that the Chief of Artillery reminded Lieutenants Camp, Church, and Fenn of their recommendations at Souge. The first was sent as instructor to the Field Artillery School at Meucon, the second to Valdahon, and the third to La Corneau.

The officers that remained, one can understand, didn't get much rest. An organization with two officers for duty was lucky.

One is reminded of the Battery Commander who was summoned to Division Headquarters to testify about some alleged short firing.

"On the day in question," he was asked, "did you have an officer with all your guns?"

He answered promptly: "I did not, sir."

Oh the disapproval of those Olympians whose lot in war lets them ask such questions!

"And why not?" this Olympian demanded with an air of, "Young man you shall be tried."

There was a map. The Battery Commander put his finger on it.

"Because," he answered, "One of my guns is here, another is here, a kilometre from the first, and the other two are here, three kilometres away. I am the only officer on duty with my battery."

****

The telephone details were at it day and night, but communication on the Vesle was kept open. Working on the lines, as they did, the telephone men became experts in judging the probable point of impact of a shell. They knew when to duck, and they did it—under orders, some of them, at first. Without this ability and this touch of common sense a telephone man wouldn't have lasted long at Les Près. It wasn't, however, always possible to duck. Sometimes there were too many shells in the air. Sometimes, too, the Huns used an Austrian 88 with a flat trajectory that was on you before you could really hear it coming.

On August 26th Corporal Schweitzer and Private Fred Isler were on the line from La Tuillerie to the First Battalion command post. A portion of this line was strung from old telegraph poles, and the pair carried a ladder as well as their testing instrument and spare wire. They had tested as far as the Chèry crossroads when they heard a big shell coming. They didn't have time to get rid of their impedimenta and duck. The shell burst too close to them. It was Isler that was hit in the temple. Schweitzer carried him to a First Aid Station in Chèry, but he died without regaining consciousness.

Two days later another telephone man went. Regimental headquarters had desired all along to establish an observatory forward with the infantry, although observation of any sort down there was difficult. A point had been located, and it was desired to run a line to it. Such a line would have to cross the open ground in front of Boston from the woods to the left, which were full of bodies and under constant fire. It was practically the same ground that so many infantrymen and artillerymen had attempted before with wire that was shot out almost as soon as it was laid.

Captain Gammell, Lieutenant Willis, and Private Frank Tiffany believed the importance of such an observatory made an attempt necessary, and, as you never get anything in war without trying against odds, they set out towards Mont Saint Martin, paying out the line as they went. It was a brave effort that should have succeeded. But the Huns sniped at the trio, probably with an Austrian 88, and Private Tiffany was hit in the leg and back. The two officers carried him to Les Près Farm. He died shortly after.

****

Such sniping was always to be looked for. It was particularly dangerous, as was also the intermittent dropping of single shells about the farm at intervals of .a few minutes all day and night. The concentrated firing of the Germans, while it irritated, was by no means so risky, because you could tell after a fashion what to expect, and when.

The Hun introduced an appreciable amount of system into his shelling of the farm and its neighbouring positions.

Let us say it is 8:30 in the evening. The last light tries to soften the shattered buildings. Here and there groups of men stand close to the walls. Several are coiling wire on an improvised hand reel. One glances at his watch.

"Most time for the evening shower," he says.

Several yawn. The groups scatter. Some slip into the cellar. Others seek the shelter of the walls where a few funk holes have been dug. In a moment there is no sign of life about the place except for a delayed ambulance plodding up the hill, and a curious head that projects cautiously from the cellar-way.

Drawn by Corporal Roos and Private Enroth, Battery D
"**The telephone details were at it day and night**"

Whiz-z-z-z—Bang!

The ambulance scurries into the courtyard. The curious head disappears.

The shells follow one another with a relentless rapidity. It is like the cracking of several whips with long lashes. The crack of one is lost in the swish of another.

These are 105s. In the cellars and behind the walls the men are safe enough except from a direct hit, and their chances are fairly good although all the shells are certain to fall within a limited radius.

The switchboard operator turns his crank and gets Regimental Headquarters for the major.

"Raining hard," the major reports to the adjutant.

"How hard?"

"Pouring."

It's not altogether pleasant to be asked such questions when you're in the midst of the storm. Somebody's got to stick his head out to verify the size of the shells. Somebody's got to count them. The first time we had this particular drubbing the major asked us for estimates of the rate of fire, so that he could tell them back at Regimental Headquarters. One officer, in an honest effort to be conservative put his reply as low as a hundred shells a minute. Another said seventy-five. A third objected.

"That's all nonsense. It can't be more than fifty a minute—a little less than one a second."

The noise made him seem like a *poseur*. We got out our stop watches. The rate of fire averaged just eight shells a minute.

****

"Pouring" was enough after a few days to indicate that particular strafing. At the end of twenty minutes everyone yawns and prepares to go about his affairs. The racket suddenly ceases. The curtains are thrust back. The men slip out, clinging close to the walls because of that intermittent firing which will continue all night, and which is more dangerous than the expensive burst we have just had.

****

It was amusing after one of these noisy, shrieking concentrations to watch men ducking at the whistle of a projectile that would probably burst a kilometre away. They did have that effect. They put one's nerves, to an extent, on edge. You never got accustomed to the flying past of many fragments with a sound like the crying out of mad witches. Always after these exhibitions there were fresh holes in the roofs and walls of the farm, and usually another piece of the cellar steps would be knocked away.

These strafings annoyed the cooks. Even here they clung to their fires as they had done in Lorraine. After one of the first concentrations we rushed out and checked up on the men. A cook was missing.

"Who saw him last?"

"I saw him in the kitchen just before the shells came in," a kitchen police answered.

Hesitatingly we stepped to the open door of the kitchen. It was quite dark in there, except for a red glow from the stove against the end wall. In that red glow we saw outstretched a body. We tiptoed in. The body stirred. The head, we could see, was hidden in the hot oven. We drew the man gently away. It was our cook, his face the colour of a well-broiled lobster. For nearly twenty minutes he had lain there with that pandemonium raging outside, his head at least protected, if rather painfully so.

Another day the surrey came up with rations. Manzo, the First Battalion cook looked them over and forgot all about the war for a time. He told everybody what Sergeant Bayer and Ramstad had turned over to him. There was fresh beef, potatoes, rice.

"No corn willy for dinner today, boys!"

Manzo was the most popular man in the army. We had lived on corn willy, gold fish, and beans for so long that the thought of fresh food was a little heady.

Manzo and his assistants set to work. Extraordinarily pleasant odours slipped from the kitchen.

"Bet the flies don't get any of my dinner," one man boasted.

It is doubtful if any Christmas feast was ever looked forward to as eagerly as that meal. Then the tragedy happened.

The Huns commenced to shell, and out of their schedule time. Mike and his assistants were forced reluctantly from the kitchen. They left the dinner cooking on the stove. Fifteen or twenty minutes' absence wouldn't hurt it. But all the time he was inhabiting a shelter Manzo was uneasy.

The bombardment lifted. Manzo and his assistants crawled out and hurried to the kitchen. A moment later Manzo came rushing out. He saw Major Easterday. He flung up his hands. He burst out:

"Maje! The Hun! He shoota dahellouta dakitch!"

The major was as interested as anyone else in the feast. The entire detail crowded into Manzo's temple. Few had the courage to gaze for more than a moment on the scene of sacrilege. A shell had come through the end wall. It had landed on the stove. It had burst there. The remains of dinner were on the floor, the walls, and the ceiling. Strong men wept. Manzo went sadly back to his tins of hardtack and corn willy. For soldiers must eat. It is such outrages that breed hate.

****

While some of these escapes had a touch of humour they were rather too close run for comfort. The affair of the dud at Regimental Headquarters, for example, might have had a very different ending.

On the morning of August 22nd a 105 ripped into the building, through a room in which Captain Fox and Lieutenants Klots and Willis were standing, tore through the wall into the next room, and passed through Colonel Doyle's cot which fortunately was not occupied. The shell failed to explode. Had it exploded, Regimental Headquarters would have needed some new officers.

CHAPTER 19

Spies and the Advance

Chèry Chartreuve did not prove to be the ideal command post the Second Battalion had hoped. The Huns undoubtedly knew the town was thick with headquarters, and, logically, shelled it a good deal. So Major Wanvig decided to move to a cave in dead space in the steep hillside to the east of Chèry.

The move was originally planned for August 24th. On the morning of the 23rd Regimental Headquarters called for a number of barrages, then abruptly shortened the lines. This meant to everyone a strong enemy attack; perhaps that vast effort we had sometimes looked for to recapture the lost ground in another drive for Paris. As a matter of fact the enemy did get La Tannerie and portions of the south bank of the river that morning, but they were unable to hold their gains for very long.

In the midst of the confusion born of this rapid and unexpected work Major Wanvig telephoned from Regimental Headquarters to move the P. C. at once. At that time the battalion staff was really too small for its routine work. Lieutenant Fenn gave the difficult task of wiring the new P. C. to Sergeant Froede, and tried to keep things going from the old headquarters.

All afternoon and evening the batteries continued their firing. At midnight a complete programme came in from Regimental Headquarters for a rolling barrage to accompany a counter attack by our infantry. It was hurriedly figured, and rapid firing went on until 5 a.m. Word came then to cease firing. It was also explained that there had been a misunderstanding and that the infantry had not counter-attacked. So much ammunition was expended that night that stray dumps were scoured for serviceable shells. Still before many hours a counter-attack was staged that reached its objectives. Without interfering with its programme the Second Battalion got into its cave where it was never once shelled.

That night was exceptional, but every day and every night an enormous quantity of ammunition was fired. Under such conditions there were inevitably charges of short firing. The Germans had a number of guns in the vicinity of Rheims that occasionally treated infantry and artillery to a few shells. These seemed to drop from behind us, although what we suffered was really only enfilade fire. It is not extraordinary that the infantry should have thought some of these puzzling shells were shorts from their own artillery.

One day Captain Whelpley was sent from Regimental Headquarters to investigate such a charge, which had been advanced by Captain C. W. Harrington of the 308th Infantry.

Captain Whelpley lost some time at Les Près Farm waiting for a guide, so that it was dark when, after a hazardous walk, he reached Captain Harrington's command post to the north of the Vesle. It seemed impracticable to return that night, but Captain Whelpley had intended to start at daybreak. With the first light, however, the Huns put down an intensive barrage which lasted for an hour, and made a shell hole a pleasanter place than the open. This was followed by an infantry attack in strength. Captain Whelpley picked up a rifle and told Captain Harrington he would help. With a party of men he moved to the edge of a patch of woods to observe and cover Harrington's left flank. He also maintained liaison with neighbouring units. His party killed ten Germans and captured three. For this voluntary assistance to the infantry at a critical time he was mentioned, after the armistice, in division orders. If it had not been for the Colonel, who asked for an explanation of his absence, the story of his courage might not have been made public.

Charges of short firing were always investigated but never amounted to anything on the Vesle. For the regiment, short-officered as it was, had developed a facility with figures and execution that left small room for mistakes. The lessons learned here made the problems of the Argonne for the 305th comparatively simple. Such experience is not gained without a continued cost.

The enemy got First Class Private Frederick J. Weeber of Battery E on August 25th. He was in his gun emplacement with another cannoneer when an over, intended for the Chèry crossroads, fell just outside.

"Look out!" Weeber called to his companion.

He didn't duck low enough himself. The other man escaped, but Weeber was carried to join that great silent army that lies in the shallow graves of Champagne.

****

The Huns favourite type of warfare seemed now and then to be aided by a brutal sort of luck.

It was said some time back that we were taught not to care as much as we had for the Y. M. C. A. in Chèry Chartreuve. The lesson came on August 28th. Even if the passage was risky it was a relief to get permission to leave one's position and dodge to the pleasant odours and companionships of that little store.

On this day there was a long line of infantrymen and artillerymen waiting in the street to get to the counter. That particular shell seemed guided by an evil genius. It fell in the middle of the line, burst, and harvested eighteen casualties. Of our regiment Private Charles C. Rosalia, Battery E, was killed; and Privates Rasmus Hanson, Battery E, Dona J. Monette, Battery E, and Corporal Alexander Landsman, Battery D, were wounded.

On the whole, though, one wonders that we didn't have more casualties in that heavily shelled, unprotected sector. We suffered a good many more than we liked, but the regiment felt that its intelligent discipline kept the list down.

There were some duties, naturally, that had to be done blindly, as it were, without using brains or anything else to protect yourself. Barrages had to be fired whether your position was being shelled or not. Rocket guards, when their comrades scattered for the funk holes at the first warning shell, had to stand their ground, and take whatever came.

Private Hackett of Battery B was caught like that one night. He remained sitting on an empty ammunition box, his glance always on Boston ridge, while his more fortunate friends got out of the way. He was pathetically reminiscent of the well-sung young man who stood upon the burning deck when he very well knew he ought to have been nearly anywhere else.

A shell burst at Private Hackett's feet. When the smoke and dust cleared away he still sat upon the box, and his gaze was still on the ridge, but now his feet were in a new crater. So he lived to become known admiringly as the Salvage King. His own description of the moment was:

"Think? When the thing went off I expected to see myself in little pieces."

****

On the Vesle spies were more dreaded than in Lorraine. The bitter nature of the fighting placed in a spy's hands the lives of more men.

During several nights we noticed the unequal flashing of a lamp on Boston Ridge. The infantry there had seen it, too. Many efforts were made to catch the operator, yet none met success. If he was a spy he was an amazingly clever one. If he was a telephone linesman, carelessly using, against all orders, a light as he worked on a wire, he was lucky far beyond his due. At any rate after a few nights the flashing ceased.

The order from General Bullard, which follows, tells its own story:

P. C. Third Army Corps
31 August 1918—21:30 Hr.
G-S Order
No. 56

1. During the attack of the enemy against Fismette, August 27th someone in American uniform ran among our troops shouting that further resistance was useless and that one of our officers advised everybody to surrender. These statements were absolutely incorrect because further resistance was not useless and no officer had advised surrender. Nevertheless, because of lack of training and understanding, the results were as follows: Out of 190 of our troops engaged in this fight, a few were killed or wounded, about 30 retreated fighting and escaped, and perhaps 140 surrendered or were captured.

2. A person who spreads such an alarm is either an enemy in our uniform, or one of our own troops who is disloyal and a traitor, or one of our own troops who has become a panic-stricken coward. WHOEVER HE IS, HE SHOULD BE KILLED ON THE SPOT.

3. In a battle there is no time to inquire into the identity or motives of persons who create panic, disorganization or surrender. It is the duty of every officer and soldier to kill on the spot any person who in a fight urges or advises anyone to surrender or to stop fighting. It makes no difference whether the person is a stranger or a friend, or whether he is an officer or a private.

4. The day before the attack on Fismette a German soldier was seen and mortally wounded by our men in Fismes, far inside our lines. He was well stocked with food. He had lived many years in America. It is possible that he was to get himself an American uniform and, because of his knowledge of our language and customs, was to be used to create doubt and disorganization among our men.

5. Division Commanders will cause this order to be read to each company or platoon in such manner as will insure that every member of the command thoroughly understands its contents.
By Command of Major General Bullard:
F. W. Clark
Lieut. Col., G. S., A. C. of S., G-S

The attack against Fismette, mentioned in the foregoing order, was one of the last determined offensive efforts of the enemy on this front. It became clear about the same time that a vast German retrograde movement was in contemplation. Any change from Les Près Farm would be a welcome one.

Drawn by Corporal Roos, Battery D
"The Artillery Would Follow in Support"

The intensity of our firing increased, while Jerry's waned. Undoubtedly we were making his plans difficult to carry through.

On the night of September 3rd the observatories reported many fires in Perles and its vicinity. A huge sheet of flame advertised the explosion of a big ammunition dump. Towards morning of the 4th the Hun-made fires thickened. Evidently great quantities of stores and the buildings that had housed them were being destroyed as an alternative to leaving them for the Americans. The Hun fire nearly ceased. Anyone who was there will recall the blessed relief of being able to stroll about those positions at last with a feeling of comparative safety.

Word came that the infantry was already moving forward. The artillery would follow in support. Strong combat patrols were already in contact with the enemy. It was understood that if a battalion of infantry were sent as an advance party across the Vesle, Battery D of our regiment would cross too. But the Hun went faster than the most optimistic had prophesied, and the entire regiment started forward on the 5th.

The old positions were policed and equipment made ready on the night of the 4th. Early the next morning the limbers came down from the echelon, whips cracked, and, after those unpleasant weeks about Les Près and Chèry, the regiment was on the road again.

Since they had been widely scattered, the batteries followed the most convenient routes while agents kept them in touch with battalion headquarters.

Regimental Headquarters went forward to the desolate ruins of Fismes and established itself in a cellar. Opposite the cellar steps an alley ran between tumbled walls. The horses, motorcycles, and bicycles were placed here as the safest place in the vicinity.

Shortly after the party had arrived Private Wallace Fisher, of the Headquarters Company, motorcycle driver for the Second Battalion, entered this alley and started to make some repairs on his machine. He was the only man there, so no one saw the thing happen. In the cellar they heard a dud fall, and another shell come over and detonate across the street. Corporal Tucker ran from the cellar to see if the horses had been struck. Two were down. The third, which, curiously, had been the centre one of the trio, was unhurt.

Tucker saw that both motorcycles had been smashed. He saw Fisher lying beside one, and called to him. Fisher didn't answer, and the scout went closer. Fisher had been killed.

Tucker reported back across the street, and a party buried Fisher in the garden behind headquarters, making for his grave a rough cross from the wood of a splintered door.

****

Battalion commanders with their captains or reconnaissance officers started forward early to select new positions in the vicinity of Ville Savoie and Saint Gilles. It rained hard, and the complaints were bitter and many—at first. A little later the men realized what a blessing the bad weather was. For the Huns still held control of the air. With better visibility he would have dropped more bombs and directed better fire on our columns which crawled by daylight along crowded roads. He would have interfered more disagreeably with the taking up of the new positions. One fellow did appear, flying low to get beneath the mist. The battery machine gunners greeted him with shouts, sending such well-directed streams of machine gun bullets at his plane that he left the cannoneers to settle their guns in peace.

While it was perfectly obvious these positions would be occupied only a short time, they were consolidated, after the habit of the regiment, as if they were intended for the duration of the war. The cannoneers dug in, and officers and details figured firing data, and ran long difficult lines for only a few hours' use. First Battalion Headquarters had moved out of Les Près Farm to a house near Mont Saint Martin. It was necessary for its batteries to be in telephonic liaison with it.

After only a little firing the order came to move again at midnight. The Umbers had been echeloned in the neighbourhood, so that there was no delay starting. Everyone knew the next stop would be nearer the enemy, and that the guns must be in position and hidden before daylight.

The batteries rendezvoused near the crossroads between Fismes and La Tannerie. Battalion Headquarters went ahead to the crossroads. It threatened to be an unhealthy place. The Huns did commence to shell it, but most of their projectiles fell to the right in low ground. Here again the rain proved its friendliness, for in the wet soil the majority of the shells buried themselves without exploding.

Nevertheless such waiting was nervous business, for there was always the prospect that the Him would sweep, or at least shift his deflection. He seemed, however, to have lost some of his skill, or else he imagined himself directly on his target. The column grew restless.

"What's slowing us up?"

"Where are we going anyway?"

Whispers filtered back.

"We're going across the Vesle. It's the bridges that are slowing us up."

There was a dramatic quality about this realization. Across the Vesle and to those very heights from which Jerry had pounded the regiment for so long!

Everyone was curious, too, as to the kind of bridge he would find, and about the cost at which any bridge must have been built in such a place. The news, moreover, brought some apprehension. If the crossing of the Marne had caused misgivings, the passage of the Vesle created graver ones. The Hun artillery must surely have it registered. It was inconceivable one could get over without a shelling. Perhaps that explained the delay. The bridge might be down, or it might be blocked by dead animals and broken carriages.

Long drawn, the command to get ahead ran down the line. Horses stumbled forward. The luminous faces of wrist watches appeared like fireflies here and there as the men took a check on the time.

Almost immediately the rumbling of wheels on planks came back. Word was passed along that there would be two streams to cross. At each men would dismount and lead their animals over most carefully, for there were no side guards or rails, and the column wasn't using any flares to guide its feet.

The carriages rumbled on the planking. Down below, between steep banks, rushed a narrow and black stream—the Ardre, about a kilometre from its junction with the Vesle.

There was no disturbance there, and the column was swallowed by the crumbling outskirts of Fismes. Just beyond the road swept to the right into the main highway to Braine and so came upon the Vesle.

The only light was from Jerry's distant flares and star shells. It wasn't much. It became clear to the men that the enemy was after this second bridge. The rustle or shriek of arriving shells was perpetual, but there was an odd scarcity of detonations, and there was no halting.

At the river itself the reason became apparent. Again the enemy had failed to register quite perfectly, and again the low ground and the rain were friendly. Most of the German projectiles were duds.

The river was scarcely wider than the Ardre, but the bridge if anything, seemed narrower and riskier than the other. Drivers led their horses and cannoneers manned the wheels. There was only one casualty, and that aroused a laugh that made itself audible above the shells. Musician Scharf, acting as messenger, was crowded over the side, and splashed in the deep, unpleasant current. They pulled him out, and he went on his way, laughing, too.

The column hurried through Fismette, into which the regiment had sent so many shells; and scattered into the positions selected during the reconnaissances of the day before.

The First Battalion commenced to dig in a kilometre south of Blanzy, near a confluent of the Vesle.

The Second Battalion, which had come from its Chèry home without taking up intermediate positions, swung more to the west, and with its batteries side by side established itself on the slope of a deep ravine across from Perles. By daylight every battery was in place.

The First Battalion settled its command post in a road repairman's house on the Fismette-Blanzy road. There was no cellar. The only protection was the stone walls of the building.

The Second Battalion chose a German dugout in the ravine between Perles and its guns.

Regimental Headquarters moved forward from Fismes on September 8th and came upon what proved to be about its nastiest experience of the war. It was the custom for our headquarters to remain with infantry brigade headquarters.

Near Blanzy was the cave of La Petite Logette, a huge hole, which the Hun had long occupied, digging from it many galleries. It was a perfect shelter except for one thing. Its very appearance proclaimed it a gas trap.

Regimental Headquarters says that it had no opportunity to judge, so it established its command post with Brigade Headquarters in the cave. Engineer and medical officers worked nearly all day to purify the air of this formidable hole. They declared the main portion was safe when Colonel Doyle arrived the latter part of the afternoon, but even then the place retained an atmosphere unhealthy and ominous. The doctors had boarded up the more suspicious of the galleries, and they warned the men against invading the remainder.

The men, however, were very tired. The mere fact that such a place had been chosen as command post was a recommendation to them that it was safe. Some of the galleries were a good deal quieter than the main portion of the cave.

Regimental Headquarters set to work at La Petite Logette, quite a different affair from Regimental Headquarters on the table in the mess hall of Jl at Camp Upton.

There were about forty men attached to it at that time. After dark, when all the soldiers, not on missions, should have been in the large cave or near the entrance, a check was taken and a number reported as missing. The searchers entered the forbidden galleries and found a number asleep or resting, quite unaware of the risk they ran. All were gassed to some degree. They were removed and treated, and the night's work went on.

About midnight a new condition stealthily disclosed itself. Men sniffed the air of the main cave. Clearly it was poisoned. So much gas could not have escaped from the galleries. The Huns, beyond question, must have buried gas shells in the floor of the cave, surrounding them with an acid, perhaps, to eat through the casings and so release the fumes when the occupants were without suspicion.

Most of those who had spent the evening in the cave were unfit for duty. There was no other shelter near by, but the colonel ordered everyone out of the cave.

"The entire medical staff (officers and men)," to quote Colonel Doyle's account of the evening, "had been gassed and were unable to give any assistance. Colonel Doyle alone remained in the cave, giving aid to a constant stream of gassed men."

As is usual with slight cases of mustard gas poisoning eyes suffered most of all, and many were temporarily blinded. After their eyes had been bathed with a weak alkaline solution the victims were hurriedly evacuated. A few were more seriously affected.

Colonel Doyle worked until 4:30 in the morning when he was forced to leave the cave. A medical officer of the Engineers, who had been summoned, took his place. The effects of the gas on the colonel were slow. He stayed by the telephone all day. It was only after a hard day's work, in fact, towards 10 o'clock, that he lost the use of his eyes. As long as he could talk, however, he insisted on staying with his regiment, and he was not evacuated until midnight. The regiment did not lose him for long, but he suffered from his experience for many months afterward.

The list of officers and men more or less gassed in this extraordinary incident includes: Colonel Doyle, Captain Gammell, Captain Mitchell, Lieutenant Klots (his second wound stripe), Sergeant Bromm, Sergeant Mamluck, Sergeant-Major Miller and Gillette, Hoffman, Kurash, Palmer, Pullen, Saloman, and Wallach.

****

The regiment had struggled through its most difficult days with insufficient officers. When the word came that it was to receive replacements, officers and men took the news sceptically. Only two or three had come in before the crossing of the Vesle, but now the rush commenced.

First Lieutenant H. J. Svenson had arrived on September 1st, but he was invalided away on the 14th. Second Lieutenants George E. Putnam and Jesse W. Stribling had reported on the 3rd, but the real influx came when the batteries were in their new positions across the Vesle.

On September 8th Second Lieutenants Stedman B. Hoar, and David J. Macleod, a veterinarian, reported. On the 9th came Second Lieutenants Osbon W. Bullen, Johnston Copelin, Raymond E. Dockery, Leon H. Hattemer, and Harold Holcomb. On the 10th the arriving stream of subalterns seemed a beautiful dream. That day brought Second Lieutenants Roy H. Camp, Thadeus R. Geisert, Edward W. Hart, Albert B. Hill, Waldo E. McKee, Thomas M. Norton, Reuben T. Taylor, John G. Teichmoeller, Philip A. Wilhite, and Charles L. Graham.

These were practically all young men from the Artillery School at Saumur. They were distributed among the three headquarters and the batteries, and made the fighting between the Vesle and the Aisne far simpler than it had been in the short-handed days of Les Près Farm.

For self-sacrificing work in the Vesle-Aisne fighting Lieutenant Thayer, Corporal Ramsdell, and Privates Shackman and McCune received divisional citations.

This campaign was in many ways far less exacting than the preceding one. The regiment, to be sure, was opposite the pivotal point of the Hun line between Soissons and Rheims, but, although there was plenty of artillery opposite, the shooting seemed poorer, and there were fewer casualties.

The weather played its share, too. The brilliant, warm days of Les Près Farm were replaced by much mist and rain. The nights, too were colder. The men, therefore, did not need much urging to dig themselves in. Very few German dugouts could be used, because their openings were in the direction of hostile fire. But German straw could be carried from its old home to the new hillside apartments of the Americans. Tiny, living souvenirs may have come with that straw, but one acquired those anyway, and it seemed a small price then, before the S. O. S. inspectors got at the regiment, to pay for warmth.

There's no point in wasting words on cooties. Practically every man and officer knows all there is to say about them.

Observation brought its difficulties here also. There was no satisfactory observatory near the First Battalion Command post, so Lieutenant Thayer pushed forward to the very front line of the infantry. On the edge of the ruins of Serval he found a deserted house. It stood on high ground in a salient of the American front line, so that it was exposed to fire from three sides. Yet while nearly everything else in Serval had been destroyed, this building was comparatively whole.

Lieutenant Thayer didn't attempt to get his men in or run a telephone line until after dark. The line was long and difficult to keep open, but for the most part communication was maintained. By using extreme care the presence of observers in the house was kept from the Germans. Only once while the regiment was in that position did the place get a direct hit. Yet it was necessary to make reliefs, to carry in food, to bring water from a well in Serval, and to have telephone men coming along the line whenever it went out.

You might hear such a conversation as this in the lower room, after a telephone man has crawled in and lies on his back, catching his breath.

"You fixed the line all right," says one of the observers gratefully. "What kind of a trip did you have?"

"As per usual, Kid," the telephone man explains as he rests. "All the way across, Jerry threw G. I. cans at me as if they didn't cost a cent. When I gets to the foot of the hill here a machine gun goes *pop-pop-pop-pop*. I plays possum, but for a long time, every time I lifts my head, *pop-pop-pop-pop* he goes again. Honest, George, I've never felt very harsh towards the Bosche, but, George, when they turn a machine gun loose on one poor linesman every time he moves his little finger, I say they ain't right-minded folks. Can't tell me any atrocity stories I won't swallow now, George."

The interior of the stone house was given over to perpetual watchfulness. Old clothing was hung across the front windows so that no one would be silhouetted for the benefit of the Germans, and behind these the instruments were placed. Day and night Lieutenant Thayer and his scouts watched the Germans, and the effect of our fire, within calling distance, practically, of his victims.

Positions very much less exposed didn't fare so well. The Supply Company, when the regiment crossed the river moved forward from Nesles Woods to the grove behind Les Près Farm in which Battery C had been stationed until September 5th. By all the rules of the game that should have been a safer place than Nesles Woods. The Supply Company had two men killed during the war, and both were lost in this place.

This tragedy recalled the earlier charges of short-firing. With all of the batteries far forward no such explanation could be advanced here. Evidently the Hun guns near Rheims were at work again. The Supply Company men indulged in the wildest hazards to account for this strange shelling. There was talk of supernaturally concealed guns left by the Germans when they had retreated. There were whispers of an extraordinary underground railway on which the Bosche moved big guns to convenient trap doors within our lines. For, until the Rheims explanation was generally passed around, this fire did look like magic.

It was on September 11th that these shells got Wagoners Jackob E. Jackson and Fiori Fillici.

There had been some firing, but at three o'clock it lifted, and the men poured from their funk holes and returned to work.

Jackson was cleaning harness at one of the wagons when the company clerk came up and spoke to him. The wagoner was very happy, for he had just that day received a letter from home, telling him that his wife had presented him with a son. He displayed the letter to the clerk, and they chatted cheerfully about the future. With the Huns falling back all along the line it might be only a few months before Jackson would be on his way home to this new arrival. The clerk promised to look after the additional government allowance which the baby's birth would give Jackson's wife.

"My wife," Jackson said, "needs the money very much, because things are so high in the States."

He said nothing more after that. The clerk climbed into the wagon to search for something the captain had left there, and at once the Huns resumed their odd shelling. The third shell, the clerk said, seemed to burst directly beside the wagon. A piece hit him in the leg, inflicting, however, only a slight wound. When he climbed down he saw Jackson lying on the ground, a medical orderly bending over him. A piece of the shell had struck him in the back of the head. He died on the way to the hospital.

Fillici was killed during the same bombardment, although he was a short distance from the echelon. He had started on a horse without saddle or bridle to get some medicine from the Veterinary Detachment. Fillici had volunteered for this service as the company veterinarian was occupied at the moment. He had been advised to take a short cut, but instead chose the main road.

The news of his death was brought by French soldiers who had been working on the road. The shell, they said, had burst very close to Fillici, knocking him from his horse. Fillici had been killed, but the horse had not been scratched. The Frenchmen said that the same shell had killed a captain and a lieutenant of the 305th Infantry.

When one considers the number of shells that fall idly it is astonishing to count up the amount of damage some one shell, better aimed, or carried by chance, will accomplish. The First Battalion got one of these at its command post near Blanzy on September 15th.

For days shells of all calibres had fallen about the place without accomplishing any more damage than tearing up the soil. Then this one arrived. It fell at the picket line. The horses stood in a row. Private Aimer M. Aasgard groomed a horse near the end of the line. Near him sat a group of telephone men, winding wire on makeshift reels—a necessary diversion of the telephone detail when there was nothing else to do. The men heard the whine of the approaching shell and realized from their acquired judgment that it would fall very near. They called out a warning and ducked. Aasgard wasn't quick enough. A tiny fragment cut into his neck, severing the jugular vein. Dr. Cronin hurried to the doomed man. Aasgard died within a few minutes.

The same shell caught Corporal Leonard Cook of the telephone detail in the knee, disabling him and putting him out of the war. An ambitious telephone man, he was evacuated grumblingly, and was never returned to the regiment. Other fragments cost the detail eight more of its vanishing horses.

But these serious moments were the exception. Life north of the Vesle was far less complicated than it had been about Les Près. There were, of course, minor casualties.

First Class Private McGranaghan gave Sergeant Hickey an opportunity to distinguish himself. McGrahaghan was hit while working on the Serval line. Hickey, who had been on duty in the observatory, picked him up and carried him over a crest exposed to machine gun fire to the first aid station.

These individual instances of courage were innumerable. Men, however, don't say much about what they do themselves. Unless someone happened to see their bravery it drifted into that vast blurred background of devotion and sacrifice against which the American soldier fought.

Between the Vesle and the Aisne the Second Battalion was even more fortunate than the First. Major Wanvig's command didn't have a single casualty in the Perles positions. Hun airmen gave it one bad night, and might have done a lot of damage.

A bomber created the impression that he had located the emplacements, for he dropped a number of flares over them, and followed with two bombs in the ravine, which missed Battalion Headquarters, and one on the slope close to the guns, which splintered a number of trees.

A group of men from Battery D had a close rim of it. They had made themselves comfortable in a large German dugout whose only overhead cover was a sheet of elephant iron. At the first flare they decided there might be safer places, and sought one. When they returned a few moments later, after the plane had throbbed away, they found their pleasant home, a mass of twisted elephant iron, ploughed up dirt, and ruined equipment. The third bomb had made a direct hit on the dugout in which they had just before been crowded for warmth.

****

The regiment fired as persistently here as it had done in the Les Près and Chèry positions. Barrage after barrage was thrown ahead of our infantry on La Petite Montagne, which because of its pivotal situation was of great strategic importance. Before it was captured the order came for the regiment to move to other pastures.

CHAPTER 20

The Argonne

The first intimation the 305th had that it would be relieved was brought by advance parties from General Garibaldi's Italian division. The sight of these strange faces and uniforms indicated to everyone that the regiment was going out for a well-earned rest. How deceitful that opinion was, everyone remembers; but the occasion was important and exciting. All our men of Italian parentage greeted the newcomers with joy and hospitality. There was much excited conversation. There were more interpreters than could possibly be used.

While the Italians reconnoitred the Americans packed—joyously, too. The prospect of billets, baths, and cooked food was alluring after more than two months in the line. The thought of quiet after a month of such fighting as the Vesle had developed, was frankly welcome.

The movement commenced on the night of September 15-16. No one had any idea where he was going, except that it was to the rear. And the belief in billets was touchingly firm.

Down roads on which they had advanced under shell fire, the columns wound through the fragmentary and odorous remains of Fismette and Fismes, past Les Près Farm, at which some fists were shaken, through Chèry Chartreuve for the last time, and to the crossroads just beyond where the two battalions rendezvoused.

When the last man was up, the regiment took the road to the left through Dravegny where our infantry was regrouping, Cohan, and Coulognes, to the Bois de Meunidre which was selected for the first bivouac. Between eight o'clock in the evening and three in the morning the column covered 23 kilometres.

After the exhausting work of the past two months it was a tired, nearly voiceless column that rode away from the flares, the flashes, and the star shells. Many drivers slept on their horses. The cannoneers, doomed to walk, stumbled forward, only half awake.

There was a delay of nearly half an hour just before reaching the biv-

Resting on the March

ouac. The column halted as if automatically. The men rested where they were, deciding it was quite like old times. Impatience seized a group of officers, and they rode forward to learn, if they could, why the halt continued. Ahead the road was open save for one obstacle. A machine gun cart rested in the middle. On the seat was a dozing driver. Attached to the cart was a mule, supremely indifferent and content. The group awakened the driver hurriedly.

"Reckon," he yawned by way of explanation, "Jinny's decided she's gone far enough tonight."

Jinny and her master suffered the application of united brute force, and watched the column go by.

It was on this first stage that Battery F wandered astray. In the dark it mistook the 306th column for our own, and followed it for some time, until scouts located it, explained the situation, and led it back to the fold.

During the day men fought the light and the noise again for a little sleep, and at 8 o'clock moved out once more. In the early morning the carriages rumbled across the Marne on an engineers' bridge at Venrmeuil. The average man's sensations were very different from those aroused by his previous crossing at Château Thierry. And again the river was a dividing line. The country seemed immeasurably less disturbed to the south. The march lost its sense of being made under the menace of aeroplanes.

And at Mareuil-le-Port, where that twenty kilometre stage ended, an officer brought joy with several motor trucks assigned to the regiment for the transportation of a certain number of dismounted men. Sixty were chosen from each organization and put in charge of Lieutenants Brassel, Putnam, and Copelin. Although it wasn't generally known at the time, the destination of these trucks was La Grange, three kilometres northwest of St. Mennehould. The rest of the regiment, condemned to the long hike, continued to foresee a glorious rest ahead. The rumour was that the billets were four days' march away.

Mareuil-le-Port had other cheering features. The weather still held fair. The country, not yet scourged by autumn, was pleasant to men fresh from the gashed slopes and devastated forests of battlefields. The gun park, the picket lines, the straight rows of shelter tents were arranged in pleasant fields; and in the village the civilian population went about its business. There were shops, for the first time since Doue, and they specialized in a fresh cheese that nearly everyone added to his rations. Best of all the column didn't form again until 10 'clock of the morning of the 18th, so that there was all day and a large part of the night for rest.

The roads now were not particularly congested. The regiment travelled rapidly, which is far less fatiguing than a snail's march with many halts.

It was generally known by this time that the French were routing the

A Well Shelled Road

Off Duty for a Moment

column, and were keeping it off the congested main lines of supplies. Therefore twenty kilometres were covered by 11 o'clock on the morning of the 18th to the summit of a high hill at Greuves, near Epernay.

The weather threatened here, but the place had matters of interest. It was in the heart of the Champagne country, and the wine was plentiful, cheap, and harmless, as far as one could judge. Thirst was excusable after the last two miles of that stage. The horses would have given up the grade if the men hadn't encouraged them and put shoulders to the wheels.

At 4 o'clock the next morning the regiment was on the road again. Its route lay through the plains of the Marne, a rich country sheltering farms and vineyards which had not experienced the harsher touches of war. There was an added spur to muscles and spirits this day. For wasn't it the fourth stage? Wouldn't night see everyone in the paradise of rest billets?

But the march closed towards noon at Ferme Notre Dame, twenty kilometres south-east of Chalons.

"That's all right," men said wisely. "They're putting another day on the march to make it easier for us. We'll sleep tonight and get there tomorrow."

Yet certainly no one would have chosen to stop at Ferme Notre Dame to make things easier. It was a place at once beautiful and abominable. There was only one well at some distance from the main buildings, so that it took five hectic hours to water the animals once.

Word passed around that the start wouldn't be made until late the next morning. It fitted in. A short march, then rest, baseball, baths, delousing!

The regiment didn't move out in fact, until 6:30 of the 20th, but the stage lengthened into twenty kilometres, and ended during the middle of the afternoon in meadows near Cheppes, on the bank of the little river Guenelle. For the first time doubt appeared in men's faces.

"What does it mean?" they asked one another.

"Ah," some answered carelessly, "we'll get there tomorrow, or, if not, the day after. This isn't so bad."

Nor was it for men or animals. The one bathed and washed clothing in the river; the other grazed contentedly in the lush meadows.

Suspicions, too, were lulled when Captain Reed was ordered by Brigade Headquarters to reconnoitre to the south in the vicinity of Bassu for the next night's bivouac. Swinging further to the south, of course, meant rest. But the next morning that hope died. A change was announced. The regiment wasn't going south, and French officers appeared and warned commanders of the necessity of seeking concealment most carefully from now on. At 5:30 on the afternoon of September 21st the regiment moved out—to the north-east, and everybody knew it meant the front again.

The attitude of the men in face of this abrupt change was stimulating.

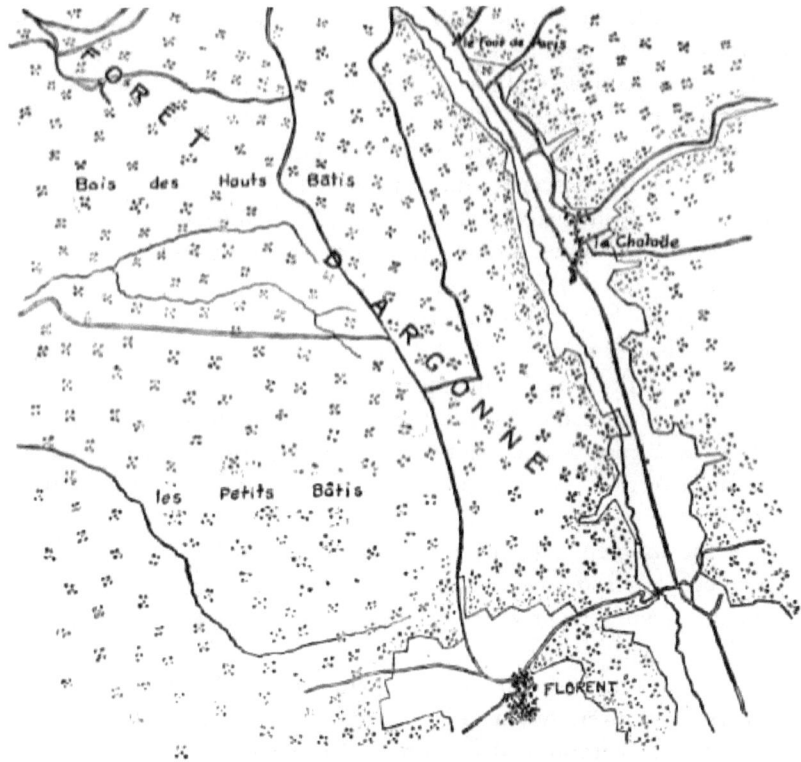

Drawn by Corporal Tucker, Hq. Co.

The jumping-off place

No matter how brave or blood-thirsty he may be, a soldier who expects rest and is suddenly shot back into the line must experience a vivid disappointment. The 305th had the air of having foreseen such a fate. They talked cheerfully of a huge, new offensive which couldn't possibly be successful without the presence of our regiment. If there was any grumbling it was done under the breath.

The march was quick. After twenty-five kilometres the column halted at 11 p.m. in Busy-le-Repos, and found a confusion already suggestive of the front. The 304th had bivouacked in and about the town. Few billets were available for headquarters, and the nearby fields were crowded. The regiment settled itself where it could.

If there had remained any doubts they would have been dispelled here. Captain Olney, from Brigade Headquarters; Captain Reed, from the First Battalion, Lieutenant Wilhite, from the Second Battalion; Lieutenant Klots, from Regimental Headquarters; and officers from the 304th and 306th were ordered forty kilometres forward by motor truck to Les Islettes to make a reconnaissance, locate positions, and figure data.

This party left on the morning of the 22nd—the advance guard of the Brigade into the Argonne.

At Les Islettes they were met by French corps artillery officers, assigned to support the Americans. These Frenchmen had foreseen everything, which was fortunate in view of the difficult and tricky Argonne terrain.

They took our officers to the point near Florent which they had selected for the regimental echelon. They led them, then, carefully forward almost to the front lines, and pointed out positions for the First Battalion a kilometre due east of La Chalade, and others for the Second Battalion a kilometre and a half north-west of the First.

These choices were clearly the best available, so the reconnaissance party set to work checking up targets and data.

While they figured in the forest the regiment resumed its march, leaving Busy-le-Repos on the night of the 22nd to bivouac a few hours the next day at Verriès. The column went on that night to the vicinity of St. Mennehould.

For the moment Regimental Headquarters established itself at the Florent echelon from where it superintended the regrouping of the command and made arrangements for its entry into position at the earliest possible moment.

The men who had come by truck from Mareuil-le-Port had had a good rest. Moreover, they were full of the gossip of the sector, and possessed rumours without end about what was going to happen.

The situation was, in many respects, fruitful of rumours.

Positive orders came from the highest command that no American soldier was to risk exposure to enemy observation unless he wore a French uniform. That made scouts and observers near the front line masquerade. It also meant that a surprise attack on a gigantic scale was in the wind. Yet no one suspected then how big the scheme really was. The terrain, indeed, seemed badly suited to anything of the sort. War here had practically paused for more than four years. The reason lay before everyone's eyes—the woods and the hills of the Argonne.

Here, one of the few points where position warfare had persisted, both the French and the Huns had developed deep and elaborate trench systems. A large proportion of the work was in cement. There was an elaborate net of barbed wire. The prospect of attacking such defences head-on was not cheerful. It was whispered, however, that our doughboys were waiting only for our support to go over.

The situation, meantime, remained placid. There was very little firing. As far as could be learned there were no raids. Either the Bosche had been fooled and didn't know what was gathering, or else he was waiting with a little surprise of his own. A day or two now would show.

Both battalions moved into the positions selected near La Chalade during the early morning of September 24th. Regimental Headquarters at the same time went forward to Ferme Ferdinand.

Those positions were trying on both officers and men, not because of enemy harassing but because of their exhausting natural difficulties. Out in front in No-Man's Land, and for a considerable distance back the forest survived only as a ghostly collection of stripped tree trunks. Two thousand metres to the rear, however, where our guns were placed, it had suffered less, and there was a dense underbrush with practically no tracks. The cannoneers, in consequence, had to chop a way in. The pieces were unlimbered on the road, then manhandled a half a kilometre through the brush to their emplacements. That would have been hard enough by daylight. Before the dawn it was a task for a Hercules with the vision of a cat. Still it was done before sunrise and the work of consolidation was got under way.

These positions were in a piece of forest known as the Bois de Haut Batis. They were near some old French reserve trenches in which our infantry waited for the great moment. The doughboys didn't seem to know exactly what was going to happen to them, or to care particularly. The difficulties of the terrain failed to appal them. They watched curiously the artillerymen as they went about their labour.

Ammunition was the chief difficulty. The firing would be intense. Consequently vast quantities of shells would be required at the emplacements. Time was short. Word to commence firing might come at any minute. Yet a point on the road about 400 metres from the guns

A Portion of the Regiment Concealed in the Argonne was the nearest place to which projectiles could be transported on wheels. The G. S. carts dropped them there, and the battery men carried them one by one through the tangled underbrush. This work went on during September 24th and 25th, while everyone wondered if the Bosche wouldn't observe such diligence and compliment it with a little heavy fire.

An odd incident happened on the 25th. There hadn't been a single high explosive burst near these positions, nor were there any later, yet that day six gas shells fell among the pieces of the First Battalion, or in the road nearby. One of these shells cost the regiment a valuable messenger. Private Carlos Montgomery was thrown from his bicycle by the explosion. Pieces of the casing struck him in the knee, and before he could get his mask on the gas had burned his eyes severely. He was evacuated and invalided to the States.

Yet within a few yards of where he was injured another gas shell fell beneath a G. S. cart, which five men were manhandling, and failed to injure or gas one of the five.

A Portion of the Regiment Concealed in the Argonne

****

From the start in the Argonne it was clear that new difficulties of observation would be met. Here and there were observatories cleverly concealed in trees or on the heights above the Biesme River which ran through the French trench system. Officers and men, disguised as *poilus*, climbed into these, but found the outlook from all unsatisfactory.

Communication, on the other hand, was comparatively simple in the first Argonne position. Regimental Headquarters, the two battalions, the observatories, and the infantry were closely grouped. Later, when the advance commenced, those in liaison with the front line had a good deal of difficulty keeping headquarters informed as to the details of a changing and hazardous situation.

At last the orders came down. The regiment would open fire at 2:30 on the morning of September 26th.

The volume of noise that burst forth at that moment was greater than the Argonne had ever known. To the men serving the guns the terrific uproar came as a surprise. They had not suspected such a mass of artillery had been collected for the drive.

The Germans, whatever they had learned, were stunned by this merciless fire. It was continued until the infantry went over shortly after daybreak. It shifted then to a rolling barrage. It had finally, because of the rapid advance of the infantry and shortage of ammunition, to cease altogether for a time.

Runners brought back word of what was happening out in front. Over the cement trenches and strong points, through the mazes of barbed wire, and the natural barriers of the forest, the infantry made that first day an advance of three kilometres. The artillery would have to move forward at once. The Umbers were hurried down and the pieces went over difficult roads through the old French trench system three kilometres to the vicinity of La Harazèe.

Regimental Headquarters established itself in the remains of the town, and the two battalions went into position side by side within two thousand metres of the new front line. There were dugouts here, large, luxurious, and fairly safe. So the personnel of the three headquarters and the batteries made themselves comfortable.

But, it developed, there would be no let up in the drive. It would go on at once. New missions were assigned. It was during those days that citizen officers and soldiers displayed an exceptional cleverness and adaptability. They located their guns and their targets on the map, and, frequently without registration, as frequently without observation even, blazed merrily away. It was like firing a revolver in the dark yet when the regiment moved forward it could check up on its accuracy. Then dead Bosche, destroyed shelters, and machine gun emplacements, a torn forest, offered their mute and terrible praise. The second day the infantry made two kilometres. After that it slowed down for a time, so that by lengthening the range the entire regiment remained in these emplacements until the 30th. On that morning the First Battalion decided to get farther forward. Major Easterday left at 7 o'clock to reconnoitre for new positions. Captain Reed was to follow with the battalion at 10 to a point near the Abri du Crochet. The infantry had captured this important and pleasant place a day or two before. On the map it appeared as a crossroads. It was, one estimated, scarcely 1,000 metres from the front line.

That distance, it was expected, would soon be decidedly widened. It was to some extent, but for a time now the progress of our infantry, was reduced to nearly nothing. There were a number of reasons. The effect of the first rush was over. The men were tired. Every battalion had had serious losses. While the Germans gathered themselves for a stand, several divisions—probably nearly 200,000 men were rushed to their support. In

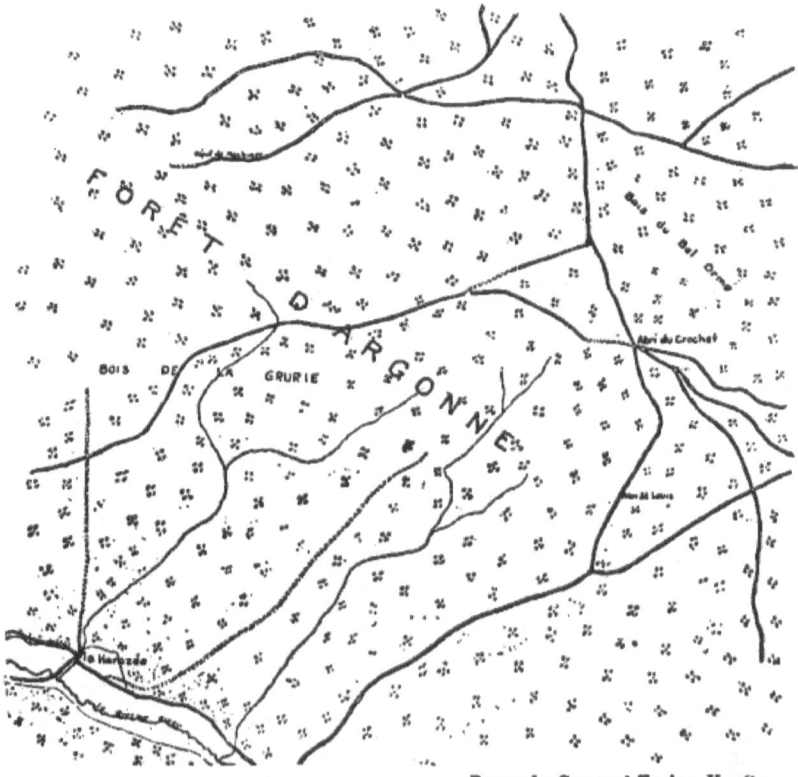

Drawn by Corporal Tucker, Hq. Co.

The vicinity of La Harazée

addition to these fresh odds, the country had become if anything more difficult than at first. Then before the advance could get fairly started once more the affair of the Lost Battalion helped hold things up. But on this day of Major Easterday's reconnaissance the advance continued, if slowly.

The battalion halted short of the crossroads while Captains Reed, Dana, and Ravenel, and Lieutenant Kane rode forward to find the major. When, after some time, they joined him, he said he had chosen positions a kilometre and a half to the rear. Coming up the battery commanders had seen these positions, and they were by no means enthusiastic. Major Easterday as usual was ready to weigh the opinions of his battery commanders. Captain Reed meantime had pushed through a fringe of trees and had seen positions on a slope to the right which he believed had possibilities, if a small amount of cutting should be done. Major Easterday approved and with the battery commanders studied the ground more closely, locating positions in which no cutting at all was necessary. in the altogether delightful Abri du Crochet.

Delightful is really the word, for here, in a sort of amphitheatre, the Bosche during four years had developed the rarest refinements of position warfare life. The place possessed enormous and intricate dugouts, some of them boring into the rock for nearly a hundred feet. They were furnished. Food, even, had been left, ready to cook, by the hurried Germans. Chlorinated water was forgotten for a time, for the dugouts were well stocked with mineral water, and some stronger liquids. Shower baths invited. Fire wood was cut and piled. Tramways ran here and there for convenience in bringing up supplies. The network extended so far that battery command posts fared as well as battalion.

The Battery A commander had an experience the first day that illustrates as well as anything else the elaborate scheme of the system. The B commander and he had their eyes on the same dugout. Captain Ravenel got to it first. Captain Dana chose another some distance away. Everyone had long since learned to examine such places for traps. Captain Dana and Lieutenant Stribling went in at once, therefore, with flash lamps, and searched through the galleries. They came to a door. They halted. For something with a slow stealth moved beyond the panels.

In whispers the two officers discussed the situation. A German spy might have been left behind to wait in this comparatively safe retreat until he could slip through the lines with a plan of the American artillery dispositions. There was only one thing to do. The door had to be opened.

The two loosened the pistols in their holsters. Captain Dana raised the lamp. He flung the door wide with a sudden gesture, prepared for emergencies. Across the threshold stood, in much the same attitude, with much the same suspicions, Captain Ravenel.

Chapter 21

Always Through the Forest

The First Battalion remained at the Abri du Crochet for a week, while the Second stayed in the position at La Harazèe, both supporting, after October 2nd, the famous Lost Battalion. The ring of fire with which the 305th circled Major Whittlesey's command was credited with a measurable share in his salvation. The Second Battalion, moreover, had an officer with him during those black days. Lieutenant Teichmoeller, of Battery D, had been in liaison with Major Whittlesey when the jaws had closed.

The story of the Lost Battalion has been told often enough. A word here will suffice to explain the artillery's perpetual support of the trapped men.

On October 2nd the infantry was forging ahead, scarcely able to maintain flank and rear liaison because of the broken and overgrown terrain. Suddenly the enemy appeared on both flanks and to the rear of the First Battalion and Companies E and H of the Second Battalion of the 308th Infantry. This party of, perhaps, 600 men and officers had made a quick forward thrust of half a kilometre or so. It became clear now that neighbouring units had failed to keep pace. Major Whittlesey's party, therefore, was in a trap from which the Huns were evidently determined it should never escape. For six days they pounded the little command while the Americans did everything possible to relieve it. For six days it went almost entirely without food. Aeroplanes were sent over to drop rations and ammunition, but in the thick woods had difficulty locating the suffering group. For six days its personnel accomplished Homeric deed, endeavouring to guide the aeroplanes and to get messengers through. Its losses were great. Of those who came back after the relief few were unwounded. Lieutenant Teichmoeller, while completely exhausted and ill from lack of food, was one of the fortunate ones who had not been hit.

During this period the strain was felt almost as thoroughly by the artillery as by the supporting infantry. Our batteries fired constantly. Our agents and observers forward did what they could to locate the command and to report on the result of the fire.

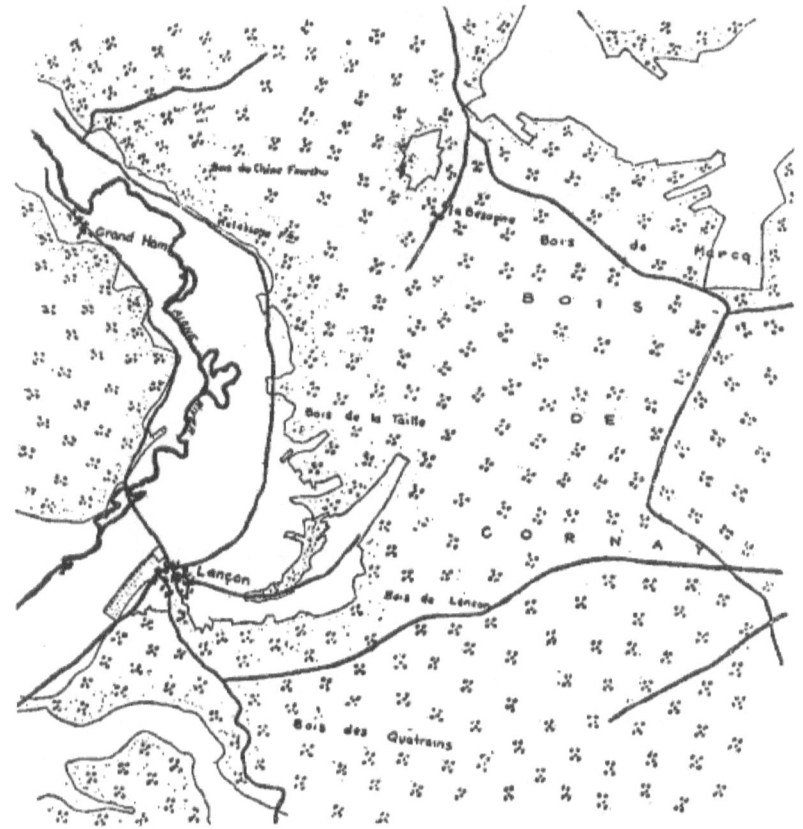

Drawn by Corporal Tucker, Hq. Co.

Lançon and Grand Ham

On the second day—that is October 3rd—Lieutenants Burden and Klots with Private Cox, of the Headquarters Company, were forward with the infantry, trying to get some light on the situation.

They were crossing an open space when they spied an observation tower in the woods ahead.

"It's an observatory," Lieutenant Klots said, "and if there's anybody in it he'll snipe at us."

Someone was in it, and he began sniping with a 77. The party took shelter in a crater.

After a time, when the sniping had ceased, the three made a dash for some trees on the flank. They reached the shelter, but the grove itself was getting a good many shells. Lieutenant Klots pointed out a low bank.

"Looks like dead space under that bank," he said. "Why not wait there and have a smoke?"

The others agreed. But the bank did not furnish dead space for a man. A number of shells fell nearby. Then one dropped directly in front of the party, and the back lash got all three. Lieutenant Burden was badly hurt in the thigh. Private Cox got a painful and disabling wound in the leg, Lieutenant Klots was struck by a fragment on the instep. Other shells would come. There was only one thing to do—make a run for it.

Drawn by Corporal Schmidt, Hq. Co.
Grand-Pré

Lieutenant Burden started first and reached the thicker woods out of the line of fire. Cox tried it, but went down after a step or two, realizing for the first time that his leg had been fractured. Lieutenant Klots carried him back to such shelter as the bank afforded and remained with him until some infantrymen came along with a stretcher and took him to the first aid station. Cox did not return to the regiment. Lieutenant Burden had had a narrow escape and was not discharged from the hospital until some time after the armistice, when he was assigned to work in Paris in connection with the peace parleys. Lieutenant Klots' wound was slight, and he returned to duty within a few days.

On October 4th, while firing in support of the Lost Battalion, C Battery lost a man in a premature burst. A piece of the tube struck Private Edgar A. Blethen. Lieutenant Robinson was the first to reach him, but the man had been instantly killed.

With the relief of the Lost Battalion the infantry resumed its advance, and it became clear that the artillery would be better off in new positions. Regimental Headquarters had left La Harazée on September 27th for Ferme aux Charmes. On October 9th it went forward two kilometres to the Depot de Machines. The First Battalion moved considerably further into the Bois de la Naza, but remained here only a few hours. After taking position it found that the infantry had gone so far ahead it would not be profitable to fire. It continued, then, to a point a kilometre west of Chatel-Cheherry where it remained for one day, firing semi-steel shells on German works near Grand Pré.

The Second Battalion on October 8th left La Harazée for the Stolzenfels dugout system in the rear of Binarville, 200 metres to the left of the Binarville-Château Vienne road. The battalion did not fire from these positions. It left them on October 9th for positions further forward, about half a kilometre to the right of the village of Langon.

The entire regiment on October 10th moved forward through the Bois de Langon to the vicinity of Grand Ham. Regimental Headquarters was established at Malassise Farm on the Aisne. The First Battalion took up positions to the east of Grand Ham, while the Second went a trifle further to the north to Hill 208. In these positions the regiment remained, by shifting its ranges, always within reach of its targets until the 77th Division was relieved on October 17th.

The regiment had a real mystery on October 10th, and it was not a pleasant one. Sergeant Orville C. Cooper, of Battery B was the victim. He had served as first sergeant of the battery since the early days in Upton, and had been much appreciated by Captain Ravenel. On the night of the 10th, according to the report made by the battery clerk, Sergeant Cooper was called from his quarters at the battery echelon near La Chalade by a soldier unknown to anyone in the battery. The soldier said that the sergeant was wanted by Captain McKenna at the Supply dump, about 500 metres away. Sergeant Cooper took a short cut. About half an hour later he was brought back to the echelon by an infantry guard detachment. He had been badly slashed in the throat and about the body, evidently by barbed wire in falling from a narrow footbridge after his assailants had

The dugout near which Lieutenant Hoadley was killed

Drawn by Private Enroth, Battery D

beaten him on the head with a club. He was in a semi-conscious condition, and was evacuated by Major Miller. Captain McKenna had not sent for the Sergeant, and a searching examination of property, and a careful questioning of the personnel in the vicinity of the echelon failed to yield the slightest clue to the assault. Sergeant Cooper was so badly hurt that he was invalided to America.

On the next day Battery D had an unusual casualty. Private Rodney J. Lecours, who had been guarding ammunition, lay down in hay on the side of a road near Binarville and fell asleep. His head was towards the road. Other men were asleep nearby. A motor truck, not seeing these men in the dark, drew up at the side of the road. One of the wheels passed over Private Lecours, killing him instantly.

It was during this last stage of the operations that had commenced on September 26th that the regiment suffered a depressing loss. First Lieutenant Sheldon E. Hoadley was killed on Sunday, October 13th. He had left his battery position and was riding along a road to the rear when a shell burst near him. A fragment struck him. He received immediate attention, but there was no chance. He died a few minutes after he was hit, while on his way to a dressing station in an ambulance.

Rumours of a relief became persistent. Horses and men were worn out. Since entering the war in Lorraine the regiment had left the front only to change position. In other words it had had no rest at all. The supply of ammunition was uncertain. The materiel needed attention. Grand Prè and St. Juvin, divisional objectives had been taken.

Rumours crystallized into fact. The 78th Division relieved the 77th on October 17th and 18th. Regimental Headquarters moved back to La Chalade, resting for a few hours at Langon. The batteries followed out. Baths, delousing, and rest waited at La Chalade.

There was, it developed, to be more than simple rest. The regiment was allowed a number of passes for three days, exclusive of travel. The fortunate departed gaily for the vicinity of Paris or the Riviera. In many cases, it will be sadly remembered, they were met as they descended from the trains at their destinations by military policemen who presented them with telegrams. These missives recalled them at once to the regiment. The reason was obvious. The division was returning at once to its place in the line. There would be a new and vigorous offensive.

CHAPTER 22

The Last Phase

The clans gathered again at La Chalade, and made ready to hurry back to the line. During the period of rest everyone had found time to read the papers. It was known that the Germans had asked for peace; that notes had passed back and forth; but at the front no one took the news very seriously. There was too much to be done. The men had become so absorbed by the war that at last they had borrowed something of the French attitude. The thing appeared eternal.

The question of transportation caused worry and wonderment. The regiment had received replacements of men, but none of horses. How was it going to be possible to move guns and ammunition with the few animals left? The answer came a little later in an unexpected form.

On October 27th the echelon was established at Chatel-Cheherry, and Regimental Headquarters and First Battalion Headquarters settled themselves in a house at Cornay. The First Battalion guns were a kilometre to the north.

The Second Battalion guns were in the same valley as the First, but to the left, near the town of Marc. Major Easterday and Captain Starbuck made a careful reconnaissance of the front. Firing opened on November 1st. Again the advance was large, and on November 2nd the regiment moved forward to the vicinity of Verpel.

First Class Private Abel S. Virkler, of Battery C was hit by a fragment on November 2nd and killed while at work at his battery position.

At midnight of that day the transportation problem was solved in a radical fashion. The orders for the move had evidently come from high up. Colonel Doyle summoned Majors Easterday and Wanvig to Champigneulles. There the colonel told the two majors that the regiment would be split. The First Battalion would continue as a combat battalion. The Second would act as its combat train. It would turn over to the First, horses, wire, telephones, and other equipment.

Such a move was inevitable. More than once in heavy weather the

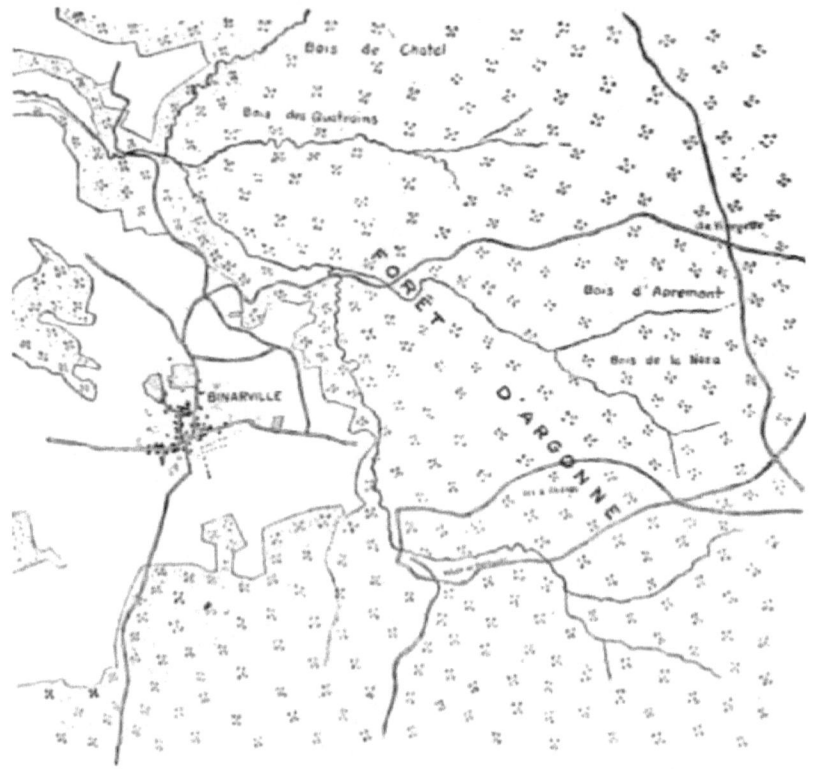

Drawn by Corporal Tucker, Hq. Co.
Binarville and its surroundings

horses had been unable to draw the pieces without the aid of cannoneers. The weather could be counted on now for much rain and the consequent mud.

The battery commanders, in pursuance to this order, met Major Easterday in Verpel, and the dispositions were settled upon. The echelon was established there. Captain Derby, who had recently been promoted with Captain Pike, was placed in charge. Captain Storer was given command of the combat train and instructed to keep always in the train 2,000 rounds. Major Wanvig and his staff, of course, were responsible for both the echelon and the train.

Under these new conditions the regiment moved forward towards the Meuse. On November 3rd the firing batteries passed through Buzancy. The town had been fired by the Germans and was in flames. Civilians, who had been under the German yoke for four years, hurried to the rear with what belongings they could save. They were clearly grateful to see the Americans, but such emotion as theirs does not express itself demonstratively.

That night and the next morning pirate guns were sent out. Lieutenant Robinson took one, Lieutenant Mitchell, another, and Lieutenant Warren W. Nissley, a third.

These officers with a piece each, and a cart full of ammunition, went forward to the infantry, and fired on whatever targets the infantry commander chose. It was dangerous work. Our officers went into position, practically in the open, and fired at German machine gun nests, and received from the infantry a gratifying amount of praise.

On the evening of the 3rd the First Battalion moved forward to Fontenoy. Regimental Headquarters also located its command post in the village. First Class Private William Kuttler, one of the regimental messengers, was killed on the road near Fontenoy that day. He was walking behind an escort wagon and was close to a party of infantry when a shell burst in the bank at the side of the road. Kuttler was the only man of our regiment hit, but seven infantrymen were killed and a number wounded.

On the same day Lieutenant Charles Graham was wounded by a shell fragment and evacuated.

The regiment remained in Fontenoy the 3rd and 4th, then moved into Stonne, placing the three firing batteries in position in the valley to the south-west.

The civilian population in Stonne welcomed the Americans as saviours. Men and women said the Germans before fleeing, had instructed them to take refuge in the church, promising not to shell the town for 24 hours. Scarcely, however, had they gone than the place was drenched with gas shells, and, of course, the civilians had no gas masks.

The next day another forward move was made to Flaba. Rations were scarce. Often the men had given of their issue to the civilians. Here the civilians gave the soldiers black German bread which the hungry men had not experienced before. The result was a sad amount of indigestion and a heightened sympathy for those who had been compelled to live for so long under the Hun food regulations.

There was no firing from these positions, and on November 6th Batteries A, B, and C, moved a half a kilometre to the east of Harraucourt, into range of the heights across the Meuse. The Second Battalion, acting as combat train, had kept pace with all these changes and had assured the supply of ammunition. Here the regiment remained until the signing of the armistice, five days later.

On the day the pieces moved into the final positions the regiment had its last casualty in action. Second Lieutenant Leon H. Hattemer, who had come to the 305th on the Vesle, was killed by a machine gun bullet, while in liaison with the infantry. The nearness of the end made his death seem all the more unfortunate.

Drawn by Corporal Roos and Private Enroth
Refugees going out, the artillery going in

Lieutenants Burden and Bullen, and Private Gormley were mentioned in division orders for their work during the Argonne fighting.

A few new officers were assigned during this last offensive. Second Lieutenant Augus R. Allmond had come on October 10th. Three other officers were with the regiment for a few weeks but were transferred away again to other branches of the service. On November 10th, the day before the armistice, Major Edwin A. Zundel was assigned to the command of the First Battalion to replace Major Easterday, whose promotion to a lieutenant-colonelcy had just come through. Colonel Easterday had commanded the battalion from Nesles Woods to the Meuse Heights, that is during its most active combat experience. For his aggressiveness, and his daring in reconnaissance he was cited afterwards in division orders. He was a familiar figure near the front lines on foot, on his horse, or dashing about in a motorcycle. Once he and his driver wandered past the pickets and into a village filled with German soldiers, preparing to depart. Easterday told the driver to turn around, and before the Huns had recovered from their astonishment, he was rushing back to his command. By virtue of his new rank he went to Regimental Headquarters as second in command.

With Major Zundel came Second Lieutenants Solomon Abelow and Horace Heyday. The next day the war was over.

The fact of the armistice had been announced during the morning, but the regiment was sceptical, and went about its business. When the firing stopped the men attended to their routine duties and grinned wisely whenever anyone tried to tell them the show was at an end. The silence at last made an impression, and, as a band appeared, victoriously playing at the head of a regiment of Moroccans, the majority conceded that there might be something in the rumour.

There were, however, cases of chronic doubt. Sergeant Joseph, of the band, for example, had been left some distance in the rear to guard a reel cart. He picked up what he could to eat from neighbouring units, but on the whole, was a hungry sentry. On November 14th a doughboy passed him in his isolated retreat, came up, and burst into a laugh.

"Hey, Buddy! What you wearing your gas mask in the alert for?"

"Orders," from the sergeant.

A guffaw from the visitor.

"The war's been over three days."

"I've heard that before," replied the sergeant drily.

Somehow this fellow managed to persuade him.

****

The minute the great fact was absorbed the talk was of home. The original word was that the 77th would go into the army of occupation. That was altered and, except for a few officers and men, who were transferred to units ordered up, the division moved out of the line.

The 305th was billeted in Verpel for a time, and the period of leaves commenced. After one or two stops by the way the regiment detrained at Latrecy and marched to Arc-en-Barrois, a charming and hospitable village in the Haute Marne, where it remained in the midst of rumours of departure until February 9th.

Here an elaborate schedule of training went into effect, based on ancient methods of firing, so that some had a good time talking wisely and extensively about aiming points, designation of targets, and P minus T. Also scandals of ammunition and equipment were laid bare at leisure. And everybody was brought into close personal touch with the *high cost of living*.

But there was a difference. Officers and men followed out the appointed schedules, but their spirits were at home. There was no desperate and necessary future to which this

Drawn by *Private Enroth, Battery D*
The Church at Arc-en-Barrois

training led. It had the air of killing time and keeping men occupied. And many soldiers wanted to learn things that would be useful to them on their return to America and work. The days slipped away beneath heavy skies, and a downpour nearly perpetual. Athletics got a start with soccer football on New Year's Day.

In the midst of rumours of our early departure came the epidemic of Spanish influenza. We had had a number of cases, and some deaths. Lieutenant Danforth Montague had gone in December, and there was an uncomfortable feeling that the dread disease was always with us. The latter part of January men commenced to report sick by the score. One day thirty would be evacuated. Another we would say goodbye to forty. The evacuations worked up to fifty or more, and we knew each day that some of the men that climbed, feverish and ill, into the ambulance, would not come back.

In this emergency, Major Miller worked day and night. Sporadic cases of typhoid complicated his labour. His success, however, permitted the regiment to leave for the embarkation centre on February 9th.

The bitter cold, the snow covering the ground, the prospect of cattle cars, didn't effect the joy the men took in this move towards home.

The train was composed of ancient cars. It crawled. A journey that one might take in a regular train in eight or nine hours consumed for us, cramped, cold, and uncomfortable, about sixty hours. We recalled the days before the armistice when we had been of more value to people generally; when we had been rushed long distances into action at express rate speed.

And that trip will be eternally coloured in our minds by Lieutenant Arthur Robinson's death. After accepting all the chances of the front with a cheerful and inspiring indifference which had won for him the Distinguished Service Cross, Robinson was accidentally killed on the night of February 10th at the little station of Chatillon-sur-Cher. He had stepped from our train which was standing on a siding. The fastest train on the road—an American special—tore by at a terrific rate of speed striking the open door of a compartment. Robinson was struck by this door. He was buried with full military honours in the American cemetery at Angers.

It was not like a death in action. Everyone, officers and men, had liked and admired Robinson. His death cast a persistent shadow over the regiment.

During the evening of February 11th the 305th entered Malicorne, a pottery town on the beautiful Sarthe River. The people were rather different from those at Arc, but after a time they learned to like the Americans. There we stayed until the 17th of April, drilling, getting reviewed and inspected, and chasing the elusive cootie, so that we should be rushed through Brest. The weather was sufficiently warm to permit us to develop a baseball team that closed an extended divisional season undefeated.

Photograph Taken by Band Leader Fisher, Hq. Co.

The Officers of the Regiment at Arc-En-Barrois

When we reached Pontanezin on the 18th we realized that we were, indeed, veterans, that we had really been pioneers in the A. E. F. For Pontanezin had grown out of all recognition since our visit of the year before. Then it had been nearly as the French had turned it over—a group of old barracks and a few tents. Now it covered many acres. The original camp was lost in the midst of countless huts and tents. Whatever horrors the place may have contained we failed to experience. We were there only two days, and the weather was clear and warm. On Sunday, April 20th, we marched into Brest, survived the mad confusion of loading baggage and men from pier to tender, and from tender to ship, and by nightfall were packed on the transport *Agamemnon,* the old German liner *Kaiser Wilhelm the Second.*

We sailed at noon of the 21st out of the harbour of Brest, "a good deal wiser," as one man put it, "than when we had landed."

The boat was uncomfortably crowded, but no one cared. We were going home. The weather, moreover, was good, so that scarcely anyone was ill, and the *Agamemnon* was fast.

At 9 o'clock Tuesday morning, April 29th we saw the low shore of Long Island and picked up our pilot at Ambrose Channel Lightship.

The story of that day of homecoming is in everyone's heart—a trifle vague still, perhaps, because it was difficult to realize that we were, after more than a year, again in New York Harbour; that, where twelve months before we had slipped out, hidden between decks, we were now steaming noisily in, surrounded by cutters and ferryboats, decorated with banners and filled with shouting friends.

Everything, indeed, was reversed. But on the pier there were still men and women who gave us things to eat and smoke. We piled on to the same ferryboats, and went around the welcoming town to Long Island City.

That night we reached Camp Mills, and the next morning, after a final delousing, half the regiment went home for forty-eight hours, the other fifty percent following two days later.

Even then you had a feeling that you were through. You could count already the hours that separated you from a return to a normal life, a final rupture from the service to which everyone had given himself wholeheartedly, but with which nearly everybody wanted to be done now that the emergency was over.

The parade alone held us. We went to New York Monday morning for that, left our equipment in the 9th Regiment armoury, spent Monday and Tuesday night home, and on Tuesday morning marched up Fifth Avenue from Washington Square to 110th Street, where we saw the last of our Division and Brigade commanders.

The return to Upton the next day was the commencement of the

Drawn by Private Enroth, Battery D.
Malicorne from the Sarthe

final phase. There, where the regiment had been born, it was to end its career. Upton had altered little, yet it seemed oddly different. That was because it was ourselves who had changed.

At Upton the machinery of demobilization seemed to be out of repair by day and to grind only during the dark hours. After three nearly sleepless nights the last formalities had been complied with, and organizations gathered in a pouring rain for their final pay and their railroad tickets home. Men glanced proudly at the red chevrons on their left arms signifying discharge. They walked, in formation for the last time, to the familiar railroad station where organization commanders and officers gave them their discharges and shook hands as they passed through the gates—civilians after one of the best jobs soldiers ever did. And with this breaking up of the 305th Field Artillery died a good deal that was fine, a good deal that you couldn't see vanish without regret. Yet, although it may seem paradoxical, few would care to watch its completest resurrection, because that would mean also the rebirth of the conditions on which it was built.

No more that great communal chorus "When do we eat?"

No more the revolt in one's heart at the best cursed music in the world, *First Call*!

No more tearing one's hair at Paper Work!

No more elaborate language or strong arm competitions with the Red Hats!

Even the first sergeant got a sympathetic thought that last morning.

His piercing whistle at reveille had a special significance.

And so did his loud, uncompromising, and final:

"Outside!"

Appendices

ROLL OF HONOR

KILLED IN ACTION

Graham, Edward F.	2 Lt.	Hq. Co.	Aug. 22	Cave near Cemenocal
Hattemer, Leon H.	2 Lt.	Btry E	Nov. 5	1 km. W. of Oches
Hoadley, Sheldon	1 Lt.	Btry D	Oct. 13	Argonne
Strong, Ellsworth O.	2 Lt.	Btry A	Aug. 25	Ville Savoy
Aasgard, Almer M.	Pvt.	Hq. Co.	Sept. 15	Blanzy
Blethen, Edgar A.	Pvt.	Btry C	Oct. 4	Abri de Crochet
Fillici, Fiori	Wag.	Sup. Co.	Sept. 11	Road near Chery
Fisher, Wallace	Pvt.	Hq. Co.	Sept. 5	Fismes
Forman, George L., Jr.	Pvt.	Btry A	Aug. 20	1.5 km. ESE Chery
Geer, Connie F.	Corp.	Btry D	Aug. 16	7 km. N. Foret de Nesles
Isler, Fred	Pvt.	Hq. Co.	Aug. 26	Chery
Jackson, Jackob E.	Wag.	Sup. Co.	Sept. 11	Woods near Chery
Kronfield, Harry E.	Pvt.	Btry B	Aug. 16	7 km. N. Foret de Nesles
Kuttler, William	Pvt. 1 cl.	Hq. Co.	Nov. 4	Harroucourt
Lucking, George J.	Pvt.	Btry B	Aug. 20	3 km. ENE Chery
Point, George E.	Sgt.	Hq. Co.	Aug. 20	Les Près Farm
Rosalia, Charles C.	Pvt.	Btry E	Aug. 28	Chery Y. M. C. A.
Rubino, Walter J.	Pvt.	Btry D	Aug. 21	5 km. S. E. Chery
Silber, Martin W.	Pvt. 1 cl.	Hq. Co.	Aug. 16	Bois de Coehelet
Tiffany, Frank L.	Pvt.	Hq. Co.	Aug. 28	Vesle
Virkler, Abel S.	Pvt. 1 cl.	Btry C	Nov. 2	Argonne
Weeber, Frederick J.	Pvt. 1 cl.	Btry E	Aug. 25	5 km. S E Chery
Whetstone, John W.	Pvt.	Btry B	Aug. 16	7 km. N Foret de Nesles

ACCIDENTALLY KILLED

Robinson, Arthur A.	2 Lt.	Sup. Co.	Feb. 10	Chatillon-sur-Cher
Lecours, Rodney J.	Pvt. 1 cl.	Btry D	Oct. 11	Binarville
Lynch, Jeremiah S.	Pvt.	Btry B	June 20	Camp de Souge
Posner, Harry J.	Pvt.	Btry B	June 28	Camp de Souge

DIED OF DISEASE*

COMPILED FROM REPORT OF DAILY CHANGES

Montague, Danforth	1st Lt.		Died of Disease	Nov. 5, 1918
Brule, Herbert J.	Pvt.	Btry D	" " "	Nov. 1, 1918
			Evacuation Hosp. No. 9	
			1st Army	
Corp. William F.	Mec.	Btry D	Died of Disease	

Reported on Feb. 4, 1919. No date given.

*Because of lack of reports, following some evacuations, this list should not be considered complete.

Klink, Joseph	Pvt.	Btry F	Died of Disease			Feb. 4, 1919
Whalen, David J.	Pvt. 1 cl.	Btry D	"	"	"	Feb. 4, 1919
Larson, F. C.	Pvt. 1 cl.	Btry C	Died Pneumonia			Feb. 7, 1919
Ford, George	Sgt.	Btry B	Died Disease			Feb. 7, 1919
Turner, Elmer	Pvt. 1 cl.	Btry F	"	"		Feb. 8, 1919
Buess, Edward G.	Pvt.	Btry E	"	Broncho-Pneumonia		Feb. 8, 1919
Burns, James J.	Pvt.	Btry D.	"	"	"	Feb. 10, 1919
Engelkes, Hildebt	Pvt.	Btry F	"	"	"	Feb. 10, 1919
Hodge, Henry W.	Pvt.	Btry E	"	"	"	Feb. 10, 1919
Pearson, Nils G.	Pvt. 1 cl.	Btry E	"	"	"	Feb. 11, 1919
Ryan, Ernest A.	Pvt.	Btry E	"	"	"	Feb. 8, 1919
Siegel, Henry	Corp.	Btry F	"	"	"	Feb. 12, 1919
Smith, George N.	Pvt. 1 cl.	Btry F	"	"	"	Feb. 11, 1919
Steen, Perry	Pvt. 1 cl.	Btry B	"	"	"	Feb. 8, 1919
Yonne, Arthur	Pvt.	Btry F	"	"	"	Feb. 13, 1919
Gittelman, Jake	Pvt.	Btry C	"	"	"	Feb. 27, 1919

LIST OF OFFICERS AND MEN, 305TH F. A., WOUNDED AND GASSED

1918	July 23	Miles, Howard G.	Corp.	Battery C
	Aug. 16	Tredendall, Douglas L.	Pvt.	Battery B
	" 16	Horowitz, Joseph	Pvt.	Det. M. C.
	" 16	Rothman, Morris	Pvt.	Btry. E
	" 16	Thomas, George A.	Pvt. 1 cl.	Btry B
	" 19	Delanoy, Douglas	Capt.	Btry F
	" 19	Graham, Edward F.	2nd Lt.	Hq. Co.
	" 19	Meierdircks, Carl H.	Pvt.	Btry C
	" 19	McKenna, Barth	Sgt.	Btry F
	" 19	Tropp, Ralph	Pvt.	Det. M. C.
	" 20	Applegate, George H.	Bn.Sgt.Mj.	Hq. Co.
	" 20	Preda, Fred	Cook	Btry A
	" 20	Scheuner, Fred	Pvt. 1 cl.	Btry B
	" 21	Cohen, Joseph	Pvt. 1 cl.	Btry D
	" 21	Metzger, Jacob	Sgt.	Btry D
	" 21	Roos, Arthur H.	Corp.	Btry D
	" 22	Klots, Allen T.	1st Lt.	Hq. Co.
	" 23	Colburn, Edward	Pvt. 1 cl.	Btry C
	" 24	Buchbinder, Marc	Sgt.	Btry A
	" 24	Cahill, John J.	Pvt.	Btry B
	" 24	Lewis, Reese H.	Pvt.	Hq. Co.
	" 25	Briggs, Lester E.	Pvt.	Btry E
	" 25	Connors, Francis J.	Sgt.	Btry D
	" 25	Forsyth, James R.	Pvt. 1 cl.	Btry E
	" 25	Golden, Charles I.	Corp.	Btry A
	" 25	Golden, Daniel W.	Pvt.	Hq. Co.
	" 25	Kilcoyne, George F.	Pvt. 1 cl.	Btry E
	" 25	Meyer, John R.	Corp.	Btry E
	" 25	Nestor, Aloysius P.	Pvt.	Btry A
	" 26	Miller, Wendell P.	Sgt.	Btry C
	" 26	Newell, Albert H.	Pvt.	Btry E
	" 26	Romer, William F.	Pvt.	Btry A
	" 27	Silver, Leon	Cook	Btry C

Date		Name	Rank	Unit
Aug.	28	HANSON, RASMUS	Pvt.	Btry E
"	28	LANDSMAN, ALEXANDER	Corp.	Btry D
"	28	MONETTE, DONA J.	Pvt.	Btry E
"	31	GAFFNEY, WILLIAM	Pvt.	Btry C
Sept.	7	BEAN, WALTER	Pvt.	Btry B
"	7	BERMAN, ABRAHAM	Pvt.	Btry D
"	7	BISSO, FRANK R.	Pvt. 1 cl.	Hq. Co.
"	7	BRAUMBACH, WILLIAM	Wag.	Sup. Co.
"	7	BRENNAN, MICHAEL J.	Pvt. 1 cl.	Btry C
"	7	BROMM, FRED H.	Sgt.	Hq. Co.
"	7	CARSON, JOHN N.	Pvt. 1 cl.	Btry F
"	7	CONLEY, JOSEPH C.	Pvt.	Btry E
"	7	CONNELLY, JAMES W.	Pvt. 1 cl.	Btry D
"	7	DOYLE, FRED C.	Col.	F. & S.
"	7	GAMMELL, ARTHUR A.	Capt.	F. & S.
"	7	GILLETTE, GEORGE	Pvt. 1 cl.	Hq. Co.
"	7	HOFFMAN, GEORGE A.	Pvt. 1 cl.	Hq. Co.
"	7	KLOTS, ALLEN T	1st Lt.	Hq. Co.
"	7	KURASH, IRVING	Mus.	Hq. Co.
"	7	MAMLUCK, MARK E.	Sgt.	Hq. Co.
"	7	MARTIN, JOHN G.	Sgt.	Btry B
"	7	McSWIGGAN, FRANCIS	Pvt.	Sup. Co.
"	7	MILLER, LAWRENCE M.	RegSgtMj	Hq. Co.
"	7	MITCHELL, C. VON E.	Capt.	F. & S.
"	7	PALMER, THEODORE	Mus.	Hq. Co.
"	7	PULLEN, EDWIN L.	Bugler	Hq. Co.
"	7	SOLOMON, HARRY	Pvt.	Hq. Co.
"	7	WALLACH, MAX	Mus.	Hq. Co.
"	7	WANNER, HENRY	Pvt.	Btry C
"	7	VISCO, ARTHUR	Cook	Sup. Co.
"	8	FRANKEL, PHILIP	Corp.	Hq. Co.
"	8	GOLDFINGER, BENJAMIN D.	Pvt.	Sup. Co.
"	11	MARGERO, CHARLES	Pvt.	Btry A
"	15	COOK, LEONARD L.	Pvt.	Hq. Co.
"	15	McGRANAGHAN, EDMUND B.	Pvt. 1 cl.	Hq. Co.
"	16	MONTGOMERY, CARLOS	Pvt.	Hq. Co.
Oct.	3	BURDEN, CHESTER G.	1st Lt.	Btry B.
"	3	KLOTS, ALLEN T.	1st Lt.	Hq. Co.
"	4	COSENTINO, FRANK R.	Pvt. 1 cl.	Btry C
"	4	DECKER, PHILIP	Pvt. 1 cl.	Btry C
"	4	EVANS, HARRY B.	Pvt. 1 cl.	Btry C
"	4	MENDONSA, MANUEL C.	Pvt. 1 cl.	Btry C
"	5	COX, CYRIL S.	Pvt.	Hq. Co.
"	5	FELDMAN, DAVID	Sup. Sgt.	Btry C
"	5	STREED, FRED A.	Pvt.	Btry B
"	8	SADLER, THOS. G., JR.	Pvt.	Btry D
"	10	NOLAN, BENJAMIN	Pvt. 1 cl.	Btry C
"	12	STALEY, OWEN T	Pvt. 1 cl.	Btry E
"	13	GERSTNER, HAROLD S.	Corp.	Btry A
"	13	GOOLEY, JOHN A.	Corp.	Hq. Co.
"	14	BULLEN, OSBON W.	2nd Lt.	Btry A
"	14	GORMLY, MARTIN A.	Pvt.	Btry F

Oct. 14	Schweitzer, Frank J.		Corp.	Hq. Co.
" 14	Whitman, Francis W.		Pvt.	Btry F
" 15	Stathes, Nicholas		Pvt.	Btry A
" 16	D'Andrea, Michael		Pvt. 1 cl.	Btry D
" 17	Englander, David		Pvt.	Btry B
" 17	Garros, George		Pvt.	Btry B
" 17	Gittleman, Jake		Pvt.	Btry C
" 17	Saucier, Joseph L.		Pvt.	Btry C
" 17	Stabile, Dominick		Pvt.	Btry C
" 18	Larson, Harold G.		Pvt.	Btry A
" 18	Thompson, Roy		Pvt.	Btry A
Nov. 1	Cronin, Denis J.		1st Lt.	Det. M. C.
" 2	Bloomfield, Edwin J.		Corp.	Btry C
" 2	Himmel, Benjamin		Pvt.	Btry A
" 2	Wing, Leung		Pvt.	Btry A
" 3	Graham, Charles L.		2nd Lt.	Btry C
" 3	Hanley, John J.		Pvt. 1 cl	Btry C
" 3	Johnston, Andrew G.		Pvt.	Btry C
" 4	Hayes, Hugh P.		Pvt.	Hq. Co.
" 5	Pearn, Robert		Pvt. 1 cl.	Btry C

DISTINGUISHED SERVICE CROSSES

2nd Lt. Arthur A. Robinson.   Corporal G. H. Johnson

ATHLETICS

By 2nd Lt. Osbon W. Bullen

ON THE morning of January 1st, 1919, the D Battery Soccer Team played a team from the Brigade Headquarters. The game ended in a scoreless tie. This was the beginning of athletics in the 305th Field Artillery. From that day until we started for Brest, there was always some contest under way in the Regiment. The Athletic hour which was made a part of the drill schedule helped to stimulate interest and started many men training for contests, which came later.

A Regimental Soccer League was organized and the first game played on January 6th, between Batteries B and E. Eight teams were entered in the league. The following summary shows the standing of the the teams on April 1st.

	WON	LOST	TIED	PERCENTAGE
Battery A	3	1	1	.750
" B	3	1	1	.750
" E	3	1	1	.750
" C	1	2	2	.333
" D	1	4	0	.200
Headquarters Co.	0	0	2	.000
Supply Co.	0	0	1	.000
Battery F	0	1	0	.000

The best players from these eight clubs were selected and a Regimental team was formed. This was the first team to represent the Regiment in outside competition. On Feb. 2nd we met the 304th F. A. and defeated them by a score of 3 to 1. From that time we played every available team, winning five games, tieing two, and losing two. The team was selected to represent the Division at the Le Mans Area Meet. As we defeated every team in the Division we claimed the championship of the 77th Division.

SOCCER SCORES

Feb 2	305th F A.	3
	304 F. A.	1
Feb. 15	305 F. A.	1
	306 F. A.	1
Feb. 22	305 F. A.	1
	302 Ammunition Train	0
Feb. 26	305 F. A.	0
	304 F. A.	0
Feb. 29	305 F. A.	5
	304 F. A.	0
Mar. 9	51st. Artillery Brigade	1
	305 F. A.	0
Mar. 18	305 F. A.	4
	305 Infantry	0
Mar. 22	305 F. A.	3
	307 Infantry	0
Mar. 28	35th. Division	6
	305 F. A.	0

On March 8th, a Brigade Track Meet was held at Malicorne, France. Again the 305th was victorious. The final score being:

305 F. A. 43
302 Ammunition Train 32
306 F. A. 29
304 F. A. 22

The men who won points for the 305th were:

2nd. Lieut. McKee   Pvt. Burns
Pvt. Bitzelberger   Sgt. Froedi

Pvt. Gillegan
Cpl. Gooley
Cpl. Kressin

Pvt. McLaughlin
Pvt. Monahan
Pvt. Wanner

Teams representing the 305 F. A. won the following places.

Tug of War—1st place.
Medley Relay—2nd place.
880 yard Relay—2nd place.

The Divisional Meet held on March 15th was won by the 152nd Field Artillery Brigade with a total of 55 points. Our nearest competitor was the 154th. Infantry Brigade with 45 points. The 305th F. A. won more points than any other unit in the Brigade.

305 F. A. 20
306 F. A. 16

302 Am. Tr. 16
304 F. A. 3

In this meet our point winners were

2nd. Lieut. McKee
Cpl. Dodge
Sgt. Froedi
Cpl. Gooley

Cpl. Kressin
Pvt. McLaughlin
Pvt. Monahan
Sgt. Parrette

Pvt. Wanner

At the Le Mans Area Meet which was won by the 77th Division, the 305 F. A. was represented by the following men.

Sgt. Alexander—3rd place 120 yd. High Hurdles.
Pvt. McLaughlin—1st place Medley Relay Team
Pvt. Monahan—1st place 1 mile Relay Team

The baseball season was opened on Feb. 22d by a game between the officers and enlisted men of the Regiment, which the enlisted men won 10 to 2.

A Regimental League was formed, the first game being played on Feb. 25th. Ten teams entered. The standing at the conclusion of the series was:

	WON	LOST	PERCENTAGE
Supply Co.	3	0	.1000
Battery A	5	1	.833
" C	3	1	.750
" B	1	2	.333
" D	1	2	.333
" E	1	2	.333
" F	0	2	.000
Headquarters Co.	0	1	.000
A. P. M.	0	1	.000
Medical Det.	0	1	.000

A Regimental Team was formed with Herman Ditzel of B Battery as Captain. The team played fifteen games, winning fourteen and losing one. The following games were played:

305 F. A. 5	305 F. A. 7
304 F. A. 3	304 F. A. 6
305 F. A. 9	305 F. A. 4
304 F. A. 2	51st Artillery Brigade 0
305 F. A. 3	305 F. A. 8
306 F. A. 2	103 F. A. 5

The team was sent to Le Mans to represent the Division in the Area Meet. The Black Hawks of the Le Mans Classification Camp defeated our team in a seven inning game by a score of 2 to 0.

A Divisional Baseball League was formed, opening games being played on April 1st. The 305th F. A. played and won eight games, finishing the series without a defeat. The last game with the Ammunition Train which the 305th won 4-3, decided the Division championship as neither team had lost a game up to that time.

The scores for the League games were:

April	1.	305 F. A. 6
		305 M. G. Bn. 2
Apr.	2.	305 F. A. 15
		306 M. G. Bn. 7
Apr.	3	305 F. A. 12
		302 F. S. Bn. 7
Apr.	4.	305 F. A. 15
		302 San. Tr. 5
Apr.	8.	305 F. A. 10
		308 Infantry 8
Apr.	9.	305 F. A. 9
		304 F. A. 7
Apr.	10.	305 F. A. 2
		306 F. A. 0
Apr.	11.	305 F. A. 4
		302 Ammunition Train 3.

The 305th Field Artillery were taking part in athletic activities from Jan. 1st to April 12th. In that time, our teams won the Brigade Track Meet, the Divisional Soccer Championship and Divisional Baseball Championship.

Where Wing Was Hurt
by Sergeant Lynwood G. Downs

Verpel, Nov. 2nd 1918

The march was nearing its end. Wearily the battery splashed thru the muddy streets of Verpel, across the brook and up the hill. "Column Right"—"Halt" It was an abandoned gun position. The piles of ammunition and fuses strewn around were evidences of a hasty retirement. The emplacements with trail logs intact were immediately appropriated and the platforms placed. In short order the guns were in position to open up on the retreating Bosche. Meanwhile the picket line and kitchen were being established below the hill. A fire was started and none too soon came the welcome call: "Chow's ready." And this time it was real chow—not corn willie or bully beef—but beans, rice and coffee.

Meanwhile Jerry had started evening serenade—in rapid succession shells were dropping on the nearby road but hot near enough to distract the hungry men. Suddenly the whine of an approaching shell grew louder, and before one could duck, it exploded. Sudden pandemonium—the air was full of rice, beans and mess kits—the diners lay on their faces in the mud. The cry "Anyone hurt" was followed from the picket line by "Medical man!"

The Captain hastened to the picket line and discovered that our Chinese driver, Charlie Wing, was wounded.

"Where are you hurt, Wing?" asked the Captain.

"In the kitchen," was the surprising answer.

The Response
by Sergeant Lynwood G. Downs

It was outside Fontenoy. The battery was lined up along a hedge behind a low bank. The Germans had hastily vacated the position leaving two 77s behind, but they were now attempting a stand. Shells were dropping in unpleasant proximity and the cannoneers had been ordered to seek what little protection the bank offered. Although there had been several narrow escapes, the battery had as yet not suffered, although a six-inch had exacted a large toll from the doughboys who in unbroken stream were filing past.

The phone rang and word came that artillery was needed to clean out several troublesome machine gun nests. The executive, Lt. Stribling, called to the section chiefs: "I want three volunteers from each gun crew to work the guns." Crouching low, the men ran to their posts and when the firing data arrived, not a single man was missing from his post.

A Trip to Germany
by Corporal Harry Tucker

When Regimental Headquarters moved forward from Verpel one morning Pvt. Pugh was ordered to take the motorcycle to the next stop, which they told him would be St. Piermont. He started out at 10 a. m. and before he had gone one half a kilo he had had three punctures, which kept him busy for most of the day. He reached St. Piermont at dusk, and was informed by a truck driver that Regimental Headquarters had moved to the next town. When he got to the next town an M. P. on a cross road told him they had not stopped and thinking they would surely stop at the next town, he continued for 3 kilo to a fork in the road with no sign boards. He took the right hand road and travelled about 6 kilo passing thru a little shell torn village. There was a field hospital here of the 82nd Div. where he stayed for the night and bummed supper from them. Next morning he refilled his gas & oil tank and asked for directions to the front, knowing that Headquarters would be farther front than a field hospital. He rode until 9 a.m. over a poor road full of shell holes and finally got off his machine and decided to consider himself lost. The gunfire seemed pretty close on both sides of him. It was very desolate and hilly and he sat and waited about a half hour, when a driver with a gun limber came from ahead and told him he should have taken the left hand road at the forks and also showed him a short way to get back to the forks. He took this driver's word although he had a funny feeling that maybe it wasn't right, and after going over a sort of wagon trail for 5 kilo he hit a good hard road and kept on down it. The firing didn't seem any closer and he saw a lot of aeroplanes and after passing a small village with a big brick wall he came to 3 Germans at work with shovels filling in a shell hole in the road. They stopped work and looked up amazed at him, and he thought at first that they were prisoners, but he saw no provost guard or M. P. and thought that very funny. He went on about 400 metres and in making a big turn saw on the right hand side of the road a village and the main street and saw nothing but Germans and so many that he did not need further proof that he was in German territory. Some of the Germans had packs and rifles and seemed to be ready to move or leave the town. He turned the machine around and went back the road he had come down passing the three road workers who were still staring and talking together excitedly. As he passed with the machine wide open they threw down their shovels and ran across the road and into the brush. He continued as fast as he could make the machine go thru the next village and down the good road, but did not meet a soul until about 6 kilo from the place he had seen the Germans when he was stopped by infantry from the 42nd Division. He was so scared he could hardly talk and as shells were going over head high over he did not stay long and travelled along until he ran out of gas, he built a fire and waited 2 hours for a truck which gave him gas and a loaf of bread. It was nearly dark so he stayed right there and didn't camouflage himself or machine as he was so scared he said he couldn't be more so. Next morning he ran into the 304th ration dump and as they wouldn't feed him on account of divisional orders he got directions and found Regimental Headquarters off to the right.

Observation
by Captain T. C. Thayer

In order to learn the sector that our Battalion was to be called upon to cover, I spent some time at the O. P of the 1st Battalion of the 16th F. A. on the hill just North of Les Près Farm during the day upon which the first two of our guns were to be put into position. As the work was entirely new to me I was directed to remain at the O. P. for the night so as to familiarize myself with the rocket signals for barrage, and the methods employed in locating the flashes of enemy guns.

The O. P. had evidently been chosen when the enemy was still on the move back, following the American thrust at Château Thierry, for it did not offer sufficient cover, nor did it have an approach hidden from enemy view. With the stabilizing of the lines the Hun had begun to search the area for observation posts and had become convinced that the activity which he noticed along the line of low brush was associated with the gun flashes which were nightly visible over the crest of the hill behind. He had decided that it was well worth while to devote a little attention now and then to discourage the use of this location for the purpose of observation, and the observers were beginning to realize this. When meals or more interesting targets did not occupy him Fritz would drop a few in the vicinity, and with better adjustment as he became more practised the prospect was not inviting.

From the series of little trenches, extending along at intervals for perhaps a hundred metres, constituting the Battery and Battalion O. Ps it was possible to view the terrain immediately to the front for a kilometre and a half. Then came an abrupt drop into the valley of the Vesle with nothing visible till the sharp rise of the far bank with scattering woods and a broad plateau reached back to Perles about due north and Blanzey to the northeast. Immediately down the slope was a mass of battered masonry—what had once been the town of Mount St. Martin.

Some time after darkness had settled down for good the Hun began an intense artillery fire upon our infantry lines along the Vesle bottom. It was not long before our guns were replying in kind, apparently putting on a greater concentration and continuing some time after the Hun had reduced his rate. While our fire was still going on some gas shelling began on the woods which lay 100 metres to our left and ran down the hillside toward the valley. As the wind was carrying in our direction, we donned our masks. The town was next given a drenching, the fire continuing for some time at irregular intervals.

The lieutenant on duty had been in communication with his Battalion Commander from time to time on the telephone reporting the appearance of rockets and the situation as indicated by the firing. We were suddenly aroused by the beam of a searchlight off to the northwest over in enemy territory. It was almost immediately followed by a terrific artillery fire sweeping the slope between our post and Mount St. Martin and apparently drawing back on the town itself. Just after the initial outburst the phone buzzed, the major reporting that the Battery Commander whose guns were located just over the crest to our rear had seen a figure outlined against the sky and noticed the flash of a light as if a signal were being given the enemy. A hasty consultation followed and Lieutenant Davidson slipped out of the trench and was lost in the night.

It was some five minutes later that a faint report sounded in the distance. Some noise in the fallen branches out in front of us attracted our attention at this moment. I challenged. A dark figure faltered up and between pauses for breath told me that he was an infantryman and that he and four or five comrades had fled from the artillery fire that had just engulfed the town. He had no idea where he was nor what had become of his comrades in the darkness. All that he did know was that his company had been relieved and on the way back from the lines had halted in the town for rest. All at once Hell-fire had been let loose beyond the town and had seemed to be everywhere when they had tried to escape as it drew back on them. I dispatched him at once to the P.C. of the Battalion Commander to report the circumstances.

It was some time before Lt. Davidson returned. He had seen flashes and the outline of a man. At his challenge the man had run. His shot had missed the mark. His search had developed nothing.

As the hours dragged on toward dawn and we recalled the incidents of the night we came to very definite conclusions. The enemy was aware that the relief was to take place and had laid down his fire in the valley while the relief was going on. Knowing that the withdrawal would in all probability be made through Mount St. Martin or the woods west of the town he had saturated the woods and the village with gas so that the progress would be held up. The flash signal from the hill immediately to our rear had announced the arrival of our troops in the town. The searchlight that had swept the sky had been a signal for the delivery of the death dealing fire.

It was toward 5:30 the following afternoon that I made my way from Les Près Farm up the slope of the hill past the two batteries of 75s which were set side by side on its bare face, only disguised by the flat green nets stretched over them. The hillside was pockmarked with shell holes. A telephone wire wrapped at frequent intervals with taping ran forward toward the woods, mute evidence of the work the linesmen were doing, and telling the story of the hail of splinters that the gunners endured to serve their pieces.

Followed at some distance by Corporal Tucker with the telescope and Shackman who was to operate the telephone I moved across the open to the edge of the woods and worked east along the thin brush which ran out to the O. P. The Lieutenant who had been on duty did not waste any time in gathering up his instruments and turning over the freedom of the little observing trench to us. Hardly had he left with his men when the slow twist of a "150" brought us to a crouching position in the shallow earthwork. There was a pause of perhaps thirty seconds and another had cleared us by a hundred metres. Corporal Tucker and I did not stand on ceremony but huddled together in the deeper end of the trench under overhead cover consisting of some light branches over which a shelter half was stretched. The next ten minutes was a succession of deafening crashes which rocked the ground and sent splinters humming overhead, each preceded by the sickening whine of the projectile, and a moment of awful suspense when our hearts sank and asked whether that was to be the last.

At length a pause came and we began to breath more freely with the thought that he had finished the allotment for this time. A call to the adjoining trench assured us that no one had been hurt and we disentangled ourselves and straightened our muscles a bit. I gasped with dismay as I saw one of our linesmen spring out from the next trench to mend a break that the shelling had caused somewhere along the line. Warning was too late, and before he had cleared us by a minute the roar of another explosion rent the air. A second blast not fifteen seconds later told us that the show was on in earnest this time. The shells were now drawing closer and closer and clods of earth began to drop with a thud on the ground about us and to strike the frail cover over our heads. The air seemed to be momentarily compressed giving a sense of friction with the whirling of each shell as it passed. Closer and closer they came. At last one struck with a terrifying crash tearing away sections of the brush and sending a deluge of earth and splinters in all directions. A dash after the next one struck seemed the only hope.

The buzz of the flying fragments was still in the air when we cleared the trench and started madly across the open. A flying leap found me in a shell hole as the whine and blast of another filled the air. Before I realized it, I was up and off again my only thought being to get to the flank. A dash of 100 feet and I landed in another crater huddled against the near edge with my helmet and a little entrenching shovel—goodness knows where I got it—protecting my head and neck. The regular whir and blast continued, now here now there and as the splinters hummed over me, I reflected in a cold sweat upon the probable error of the "150" howitzer, and experienced with bitter irony the practical demonstration of dispersion.

After what seemed an interminable period the bombardment came to an end. For about five minutes I lay still lest a move precipitate another deluge. Not knowing what fate my comrades had met with I began to call and whistle in the hope of determining where they might be before I made a move. Getting no reply, I crept out and started cautiously back in the direction of the O. P. to find that my telephone operator was at his post and the line again in operation. The scant fringe of brush had been torn and uprooted all about; the ground was gouged up and everywhere were clods of sticky clay that clung to the shoes. Crawling through the tangle of fallen branches, I reached what had been my neighbour's trench. The telescope blown against the side had a hole where a splinter had cut through and carried away the glass. Blankets and coats which had been lying on the ground were cut into shreds as though an axe had been used on them.

A terrible sense of depression seized me as I came to the edge of the trench. Death had claimed one of the number that had been with me but a few moments before. Perhaps Private Silber died thinking he had played but an empty role in the great struggle, yet it was his death that taught me the prime necessity of utmost caution when undertaking observation work and led me to an immediate decision to abandon the place. What the price might have been, had we continued to remain there, one can only conjecture. Certain it is, that the Him shelled the place unmercifully long after we had left it.

Dusk had now settled, and with the prospects of spending the night amid surroundings so desolate, it was a relief to learn over the telephone that Corporal Tucker had escaped unharmed and would join me again in a short time. I began to bethink myself of where we might move to. It was perfectly evident that to attempt to maintain an O. P. in the immediate vicinity would be suicidal, but no move could be thought of while we must keep our watch for barrage signals during the night. As the hours wore on, the Hun began to deliver gas on the woods to our left and the air was filled with a pungent odour as of mouldy hay. It was two hours before we dared to remove our masks and breathe freely again. The only possibility for re-establishing ourselves, however, seemed to be in the front edge of this very block of woods. I directed the telephone detail to report before daybreak with wire prepared to lay a line to such a place as I could find there. Before leaving, Corporal Tucker and I re-arranged the branch camouflage and improvised a fake telescope and figure out of some white birch branches and the tattered blankets in the hope that Fritz would think the place still occupied.

The thin mist of early morning was beginning to dissipate when we completed the transfer. A shallow dugout about five by seven feet located just inside the wood had been abandoned by one of the regiments that had been relieved and I decided to employ it. The roof offered protection from splinters to be sure, but unfortunately the foot or so of earth was supported upon stringers not more than three or four inches through and could only be expected to cave in with anything like a direct hit. A screen of brush about four feet in height immediately in front of the woods' edge and blending in with the surrounding underbrush allowed the setting up of our telescope. As the observer must sit entirely exposed to fire it was a case of waiting for the first one to strike and trusting that it hit at a respectable distance. After it had struck you made your decision as to whether you had best retire to the dugout, or would try your luck with a few more.

During our stay on the Vesle, this O, P. was in operation day and night 24 hours every day. Small details of men, when shelling did not prevent, were almost constantly at work in making the place as safe as could be done with the means at hand. Eventually observation was had from a wooden box, about the size of a telephone booth, which was sunk in the ground to a depth of about five feet and had a prow shaped front of ½ inch steel protruding perhaps eight or ten inches above the earth's surface. From the rear a narrow six foot trench ran back a ways, and, turning squarely, extended on to the dugout in which we slept. Under severe shelling we would leave the dugout and crouch in the bottom of the trench.

Movement visible in German territory was almost nil. Now and then a man might be seen walking about, but seldom more than two were ever together. Our guns were registered almost daily on the dull grey walls of the once peaceful village of Perles, and fired on batteries of the enemy that we picked up under favouring conditions by their smoke. One day I was much interested by observing half a dozen horse drawn ambulances that passed along the roads at intervals during the day. I learned with satisfaction that we had delivered a gas attack on the left. Had I at this time been initiated, as I later was, into some of the methods of waging war that the Hun considered legitimate, I would have called for fire upon these wagons.

Barrage calls by rocket were frequently relayed back from the O.P. to the batteries by Very pistols, fired from behind our hill, a man running back through the woods to do it. This was some times our only means of reaching the guns quickly for wires were cut at all hours of the day and night. Projectors were also set up and used for this purpose.

One of the most glorious exhibitions of the obliterating power of the artillery came on the afternoon preceding the night upon which the Hun withdrew to the Aisne. For two days previous we had picked up movements of troops on the heights across the Aisne, fully fifteen kilometres away, and had seen large numbers of horses grazing. Toward four o'clock our "155s" opened up on the town of Perles and on the region to the east and west. With the burst of each shell a great cloud of dust would rise up and crawl along westward. At times, the town was lost completely in the blanket which extended for more than five hundred metres, and rose to a height of a couple of hundred. Zone fire over an area west of Blanzey drubbed the ground like heavy rain drops. All at once a great burst of flame shooting skyward recorded a direct hit on an ammunition dump. It was not long before the fire was creeping along the ground and apparently licking up new stores as it went. At least two hours elapsed before the flames subsided and died away. We found later when we moved forward into this region that two Battery positions had been swept by the fire, their camouflage burned away and a great deal of their ammunition destroyed. Over on our left, north of *Bazoches* another dump went up under a terrific downpour of the "how's."

During the night, the Hun announced his retirement by fires started for the most part toward early morning. It was a strange and uncanny feeling to be able to move about with freedom and to view our infantry in a thin line working across the open the other side of the Vesle in the direction of Perles. Our barrage line was well forward and we adjusted with semi steel shell at a range of 8,500 metres. The following morning we picked up our instruments and moved forward. It was really quite a blow to leave our little *Gibraltar* for it had been our home for many a long hour and had protected us from a hail of wicked splinters.

The Battalion P.C. was now located near a sand pit some distance down the valley from Blanzey and I was directed to go forward to reconnoitre a new O.P. which would cover the region between *Oeuilly* on the west and *Cuisy farm* on the east. My first effort did not give me the sweep required and Lieutenant Colonel Easterday—then our major—arriving on the scene with his Battery Commanders on reconnaissance of positions forward, started me off in the direction of Serval.

Dusk was coming on when I reached the cross roads 500 metres from the end of the valley in which the town lay. It would have been folly to go out on the bare hill that I expected to get observation from for the Hun was pounding the tar out of the town and the hill itself was receiving a full share. For some time we watched the powdered dust rise from the battered ruins. When the fire had slackened I sent Braun, my telephone man, back to start the laying of a wire to a point which I designated. Michel and I waited a while longer and then began our reconnaissance for a suitable place to establish ourselves. A couple of battery emplacements from which the enemy had retired were in the vicinity but offered no view of our sector. We extended our search over the entire face of the hill only to find it barren of possibilities. It had now become too dark to warrant a continuance of our efforts on unfamiliar ground with our own line only a short distance away. We seated ourselves in a ditch at a road crossing and awaited the arrival of the wiremen. A misunderstanding resulted in our remaining here all night during which time the Hun tried out every form of gas he had in stock and put down a barrage that dropped splinters in the road near us. Expecting the detail to arrive at any time, we fought off sleep, though it required a tremendous effort. When it became light enough for me to make my way about I set out for the town on the chance that I might find some possibility there. Working along the brush that fringed the top of the valley, I reached a point from which I could see a house that was still intact and which stood out from the other buildings like a lighthouse on the nose of the hill. Exercising extreme caution, I dodged from cover to cover until I got within a stone's throw. Then I had to move directly across the open. A hasty examination of the interior developed the fact that we could get excellent observation, that it had good walls and that it had a roof. As the rear door by which we must enter was opposite a window I hung some old clothing, found in the attic, over a wire in such a way as to break the light and prevent our being outlined against the sky as we passed in and out. This done, I began to look for some stairway leading down to a cellar. There was none, and with visibility now sufficiently good to permit the enemy to pick up any movements outside. I did not dare go out the front door and down the flight of steps to carry my investigation further. I wasted no time in retiring from the house and making my way back to the little shelter in which I had left Michel.

Still in doubt as to why the wire had not come we separated and plodded back to Blanzey by different routes so as to meet up with the detail if it were on the way. Arriving at the Battalion P. C. I found orders awaiting me. I was to establish an O. P. immediately and proceed to the registration of the guns.

The thought of laying a wire out to Serval over the face of an open hill upon which the enemy had direct observation was a bit flabbergasting. Furthermore, the fact that my observatory was on a point which projected into the enemy line and exposed to view from two sides due to the bow to the southeast that the line took, would simply mean that to carry a wire there in the day time would give the place away at the outset. "Orders is Orders" and in a couple of hours I was leading a procession from Blanzey that was telling out wire behind me. Lt. Hoar, just arrived with the regiment, and Corporal Rice who was to act as telephonist followed me at intervals. We took a course as direct as possible owing to the length of the run and upon reaching the valley we crouched and crawled along, keeping close to the cover afforded by the brush on the very edge of the precipitate side. Reaching a point protected by a heavy growth of tree tops, we set aside our instruments and equipment and waited for the linesmen to come up with us.

Kind circumstance had a surprise in store for me. The run proving longer than was anticipated, it was necessary to send back for more wire. The wire available had suffered under the service at the Vesle and required considerable testing to locate leaks before it carried through. While we were lying there, the Hun began to shell the town below us and to deliver some scattered shots where he had picked up the movements of our linesmen. We were still a couple of hundred metres from the house which we could see from our location, but I did not propose to make the move across the open to it until the line was in operation as far as we had come. It was, to say the least, somewhat disquieting to have the Hun now register a battery of "105s" on a tree which stood a couple of hundred metres behind our observatory to be. As the rounds whined over we passed judgment as to whether they were going to be "shorts" or "overs." Some of the fragments sang over our heads and kept us on the anxious seat, but none was labelled for us as it turned out.

At length the line was in operation and the decision must be made as to whether the parade to the house would be staged immediately or delayed till dusk, which was rapidly coming on. I decided upon the latter.

The wire to complete the run proved insufficient, and Corporal Rice with Sergeant Hickey who had come up with rations, went out in the darkness to salvage some German wire. Lt. Hoar and I immediately began to search for some place to which we might retire in the event of shelling. Passing down the flight of steps from the front door to the ground level of the front of the house we found that the room under the main house was a cow barn. Feeling our way toward a dark passage in the far wall, we descended a flight of steps to another level. Here I lighted a match and examined our surroundings. The room we found ourselves in had evidently been employed by the Germans as a dugout for there was straw on the ground and a chair or two. A smaller room separated from the main one by a wall had some 20 or 30 unused "150s" and "155s" lying on the floor, but our attention was chiefly taken up with a shell that was lying in the centre of the main room. It was placed in a very suspicious position, was fused, and had an oblong brown box resting against its nose.

The possibility of having the house blown up from the explosion of this device had no appeal for me and I knew that our work would be doubly taxing if we had this possibility hanging over us. A few minutes later I was outside holding the end of a wire that ran down the passageway and around the nose of the shell. A moment of suspense, and I returned to find that I had succeeded in pulling the shell away from the brown box without causing it to detonate. I made two trips, throwing the box over the cliff and depositing the shell some distance up the street where it would do us no harm. We cut a hole through the floor the following morning and constructed a ladder which permitted our descending to the cellar without being observed.

I will never understand how this house failed to be hit more than once during the next nine days for shells of all calibres struck all about us and splinters even cut through the roof. We slept, that is the two of us not on duty, within six feet of a window facing the direction of enemy fire, but they never got the grove. Rations came up at night, and water was carried from a water spout down in the town, that was regularly shelled as a likely place by the Hun. No one was permitted to approach or leave during daylight. One night a German dog with a bell on its collar could be heard running along in the street below us. It was possible to see our infantry outposts a few hundred metres way, though they were not aware of our presence.

Perhaps, one of the most amusing experiences I ever had was my night and day with the Italian officer who came up to take over this O. P. My French consists of the salvaged variety that the average American soldier has to offer, and my efforts to convey information as to where to look for barrage signals and the points that we used to adjust fire on, convulsed him. Thanks to his ready wit and intelligence, most of my attempts ended successfully. I hated to turn over such a Hell-hole to anybody, for the morning of the day upon which he came up, it had been necessary to evacuate one of my men who had been wounded by a gas shell fragment, and this could not fail to result in the O. P. being spotted and destroyed if the Hun was wide awake. I fled from the place as if a fiend were following me, when the time had arrived for me to go.

The towering oak that served as the O. P. at the outset of the Argonne Show September 26, was only necessary for a day. My next move was to the 307th Infantry which was cleaning up the Fontainaux Charmes above La Hara-zee and starting into the heavily wooded region in the area back of the German trench system. Observation of fire was practically impossible, and although I went forward to the infantry front line, and even beyond it, in an effort to obtain information that would enable us to fire more effectively, it proved almost useless. On one occasion when Lieuts. Bullen and Burden and I made up the party, we worked well out in advance of our own line in hopes of being able to observe the effectiveness of a rolling barrage which they were to follow up. Sniping fire from enemy machine guns stopped us and for a quarter of an hour during which time we had to work back across a twenty foot band of barbed wire and dodge across a wood road that he had covered with a machine gun, it was a toss up as to whether or not we wouldn't be picked off by our own people as they came up.

Although I extended my search over all of the high ground in the vicinity and did manage to find a couple of places from which some view could be had, observation of fire in the Argonne Forest proved a failure. The first real sweep I obtained, was from a beech tree which was located on the summit of the hill north of the Moulin de Charlevaux near where Major Whittlesey's battalion had been cut off. Although this was out some two or three hundred metres beyond our outposts and offered an excellent target for snipers, Fritz either was not in the vicinity or else thought he would wait until I established myself. For 15 or 20 minutes, I looked off to the northwest to where the woods ended and I could see German guns along fences in open fields firing upon the French Division upon our left. Before I was able to get a wire laid to this point, our infantry was on the move again, and I was trudging along behind them.

Our infantry was now roughly drawn up along a line before Grand Prè on the west and St. Juvin on the east. I was directed to go forward to Chevieres for the purpose of ascertaining the condition of the roads and bridges for the passage of artillery across the River Aire. In order to obtain a view of the crossing, it was necessary to work down toward the river in advance of our line, but as was so often the case, Fritz did not prevent an individual reconnaissance, though he probably would have shot up a squad of men if they had attempted to show themselves anywhere near there a few minutes later.

The attack on Grand Prè, on the 15th of October, 1918, found me leading a string of 8 runners down across the open toward our infantry line which was dug in along the railroad embankment. Machine gun bullets striking in the grass around us brought us to the ground, and a burst of shell fire drove us back into the woods we had just emerged from. I later succeeded in reaching the embankment with two of my men, but it was only at dusk that a crossing of the river was effected and the companies began to feed over in single file. During the night, while the 307th was engaged in house to house fighting in the town and we could hear machine gun fire rattling intermittently, the officers of the 312th Infantry of the 78th Division arrived at the shelter by the railroad which was the first Battalion P. C. and preparations for relieving were begun. In the morning, I made my way across while the 312th was attacking and reported to their Major who had taken for his P. C. a cellar which had been similarly employed by one of the Company commanders of the 307th, the night before.

Owing to the relief taking place before the 307th had been able to clean up the nose of high ground in the north-eastern section of the town, the Hun was able to snipe and harass from here most effectively. This, together with the splendid observation he had on the whole region from the heights to the north, made it possible for him to employ his artillery to cover the river crossings and the flat-land of the broad valley so thoroughly that it was well nigh impossible for anyone to get across, much less evacuate the wounded. When I pulled out late the following afternoon, the town was receiving a terrific shelling from the northeast and I couldn't help recalling my departure from the house in Serval and experiencing much the same feeling of foreboding for the fine fellows I had just left.

After ten days out of the line our guns took up positions near Cornay and I went forward to St. Juvin to reconnoitre a forward O. P. for the attack staged Nov. 1. The place was reeking with gas and the bridges thrown over the river were under heavy fire, particularly that which must be used for the passage of our guns. Our infantry had not yet relieved, and the 82nd Division which was in the line had a Battalion P. C. in a building down the street running east from the church. The Major informed me that observation could best be obtained from the church steeple but as I evinced no enthusiasm for the project he added that it was possible to see a bit from the trenches their line occupied some 200 metres from the church. Going out with a runner I found the men occupying an old German system, shallow and pretty mussy. It was getting hazy and as I couldn't get the view I wanted, I went out about a hundred metres beyond some loose wire that had been put out. Fortunately, the Hun was some distance away, could not see very distinctly, and his aim was a trifle short, so I made my way back to the town, and after investigating the church decided it met my requirements.

During the day of the attack, it was possible to see Hun activity to the southeast of Champigneulle, which our infantry was working on, but due to the fact that the exact location of our line was in doubt, fire was not permitted upon one nest that raked the bare slopes of the approach and put a withering fire on our men when they attempted to advance. When the break came the following morning, there was a rapid forward movement to Thenorgues and the next day to the crest south of Oches. It was here for the first time that I noticed white flags flying from the towns. Activity on the roads leading into Stonne, which stood on a crest 8 kilos to the north, and some smoke now and then from buildings led me to believe that we were close on the enemy's tail, and I called for fire from the heavies. Fortunately, they had not yet pulled into position, due to the heavy going and the congestion on the roads, for, as I learned the next day from a French civilian, the white flags indicated the presence of civilians.

Machine gun pits hastily dug in the face of the hill opposite us, allowed of our "75s" executing some telling fire, and I took especial delight in directing the fire of one of our own machine guns upon some of the Bosches as they retired under the shelling. The fun was not all for me, however, for later on when I endeavoured to adjust our fire on the Polka Farm lying out on the forward slope under a couple of low fir trees, Fritz got the range pretty well with a sniping "77" and spanked the ground just above me quite successfully with machine gun fire.

Stonne was being shelled when I entered the town. It was a pathetic sight to see the wretched old men and women with the little barefoot children just evacuated by the Huns from around Sedan, all crowded together in the church in a frenzy of fear as they experienced for the first time the crashing horror of shell fire. By good fortune one of my men was of French descent and we succeeded in persuading the people to scatter through the buildings of the town in the hope of reducing the casualties. One direct hit on the church might have precipitated a terrible catastrophe.

Raucourt welcomed us with open heart, and it was almost impossible to persuade the people to take money for the heavy German black bread that they doled out to us with a layer of plum-coloured apple butter. Only to keep as a souvenir of the arrival of the Americans could they be brought to the point of accepting it.

Our guns went into position east of Haracourt and we set up a telescope on a commanding hill overlooking Remilly and the far side of the Meuse, after an attempt to establish an O. P. in the church there had resulted in two hits. Something was in the air, for we didn't receive the usual orders to pick up targets and fire on them, but rather instructions were to record all information of this nature for future information if called for. When, at night, I heard the rumbling of heavy traffic on the roads across the River, but was told that we were not to fire upon it, I became an optimist myself, and joined in the speculations of the hour.

As the hands of my watch crept on toward 11 a.m., that memorable morning of November 11th, I could not help but look back over the vista of the past months and marvel at the enduring loyalty to The Cause that had characterized every man with whom I had come in contact. If it had not been for the pluck and spirit that thought nothing of the cost, so long as it was a job to be done, I doubt if lots of us would be here today, for there is nothing like knowing the other fellow is absolutely sure to deliver, to stiffen a bowing back.

A word for the fellow who carries the rifle—though perhaps I was something of a doughboy myself. After sitting in on the going up through the Argonne Forest with its machine gun nests and barbed wire placed with all the craft of the evil one himself, I am proud to take off my hat to the men who could "carry on" through all of it and then with a black night and rain to boot, had the drive to "carry through" and snatch Grand Prè from a very unwilling Hun.

As for the fellows who rode the barking guns,—perhaps Fritz is the best man to apply to—for I only saw them as they went and didn't see them as they came. We'll let it go at that, for we of the artillery will stand on the record of our infantry well realizing that there's nothing like the crackle of your own guns to put pep in the old carcass when the going's rough.

A Memorable Forty-Eight Hours
by Private John R. Egerton

The date of September 5th, 1918, and the name of St. Martin brings very vivid memories to my mind, for it was on that date and from the village of St. Martin that I saw the beginning of the first complete advance of the Seventy-Seventh Division on the so-called Fismes Front.

Together with three other men, I had been stationed for three weeks in the village of St. Martin doing observation work for the First Battalion of the 305th Field Artillery. These weeks had been strenuous ones for us, as during that time the Germans seemed possessed with the idea that a portion of our army was located in this village, and so shelled it continuously.

Had you walked through the deserted streets to the end of the village, and then through an entrance in a stone wall surrounding what had once been a well kept garden, you would have seen through the grey mists of the morning, two figures huddled closely together in the farthest corner of the wall, one with his eyes peering anxiously over the top of the wall and the other standing by with his telephone in readiness. You might have thought that nothing could be seen by these men, but you would have been mistaken, for from this point our entire sector was under observation, and record of every flare and rocket was immediately transmitted by 'phone to headquarters some distance away.

As day began to dawn these men, realizing their night's vigil was over, and finding, as was most always the case in the early morning, that visibility was poor because of the mist in the valley, rushed to the centre of the garden and rapidly descended a flight of stone steps which led to an old wine cellar. At this point I was somewhat rudely awakened (for we could sleep even with shells bursting around us) and hearing the familiar words, "Hurry up, men, we must have breakfast before the haze lifts in the valley and we can observe the enemy again," I arose, and prepared for our meal.

Up came our floor, a much walked on board which, when placed on two Chippendale chairs, formed our table. This was then covered with linen of newspaper quality, and a can filled with white phlox from the garden above us formed the centre decoration. A brass candlestick at either end of the table furnished just enough light to enable us to eat and yet hide our bearded and unclean faces. An assortment of china of the mess kit variety completed the scene. This began our day.

From that time on, it was a busy day. It seemed as if all Hell had been let loose, for the Huns were shelling not only St. Martin but every point around us, and we were not only getting the shells that were intended for us but also those that fell short of their targets. Our telephone line was broken by shells more than a dozen times that day, and we were forced to repair same both under fire and aeroplane observation.

Our greatest troubles were always during the three or four hours after dusk, as it was at that time that our supply trains went down to the trenches, and our observation post, located as it was at the very intersection of the two most travelled roads, received the full benefit of the fire that a cross road always attracts. We had educated ourselves not to mind the six inch shells and so called "minnewefers," but the "Whizz bangs" were always a constant terror to us, for hardly would we hear the report of the gun before the shell would be upon us, and many times we had miraculous escapes from their bursts.

As night drew near on the 4th day of September, the shelling became more furious than ever, and we were forced many times to seek for the period of a few seconds a more substantial shelter than the crumbly rock wall behind which we usually stood. It was a remarkably clear night and we could see many miles of the battle front. Up until about nine o'clock we had been listening to the music of German shells, but not long after that time our batteries began to fire a seemingly continuous barrage. Towards midnight the enemy firing became less vigorous, and in fact almost ceased with the exception of a few long range guns. We began to observe flares here and there, and before long the sky was a vivid red. What did it mean? Were the Huns retreating and burning their supplies, or were our men touching Uncle Sam's matches to their ammunition dumps? Both things were true, but our batteries were the cause of the greater number of the flares, and we could not help from doing a little silent cheering at our posts.

The firing continued for the greater part of the night but morning dawned upon a practically strange country, for the firing had ceased on both sides, with the exception of a few stray shots, and the silence was almost appalling, coming as it did after the din of the night before. For the first time since we had been at the post, we viewed our outlook from the outside of the wall and marvelled that we could stand there without attracting enemy fire.

Before noon the fields were swarming with our troops of the reserve infantry, advancing to occupy the newly won territory. What a difference a few hours had made. Only the night before found men cautiously making their way through the grass to the trenches, each with a serious yet determined look on his face, while not twenty four hours later more of their comrades were traversing the same route in a care free manner.

We remained at our posts all day, but all we could observe was line upon line of our men travelling onward. The roads were getting more and more congested, and at dusk as we stood at the gate we could see nothing but a continued procession likened as it were to the Crusaders of old, all pressing forward each man with but one objective in view.

That night in our little French wine cellar, where we had previously sat in the dark and listened to the bursting shells above us, we were visited by the Commanding Officer of our regiment, and heard these words "I shall be at the Hotel de Fismes tonight" which, as he sent them over the telephone, reminded us at that time of Caesar's famous message *"We came, we saw, we conquered!"*

Surely these forty-eight hours were memorable.

The Accompanying Gun
by 1st Lt. John R. Mitchell

I have hunted sparrows and frogs with an air rifle when a youngster, and some larger game with a shot gun and rifle, but for an all-around sporting proposition to those interested I can recommend hunting Bosche with a 75mm gun. You can have all the thrills of an ordinary day's shooting. You get up very early in the morning. You find that your careful arrangements for breakfast have all miscarried. You tramp all day, sometimes getting a shot and sometimes not. It usually rains. All your superior officers, from the generals down, cuss you out for being where you are, and for not being where you are not. I may say in passing that a General as a rule rarely notices a battery, but a pirate gun and its hapless commander are never overlooked. However, if you can arrange things so as not to arrive at any one point at the same moment as a Bosche shell, it is a reasonably happy and healthy life.

About eleven o'clock on the night of November 4th I was awakened from a beautiful dream, that I had never been a hero and joined the army, by the following conversation on the telephone:

"Yes, we have Mitchell with us from 'E' Battery."

"Yes, he is a 1st Lt."

"I think he will do, anyway, he is the only thing we have in the way of a first lieutenant."

"Just a moment until I get a pencil."

"All ready, sir."

"One gun, a kilometre of wire, 200 rounds of ammunition, a G. S. Cart."

"Yes, sir."

"Yes, sir."

"Yes, sir."

"To report to Col. Sheldon, 307th Infantry, at Oches, at 5:15 a.m., November 5th."

"Very good, sir."

That "very good" certainly did not apply to me, for I was very comfortable, thank you, just where I was, and at that moment my idea of a good time was not going out on a pirate gun expedition. So when Capt. Ravenel turned to me, with a smile that a man from the warm depths of a bedding roll always gives to another man who is to be routed out forthwith, and said, "I've a little job for you," I just naturally cussed the army and the Bosche.

We were on the road at 3:00 a. m., and reported as per schedule. Upon arriving at Oches I was told to take up a position to fire on some machine guns on the northern outskirts of Oches. We hauled our guns up on top of a hill behind the town, and prepared to make things unpleasant for Mr. Bosche. Unfortunately, the machine gunners departed with the night, and we duplicated the action of the Duke of York. . . .

Who had ten thousand men,
He marched them up the hill
And marched them down again.

As the Bosche had very considerately blown up the only bridge out of Oches, I managed to get some food and rest for my men and horses. At 1:00 o'clock the bridge was finished and to our great satisfaction we were the first wheeled vehicles over and after the Bosche. By night we had caught up with our advanced infantry at Stonne.

The next morning the infantry beat us out. When an infantryman gets up in the morning all he does is just that and he is ready to move. Horses, unlike the infantry have to be fed in accordance with G. O., A. E, F., G. O., Hq. 77th Div., and G. O., 152nd F. A. Brigade, which all takes time, and then harnessed and hitched.

The next time I take out an accompanying gun I am going to apply for a tank, for the road between La Besace and Raucourt would have given an energetic tank a good morning's exercise. The Germans had blown holes in the road, completely destroying it, and making cross-country riding and driving a necessary accomplishment.

The commander of the advanced battalion of the 307th Infantry, which I was supporting, was a most elusive person that morning. He had been reported to me to be in several different places at the same time, which, though that regiment was accomplishing the seemingly impossible, I was loathe to believe. To settle the matter I rode ahead, leaving my gun to follow. As I rode along the La Besace-Raucourt Road I met several parties returning, wounded, which indicated that I might do some work shortly. Immediately south of Flaba I met General Price, commanding the 154th Brigade, and Col. Sheldon, of the 307th Infantry. Word had just come back that our advance was delayed by stubborn machine gun action from points southwest and southeast of Raucourt.

In my precarious existence as a lieutenant I have had a variety of jobs, but never before had I been called upon to act as a Brigade Commander. True, my force consisted of but one gun, but for this one engagement I represented the artillery, and we had all the elements of a regular battle. The general simulated the action of the aforesaid machine guns by his questions of: "How long before you can fire?"

"How long do you want to fire?"

"How much do you want to fire?"

Three seconds is no proper time for much mental gymnastics, but I had to beat the next question. We were to open fire at 1:45 p.m. on the point southwest of Raucourt for fifteen minutes, then shift for fifteen minutes to the second point, southeast of Raucourt Immediately upon the lifting of our fire the infantry were to advance.

All I had to do was to get back to my gun, put the gun in position and lay it, compute the data, find an O.P. where I could see and fire; and I had forty-five minutes to do it in. I don't remember exactly how we did it, but we did. It took a kilometre of wire and all my wind to establish that O.P. Capt. Pike, of the 305th F.A., then liaison officer with General Price, contributed very great physical, mental and moral support. Our range was three thousand metres, and therefore there was not a chance to see the target from near the gun. My "P-T" training failed me, for there never is a convenient steeple or "the flagpole on Division Hill" around when you want to use them. So on my way back to the gun, I prayed for a goniometer, the *alpha* and *omega* of modern artillery. We have all dreamed of some nice kind old gentleman, casually presenting one with a million dollars or some other little thing like that, or of an inspecting officer saying something is good, but if that ever happens to me it will be nothing compared to my feelings when at the gun I found Lt. Hoar with a goniometer out on an advanced reconnaissance for the 305th F.A. To be strictly correct, I saw that goniometer and rather vaguely took in the lieutenant.

The miraculous continued, for our first shot dropped just about where we wanted it. From the O.P. we could not see the machine gunners, but we could see our infantry waiting under cover of the crest behind which the machine gunners were operating. With sweeping fire we walked across the area indicated by the co-ordinates furnished and then decreased the range, to be sure of a bracket. At the end of fifteen minutes the fire was shifted to the second target, and the operation repeated. It was a great moment when our fire shifted and we could see our infantry go over the crest, apparently without resistance. That is a satisfaction an artilleryman rarely gets.

As to the direct effect of the fire I have had reports varying from a direct hit to scaring the Bosche to death. My own opinion is that the Bosche decided he was in a rather unhealthy neighbourhood and executed a typical German "successful operation," worthy of his high command.

My gun was in position immediately behind one of the German mine craters on the road, and as he was shelling quite heavily on our right, and now that the party was over, I was tremendously interested in getting on and away from behind that crater, for I guessed the Bosche would shell that part of the road as soon as he thought wheeled material would be on it in the hope of catching someone held up by the crater. As a matter of fact, I guessed correctly, as he did drop a few there before we left; fortunately, however, with no more effect than to cut our telephone line and to cause us to do some prompt ducking. My total losses consisted of a pair of field glasses and a raincoat. These I had left forward of the gun position, and upon inquiring from some men near where I had been as to whether they had seen them, they replied, "No, but we have seen a General and a couple of Colonels hereabouts." I never quite determined whether that was an explanation, or merely a bit of information.

About five o'clock that afternoon we rolled into Rau-court. There had been demonstrations when our infantry came in just before us, but when those liberated French civilians saw once more their beloved *soixante-quinze* their joy knew no bounds, and we had a triumphal procession. We could not understand their French, but we had a very good idea of their intentions when we saw the plates of bread and jam they had for us. The men decided that this was the place to stay for life, but as the infantry had gone on our job was to go on, too. So, after ten minutes' rest, we moved on to Harraucourt, a rather unmilitary looking outfit, with jam inside and out, but satisfied with the world. At Harraucourt the bread and jam operation was repeated with the addition of other food and beds for men and horses. Our troubles were not yet over, for the G. S. cart was pressed into service as the only wheeled vehicle in the vicinity to haul a supply of captured German bread to our front-line infantry. This took most of the night.

I shaved and washed that evening in somebody's kitchen, surrounded by an admiring group of French civilians who would burst put on an average of once a minute with a rousing, *"Vive la Americaine,"* whereupon I would have to suspend operations and return in my best American, *"Vive la France."* I have now the greatest sympathy for a trick bear or a film star. That night I slept in a Bosche colonel's bed. Altogether, it was a fair day's sport. The next day we went into position southeast of Harraucourt, but had no chance to fire as rather complicated orders came out which prevented our firing where a Bosche might be. As about the only alternative was to shoot up our own troops we lived as all good people should in peace and happiness until the armistice.

Gassed Cave at La Petite Logette Near Blanzy
by Colonel Fred Charles Doyle

On Sept. 8, 1918, the regimental command post went forward from Fismes after two days of incessant shelling and occupied a large cave recently deserted by Germans. The engineers and medical officers had worked diligently all day neutralizing the air of the cave and taking all possible steps to degas the cave. The cave was pronounced safe for occupancy about 4.00 p. m. Col. Doyle arrived about that time and inspected the cave. Things did not look any too well and evidence of possible German trickery existed. The cave was very massive and could hold possibly 1000 men in ranks. Outlying galleries of the cave were pronounced unsafe but ventilation and boarding up of some of the galleries offset this difficulty and apparently rendered the balance of the cave safe. About 9:30 p. m. Col. Doyle instituted a check of all his men (about 40) to ascertain if they were in safe, ungassed parts of the cave. This check turned out to be a remarkable safety precaution, as despite all warnings many men had wandered into gassed galleries and were even then gassed, some badly, others undetermined. Many of the men gassed were blissfully asleep. About 11:30 p.m. leaking gas from buried gas shells rendered the entire cave uninhabitable and all men were ordered out. This was a severe measure as no protection against bombing planes or shell fire existed. However, drastic action was imperative. About this time many men began to show the effects of the gas and were in great agony some blinded. The entire medical staff (officers and men) had been gassed and were unable to give any assistance. Col. Doyle alone remained in the cave giving aid to a constant stream of gassed men. This aid consisted of his locating some potassium tablets left by the medical detachment and making up an alkaline solution from the water in his canteen. Gauze from a first aid bandage dipped in the solution served as an eye dropper. Many men were in the greatest agony from their eyes. Many were blinded for the time, only a candle existed for light and no assistance whatsoever was at hand. Col. Doyle worked unaided over the cases until 4:30 a.m., at the time he knew he was being gassed as he had been continuously in the same place where some of his patients had been rendered blind. At 4:30 a.m. he felt he had endangered himself to a point where it was wise to get out, but not until a medical officer attached to the engineers had been requested and arrived. This officer gave the men, still streaming in, the same treatment but only for a few moments. During the four hours one of the greatest problems consisted in getting men out of the cave at once after treatment. Many had to led in and led out.

During the day Col. Doyle's long exposure developed and that night about 10:00 p.m. his condition was such as to deprive him of any ability to see although he continued to personally stay by the telephone, receive several missions for fire and assigned such missions to his battalions. About midnight he realized that his effectiveness was practically terminated as he was in great pain, and calling for assistance he was led away for treatment and evacuation.

The Germans in this case had buried gas shells and apparently using a corrosive acid the shell cases had been eaten through. I suppose somewhat about 7:00 to 8:00 p.m. the gas had then leaked out, worked through the covering over the buried gas shells and fouled the air of the cave. A very nasty vivid impression of this incident will remain for years in the minds of all. Some of the men have not recovered as yet. Col. Doyle plainly felt the effects for three months after. Capt. Mitchell and Lt. Mots had been in the cave but a short time, possibly 3 hours and prior to 11:00 p.m., yet they were gassed and evacuated to the hospital.

The Dud
by Colonel Fred Charles Doyle

On Aug. 22, after an all night engagement during which no one had slept, Col. F. C. Doyle went to his bunk about 8.00 a. if. for the purpose of laying down for ten or fifteen minutes. He however changed his mind and decided first to talk over some matters in general with the Infty Brigade Comdr. Within 5 minutes after quitting his quarters a 105 shell ripped through the wall, passed through his mattress and dropped on the floor of his room. It failed to explode. Lieuts Willis, Elots and Capt Fox were in an adjoining room through which the projectile had also passed. Had the projectile exploded during its passage through this room all would undoubtedly have been killed.

The Dud Again
by Some Ear-Witnesses of the Headquarters Company Orderly Room

The following in a verbatim report submitted by Tailor Smith, Hq. Co., 305 F.A., of an incident at La Tuilerie. A shell passed through two rooms of the officers' quarters above Regimental Headquarters, landing in the second room—a dud. While a fair measure of success was attained in reproducing the pronunciation and accent of the narrator it is with exceeding regret that it is impossible even to indicate the dramatic delivery with which the story was told.

DE BIG EXCITEMENTS FON DE DET (DUD)

In a nice mornink I don't rember it de day, before Duffy vent aveg, in a nice Mornink standink in the Kroinel's (Colonel's) room vaz located five officers; two rooms ind five officers. One mornink vaz hot German shellinks; ven de shellink landit all vaz in de house and all big excitements. Understand it, all big excitements, 'n I vas in a little house vere de Kroinel's officers' quarters leaves. Ven de big shellink started de Kroinel vent out fon dis house, ind he vent aveg 'n I don't know vere. After ten minutes ago, der comes arahn Capt. Whelpley, ven de big shellink fall near de house, 'n Pvt Smith vaz in de house, ven Capt. Whelpley come in in de house,'n he grabbit his gez mesk 'n helmet; 'n Pvt. Smith vaz in de house ven he qvick he grabbit 'n run out 'n run out. 'n de excitements ven he got out 'n grabbit it, he don't know vat to do; 'n I vas stock in de same house, in de big excitements.

In de moments fon excitements it takes him about tree minutes ind he heard it a shelf vaz comink 'n hit de hill ind soon de shelf hit. De vile I vaz so excited I dug dahn, 'n I gorrup a minute later 'n I start to run; I start to run 'n I vaz tinkink, ind I run *to* de dughouse, 'n I run *in* de dughouse, 'n I come in; I come in de dughouse 'n I couldn't speak aus, 'n eferybody tells me: "vat is de matter," 'n I couldn't tell me vat is de matter. After I vaz run in de dughouse ind I could not nobody answer, as de whole Regimental Headquarters, dat's Capt. Gammell, all de cloiks 'n de rest of de officers vot's dere, I couldn't remember, dey run after me in de big excitements. Dey vaz take dahn de telephone in dis dughouse ind it vaz in dis dughouse; de telephone vaz standink for five minutes later. Dey couldn't get any answer from Pvt. Smith vat vaz happink for de big excitement, Pvt. Smith couldn't speak for de last ten minutes.

Ten minutes, you know after de ten minutes, dere come Lt. Klots, Lt. Willis 'n Capt. Fox mit de big excitements vot's happink in dis sleepink quarters. Dat's de same room vere vas Kroinel located in dis two rooms, ind oder officers, ind vaz start to tell it how de shellink landet in dis room. You couldn't believe me; you know in de same moment vat's all vaz big excitement; (here the narrator carried away by his own dramatic delivery of "de big excitements," becomes rather involved), dere vaz very big excitements in de same moment; in de moment ven ve vaz excitement, I vaz you know like some of dem, could not believe it in anytink you know, ind a minute after ve vaz standink dere, 'n all odder officers, I mean it Lt. Klots came it dahn vit all suits covered like tree painters. Dey tell us how de shelf landit in de room. Veil ve standink few minutes ind vere listenink; ve standink in de room ind listen maybe come more firing arahnd here.

Ve passed de time by ten minutes ind he is gettink quiet. Den de excitement vaz over dey vent out lookink on dis excitement, ind dis is vat vaz happink mit our excitements. Comink near de house, de door vaz opink ind laining up vaz bik 155 shelfs ind not esplozhit (exploded), Den, de whole Regimental Headquarters togedder in dey come togedder look on it, how de shelf vaz comink in de house. (Here follows description of course of shell) De shelf hits first de vail outside; den de shelf vas hittink in de first room vere vaz Lt. Willis shavink 'n Lt. Klots vaz shavink. 'n Capt. Fox vaz sleepink on his rolling bed on de grahnd ind de shelf vaz hittink, ind hit tru de vail near his facet, ind hit Kroinel's bed in de odder room, ind smashed de bet, 'n turned arahnd de bet; ind de shelf hit in de end of de vail fon de bet; de shelf hit ind of de vail fon de bet ind jumped back; de shelf jumped back 'n he landit in de grannd tree feet aveg fon de door (very dramatically) 'n

Pvt Smith vaz standink by de door; dat's only tree feet, one yard American langvage; tree feet aveg vaz Pvt. Smith. You can immeasure how happink he vaz de shelf vaz not esplozhit.

'N de same time Sgt. Gruber came up to see Capt. Whelpley, ind he started to tell vat a shelf landet in de room; in de same moment he couldn't believe it for big excitements; de von tink, he goes over vit me 'n dere vaz de bik long shelf vaz laining in dere in de room. In de big excitements fon de officers, dey vaz afrait to touch it; even to get five feet nearer, den dey order Lt. Willis take de shelf fon dis house. Sgt. Gruber take, how you say it, grabs dat's courage, 'n a vire 'n a pail, I meam to say he's not afrait, for it fealressle, you know fealressle, like he vaz not afrait you know; he take de vire ind hook it dahn in de shelf, in de bik Germish shelf, 'n he pull it out fondisroom. 'n dey make a bik whole 'n dey bury it him.

Ven de Kroinel comes back he vas bik excitements, very bik excitements. You immeasure how he happink he vaz, he vaz not dere. Sure he vaz glat he didn't hit him. Capt Whelpley come back in an hour later, 'n dey tell him de whole story 'n he couldn't believe it till he's going see it. Ven de saw it, he believe it. Dis Kroinel ind dis Captain dey vaz not afrait, 'n de same day ven de shelf hit, dey vaz sleepink in de same house. For de last veek, till ve left dis place, dey vasn't afrait to leave in dis house in de same room in de same spot.

Praise and Advice
by Paper Work

Headquarters
154th Inf. Brigade
American E. F.
October 18th, 1918
From: Commanding General 154th Infantry Brigade
To: Commanding General 152nd Field Artillery Brigade.
(Thru Division Commander)
Subject: use of artillery during recent operations.
1. I desire to express to you and through you to the officers of your command, my appreciation of the assistance which was rendered during the recent operations of this brigade by your artillery, particularly during the last few days, where there was possibility of observation and where artillery assistance was of the highest value. I may say in fact that had it not been for the effective and efficient support which was given to me by both the heavy and light artillery, placed at my disposition by the Division Commander, the taking of Grand Pre by the troops of my command, under the conditions as they existed, would have been an impossibility, and that the success of the operation was due in large measure to the effective artillery support.
(signed) *Evan M. Johnson*
Brigadier General
N. A. Commanding Brigade

1st Ind.
Hq. 805 F. A.
American Ex. Forces
23rd Oct. 1918
To Organization Commanders

1. The foregoing letter is published to the command for the information of all concerned.

2. Each officer must feel a sense of gratification to learn that the efforts of this command during the past operations have been successful and effective and will inspire all to further continued efforts and sacrifices with the same aims in view.

3. It is directed that this letter be read to all members of this command.

By order of Major Easterday:
C. vonE. Mitchell
Captain, 805 F.A.
Acting Adjutant

Headquarters
305 F.A. N.A.
1st Bn. American Ex. Forces
July 29, 1918
MEMORANDUM
For Organization Commanders

The Regtl. Commander, after the past 3 weeks observation of the work of this regiment, desires to call the attention of all concerned to the point that the entire command, from the most newly arrived private, to include all officers, must realize the stern obligations imposed on all by our present calling. Initiative, that means grabbing any and all situations by the scruff of the neck and jamming it forcefully through to a quick and successful conclusion is the first duty of all; this means putting a punch into your work, and applies to enlisted men as well as officers. If officers, for any reason, are not present, and N. C. Os understand the idea to be carried out, let us make it an artillery standard to get the work done, in all cases of emergency, and done quickly.

All work of the gun crews must be done with life and perfect team work. The crews have had sufficient drill by now to make this possible, It is earnestly advised that every enlisted man think carefully of his particular work. Run over your work in your mind, when not at drill, and fully master same. All cannoneers by now should know all the duties of other cannoneers. Slowness on part of gun crews is the greatest crime they can commit. It means the loss of lives by our infantry, and what is worse, the loss of standing of the artillery in the eyes of all, and loss of confidence to attack by the infantry. Officers will make a special propaganda of this issue with the men.

The New York papers, in front page letters, are spreading broadcast to the country the pride taken by the City of New York in the 77 Division. The city is thrilled to the depths by the information that we are on the front line. The articles fairly glitter with comments of our highly trained condition. All papers exult in stating that the 77 Division has earned the distinction of being the first N. A. Division to appear on the front. We have done this, because we were the most proficient and highly trained. This fact will go down in American History, and you cannot realize the pride our friends, relatives and families must have in us to know that we, each one of us, earned our place of distinction by hard, patriotic work.

It is now up to each member of this command to maintain this high standard. Let every one of us get the jump into our work to such an extent as to give our families additional cause to be proud of us. They are proud of you, you will never know how pathetically proud.

Every regiment on the battle front is striving to outdo others. Remember we are doing the same.

F. C. Doyle
Col., 305 F. A. N. A.

Doing Scout Duty for the Artillery
by Private Everts

Around noon hour, a call came in from Headquarters for Battery E to send a scout as guard for an advanced gun position. It happened at Perles and I have the honour of being selected to pack my duds, stow away a day's rations and report to the P. C. in fifteen minutes notice. When a pirate hammers away at your position, it's immediately decided upon to bring the bandit to a lamb like disposition. This particular "kiss thrower" was annoying us when the time came for my departure for a night's sojourn to unknown parts. Being on familiar terms with the cook (mess was always attractive to me) I told him of my intentions to locate the *siesta* disturber and also to remain as a squatter for the battery's future rendezvous. He, *la chef des armes*, broiled me a steak, evidently deciding I was dead already. (I'll admit I thought I must have been in heaven as "corn willy," predominated my digestive organs for weeks). As a farewell gift, I was allowed a can of "gold fish" and a litter of beans, accompanied by a half-loaf of bread. I was soon on my way and by evening, located the claim and prepared to guard. The location selected was just beyond a slope and must have been an old French gun position. It had two dugouts with a trench leading between, scantily camouflaged and muddy. After striking a few matches, I saw a German helmet protruding through sort of a barricade that "made up" the dug out. To be sure, I fired two shots at the "intruder." Satisfying myself it was *finis*, I sheepishly advanced rather ashamed of my cowardice. But being a New Yorker you soon learn that "Safety First" is a pretty good motto to follow. On close inspection, I noticed one hole clear through the top of the "cranium protector" but to my disgust, blood trickled through the aperture. I was certain I had little intention of sleeping in that particular dugout so moved to what must have been some Hun generals'. All conveniences were to be had, such as straw for a bed, half empty cans of solidified alcohol, two chairs, and in the evening, rats for company " It's only for a night" I said, so prepared for a sleep. I believe I slept for an hour or so, but that was brought to an abrupt end by a shell falling uncomfortably close to my private residence. I said shell but can easily make that plural. At that moment I thought I was the whole American Army consolidated, as I swore enough for a regiment. Even that was cut short, by a shower of dirt thrown rudely in my direction by an insulting direct hit. Our artillery must have heard my mixture of prayers and slaughter of the English language because a barrage began that continued for a good five hours. I smiled contentedly and continued to show my appreciation to "Morpheus." When the daylight came, I awoke lazy and hungry (as usual) Partaking of beans and bread, isn't very encouraging for one who has slept uneasily but eating is essential, regardless of the condition of your feelings. After saving half a can of "fruit" for dinner, I pulled in a hitch on my belt and prepared for the day. A half hour later found me in the infantry trenches with machine gunners. They had heard the pirate German gun but couldn't locate it. When I saw coffee coming down the narrow lane, I decided then and there, that if they couldn't find an enemy gun—neither could I. After a gulp of "java" I felt better and went to my home to await my relief. When it became night again, I figured they had either forgotten me, or left me for "the army of occupation." I still had a can of salmon to take out my vengeance on but discovered on opening same it was ancient and beyond eating. The next best thing to do was to impose upon my soldier brothers a kilo away. Arrived with greetings and after explaining my predicament, was rewarded with a whole box of hard tack and a canteen of water. On my way back rejoicing, I was cut off from my "home" by a succession of one-pounders coming in close proximity to my person. Lying flat in a shell hole with a foot of dirt higher than your head, is much more comforting than being the same distance, above. Figuring, they—the Huns, had discontinued the barricading barrage, I "rabbited" to my hovel with enough prayers said and saying, to save my soul from Hades twenty times over. The question of slumber was far away so I layed counting shell bursts until I finally "passed out of the picture of light." I received word next day to return, as our battery had decided to move to another front. Two days later the Italians, who took the same positions, were driven back. The dugout, forty eight hours ago my shelter, was now in the hands of the Bosche. And to think how fussy I am about having a German "P. G." on my spinal column.

Rustling Supplies
by Corporal Louis A. Cohen

The greater part of the personnel of a Supply Company being "mule skinners," this story will necessarily—if the real work of the company is to be described—have to centre around mules, horses and wagons, not forgetting the men who handle them and who, in the army, are officially known and rank as "wagoners." As is probably known, the Supply Company escort wagon is the means of bringing rations and ammunition to the Batteries at the front. Since this is true, it can readily be appreciated that the escort wagon to the Supply Company is as important as the gun is to the Battery.

Of what use is a gun unless you have the animals to pull it into position for you; on the same basis of what good is an escort wagon unless your animals stand up and help you? It follows, therefore, that you must be good to your mule if you want her to be good to you. Nearly all our "mule skinners" named their mules and the names ran from "Jennie" to the names of Queens. One man in particular named his mule after his intended wife; *their* name was Nora Bayes. This particular mule had the distinction of driving the water cart.

It is also interesting to note that one entire battery might be wiped out and yet the regiment would be able to hold its ground while, if the Supply Company was destroyed the entire regiment would cease functioning.

The task of feeding and supplying an Artillery regiment is not an easy one, and as for the Commanding Officer of the Supply Company who is also the Regimental Supply Officer he is responsible that the men and officers are fed, supplied with clothing and otherwise equipped. In a sense, he is father and mother to nearly 1,500 officers and men always worrying about the condition of the men's shoes, clothing and other equipment. So is he always concerned about the rations of the men, being on the alert to see that the components of the ration, are such as to give the men the necessary variety. Of course, this is the most difficult part of the Supply Officer's task since the army menu is so limited. If bacon happens to be issued one day the entire regiment wants to know why hash wasn't issued instead, and if hash should be in order the cry is "why can't we get bacon?"

The Supply Company had its first casualties at Fismes. While at Chèry, 2 men were killed and 3 were gassed. Wagoner Jackob Jackson was one of the men killed. About five minutes before he was hit he was cleaning his harness in front of his wagon. The Company Clerk who was passing was stopped and shown a letter which Jackson had just received from his wife. The glad tidings that he was the father of a little boy was conveyed in the letter. Jackson asked the clerk to get him the additional allowance from the Government because of the birth of the child, adding "my wife says that things are very high in the States and she needs the money." The clerk promised to attend to it immediately and then jumped into Jackson's wagon to look for some candy that the K of C had distributed the day before. It wasn't a minute after that that the Hun commenced shelling again, the second one hitting and breaking within five feet of the wagon. On investigation it was found that Jackson was hit in the back of the head. He died on his way to the hospital.

In the last months of the campaign, the rout of the Hun having been so complete, they were forced to retreat so fast that our Infantry and Artillery experienced difficulty in keeping up with them, the roads and bridges being destroyed after the enemy had vacated. We were hot on the trail always keeping within a few hours of the batteries.

In addition, the roads were almost impassable, the heavy traffic and the continued rain having helped to make matters worse. Not only were these conditions to be met with; at several places between Thenorgues and Raucourt the road was mined by the retreating enemy each explosion having torn up the road for about 25 yards and each excavation being 40 feet deep. This, of course, prevented the movement of the long supply trains and even the guns. Troops on foot had only to walk around these holes but vehicles could not do this. The engineers were early on the job and built roads around the torn up places; to attempt to fill in the roads would require days of hard work, the holes being so large. These were not the only troubles of a Supply Company. We could only move at night. The mules were exhausted after the continuous advance and it was not unusual for 10 or 15 of us, with heavy packs on our backs, to help the mules out of a bad spot. Some of the men would get on the wheels while others would push from the rear. Of course the men were just as tired and exhausted as the mules but the difference was that American soldiers can understand why they must go on while the mules had not the intelligence to know. It does seem strange for the very same mules always knew when it was time for them to be fed, watered or groomed and if by chance they were not fed on time every men within a radius of miles knew what the trouble was.

The composition of the personnel of the Supply Company was quite varied. It ranged from cobblers to poets. It can truly be called a melting pot. The following was written by the company poet one afternoon while all traffic was held up for about an hour due to breaks in the road:

The old Supply is lumbering,
Along the muddy road;
The Guns up there are slumbering,
They want this heavy load.

No glory in this hovering,
In shell-torn village streets,
No glory in the covering,
From hostile airship fleets.

The boys up there are hungering,
We must push on—that's all;
There's no use in our buggering,
We've got to heed their call.

The drivers now are whispering,
They urge and cuss the mules,
The hubs are all ablistering,
But who cares for the rules.

This is no time for faltering,
The boys must have their chow;
Drive on, though all are sweltering,
We must get there somehow.

You may not call this soldiering,
I know they have the stuff.
Within no fear is smouldering,
They all are brave but gruff.

And when there is a reckoning,
Back home where all is fair,
From those who do the beckoning,
I know they'll get their share.

A Good Dinner Shot to H—
by Corporal Henry Goldberg

Don't ask me the date, for when we were at the front, and we were seldom away from it, that was the last thing we thought of. I remember it was a Sunday and sometime in August. Sunday I am sure, for Mike, who was our cook, said, "Boys, a good Sunday dinner and no Corned Willy."

The place where we were to have this feast, was near Chèry Chartreuve, and anyone who was in that sector knew how Jerry would shell it, especially around meal times. But for the benefit of those who were not there, let me say that there was hardly a square yard of open country that did not bear evidence of Hun artillery.

Well, the rations had come up and Mike and his able assistants were busy preparing, what we thought, was to be a good meal. Not that our meals were bad, but after eating corned beef straight, camouflaged and otherwise for almost a week, I assure you that Roast Beef, Mashed Potatoes and Rice Pudding was a feast. They were progressing wonderfully well, when about 5 p.m. Jerry started his customary shelling. One hit near the kitchen, which by the way was in a direct line of fire, which caused Mike and the K. P's to *"Partee tout de suite."* Not that I blame them the least bit for doing that, for the farther you were away from the shells, the better you felt. They were about to go back and get the meal ready for serving, when *zowie*, along comes a Hun 150, crashes right through the wall in back of the stove, and spreads dinner, in fact our next two meals, all over the walls.

Our Major came running out of the P. C, which was in the same building, to see what had happened, and the first one he should meet was Mike. All Mike could say, was, "Major, they shoota de hell out of the kitch."

That's all there is to it, except that it was Corned Willy again for supper and, well I guess you imagine what we wished the Hun.

THE FIRST AND LAST SHOTS

The First shot fired by the 305th Regiment, F. A., was,
(1) July 11th 1918, 3:10 P. M.
(2) Battery "A" 305th F. A.
(3) One kilo. east of Neuf Maisons
(4) Gun Crew:
Sgt. Wallace
Corp. Anselowicz
Pvts. Elsnik
Lundy
Berg
Christy
Zuccola

(5) Remarks: The gun was laid for registration on an angle of a German communicating trench. The first shot was lost. The change was then made from high explosive to shrapnel and the second round, with the same data, showed the burst about three mils off the target. Not only was this the first shot of the Brigade, but it also was the first shot fired by any National Army Artillery in the war.

The last shot fired by the 305th Regiment, F. A. was
(1) November 10th, 1918 Sunday 4:10 P. M.
(2) Battery "B" 305th F. A.
(3) Harravcourt Dept. Ardennes
Approximately 12 kilometers south of Sedan dept. of Ardennes; 4 kilometers north of Raucourt dept. of Ardennes and 27 kilometers north-west of Montmedy dept. of Meuse.
Battery position on a high hill to the east of the town of Haraucourt at a distance of ½ Km. from the center of the town and the main road to Sedan.

Co-ordinates of the Battery position:
X—300,450
Y—317,300
(4) Gun Crew:
Sgt Geo. Foose, Chief of Section
Acting Corp. Hunt, Gunner
Pvts. Burgeron, No. 1
J. Stavish, No. 2
Tom Moore, No. 3
E. A. Olsen, No. 4
J. Brennen, No. 5
(5) Remarks: Fire for registration.
Target, Farm house to the north.
Total number of rounds, 38.
Last shell, cleaned by No. 5, Pvt. Brennen.
fused by No. 4, Pvt. Olsen.
fuse set by No. 3, Pvt. Moore.
loaded by No. 2, Pvt. Stavish.
fired by No. 1, Pvt. Burgeron.

CHANGES OF STATION OF REGIMENTAL P. C.

STATION	ARRIVE	LEFT
Pontanezen Barracks	May 6, 1918	May 7, 1918
Camp de Souge	May 9, 1918	July 5, 1918
Neuf Maisons	July 8, 1918	Aug. 1, 1918
Magnieres	Aug. 2, 1918	Aug. 2, 1918
Bainville	Aug. 3, 1918	Aug. 6, 1918
Doue	Aug. 7, 1918	Aug. 9, 1918
Chezy-sur-Marne	Aug. 10, 1918	Aug. 10, 1918
Bois de Courpoil	Aug. 11, 1918	Aug. 12, 1918
Nesle Woods	Aug. 13, 1918	Aug. 17, 1918
La Tuilerie	Aug. 17, 1918	Sept. 4, 1918
Fismes	Sept. 5, 1918	Sept. 6, 1918
La Petite Logette	Sept. 6, 1918	Sept. 15, 1918
Bois Meuniere	Sept. 16, 1918	Sept. 16, 1918
Mareuil le Porte	Sept. 17, 1918	Sept. 18, 1918
Grauves	Sept. 18, 1918	Sept. 19, 1918
Ferme Notre Dame (Near Fibbes)	Sept. 19, 1918	Sept. 20, 1918
Cheppes	Sept. 20, 1918	Sept. 21, 1918
Bussy le Repos	Sept. 22, 1918	Sept. 22, 1918
Chatrices	Sept. 23, 1918	Sept. 23, 1918
Florent	Sept. 24, 1918	Sept. 25, 1918
Fme. Ferdinand	Sept. 25, 1918	Sept. 27, 1918
La Harazee	Sept. 27, 1918	Oct. 3, 1918
Fme. Aux Charmes	Oct. 3, 1918	Oct. 9, 1918
N. Depot d'Machines	Oct. 9, 1918	Oct. 10, 1918
Bois de Lancon	Oct. 10, 1918	Oct. 11, 1918
Malassise Fme.	Oct. 11, 1918	Oct. 17, 1918
Lancon	Oct. 17, 1918	Oct. 17, 1918
La Chalade	Oct. 18, 1918	Oct. 26, 1918
Chatel Chehery	Oct. 26, 1918	Oct. 28, 1918
Cornay	Oct. 28, 1918	Nov. 1, 1918
Martincourt Fme.	Nov. 1, 1918	Nov. 2, 1918

STATION	ARRIVE	LEFT
Champigneulle	Nov. 2, 1918	Nov. 3, 1918
Haraucourt	Nov. 3, 1918	Nov. 4, 1918
Fontenoy	Nov. 4, 1918	Nov. 5, 1918
Oches	Nov. 5, 1918	Nov. 5, 1918
La Berliere	Nov. 5, 1918	Nov. 6, 1918
Stonne	Nov. 6, 1918	Nov. 7, 1918
Haraucourt	Nov. 7, 1918	Nov. 12, 1918
Woods North of Sommauthe	Nov. 12, 1918	Nov. 14, 1918
Beaumont	Nov. 14, 1918	Nov. 20, 1918
Verpel	Nov. 20, 1918	Dec. 1, 1918
Autry	Dec. 1, 1918	Dec. 2, 1918
Arc en Barrois	Dec. 3, 1918	Feb. 9, 1919
Malicorne	Feb. 11, 1919	Apr. 17, 1919
Pontanezen Barracks	Apr. 18, 1919	Apr. 20, 1919

ROSTER OF THE OFFICERS OF THE 305 F. A.

ARRANGED
ACCORDING TO ASSIGNMENT TO THE REGIMENT

Officers transferred before Regiment sailed overseas not included in this List

DATE 1917	NAME	RANK	ORG.	
Aug. 26	DOYLE, FREDERICK C.	Col.		
" 31	HOADLEY, SHELDON E.	1 Lt.	Sup. Co.	Killed in action, Oct. 13, 1918
" 31	THAYER, THORNTON C.	Capt.	B	
" 31	THIRKIELD, GILBERT H.	1 Lt.	Hq. Co.	
" 31	THIRKIELD, NORMAN	1 Lt.	Hq. Co.	
Sept. 1	BROOKS, GEORGE B.	1 Lt.	E	Returned to U. S., Aug. 25, 1918
" 1	DELANOY, DOUGLAS	Capt.	C	
" 1	HOYT, LYDIG	1 Lt.	Hq. Co.	Transf. G. H. Q., June 6, 1918
" 1	WANVIG, HARRY F.	Major	2nd Battalion	
" 2	BRASSEL, THOMAS M.	1 Lt.	A	
" 2	BROWN, LEE D.	2 Lt.	Sup. Co.	Transf. July 2, 1918
" 2	BURDEN, CHESTER B.	1 Lt.	F	Wounded in action, Oct. 14, 1918
" 2	CAMP, CHARLES W.	2 Lt.	Hq. Co.	
" 2	DERBY, JAMES L.	Capt.	F	
" 2	GAMMELL, ARTHUR A.	Maj.	Adjt.	
" 2	JONES, PAUL	1 Lt.	C	Transf. Aviation July 23, 1918
" 2	PIKE, H. HARVEY, JR.	Capt.	D	
" 2	STARBUCK, FREDERICK L.	Capt.	Adj. 2nd Batt.	
" 3	CHURCH, OLIVER A.	1'Lt.	Hq. Co.	
" 3	LITTLEFIELD, ROBY P.	1 Lt.	D	
" 4	FENN, WILLIAM H. M.	1 Lt.	D	
" 4	KANE, WILLIAM M.	1 Lt.	C	
" 4	KLOTS, ALLEN T.	1 Lt.	Hq. Co.	
" 4	MITCHELL, CORNELIUS VON E.	Capt.	Pers. Adj.	
" 4	MITCHELL, JOHN R.	1 Lt.	E	
" 4	MONTGOMERY, GEORGE P.	1 Lt.	B	
" 4	NISSLEY, WARREN W.	1 Lt.	F	
" 5	STORER, ROBERT T. P.	Maj.	E	
" 5	WHELPLEY, MEDLEY G. B.	Capt.	Hq. Co.	Trans. Hosp. Dec. 21, 1919.
" 5	WILLIS, HAROLD S.	1 Lt.	Hq. Co.	
" 6	BECK, FREDERICK L.	2 Lt.	B	Returned to U. S. Aug. 25, 1918

DATE 1917	NAME	RANK	ORG.	
Sept. 6	Fox, NOEL B.	Capt.	C	Returned to U. S. Aug. 25, 1918
" 6	MONTAGUE, DANFORTH	1 Lt.	Hq. Co.	Died of Disease, November, 5, 1918
" 6	RAVENEL, GAILLARD F.	Maj.	B	
" 6	SAWIN, MELVIN E.	2 Lt.	B	Returned to U. S., Aug. 25, 1918
" 6	SHUTT, GEORGE P.	2 Lt.	D	Returned to U. S. Aug. 25, 1918
" 6	STIMSON, HENRY L.	Lt. Col.		Returned to U. S. July 31, 1918
" 6	STRYKER, LLOYD P.	1 Lt.	A	Returned to U. S., July 25, 1918
" 6	WASHBURN, WATSON	1 Lt.	E	Transf. Hqrs 4 Army C. Aug. 1, 1918
" 6	WASHINGTON, LAURENCE	2 Lt.	C	Transferred to aviation, July 23, 1918
" 7	SAVAGE, EDGAR W.	1 Lt.	Sup. Co.	Transf. 2. F. A. Bn. Am. Tr Nov. 16, 1918
" 12	CRONIN, DENNIS J.	1 Lt.	M. C. Det.	
" 12	MOORE, MARSHALL A.	1 Lt.	M. C. Det.	
" 12	PARRAMORE, JAMES B.	Capt.	M. C. Det.	Transf. Base Hosp. 24 August 19, 1918
" 19	McKENNA, DREW	Maj.	Sup. Co.	Transf. G. I. 77th Div. Jan. 14, 1919
" 27	SHERIDAN, JOHN J.	1 Lt.	Chaplain	
Oct. 8	NORTH, LEON N.	1 Lt.	Vet. C. Det.	Transf. 304 F. A. Sept. 6, 1918
" 14	JOHNSON, THOMAS J.	Lt-Col.	1 Batt.	Tranf. Gen. Staff, July 10, 1918
" 16	BROPHY, FREDERICK H.	Capt.	D. C.	
Nov. 12	HODENPYL, GEO. H.	2 Lt.	C	Tranf. to Aviation July 23, 1918
" 12	McNAIR, KARL R.	1 Lt.	Hq. Co.	
" 12	WALSH, WILLIAM A.	2 Lt.	A	Returned to U. S. Aug. 25, 1918
" 22	WANZER, H. STANLEY	2 Lt.	E	
Dec. 10	STRONG, ELLSWORTH O.	2 Lt.	A	Killed in action, Aug. 25, 1918
" 16	DODWORTH, WILFRED K.	1 Lt.	C	Returned to U. S. Aug. 25, 1918
" 17	MOORE, LLOYD E.	2 Lt.	M. C. Det.	Transf. Mob. Vet. Hosp. C, Jan. 2, 1918
" 17	PENNOYER, PAUL G.	1 Lt.	B	Transf. Art. Inform. Service, July 4, 1918
" 20	GRAHAM, EDWARD F.	2 Lt.	Hq. Co.	Killed in action, Aug. 21, 1918
" 27	GURNEY, ALBERT R.	Capt.	Hq. Co.	
1918				
Jan. 14	ESSEX, JOHN J.	Capt.	V. C. Det.	
Feb. 14	DANA, ANDERSON	Capt.	A	
Mar. 22	REED, H. H.	Capt.	Hq. Co.	

DATE 1918	NAME	RANK	ORG.	
Mar. 24	SCHILPERT, JOHN W.	1 Lt.	M. C. Det.	Transf. 302 A. Tr. Aug. 19, 1918
Apr. 22	ROBINSON, ARTHUR A.	2 Lt.	Sup. Co.	Killed by accident, Feb. 10, 1919
July 1	EASTERDAY, GEORGE W.	Lt. Col.		
" 10	WEMKEN, CHAS. F.	2 Lt.	F	Returned to U. S. Aug. 25, 1918
" 20	PERRY, CHARLES F.	2 Lt.	B	
Sept. 1	SWENSON, HERBERT J.	1 Lt.	Hq. Co.	Adm. S. O. S. Hosp. Sept. 14, 1918
" 3	PUTNAM, GEORGE E.	2 Lt.	Hq. Co.	
" 3	STRIBLING, JESSE W	2 Lt.	Sup. Co.	
" 6	HOAR, STEDMAN B.	2 Lt.	Hq. Co.	Transf. 15 F. A. November 16, 1918
" 6	MACLEOD, DONALD J.	2 Lt.	V. C. Det.	
" 9	BULLEN, OSBON W.	2 Lt.	A	
" 9	COPELIN, JOHNSTON	2 Lt.	C	
" 9	DOCKERY, RAYMOND E.	2 Lt.	B	
" 9	HATTIMER, LEON H.	2 Lt.	E	Killed in action, November 6, 1918
" 9	HOLCOMB, HAROLD	2 Lt.	Hq. Co.	Transf. 2 F. A. Br. Am. Tr., Nov. 16, 1918
" 10	CAMP, ROY H.	2 Lt.	Hq. Co.	
" 10	GEIBERT, THADDEUS R.	2 Lt.	C	
" 10	GRAHAM, CHARLES L.	2 Lt.	C	
" 10	HART, EDWARD W.	2 Lt.	D	
" 10	HILL, ALBERT B.	2 Lt.	F	
" 10	McKEE, WALDO E.	2 Lt.	Hq. Co.	
" 10	NORTON, THOMAS M.	2 Lt.	E	
" 10	TAYLOR, REUBEN T.	2 Lt.	F	
" 10	TEICHMOELLER, JOHN G.	2 Lt.	D	
" 10	WILHITE, PHILLIP A.	2 Lt.	Hq. Co.	
Oct. 10	ALLMOND, ANGUS R.	2 Lt.	B	
" 10	GLUCK, ARTHUR C.	2 Lt.	D	Transf. to Aviation. Oct. 17, 1918
Nov. 7	CLEARWATER, JOHN H.	2 Lt.	Hqrs.	Transf. 2 F. A. Br. Am. Tr., Nov. 16, 1918
" 7	MURRELL, ARCHIE	2 Lt.	E	Transf. 2 F. A. Br. Am. Tr. Nov. 16, 1918
" 10	ABELOW, SOLOMON	2 Lt.	Sup. Co.	
" 10	HAYDAY, HORACE	2 Lt.	A	
" 10	ZUNDEL, EDWIN A.	Maj.	1 Batt.	
" 17	DEBELL, JOHN MILTON	1 Lt.	Sup. Co.	
" 19	KILBOURNE, HAROLD H.	2 Lt.		
1919				
Jan. 21	VON SALTZER, PHILIP W.	1 Lt.	F	
" 27	VOLLMER, WILLIAM A.	1 Lt.	C	
" 29	GILLESPIE, GEORGE A.	2 Lt.	A	
Feb. 11	McNEVIN, ALFRED C. B.	1 Lt.	F	
" 19	KIRKPATRICK, JERE W.	Capt.	M. C. Det.	

In France with Battery F 305th F. A.

Ben Jacobson

Dedicated to
Captain James Lloyd Derby

Introduction

Words shall be few and explanations less in this little diary. However, the author does want it understood that his disproportionate sense of humour has overbalanced all other things in these accounts. He regrets that it has been impossible to mention everybody in this book. Only those who have been more or less incorrigible or spasmodically amusing will find themselves in the limelight, while the names of a great many heroes in our battery will forever remain unsung.

In the first place, this little book would ne'er have been were it not that it rained continually in France following the armistice and that we held drills daily and relentlessly in those rains. The birth of this little book is due directly to the fact that by creating it the author could dodge, avoid, or be excused from the majority of these '"wet" formations, which were the bane of our existence in France after the signing of the armistice.

The historical data contained herein are facts—the stories perhaps so. The book is a great deal shorter than the author ever intended it should be. He could not relate all individual happenings, and many an interesting story had to be left out. His aim will have been achieved, if, from this meagre history the personnel of the battery can individually recall their own personal adventures and trials, brought to mind in this general way, and in relating their stories, clothe and adorn them, each in his own imaginative speech.

B. J.

In France with Battery F 305th F. A.

Not with the sound of bugles, not with bands playing and standards unfurled, but in the still of the night with packs and full equipment, and our every move concealed, we began that memorable march "for Berlin."

At 2.00 a.m. Thursday, April 25th, there was a half-hushed blast of the first sergeant's whistle and all men started from their resting places on the floor of the clean swept barracks. As they formed in column outside, speaking in whispers, there was not a word of discontent. We were a happy, bustling bunch. A delay of an hour before starting, and then began a slow, grinding march to the Camp Upton Terminal. Everyone was littered with packages. Boxes of cigarettes, cakes, and articles never used were tied to the long heavy packs and rolls on our backs. In the rear of the column marched a slow solemn procession; a stretcher carried by four men and containing one Jimmie Houlihan with badly bent and twisted ankle received the day previous in a victorious basketball melee. Halts on the march were frequent as the 1st Battalion was entraining. The cars were boarded at 5.00 a.m. and fifteen minutes later they pulled out. Packs were piled on top of men and men on top of packs. There was scarcely room in which to breathe. Those near the windows were the lucky ones, and some hung half way out to get the fresh air. Still, everyone was in good spirits, and with difficulty the Sergeants in charge of each car restrained the men from singing, and, as the cars swung madly through each little hamlet, and the groups of villagers would wave and cheer, there burst a yell from every throat, and quickly the Sergeants would put an end to the racket. as our destination was neared, a lieutenant came through the cars, and, discovering the guidon unfurled and showing through one of the rear windows, hastily bade the holder to cover it at once—with it's simple message to the world: *Battery F, 305 F.A..*

Long Island City was reached at 7.30 a.m., where the ferry "Manhattan Beach" "lay in dock. On the trip around lower New York and into the North River no cheering or waving was permitted. When

Hoboken was reached, there was a final check and roll call. One by one, in alphabetical order, the boys went up the gang-plank and stepped on deck the U.S.S. *Von Steuben*, the renamed German auxiliary cruiser *Kronprinz Wilhelm II*. The Red Cross women worked feverishly along the line of boys on the pier, distributing hot coffee and buns and a pack of cigarettes to each.

We spent the rest of the morning and afternoon writing our safe (?) arrival cards and watching the hurried loading of the ship. It was a hot, stuffy night below decks in our crowded sleeping quarters, and, not enough hammocks to go round for everybody, some of us had to be S. O. L. and slept on the floor.

Friday, the 26th, was a bright, sunny day and we could now look around and get our bearings. We were at Pier 1, North German Lloyd Line. The old familiar buildings of lower New York were plainly visible to us, and what would we have not given to have been able to telephone over and say "goodbye" to the ones we loved dearly.

The ship's crew were busy all day, scrubbing decks and polishing her guns. She carried four 5-inch guns, ten 3-inch, four one-pounders, and two 3-inch anti-aircraft, twenty guns in all. Her passenger list consisted of 1,107 men and 27 officers.

Late in the afternoon came the order "Everybody below decks," and we were all locked in, hatches down. At 5.30 p.m. we pulled out of the dock silently, with no blowing of ship's whistle—bound for France! We were convoying the *Northern Pacific* transporting our 1st Battalion, and together the two ships passed through the harbour and out into the ocean, keeping abreast in the broad expanse, about a thousand yards apart.

No lights were permitted and all in all it was an uncomfortable night for everyone except the officers. How we wished we had gone to Plattsburg. Staterooms for each one, and their meals were of the finest, silver dishes and cutlery adorning their tables. And as for us, we had to stand in line for an hour or more perhaps, to be served our mess, and would then climb somewhere upon the deck, where the wind would blow our bread overboard, or the ashes from the ship's funnels get into the stew.

Saturday was a quiet day, wonderful weather. Our first lifeboat drill was held at 1 p.m. and we were all issued cotton-filled life-jackets to be worn at all times, even when sleeping. About forty men began the Lookout Guard at 4 p.m. to watch for submarines and mines from every part of the ship.

Sunday found a great many of the boys seasick, and it also found us dirty. By Jupiter! it was tough to keep clean in that miserable hole, and no water to wash in except saltwater. When it came to shaving, if the barber shop was too busy, the drinking water in our canteens answered the purpose. As there was a guard placed at the drinking cooler to see no one wasted any fresh water, or took any to shave or wash with, we had a pretty lively time dodging him with a little unauthorized issue in our mess cup.

We ran into rather heavy seas on Monday and a strong north wind. Pretty rough and nearly everybody sick. Boat drills went on regularly every day, however, and our "Lookout Guard" corporals were pretty busily engaged chasing all over the boat to find some soldiers who had weathered the storm sufficiently well to take the places of the sick ones in the lookout booths. Kingston, with a red band on his sleeve, had a hell of a time trying to rout out the desired parties for details. It was more like a game of hide-and-seek, as everybody dodged him when they saw him coming, and he roamed ceaselessly from one end of the boat to the other.

Monday was quiet compared to the pitching and rolling of the ship on Tuesday. The sailors endeavoured earnestly to relieve the sufferings of the seasick soldiers. To some of us it was a week of terrified agony, mingled with an acute desire for an instantaneous death. Poor Gee Tung was a sorrowful spectacle. The courtesies and kindness of the crew to us on that trip will never be forgotten—'twas like the gentle cheerfulness of a Red Cross nurse.

Again on Wednesday we encountered high seas and stiff winds, and after more boat drills we were mustered in, it being May first. Then the officers would take turns reading to us several columns on governmental censorship, articles of war, and lots of other bunk. The majority of us listened to it all with pain in our faces and nothing in our stomachs. We entered the Submarine Zone about 4 p.m. and began zigzagging. For two hours at twilight all hands remained above decks.

This was repeated just before dawn the next morning, pursuant to orders, and we sat around on deck from 3.30 a.m. to 5.30. The sun poked its nose out for an hour or so Thursday morning, but was lost soon in the black clouds rolling up on our starboard. Plenty of rain in the afternoon, and again our two unpleasant hours above decks waiting patiently and merrily to be torpedoed.

The sun came out to stay Friday morning, and the sea was fairly calm. All signs of seasickness among the boys disappeared, and as the morning went on the sea became more and more gentle. At 8 a.m. we sighted smoke on the horizon, and in fifteen minutes we were close enough to discern with the naked eye our little protectors of the sea, five American destroyers. They darted in and out and around the ship, and then spread out in fan-shape to our right and left.

We were ordered to pack up towards evening, as we expected to make port by morning. We were all on deck as usual at 3.30 a.m. Saturday, but all hopes of making the harbour in the morning were gone. It was dangerously foggy. Early in the day we narrowly missed running down one of the destroyers. Twice we tried to make the harbour while the fog lifted a bit, but both times it immediately after became denser than ever, and the ship pointed its nose away from land travelled in circles. We lost our consort for one hour and it was only about noon when it became clear that we were again together, with a great many French destroyers, and more American added to our convoy. Land was sighted at 1.30 p.m.

Never will we forget the view of the port of Brest with the old stone fortresses on steep promontories booming its welcome salute to us as we steamed up the harbour. We were met by American aeroplanes, a French dirigible and English submarines. It was a perfect Spring day and the hills enclosing the port were gloriously tinted with various coloured foliage. We anchored at 4 p.m. and amused ourselves as long at it was daylight, and that was until 9 p.m., by pitching our nickels and dimes to the French stevedores on a barge moored alongside, and watching them scramble frantically for the coins. No one was allowed shore leave except Lieutenant Nissley; and it has always remained a matter of great debate to the entire battery as to just what he did ashore that night.

Sunday they recoaled the ship. Everybody got more or less blackened from the clouds of dust that settled over everything aboard. Wonderful souvenir booklets of Brest views were sold on ship, and we all bought copies at fifty cents a throw and mailed them home, thinking in this way we could beat the censor and let the folks know just where we were in France. But the censor fooled us, after having said they would be O.K.d, for nary a booklet reached its destination.

Sunday morning, May the 6th, we were aroused bright and early. Inspection on board and then landed on French soil at 9.15 a.m. amid the cheers of the sailors and the playing of the ship's band. We then marched in the boiling hot sun with full packs to the Pontanezen Barracks, three miles from the port. At every stop along the road we were besieged with French children asking for *monniaie* and *Americaine cigarette*. What little clothes the kids wore were of a cheap black cotton material. Boys and girls alike dressed in thin loose smocks and wooden shoes. Those who did not ask for cigarettes begged for our biscuits and rations carried on our packs. Our first impression of France was one of poverty and starvation.

Our so-called "rest camp" was reached at noon. It was an old walled camp of Napoleon, and we considered ourselves lucky by not being housed in the antique barracks. Instead, we were put in large squad tents. We nearly froze to death at night, as it turned extremely cold.

The next morning we were up before daybreak, sitting around the kitchen fires to keep warm. Orders were suddenly received to leave our rest camp. At 10 a.m. we were on our hike back again over the road we came up yesterday. The railroad station was on the outskirts of Brest. It was here that we were initiated into the wiles and witcheries of corned willy and 'twas here we had our first nip of *vin ordinaire*, *cognac* and Benedictine. And praise be to Allah, what a long nip it was! All the way from Brest to Bordeaux that nip lasted—something around forty hours. Maybe the civilians didn't soak us for smuggling the stuff aboard the train. For many a bottle of *vin* worth about two *francs* we had to shell out a nice crisp two dollar bill. But 'twas well worth the price, for half the misery of that nightmare ride was forgotten with the aid of those bottles.

We were crowded as all other troops were, into the proverbial French box car with the sign *"40 Hommes ou 8 Chevaux."* Some cars held 45 men and had but one little opening about two feet square for ventilation. At 2.20 p.m. the train pulled out. We passed through Landerneau, Chateaulinm, Quimper and Rosporden before night set in. Our old horse cars of twenty years ago went faster than the imitation engines we had. And just when the train started to make good time, about 10 p.m., our *frog* brakeman fell off. We thought we would have to dynamite the train to stop it. There was no way of communicating the loss of our valuable brakeman to the engineer, so we yelled and tooted the bugles and one sergeant fired a few shots from his revolver. The engineer was finally convinced something had happened when someone who could talk not a word of French crawled out of and over the cars to his box and made wild motions. The train was stopped on a side track about five miles from the scene of the accident. We waited patiently while the engine was run back and gather in our frightened but unhurt brakeman.

We stretched our legs a bit at Nantes where we arrived at 7 a.m. Wednesday. The French Red Cross served us black coffee in our mess tins, and at first it had a horrible taste. Then some genius discovered it was the cognac flavour from the barrels which contained the coffee. Immediately there was a rush for "seconds" and "thirds." We quickly bought out the lunch room at the station and the old ladies were so excited over getting such extravagant prices for their wares that not one of us bothered to pay for the drinks they dished out. During the day we passed through Glisson, La Roche-Sur-Yon, Lucon, Rochefort-sur-Mer, and Saintes.

Again followed an enjoyable half suffocating night in our delightful roomy and clean box cars. At 3 a.m. we were at the railroad station in Bordeaux. To cheer us up we were served *hot* coffee that was black, tasteless and ice cold.

A real American engine pulled our train to a point about twelve miles north of Bordeaux called Bonneau. We detrained and hiked along a good road for about two miles to our destination, Camp Souge. The road was congested with huge American-built trucks carrying supplies and our blue bags. It was here we had our first glimpse at trance's famous gold-bricks—Chinese coolies. What a mixture of sloth, slovenliness and slime. They were clothed in just enough garments to keep Anthony Comstock from serving a *subpoena* upon them. Each was more curiously decorated than the other. They carried either a raincoat or a parasol; some held canary cages in hand; others, teapots; more still were loaded with fresh vegetables; and all wore the oddest collection of head-gear from a milk maid's bonnet to a silk dress hat.

Our barracks were fine, better than we had ever dreamt of. We had latrines and even a shower bath. The day was spent getting our wooden bunks together and filling bed-sacks with straw. Everybody had a good night's rest, the first in fourteen days. The night was bitterly cold and damp, yet during the day it had been terribly hot. During our entire stay the weather was pretty much the same—a penetrating told at night and from hot to boiling during the day.

The next couple of days passed by in cleaning equipment, resting up and buying lots of eatables at the commissary and from the French carts allowed within the camp limits. Our purchasing capacities were enlarged by changing at the Y.M.C.A. our good American money into vast quantities of strange looking, tissue-papered *francs*, which we all reluctantly did. Captain Mitchell announced we would stay here for approximately two months—good guess, to the day—and by the new schedule to take effect Monday we must arise at 5.30 a.m. have but forty-five minutes apiece for breakfast and dinner and hold retreat at 5.30 p.m. Ten and a half hours of actual work—real intensive training.

Saturday morning we were allowed outside the gate marking the camp limits, to imbibe freely of stipulated light French *vins* only, in *orderly* and well-chosen *estamines*. Fine! We had everything, anywhere .

Nineteen men from the battery were given passes to Bordeaux, by mistake reading for overnight. And, by their quiet, mannerly and *lady-like* behaviour, killed the act for all of us.

Sunday, May the 12th, was Mother's Day and, of course, everyone more or less full of *vin* wrote letters sparkling with enthusiasm for that wonderful part of France we were in, with its beautiful scenes on the lake, and the days that would be light until 9.30 p.m.

The next day, however, started the process of squashing the sentiment and romance in our systems. A stiff schedule of drill periods; school for the officers: school for the enlisted specialists; meals tasting of horse meat—these were the things warranted and guaranteed to knock out all sentimentality and artistic temperament from the tenderest to the most stoic.

The artists chosen for telephone school consisted of Sergeant McKenna (bless him), Corporals Dupree, Duckworth, Spiegel, Jacobson; Privates Houlihan, Brown, Stengren. The radio experts were Corporal Horton, Privates Carson and Fried. The *wildcats* chosen for machine gun instruction consisted of Corporal Skillmen and Privates Liebler, Kehoe, Sammler, Neuwerth, Rolke. All of the above details were immediately set down by the remainder of the battery as qualified A-1 "goldbricks!"

The battery had its first gun drill. It was an exciting moment—our first handling of a French "75." There was a medical inspection, and five men were taken to the hospital; two for scarlet fever, a couple for measles and one for mumps;

The week was a corker. Schools in the forenoon and drills in the p.m., including close order in our famous sand fields under a perfectly healthy and broiling hot sun. Wednesday we received our first mail from the U. S., transferred from Camp Upton, and also the bounteous assignment of four horses to the battery. Friday was the day of the horse shoe nail found in the stew at noon, convincing all disbelievers that we really were thriving on horse flesh. Immediately there was a rush on the egg market resulting in a boost of a half *franc* a dozen by the French peddlers quick to see that for some unknown cause there had arisen a sudden urgent demand for their wares. The bull market continued as, day by day, more and more men of the more dubious sort were convinced of the presence of "horse meat" and joined the ranks of the egg-eaters. It was luxurious living, but that made no difference. At mess time the kitchen was jammed with so many fellows frying eggs and making omelettes *a la* Duckworth, that Mess Sergeant Greenlee was certain he had now succeeded in reaching that stage where he could afford to give a full portion of mess to the rest of the battery waiting in line, and seconds, too, plentifully.

Corporal Dupree and five men, Privates Foray, Rosenzweig, Eddie Miller, George Johnson and J. A. Williams, were quarantined in a separate barracks being under a suspicion for contact with contagious cases that had been sent to the hospital.

Saturday was a half holiday—drills in the morning and off in the afternoon. Hot day, as usual, and quite a bunch went swimming in the lake. Five more horses were assigned to the battery. Sunday was a real rest, and plenty of time to wash clothes, write mail, and go swimming in the lake. The *estamines* were very popular, particularly one, where Sergeants Pohlman, McHenry and Garry were wont to frequent. It was a little shack that had a thriving business, overflowing the premises and out into the backyard where tables and wooden benches were set around. Way in the back was a well in which the proprietor would keep cool his bottles of *vin*. The "Garry" bunch had the table nearest the well reserved for them, so that while the proprietor was engaged in lowering a basket filled with warm bottles to float in the ice-cold water of the well, they could *salvage* about three cold bottles unbeknown to the proprietor, from the basket he had just pulled up, and so get four bottles of *vin* for two *francs* instead of only one bottle.

The one thing that stood out above all others during the week May 19-25, with heartbreaking prominence, was the quarantining of the battery and regiment, to the limits of the camp. This was due to the alarming daily increase of contagious cases taken to the hospital. Of course, we couldn't get it out of our heads that the quarantine was not due to the major general's desire to inflict a little punishment for the Bacchanalian revelry enjoyed by the bunch that spent the night of May 11-12 in Bordeaux.

It was hot as hell all week. Schools in the morning, drills in the afternoon, and Sergeant Anderson's gas mask instruction at odd periods helped make us look like *drowned rats*, by the time retreat rolled around.

Wednesday forty-four horses were assigned to the battery, good ones, so good that when Sergeant Ecock put the two best ones in harness to an empty *fourgon* wagon they couldn't even budge it until he administered his patented massage treatment.

Thursday night of the 23rd we received our money for April. It was the first pay-day in France and it was late at night, almost 10 p.m., as we stood in line each one awaiting his turn to bellow "here" and salute reverently the stacks of dough piled on the table that he was *not* going to get. We were paid in *frog* money and everybody agreed that the reason we had to wait until after dark to "collect" was that the paymaster decided on this course so we couldn't see the *stage* money we were getting. Lights were going in the barracks until midnight disclosing groups of the boys scrambled on the floor, paper and pencil in hand, trying to figure out just how much real dough they had received. Oh, yes, we finally calculated how much that bunch of tissue paper represented, but it didn't look like it. Nobody has ever respected the value of a *franc*—or of a hundred—to this day. It has never seemed to impress us as real money.

On Saturday, after a gruelling hot day at drill, we had our first gun competition for the battalion. Nobody felt like working, so as a reward for our excellent showing all non-coms were called together by Captain Mitchell in back of the latrine and informed that their jobs were not likely to be steady unless there was a material improvement.

Sunday was a beautiful day and it was our turn at Regimental Guard.

The week of May 26-June 1st began our really interesting work, firing on the range. We began with 400 rounds Wednesday afternoon and knocked 'em dead—showed 'em all up. We might not have been good on a drill field, but when it came down to shooting—the real test—we couldn't be beaten. We had received 26 more horses in the morning to help us get the guns to the range and we needed 'em. The quarantined boys returned to our barracks before nightfall with the joyous tidings that we would now be allowed outside the gate—the quarantine had been lifted so that we could go to Bordeaux for Decoration Day—tomorrow.

The party was spoiled a bit by our going out to the range in the morning on Decoration Day and shooting some more. The firing battery and telephone detail did not get back until 2 p.m. and were just about in time to see their more lucky comrades go dashing for Bordeaux in two of the trench mortar trucks. A real party in Bordeaux all right, and most of us got in somebody else's truck in front of the "Y. M." at 9 p.m. without being invited to do so by the M. P.s, and without being able to find the "P. S."

The hot weather continued right along and made muster particularly uncomfortable with blouses on. So somebody balled it up Friday afternoon and we had to do it over again to please the "majuh," Saturday, June 1st at 3 p.m., and that killed all chances of making another trip to Bordeaux. We also received 30 more horses and that kept the drivers a little more occupied. The only pastime left to us now standing in line at the Y. M. C. A. to get a chance to buy enough oranges for the whole week and eat 'em all in one day.

Sunday, June 2nd, white passes were issued, good for the towns of Bonneau, Isaac, St. Medard, Martignas and St. Jean d'Illac. Only noncoms and first-class privates received these cards, but what wouldn't a fellow do for a friend? And, naturally, everybody that wanted to visit the above *vin*-joints had a card. So, although in this first week of June drills were twice as hard, gas masks had to be worn twice as long, and the stables now meant four times as much work—who cared In the evening there was always a good meal awaiting us at St. Jean d'Illac, with all the good *vin* and cherry brandy a man could drink, and pay for.

Monday, the 3rd, we were roused at 4.15 a.m. for target practice on the range and did not return until 6.15 p.m. for supper. We fired 709 rounds and it was a hard day's work. The battery was pretty much all in after the long hike back in the thick hot sand, and everybody tumbled into their bunks early for a solid night's rest. On Tuesday, 22 casuals were assigned to the battery—not horses—casuals, including our famous Manwaren-Swada delegation. Regular routine continued in force and we began to realize the necessity of good long sleeping hours.

Thursday we fired all day on the range again, this time using shell-reduced.

Friday evening the boys were down to *four corners* in bunches as Saturday was a soft day, the usual drills in the morning and the mean-less-than-nothing gun competition in the p.m. Passes for Bordeaux were granted to a lucky few and a great many unlucky ones went along solely for companionship.

The flies around the camp now became a serious menace to the health of the soldiers. Day after day another batch of men would be sent to the hospital. An official count was made of the men suffering from dysentery by the first sergeant, and it was found that 62 were severely ill at this time in our one battery.

But a little thing like dysentery couldn't keep a man from going to Bordeaux, as Carl Schaeffer will testify, even if it was a trifle embarrassing to him and absolutely mystifying to his *lady friend*.

The week of June 9-15 particular stress was laid by the signal detail on work with projectors, semaphore and wig-wag, stuff we never used at the front.

We were paid on the 11th for May, not so bad, and the rest of the week small *egg* omelettes consisting of eight to ten *oeufs* for one person were frequent and not alarming.

Wednesday, the 12th, was another early morning target practice at the range. We were routed out of bed at 4 a.m. We fired with reciprocal laying and used the quadrant for the first time in firing the pieces.

We had regimental guard on Friday and, of course, far be it from us to gossip, to wantonly tell tales about the officers in this logbook, but, being as the offenders were not our officers—this time—the above facts must be recorded. Our Private Goodwin, on guard Saturday from 1 a.m. to 3 a.m. at the officers' quarters, had considerable difficulty in maintaining quiet and order at the officers' luxurious mess-halls and had to several times threaten to pinch the bunch, "Goody" was finally reconciled by getting a couple of swigs from the coloured waiter, and patrolled his beat in peace until, as he reported to the corporal of the guard and to the O. D. on their rounds that there was no use of having a guard there. He had challenged a couple of officers approaching him and one lovingly assured him that he was *pure as a lily*, and the other that he hadn't touched a drop, but couldn't find his house.

Saturday we again had target practice in the a.m. Passes were issued for Bordeaux. *Four corners* rapidly began losing its popularity now with the white card permitting us to visit Medard and Jean d'Illac. Of course, 50 percent of each section had to remain around barracks to water the horses and attend to other details. The bunch that were off Saturday stayed at the Barracks Sunday, washed clothes and let the other fellows have a chance to get a sore head and an empty pocketbook.

Monday, the 17th, our regular routine was broken by everybody being called out (just before eating) at 11.30 a.m. to fight a fire on the range. No water, so we had to use sticks and shovels, and ask anybody if it wasn't real hard work. We got back at 5.30 p.m. starved and blackened, and cussing the world in general, as the water supply was turned off at 5.15 and we couldn't even wash up. Of course, there was the lake but we were too weary to walk way over there through the thick sands.

The Limoge party left today, consisting of 28 men, three corporals and one sergeant. They were gone for four weeks and the remainder of the battery always pitied the poor fellows "stuck" on this detail. But we didn't know at that time just how they were getting along or our pity might suddenly have changed to envy.

They were supposed to have been quarantined in a half cleaned stable in Limoge, but we are now assured no one ever slept there except the guard. Limoge will remain forever in the minds of those unfortunates as a place where money was not essential to have a good time. Everyone was broke, yet the French people treated them like lords. They had plenty to eat, all they wanted to drink and any French home was theirs. Corporal Michael Lyons has a particularly healthy smile when we ask him about Limoge, and we understand, from a little inside information, that he had a shade on everybody's. Pretty soft!

Working hours were short and consisted only in taking care of the horses as they were delivered to the regimental corral. A French soldier picked the mounts as they arrived, for the French outfits; and a French woman chose the horses for the Americans. We all agree she was a good picker—for the French army.

Before we go back to the battery news at Souge, the 4th of July dinner the boys received at Limoge, must be mentioned in all fairness to the French. They killed two pigs, served a wonderful meal and furnished their own champagne in honour of the day.

At Souge there was plenty of work for the drivers the week of June 16-22. The new French harness was received on Tuesday, the 18th, and Lieutenants Burden and Steis were quite occupied instructing the drivers in the proper application of same.

Thursday a.m. we were at the range and fired our first barrage in practice. One of Battery B's guns blew up, killing two men and the boys' spirits were a bit dampened by the news of the accident. It was forgotten entirely the next day, however, and never has our confidence in the wonderful French 75s been shaken again.

Early Friday a.m. we were firing again on the range, gunners and numbers one riding their pieces carelessly. After one-half hour's practice word was received to cease firing as there was a fire on the range. We hiked five miles to fight it. It was two o'clock when the fire was finally checked and put out and we started back for the barracks. When in sight of it we were turned around and hiked again to the range. Completed our firing and then returned weary and footsore to our barracks to eat.

Saturday morning we had more target practice, and at last the reason was learned why the kitchen persistently arrived late with the mess. A man was despatched to locate them on the road and discovered that the kitchen force took the longest way round, far beyond the camp limits, in order to stop at the gin-mills and get a few drinks. We had the usual unsatisfactory battalion gun competition on the range in the p.m.

Sunday, the 23rd, there were lots of passes to Bordeaux. There were only two or three trucks for the regiment and it was always necessary for half of us to get a lift on somebody else's truck going in probably as far as Medard, or walk there—five miles—and then take the dinky trolley line to Bordeaux for six cents.

Coming back the trucks were crowded beyond their limits. It was with God's own grace that we always managed to come through without a serious accident. The 9 p.m. trucks were one struggling mass of more or less fizzled humanity. Arms and legs were stuck out in all directions and men hung limply to any part of the truck body, seat, top, or tail-board, they could grab hold of. It was a sight that will linger forever in our memory. Waiting for the departure, crowds of French civilians surrounded the loaded trucks and the boys merrily sang the *Star Spangled Banner,* the *Marseillaise,* and the latest Broadway ragtime hits to them. With a lurch the car was off, it's powerful motor throbbing restlessly under the strain of the heavy load. As the line of trucks swung through the streets of Bordeaux to the outskirts, headed for camp, store-keepers, villagers, old men and women, waved gleefully from doors and windows, to the happy singing American boys, who had left the best part of their month's pay in town without remorse.

We had target practice at the range every day this week, June 24-28 and in compliance with regimental order everyone had to wear his gas mask for one entire hour every day that week at a certain specified hour, no matter where he was or in what work has was engaged. It was a severe test as the weather was unbearably hot. Starkie, however, did it with ease. It was like eating pie to him. He had been in the habit of ducking out of the supply room and crawling into his bunk every day for the last month or so. He slept right through the morning and afternoon only getting up for mess. In order to keep the flies from disturbing his peaceful slumbers, he had tried sleeping with his gas mask on. It worked wonderfully, better than mosquito netting, and any time of the day when the flies were the thickest and the heat the hottest Starkie could be found, his thoughts in dreamland and his face in his gas mask.

Friday, after target practice, a fire broke out on the range and was not extinguished until Saturday morning.

Saturday the guard at Bonneau fell to our battery and the boys who were stuck went down in anything but a happy, playful mood. The coolies there had just been paid and were pickled to the gills. So, naturally, whenever one of the above usually timid, unmolesting Chinks got pesky with one of our docile guards, or two Chinks would start a little Château Thiery of their own in ninety-six different sharps and flats, our boys, just to give vent to their satisfaction at spending Saturday with them, instead of with friends in Bordeaux, and also to demonstrate how fervently we loved 'em, would belt a couple on the bean and then bump another one, about a mile away from the scene of trouble, for luck.

Sunday, the 30th, was muster. All the guns were cleaned. The sections of the battery, reorganized and horses assigned to certain drivers. Something was in the air.

The next day, July 1st, came the rumours of our departure for the front. We began to speculate, then to bet, on what front we were going. From what the papers said it looked as if they would only leave us where we were for another month, the Germans would move the front down to us, and so save our being transported 'way up to the battle line. But it probably wouldn't have been a safe procedure, so we began packing. Target practice went on as usual in the afternoon.

We received more horses Tuesday. Went out to the range after dark and had night firing. Quite a spectacle. We would call it a Fourth-of-July celebration with fireworks. Shrapnel was exploding at about a 50-mil height of burst and the flashes of the guns along the whole battalion front made one think of Coney Island.

Wednesday we unpacked to get ready to parade in Bordeaux tomorrow. The battery, consisting of the first gun crews—four pieces and the caissons—left at 2 p.m., just as it started raining. The boys were greatly disappointed when they pitched tents outside of Bordeaux at the old racetrack, and were not granted passes to town. Lieutenant Steis took Corporal Duckworth as interpreter to find water for the horses, and were the only lucky two. Duckie, with his usual ingenuity, managing to discover some good bottles of *vin* instead of locating plain water.

The battery paraded in Bordeaux 4th of July morning, along with the others, and then back to Camp Souge. arriving about nightfall. The rest of the boys who spent the day in Bordeaux on pass, and not in parade, had a wonderful joy-party celebrating over Declaration of Independence with more than the usual amount of cognac.

Friday, the 5th, was a perfect day. Lots of mail in and pay-day. We needed it.

Saturday was a fine day and quite a bunch of the boys went to Bordeaux to buy souvenirs for the folks back home, as we knew we were leaving soon.

Sunday morning we washed all soiled clothes, and got everything in readiness to leave. Captain Mitchell succeeded in getting a motor truck for the battery to take us to Bordeaux for the p.m. About thirty of us had passes, yet more than seventy were aboard the truck as it swung through the gate of the camp going to town.

Monday morning bright and early our battery started cleaning out the gun parks, the officers' quarters and the stables for the entire 1st and 2nd Battalion.

We then started cleaning up our own barracks. Brody was given a detail of burning up the piles of rubbish that the other bucks were carting out of our barracks. He displayed his usual cunning by bribing the two Chinks who were hanging around with two bags of "Bull-Durham" and a pack of cigarette papers, to do his work for him. He immediately retreated to the Y. M. C. A. and camped there all day while his two Chinks laboured silently and diligently completing his job in a much more meritorious manner than Brody could have done.

John Bohannon, first sergeant, and Ben Jacobson, instrument corporal, managed to work Captain Mitchell for a pair of theatre passes to Bordeaux good until 1 a.m., in order to celebrate our departure for the front. They came back in a velvet-cushioned taxi to Souge and no sleep. The battery was awakened at 3.20 a.m., packs rolled, less than no breakfast, and all arrangements completed. We left Camp Souge at 7 a.m. Tuesday, July 9th, in a broken line of march—some on foot, some on horse, and others by motor truck. We entrained at Bonneau in two hours, even rigging up telephone lines along the whole train. We had mess at the station consisting of canned tomatoes and *willy* and other similar delicacies.

We left Bonneau at 1.15 p.m. and rode for 56 hours. It was another case of *couchez* in the hay in box cars but we were all happy. It wasn't half as bad as the trip from Brest to Bordeaux and the consolation of it all was that we almost lost Greenlee, our beloved mess sergeant. He fell off the train while it was in motion on the second day out and we all prayed while the train was being stopped and a detail was sent back to pick up the pieces. It was the closest call Battery F ever had to getting good mess.

The big *burgs* we passed through on this trip were:

Libourne, Mussidan, Perigueux, Limoges, St. Sebastian at (7.05 a.m., July 10), Chateauroux, Issoudun, Bourges, Sancerre, Clamecy, Mailly-la-Ville, Château-Villain (at 7.15 a.m., July 11), Bricon, Chaumont (at 9.15 a.m.), Langres, Culmont, Hortes, Barges, Passavant, Darney, Thaon, Vincey, Charmes, Bayon, Einvaux, Blainville, Luneville and Baccarat.

We reached Baccarat at 11 p.m. and detrained. We were alarmingly informed that it was only three kilometres to the front line trenches, and all precautions should be taken so as not to apprise the enemy of our arrival. We first of all unloaded the blue bags and took all helmets out, as we were assured the German aviators bombed the station every night and we needed the helmets for protection. Say, the war began to look serious! No lights were allowed, and we talked in whispers. The unloading progressed quietly and quickly and was completed at 1.30 a.m., and not a Boche plane in sight and not a shell had fallen.

Everything went along smoothly until we started off and then—woe be unto us—our rolling kitchen could be heard along those roads for ten miles—*klankety, klank, klank!* We expected any minute a ton of shot to fall on us, but it never came.

We reached Bertrechamps about 3.30 a.m., watered the horses and rested up all morning. We made our "echelon" in the woods and in the afternoon drank a little *vin* in town and wrote our farewell letters home. We were going into firing position the following night. We left at 6 p.m., July 13th—the 3rd and 4th guns only went up with the telephone, machine gun and camouflage detail. Reached our position about 1 a.m. in a black night and pouring rain. There was no sleep for anyone. Position was about 200 metres north of the road between Neuf Maison and Vacqueville. It rained all day and we got little chance to sleep. This was Sunday, July 14th, the French National holiday. We laid our first lines to E Battery and began camouflaging.

The 1st Platoon came up at night. There was more digging and no sleep for us.

Monday, the 15th, everything was quiet. The telephone men made their first trip to the dreadful "No Man's Land" and we had the pleasing and interesting sensation of watching the Boche aeroplanes overhead being shot at. Sergeant Dooley is the acting first sergeant at the gun position.

Tuesday we did more digging, as our pits didn't fit the elephant irons just so, and somebody thought we ought to change the line of fire. We also turned around our camouflage nets a few times for ditto reason.

Wednesday all day there was considerable aerial activity which lessened our working hours at digging—*"It's an ill wind, etc."* Also somebody discovered good champagne could be bought at the farm and the officers soon had three bottles. We finally received our revolvers and ammunition, and as soon as we got the chance we would go off somewhere and see how near we could come to hitting the side of a house.

Thursday, July 18th, the battery registered, and Corporal Spiegel was sent down to the infantry front line trenches as liaison agent. The Germans shelled the Peronne road last night and that put a stop to bringing the wagon-trains in by that roundabout way and somebody we know very well was not a bit sore that he could now get a little sleep.

Friday, the 19th, five men were detailed for instruction on handling the 60 and 95 mm. guns, made in 1882 and 1890, respectively. Communication with O. P. was very difficult to maintain (see Sergeant McKenna).

Saturday, the 20th, was a beautiful summer day with an occasional air battle to lend *atmosphere* and setting to this busy front.

Sunday we had nothing to do all day—*mirabilé dictu*. Even First Sergeant Bohanan at the echelon allowed everybody there 1½ hours off to go to Bertrechamps and wash clothes. Our blue bags were taken away today—never to be seen again.

On Monday night the second gun, under Sergeant Parlee, moved forward about two kilometres to the *pirate* position. It was dark and rainy and we had a lovely time getting in. The medico and assistant gas N. C. O. went along in case of need.

It rained all day Tuesday and the extra men dug two gun positions in the wood directly in front of Parlee's position. A lookout station was formed called Madison' connecting the pirate gun to the main position which we called Hunt station.

Wednesday night Captain Mitchell mistook two trees for a couple of spies and ran around them in a circle hollering: "Halt! or I'll fire!" and would have shot, only he didn't have his gun.

Thursday, the 25th, Father Sheridan visited us and stayed overnight. We sent Sergeant Tingle and five privates on detached service to Battery B, as their gun crews were quarantined.

Friday it was still raining. We lost Lieutenant Steis—transferred to the Gas Service. Sergeant Parlee left in the p.m. for Officers' Training School and Jacobson was put in charge of the pirate gun.

It rained heavily Saturday all day. We played the game of *trial barrage* on and off during the day and night. It was a hell of a lot of sport trying to see how fast you could get a shot off, but Schaeffer almost lost his life on one occasion at the pirate position while repairing the line to the aiming light. He was directly in front of the muzzle when the command "Fire" was given, and he saved his life only by dropping to the ground, getting his blouse badly scorched and his hearing somewhat jarred, not to mention anything about the fit Corporal Dupree had while trying to stop the piece from being fired.

Monday, the 29th, we all signed the payroll and also were deloused at Indian Village.

The night of Tuesday, the 30th, about 10 p.m., Jerry came over in one of his bombing planes and came very close to putting Battery F off the face of the map. He dropped three bombs in rapid succession from a very low altitude and they landed squarely among our shelter tents, one just narrowly missing Lieutenant Derby and Private Hundt at the telephone station and another barely escaping destroying our kitchen. It was a close call and nobody was injured at all.

Wednesday we received word that we break camp tomorrow and leave for a *regular* front. Our schooling was at an end—now for the big fight! Everything was being put into readiness and just while we were having dinner at 6.15 p.m., over came a shell, exploding in the woods right near us. It spoiled everybody's dinner and broke up the mess. Beans were thrown in all directions and the battery dove headlong into our huge dugout to await the next shell. We were then ordered to crawl to the other woods by No. 1 gun and sleep there.

At the pirate position the gas alarm was going all night, but we never even got one sniff of any gas. If the Germans were sending any gas over, all the harm it was doing was to keep us from getting any sleep.

Thursday, August 1st, the telephone lines were taken up, wagons packed with everything in sight, and the gas stores left behind. We were to pull out of positions at 11 p.m. and did so on the dot. The main battery under Lieutenant Derby met the pirate gun with Lieutenant Nissley at Vacqueville at midnight.

We travelled on the road all night and morning, passing through Vacqueville, Baccarat, Fontenoy, Domptail, St. Pierremont, and camping in woods near Magnieres at 11 a.m. We caught a couple of hours' sleep, had a corned willy meal and hardtack and harnessed up again at 6 p.m. We waited in formation with our carriages until 12.30 a.m. before the regiment had pulled out of Magnieres and we resumed our road march.

We again travelled all night passing through Bayon and arrived at Bainville at 8 a.m. It was tough, all right, and we were all more or less asleep on our horses, and at every halt along the march the boys who were walking would flop on the wet ground for a few minutes' sleep.

We were given billets in Bainville, sleeping on cots with hay mattresses, located in empty dwellings—upper lofts of occupied houses, and in stables and barns. In one particular billet the boys slept with a nice young pig as a companion, and the rooster and hens would come in and visit them occasionally and perch all over their beds.

We were the first American troops to be billeted in the town and we were treated excellently. They had wonderfully good beer, just like home, and any and every house woman would cook us up a corking good dinner for little money.

Sunday, the 4th, Sergeant Dooley appointed first sergeant. The articles of war were again read to us, but this time to the *non-coms* only and in an even, calm, but firm tone, each word hardly more than a whisper, but as clear and distinct and impressive as the chimes of an old church bell. And the crisis was passed. We loved and honoured the reader of those words and our decision was as one man—we would all go through hell for him without a whimper.

Mass was held in the church next to the ruins of an old monument built in the 9th century, and in the p.m. we went bathing in the Moselle. Pat Kiernan went fishing with a bent pin, but had no luck as he forgot to put bait on his line.

Monday we had a good time. Little to do and we had lots of beer and good meals. Quite a bunch more had a bath in the river and to bed early, the cafes being closed at 8.30 p.m.

Tuesday, the 6th, we were ordered to move. We packed up and left Bainville at 5 p.m. Entrained at Charmes at 8 p.m. and the train pulled out at 11 p.m. Our line of travel was through Neufchateau, Bar-le-Duc, Revigny, Pargny, Vitny-le-Francois, Sompuis, Sommesons, Connantre, Sazanue, Esternay, Joiselle, St. Simeon, and arrived at Chailly-Boissy at 7 p.m. the next day, which was Wednesday, the 7th. We lost Lieutenant Derby at the last station before our destination was reached as our train had pulled out without him, but he came along all right on the next train.

We detrained at 10 p.m. and harnessed up our pretty sick horses. As we started our march No. 3 caisson held us up a bit by falling over the little bridge we had to cross and down into the river below. Luckily, the horses were not pulled in with it and more luckily they call any old mud puddle a river in France. Nobody was drowned and we were off again, marching all night until about 4 a.m., when we reached a little cluster of farmhouses called Le Petit-sur-Nois (near Doux) and after tying the horses up to the picket lines, crawled in hay lofts and barns. We slept until 7.30. Were assigned to billets and then cleaned material. We are about 25 miles due east of Paris and about the same distance south of Château-Thiery.

During the night of August 8th the camouflage net on the 4th piece mysteriously caught fire and burned up and Masterson did a Paul Revere up and down the road on horseback yelling: "Fire! "Fire"! While he was arousing the army to fight the flames, Farina, on guard at the time, was doing a *hula-hula* around the burning net, trying to put it out without scorching his hands.

Friday, the 9th, we packed up to move and then unpacked again. We had pistol practice in the p.m. and "Red" Hinds was almost winged.

Saturday, the 10th, we left at 3.20 p.m. and marched all the rest of the day and all night, passing through Coulommiers, Rebais and Sablonmieres. We made camp at 5.30 a.m. in the woods overlooking Chezy-sur-Marne and as worn out as we were, we started right in cleaning material.

Corporal Hovey fell asleep on the march while dismounted and lost his horse and his pack. Our corned willy tasted good to us today, and most of us took a swim in the Marne to refresh us a bit.

Pulled out at 7 p.m. Passed through Château-Thiery at 10 p.m. and again kept going all night. At daybreak camped in woods north of Courpoil, called Forèt de Feré. It had been a scene of recent severe fighting and the spoils of battle lay on the grounds amid the newly dug graves of Americans and Huns. Quite a number of dead horses were strewn around and the stench was far from pleasant. We slept a bit, cleaned material and pulled out again at 7.30 p.m.

Arrived at 4 a.m., August 12th, at Forèt de Nesle. Quentin Roosevelt's grave was about one kilometre away from our camp. Very near our watering place was Château Nesles, once visited by Joan of Arc and where Napoleon spent his honeymoon with Josephine.

We lost our kitchen and were out of luck until the next day for coffee or any warm food. The flies were terrible. There were millions of 'em round the camp. 80 per cent of the battery's effectives were down with a most severe dysentery, too weak to stand. It was now ascertained that this is to be our echelon and the guns go into position from here.

We slept in our shelter tents in the woods and it was a dizzy night. The Boche bombed the woods all around us from aeroplanes, and during the entire night we were kept awake by some damn fool gas alarms.

Wednesday, August 14th, after our kitchen arrived we were served rotten cabbage and it added another bunch to the sick list. Captain Mitchell was transferred to the Battalion Field Staff and Captain Delanoy assigned to our battery. As a protection from aeroplane bombs, everybody had to dig little graves about six inches deep, for themselves to sleep in at night. Towards evening the roar of the distant cannon increased gradually in intensity, as barrage after barrage was repeated and by dark the black skies were rent with ceaseless crimson jets of flame.

It was the *call of the wild*, and our blood tingled with the excitement, the desire, the knowledge that tomorrow we'd be in it—the *Big Push*! And we gathered around the old battery quartet and sang those songs we loved so much. A dizzy night again, every half hour another false alarm for gas. Corporal Lasher almost had apoplexy when awakened by the gas claxon and he couldn't locate his gas mask under the caisson.

Thursday, the 15th, was a peach of a day, hot and sticky, perfect weather for flies. The picture will long remain with us that Lieutenant Burden made at noon mess trying to eat bread and jam without getting it full of flies, by wrapping his head in a bundle of pink mosquito netting and sticking the jam under it, in his wild efforts to evade the hungry pests.

In the p.m. we were notified two guns were going into position. They left at 7 p.m., the first and second guns under Sergeants Mc-Henry and Jacobson, and were led into position by Captain Delanoy and Lieutenant Nissley. There were clouds of dust along the road, the only place we ever encountered that so much heralded plague of the artillery.

The incessant rumble of the artillery on our left slowly became more and more distinct. A hell of a battle was going on in our adjacent sector. As we neared Chèry and passed through it, the Boche began shelling. There was quite a lot of sneezing gas in the air. We had to put our masks on and one piece not being able to see the turn in the road went straight on ahead towards the German lines till Nugent stopped it.

We relieved the 16th U. S. Artillery and no sooner had we gotten into position, packs hardly off our backs, than we got a call for *barrage*, and it was repeated several times throughout the night. It was our first real battle. Jerry was putting 'em over, too. Shells were falling all around us, but not within 300 yards, and he gave us plenty of sneezing gas.

The evening of August 16th the 2nd platoon under Sergeants Tingle and McCormack escorted by Captain Derby arrived amid severe bombardment of Chèry and the crossroads.

Our O. P. was on Lesprey Farm. Shells were falling continually round us and at night we got a good deal of mustard gas.

Saturday the telephone lines were heavily shelled by the Boche, causing continual work at repairing same. We had more gas on and off during the day and occasionally their vicious time H. E. high overhead. There were plenty of splinters flying about at all times and we were ordered to enlarge our two by two dugout so that ultimately everybody could sleep under ground. Lieutenant Derby told the telephone detail to deepen their dugout a bit and they immediately complied, but soon hit upon bones, and then ribs and finally a hoof. They found they had constructed their dugout right over the spot where someone had buried a horse, so they quickly threw back again a few inches of the newly disturbed earth on the dead horse, calmly lay their blankets down on top and let it go at that. It was easier than digging a new dugout.

Sunday, the 18th, we pulled off a couple of barrages before breakfast. More gas and continual shelling of the woods just to our right and the little farmhouse used as a first aid station about 500 yards in front of our position. We got quite a little gas at night.

Monday, the 19th, Captain Delanoy and Sergeant McKenna were wounded at the O. P. during a heavy shelling. We received our first American mail since Lorraine front. Captain Derby in charge of us now.

Thursday, the 20th, we did more than our usual firing and got more gas in return and more shelling all around us. At night we had our masks on from six to eight hours. We had been getting only two meals a day, breakfast anywhere from 8.30 to 10.30 and dinner about 2.30 to 4 p.m., according to when the ration cart arrived with the food. Captain Derby now arranged with the echelon to send us hot coffee and bread every night at 10 p.m. and it certainly was a blessing, providing we could get down to the wagon in time before the hash-hounds in the first section had grabbed all the eats.

Wednesday, the 21st, the battery had a good day, firing 700 rounds in all, 200 of which were gas shells—and we were happy. We were contented only when we were firing our pieces. Two of our guns kept up an harassing fire all night.

Thursday we continued the fire of the preceding night with about 600 rounds. Things began to look serious for us. Barrage calls from the infantry were getting frequent. From 9.30 a.m. to 2.30 p.m. we fired five barrages, and then began cutting our range down.

In the afternoon we got word of our counter-attack on a large scale and at 4.30 p.m. we opened the attack. There was not a moment's rest until 11.30 p.m., by which time our battery had fired 3,068 shots. Our guns were terribly hot, so hot that the paint blistered and boiled on the barrels.

At 12.10 a.m. we got orders to re-commence firing and with shortened ranges. We had to dig away the little mound of dirt on the edge of the machine gun trench in front of us to be able to fire at the required elevation and got to it eagerly. We fired all day Friday and up to midnight had gotten off 1,655 shots, a total of 4,723 rounds in 31½ hours of practically unbroken fire. One by-one our guns were rested for 15 minutes and cooled by pouring buckets of cold water through the barrels. Everyone from buck to sergeant helped carry the ammunition from the road to the gun position.

Saturday, the 24th, we did our first firing at 12.05 a.m. There came a verbal call for barrage. We got six rounds off (per gun) and then the barrage was stopped by orders. Ten minutes later the call was repeated by telephone and we completed our barrage in quick order. We have since learned that the second barrage caught the Germans coming out of the trenches and cut them up severely. They had come to the attack thinking our first barrage had ended. All day we fired 759 rounds. We got more gas at night and it was raining. Chèry got heavy shelling as usual and six men were killed there in the Red Cross station. We gave the Germans harassing fire all night and felt better for it.

Sunday, the 25th, the battery had a soft day, 472 shots, spent in normal barrages, counter battery work and retaliatory fire. The night was cool and rainy and we had a gas attack for one hour. Benny Polack again carried coffee to Lieutenant Nissley at the O. P. at night. He fell in a straddle trench in the darkness on the way up and turned his job down, complaining to the lieutenant that he didn't want to do it again.

Monday we discovered that during the night the Boche had put 8 direct hits on the road between Chèry and on our position and had also knocked down the church steeple at Chèry. This was a busy day for the telephone detail.

Tuesday, the 27th, we continued our barrages and counter-battery work, firing a total of 592 shots. We repeated a normal barrage three times in rapid succession just after daybreak. At night we got mustard gas, but were quite accustomed to it now and thought nothing of it.

Wednesday, the 28th, the boys at the echelon received their July pay. The firing battery got off 385 rounds and called it a day's work. But the telephone men had a busy time of it, day and night work on the lines and the boys had several narrow escapes from shells.

Thursday the firing battery received their pay, but there was no place to spend it. We amused ourselves with some counter-battery work—100 shots—for which we had to dig our heads off to get our anti-craft elevation. And then the officers would devise a scheme for winning the war by shooting 900 mils to the wrong side of our normal line of fire and we had to dig all over again and in solid rock, too. The 4th piece was particularly fortunate in having the good luck to strike solid granite to dig through. All four gun pits had enough rock, but the pit of the 4th piece resembled a stone quarry when they got through. In the evening Sergeant Schwitchenberg again came up with the *fourgon* wagon. This made his tenth successive night trip to our position and he has had some pretty close calls along the roads. The past few nights we had a beautifully clear moonlight and the drivers coming up from the echelon with chow and wire netting had anything but an enjoyable trip through gas and shell fire.

Friday, the 30th, we again had counter-battery work and one hour's gas. Last night two Camembert cheeses had come up in the wagon for one of the boys and by mistake had been put in the officers' dugout. Captain Derby spent a miserable night insisting that a rat or something worse had crawled into his quarters and died. In the morning the cheese was discovered and the Captain immediately got rid of it by dispatching one cheese to Lieutenant Nissley at the O. P. and the other to its proper owner.

It started raining early in the morning of Saturday, the 31st. We had barrages and counter-battery work, 245 rounds, and it was becoming more evident that the Boche gas was dwindling in frequency and strength. Corporal Hovey took the G. S. cart up with a German pill box to the O. P. under severe shelling, and he wasn't a bit sorry when he got back.

Sunday, September 1st, we fired our last normal barrage at 10.30 a.m., and then continued with counter-battery work. At about 2.30 p.m. we thought it was all over with us when Jerry started dropping shells right on top of us and our gun position. They had the exact range. The first one was a dud and hit squarely among us. It would have killed ten men had it gone off. There were six more that did explode, all within a radius of 25 yards of our guns. One fell in the 306th Machine Gun trench, 10 yards in front of us, killing three and wounding seven. That none of our battery was killed was a miracle. In a few minutes it was all over and our firing continued, as usual, totalling 350 rounds. Cheese and chocolate was received for our canteen and which we divided equally among the sections. At night the gas was very slight.

Monday, September 2nd, we fired only 172 shots in counter-battery work and we had a chance to go down to the water trough and take a bath—while the Boche shells were breaking on the crest of the hill not far away.

A new position had been picked out for us yesterday in case of renewed shelling of our present position, and camouflage nets set up. This morning it was discovered that a German 210 had gone through the net and tore a big hole in the ground just where our gun would have been. The boys at the echelon were entertained at night by the band of the 308th Engineers. Jerry broke up the party, however, by appearing on the scene in a war chariot and dropping a little confetti.

Tuesday, the 3rd, we had counter-battery work—265 rounds and a little gas in the air. It was reported the Germans are beginning to retreat and they certainly made desperate but unsuccessful efforts to cover the movement of their troops by bringing down our observation balloons. Air fights had been frequent, but now the skies were speckled with bristling, sputtering machines and we witnessed some interesting battles. Fires were burning behind the German lines most of the night and we knew their retreat was imminent.

Wednesday, September 4th, we fired only in the morning, at long range, 72 shots. We received word about 3 p.m. to advance. The echelon broke camp and moved forward in twenty minutes. We left our excess equipment behind at the gun position and towards evening pulled our guns out and harnessed up. We remained all night in march formation in a drizzling cold rain, without any sleep. The roads were blocked and it was 3 a.m. when we started forward passing through St. Martin and Villa Savoy.

We crossed the Vesle at 5 a.m. (Thursday) and kept going. Everywhere was visible the *price of honour*—our unburied dead. They lay along the whole route, some terribly mangled, others as calm and serene as in sleep. We had a salmon and hardtack breakfast in an open field, rested for an hour as our horses had had a hell of a time pulling through the mud and shell holes in the roads and then continued on passing through Fismette under heavy shelling from the Boche. We remained in the open roads, broad daylight under continual observation by enemy aeroplanes until

2 p.m. We arrived at battery position about 6 p.m. and started digging. Moved a quarter of a mile to new battery position at 8 p.m. and began an all night shift of digging. Privates George and Carson were gassed in German dugouts and left for the hospital.

Friday, September 6th, the line was laid to the infantry trenches. We had our first hot meal in 48 hours. Somehow our kitchen always managed to get lost. It was some night. Jerry was upstairs dropping lights, star shells. He put one directly over us. Again we were saved by a miracle. He dropped his bombs just to the rear of us, between the echelon and our position.

Saturday the rain began and for a stretch of six successive days and nights it rained on and off—mostly on—us. Today was a veritable cloudburst, and everybody slept in the mud and water. Sergeant Bohanan was put in charge of the first section, while Sergeant Mc-Henry was given his "Coney Island" barker job, acting as executive at the guns. For nearly a month we were short two officers. All the work devolved upon Captain Derby and Lieutenant Nissley to figure data and ranges. Our problems were such that called for instant computation. We tried to register, getting about 30 shots off, but observation was too difficult and it had to be given up for another day.

We were some army! We stole everything in sight, from a piece of tin to the side of a house and got away with it by calling it *salvaging*. Anything you'd see that you would like, just take it—it's yours—*salvaged*. And maybe we didn't become experts in a short while! It was wonderful. Put a bunch of men out there in the barrenness and desolation of war-beridden France, leave 'em to their own initiative to find the necessities of life, and we don't know where it comes from, but they'll soon have everything that belongs to the comfort of a home, from a mattress to an egg-beater!

Sunday, the 8th, was still raining and the linemen had great difficulty in maintaining communication over the long lines to the infantry. We fired 316 rounds all day.

Monday, the 9th, we fired our barrages and did some counter-battery work, totalling 186 shots. The rain still kept up and it was a tough time trying to keep our sleeping quarters dry.

Tuesday we registered, the weather cleared a bit. One of the guns fired fifty semi-steel and never could the O. P. locate one of them. We got off a little counter-battery and harassing fire totalling 186 rounds. Lieutenants Taylor and Hill—regular fellows—joined the battery today. At night plenty of shelling on the crest just in front of us, and *beaucoup* rain all night.

Wednesday, the 11th, we fired 440 rounds getting our first normal barrage off at 7.30 p.m. There was lots of trouble on the lines again caused by shell fire.

Drivers had their share of the dirty work at this front, working day and night, bringing food and ammunition from the echelon up the steep slopes to our battery position under constant shell fire from the Germans.

Thursday, the 12th, we had more rain and more mud, fired 208 rounds during the day and got all the chance we wanted to sleep in the slush at night.

Friday, the 13th, and raining—but none of us got killed. Only 75 rounds today.

Saturday was a grand day. We did some real fighting again like the big day at Chèry. Just before daybreak our guns opened up and fired for twelve hours without a let-up, the battery getting off 3,200 rounds. The weather favoured us, too. It was the first sunny day in a week, and during the hurry call to the echelon for more ammunition, every available man, driver, spare cannoneer, or non-com—all did their damndest, passing the ammunition up the steep slope from the road to the gun position.

Sunday, the 15th, we learned we were going to be relieved for certain in the p.m. The combat train pulled out of the echelon at 3 p.m., starting back along the road through Fismes. While passing through the road the Huns began shelling just ahead of us. The carriages were turned around and had to come back through Fismes and go around by the other road. Some of the other batteries lost quite a few horses by shell fire, but again we had our streak of luck with us and no one was injured. The guns pulled out at 7 p.m. relieved by the Italians. We met the combat train along the road and travelled all night. Jerry bombed the roads in a wonderfully clear moonlight and again the regiment lost some horses. Passed through Fismes, Chèry, Travegney, Coulouges and Cohan.

Just about daybreak of Monday, the 16th, we went into camp in the woods near Cierges. We got a few hours' sleep. We were paid for the month of August. Harnessed up at 6.30 and waited in woods. Pulled out at 10.30 p.m.

Had another all night march, going through Goussacourt, St. Geminee Passy. We crossed the Marne near Mareail le Port just after daybreak and camped in a stubble field—Chene la Reins. Tuesday, the 17th, we spent the day there, packed up about 6 p.m. and then the order to leave was cancelled. Forty men with their packs were sent over to the headquarters detachment. We lay down to catch a little sleep just as it started to rain. Called at 2 a.m. (Wednesday) and began our march at 4 a.m. We were now passing through country unscathed by the war. Wonderful vineyards walled the roads, and the boys, tired, wan and thirsty, ate ravenously the handful of grapes taken on the march. It was well on towards noon that our weary horses were made to pull up to the top of the long, steep hill overlooking Avize, and we camped in the woods along the road. While the cooks were trying to prepare us some corned willy, most of us paid a visit to the town—Avize—and bought lots of eats and *vin*. It was a real Champagne town and soon everybody was more or less drunk. Corporal Goodwin had somebody's goat for a while and John Foray-slept in the cemetery all night. It was our first chance to get a drink since going to the front in August and the stuff had double effect as we were tired and empty-stomached.

We had a good night's sleep, though it rained continually and most of us did not have our shelter-halves pitched. We were aroused about 3.30 a.m.

Thursday, the 19th, turned all the carriages around a couple of times first in one direction and then in another and finally got going in the right direction at 5 a.m. It was necessary in order to hide our worn out uniforms and dilapidated appearance to don overcoats or slickers on the march before entering any towns. There was a long halt in Avize and when we started again we were a sight for the Gods. Every man was stocked to the limit of his carrying capacity with honest-to-goodness bread, sardines, cheese and champagne. It was another entire day's hike, the battalion losing the route. Reached our destination at 5 p.m. Camped in a large open field—Farm de Notre Dame (near Cheniers) and ten kilometres from Chalons. Sergeant Bohannan, still dizzy from Avize, right-dressed the tent-pitchers to the great amusement of everybody present. Wild and varied were the rumours afloat. Chalons was in all probability our rest camp. Huge barracks had been constructed for the housing of men and horses, and we would draw new uniforms and equipment, get baths there and have a good month's vacation in the city itself. We went to sleep happy—particularly that Captain Derby told us to throw away our aiming stakes and camouflage poles. We were not going to another front without a rest, as the pessimistic ones had preached.

Showers were frequent during the night and morning. We were aroused by bugle at 3.30 a.m. Had an early breakfast in the rain and on our way at 6 a.m. But we went directly away from Chalons. Something was wrong—and our dope changed into doubt. We made good time on the march and made camp in a field at La Cheppe about 2.30 p.m. Pitched tents and spent the rest of the afternoon cleaning material and repacking wagons. We bought some real eats in the town, got a good night's sleep.

Up at 7 a.m. the next morning (Saturday, September 21st) and again repacked the wagons and cleaned material. We left our field at 3 p.m. and hiked through Pogny, Franceville, Coupyville, Le Fresne and reached Bussy-le-Repos at 2 a.m.

We camped in a little orchard in the village. It was raining cats and dogs and after daybreak some of us took refuge in a deserted Y. M. C. A.

hut nearby and slept on the tables and floor. It was impossible to buy a thing in the village, reputed as the poorest town in France—in contrast to Avize, which we had but shortly left and was classed as one of the richest and cleanest towns in the country. We pulled out at 7 p.m. and marched all night in the pouring rain. We made camp at 5 a.m. in the thick woods alongside the road about one kilometre from Chatrices. Everybody was soaking wet, cold and hungry. The rain had gone through our slickers and our clothes were wringing wet. No one pitched tents—we were too tired. We contented ourselves with rolling in our blankets and shelter-halves, and threw ourselves on the ground, dead tired. After two or three hours' sleep the horses were groomed and then we had a joy party making pancakes for ourselves with the dough that Larue spoiled by knocking the can over. We were informed in a little speech by the B. C. that we were nearer the front than we had imagined and would go into position in the line direct from here. "Our rest is at an end," he said with a smile, and we heaved a sigh of relief. The front was better than this hiking. At 7 p.m. we started out marching and kept it up all night.

We passed through St. Menehould and arrived at battery position in the Argonne Forest at 6 a.m. (Tuesday, the 24th), near La Harazee. We were greeted with a warm reception by the Boche—the scream and bursting of the big shells round us celebrating our entrance into the Argonne front. We were given no time for sleep. To work at once, on our gun-pits, ammunition pit, and shelter trench. Luckily, we had any number of old French dugouts in the vicinity, and at night while half of the crews worked the others caught a few hours' sleep on their wet, cold blankets.

The next day was spent at hard labour enlarging our pits to their 1600-mill sweep and as soon as night set in every available man got to work with brand new axes borrowed from the engineers. By midnight we had cut down a good part of the Argonne forest, permitting us to fire from our position at the required short ranges. At our battery position, tired as everyone was, there was no chance to sleep after midnight. The battle was to open at 2.20 a.m. and ammunition was arriving every minute and had to be carried back from the road to the gun position. Everybody was stepping round lively. In the P. C. both Captain Derby and Lieutenant Nissley, without sleep for 48 hours, broke down under the strain of ceaseless figuring and reconnaissance, and fell asleep across the little wooden table with the dim light of the low burning candle in the corner, and left Lieutenant Hill to figure his first barrage. At the last minute our battery received orders to cover the entire battalion section, which required a further shift of three hundred or more miles and while the section chiefs were going crazy trying to get the pits completed for the new laying, Lieutenant Hill, watch in hand, emerged from the P. C.

and after the preliminary caution that it was one minute to firing time, began: "Ready—Fire!" and not a gun responded. The first piece had slipped off the platform and rolled down into the trail pit and the second piece was busily engaged chopping down a tree about two feet thick that was only five feet away and directly in the path of our new line of fire. The third piece had its trail in the ammunition pit and the fourth was busy tearing down their beautifully constructed sandbag and log roof and walls, as it interfered with the muzzle of the gun.

The swearing that we indulged in for the next ten minutes before we got firing was good for our constitutions, but not very good for our souls. Our guns started. At about the same time Hell itself was turned loose on earth. The battle that was to put our division forever in history—the Argonne—was on its way—opened by the *million dollar barrage*. The noise was so terrific that one had to holler at the top of his voice to the man standing next to him to make himself heard. The first shot from McHenry's piece carried away the *frog* telephone line that had been put up during the night directly in front of his piece.

We fired without a break from 2.40 a.m. to 3.30 p.m., getting off 2,725 rounds. As the morning went on and the rate of fire decreased, the exhausted crews were given a chance of getting a couple of hours' sleep.

In the p.m. after waiting impatiently for the limbers to come up from the echelon, the 2nd platoon went forward with Lieutenants Nissley and Taylor. Passed through La Harasee and up a steep hill to the east of it. Lieutenant Nissley had no map on hand and the two guns had moved unbeknown to him, to within 2,000 yards of our front line. We slept all night on the ground by the pieces while waiting for orders—with machine guns and snipers' bullets occasionally whizzing by. The G. S. cart from the echelon had failed to reach us with food, and all we had was three hardtacks apiece before going to sleep. Lieutenant Nissley took a little joy trip with Ken Miller to the infantry trenches to get our targets from the major. They had an exciting time crawling back through mud, barbed wire and machine gun fire, and if it had not been for Miller the chances are neither would have gotten back alive.

Sergeant Smith left us to attend Officers' Training School.

In the morning of the 27th, Friday, while the 1st platoon was getting off 586 rounds, the crews of the 2nd platoon were trying to grub a little food from the infantry kitchens that lined the road at La Harasee. The 1st platoon pulled out of position about 4.30 p.m. and moved forward to a new position among the dead trees just to the east of Le Four de Paris. The 2nd platoon was unable to fire from its position on account of the heavy forest, and late at night was ordered back to the other guns. They joined the battery about 3 a.m. It was a hell of a position for our guns.

The ground was spotted with shell holes two yards apart, and in trying to pull the pieces into position, one of Corporal Spenzola's white horses fell into a shell crater and simply would not try to get out. The poor horse was dead tired, and as this was his first chance to rest in a long while, he was contented to choose the comfort of lying in a shell hole to standing up in harness. We fired 145 shots during the day here.

Sunday, the 29th, we had some barrages and harassing fire, totalling 684 shots. The scarcity of horses was now beginning to be felt. Half of the stuff that we had to leave behind yesterday was brought up only this p.m. and the few good horses we did have we worked to death hauling ammunition. We also received a little new clothing today—we were badly in need of it.

Monday, the 30th, our limbers and horses were up to battery position at daybreak. We rolled packs, pulled our guns out from among the shell holes to the road, everything put in readiness to move forward, and then the order was cancelled. This stunt was repeated at odd intervals during the day. And every time the darn order to move was cancelled we had to rush our guns back in position and rip off a dozen or two rounds at some pesky machine gun nest that was holding up the advance. During this game of *tag, you're it*, the 3rd piece was always the winner, being the first gun in the battalion to report in firing position and *in order*, due principally to the physical efforts of Lieutenant Taylor.

We remained in this position exactly one week more. It was during this week that the *lost battalion* of the 307th and 308th were sticking it out in their death trap, and every day from Monday, September 30th to Sunday, October 6th, it was practically day and night firing, barrage and zone firing and exterminating fire on machine gun nests. There was little rest for anyone these seven days, firing in all a total of 4,516 rounds for the battery. We had plenty of rain, too, which didn't make things a bit pleasant, as our dugouts would have an inch or two of water in the bottoms. The mud and slush on the long narrow staircases made it easy for anyone to slip and fall in it.

Our fire was particularly accurate and destructive and was instrumental in bringing upon our heads two letters of commendation, one from the corps commander to the division commander and another from the regimental C. O. to the battery commander, which bore the major's personal endorsement and commendation. Both of these documents are reproduced in the appendix page.

Back at the echelon our horses were dying so fast that First Sergeant Dooley had to appoint someone to handle the job of burying them. Corporal Hovey was elected official undertaker and his detail of gravediggers had plenty of work.

But outside of burying horses and grooming those that weren't quite ready to be buried, echelon life was not so bad at that time. Banquets and champagne dinners were often held in the little elephant-ironed orderly room and some of our purely local talent would help to entertain the guests while the crash and roar of the bursting shells and booming guns would be drowned in laughter and songs.

October 6th, Lieutenant Hill left us to join the infantry as our liaison officer. Varied and exciting have been his adventures, in that capacity, but he never tells of his many close calls to death. We have tried to get the personal side of his story from him, but all we could learn was, to put it in his own language, that he "ran all over France, and got damn good and wet."

The night of October 6th the firing battery moved to Vienne le Château, better known to us as German Village. We pulled into position about 3 a.m. October 7th in a dark night and the pieces had to be manhandled three or four hundred yards through soft, muddy soil covered with shell holes half full of water. In trying to bring in one of the *fourgon* wagons over the narrow plank bridge that spanned an old trench in front of our position, at Lieutenant Nissley's suggestion, the lead and swing teams were changed, and the wagon promptly fell overboard into the ditch pulling the off horse with it. Lieutenant Nissley admitted, for the first time, that he was wrong, and Sergeant Schwitchenberg went ahead with the rest of the train.

When daylight came we discovered our position was a *cuckoo*. Wonderful German dugouts nearby made of solid concrete and iron with electric lights, stoves and even bath tubs. We dug our gun-pits and lay in a store of ammunition. But in the three days we were here we did not fire a shot—the Boche kept pulling out of range.

Tuesday we all took baths in the German bath tubs—real hot water. Lordy! what wonders a little water can do! It began to rain pitchforks at night, so, naturally, even though we didn't fire, they had the section-chiefs get up and report to the P. C. a couple of times in the downpour. It was unbelievably dark, and the P. C. could only be found by wandering around about fifteen minutes floundering in the mud, and then for consolation the sergeants would get hell for taking so long to report.

Peace rumours were afloat Wednesday, the 9th, and the boys were beginning to believe them. Got ready to move forward at 5 p.m. and the order was cancelled at the last minute. There were several *peace celebrations* that night, the one of the most social prominence being held in Sergeant Anderson's dugout (please take note, he always had a dugout) and the invited guests and entertainers consisted of Corporals "L. I. Farmer" Horton and "Shoe Lace" Spiegel, and Sergeants "Black Jack" McHenry, "Whizz-Bang" Garry and "Silk" Jacobson. Said party lasted until 11.30 p.m., whereupon the guests went to sleep on the hard but inviting floor.

Thursday we were aroused at 4.30 a.m. Had a wee bite and pulled out. Travelled all day along shell-torn and muddy roads. German signs painted in big black letters on huge board frames confronted us on all sides. The Boche had left here only yesterday and the roads and underbrush were spotted with dead Frenchmen. We pulled into position near Lancon late in the afternoon, laid our pieces and to bed at 8 p.m., pitching our shelter tents in the camouflage of a little wood, while the Boche were shelling about a half mile to the right of us.

Before dawn on Friday, the 11th, the first platoon went forward with Lieutenant Nissley on his famous *pigeon shooting* contest. After having been assured by some American infantry colonel that the guns could go right on into Grand Prè, he learned from a French officer that the Americans had not yet succeeded in even crossing the river. After some close shaves the two guns were gotten into position and in the week they stayed there did some of the most remarkable shooting in the war, bringing forth high comment upon this successful undertaking.

The second platoon under Captain Derby pulled up a steep hill to within 3,000 meters of our front line, a bit S.W. of Grand Prè. The Boche was way in on our left flank and there was *beaucoup* machine gun fire on the hill directly to our left. Big shells were dropping by the carload. Shelter tents were pitched in the pouring rain and the crews worked in shifts all night digging a safety trench.

Both platoons stayed in their respective positions exactly one week, until the evening of October 17th. The firing was mainly at special targets, such as the church steeple in Grand Prè, German trucks and wagon trains along the roads, and exterminating fire on machine gun positions.

Captain Prentiss, in command of a machine gun battalion, visited Captain Derby the night of October 12th and brought rumours of Germany's consent to withdraw to the Rhine and sign peace.

We managed to salvage two nice new camp telephones that belonged to somebody else, but it helped the battery out of a hole.

Lieutenant Hill lost everything he owned and over and above that, Captain Derby's overcoat, while advancing with the infantry. He tried to salvage some blankets to keep warm at night from the bodies of dead Frenchmen lying around, but found the blankets were about the size of table napkins. Finally he succeeded in getting a good one out of a German pack.

The morning of October 14th Private Whitman, while acting as runner to the infantry, had both legs blown off during a violent gas attack. Gormley, who was with him, removed his mask to give Whitman "first aid" and carried him to a place of shelter. Gormley was gassed seriously in saving his friend and later was himself taken to the hospital, receiving a divisional citation for his brave conduct. The same day, during some three hours' steady fire, the 4th piece, under Sergeant McCormack, blew up. Again Battery F had its marvellous luck with it, and by a miracle no one was even so much as scratched.

Tuesday, the 15th, we received a sweet, comforting little note which read to the effect that we should not believe the war is over, but to fight our damndest to bring it to a close before winter sets in. The 3rd gun being alone in our main battery position, we received orders to put it in position in Battery D's line, as they were also short two guns. This left all the shooting to our 1st platoon, but they made up for the missing pieces. The telephone detail had the extreme delight here of having a French caisson come across the field and roll up about 500 metres of their line to the Battalion O. P., which had to be immediately replaced while firing was going on. It is worthy of mention to say Corporal Schaeffer stated that he counted 15 splices in this line on the last day, all of which were bare, owing to the impossibility of procuring tape, and that part of the line was composed of captured German wire. From this we might gather an inkling of the trials and difficulties that befell our plucky, resourceful crew of telephonists and linesmen. Quite a bunch of gas was being sent over by the Germans and a few G. I. cans came down pretty close. But we did no digging. It was pouring rain and we lay in our little pup tents, laughing and smoking as it was raining too hard for aeroplanes. We even lit candles at night. Nothing could dampen our wonderful cheerfulness.

Thursday, the 17th, we tried to dry out our blankets and other things with the help of small bonfires. We were relieved in the evening by the 78th Division.

The 1st platoon went on ahead of the 3rd piece, which followed in Battery D's line of march and all three sections met at our echelon near La Harasee. It was a tough night. It was raining, ice cold and the roads were filled with slush. We hiked for ten long hours—most of us with packs, and only a short halt along the road. We waited, shivering and wet, while the echelon was roused and packed up, and when the captain got through fuming, we renewed our march just as day was breaking. We made our camp near La Chalade at 8 a.m., making it a hike of nearly 32 kilometres overnight. Those of us who didn't have to go back with the teams to help move up the echelon, or start the kitchen work, threw our wet blankets on the ground, and rolled into them for two hours' sleep. There was nothing but corned willy to eat all day. We were assigned to numerous little dugouts in the edge of the forest, and the boys were asleep by 6 p.m.

Saturday, the 19th, we had reveille at 6.30 a.m., first in months. We immediately got to work after our corned willy and coffee breakfast cleaning material, grooming and feeding horses and checking personal equipment. Our battery canteen opened in the afternoon, and we bought lots of wonderful stuff—Camembert, butter, sardines, cigars and cigarettes. Again we pulled under the cover early—7 p.m., finding everybody in bed except the luckless guards.

Sunday, the 20th, we got out in a pouring rain to hold reveille. Lieutenants Nissley and Taylor left on their furlough at 2 p.m. Three guns, the 1st, 2nd and 3rd pieces, left for overhauling at the Ordnance Department. Three men of each section accompanied the guns and hiked in the rain to Les Iselettes. Got pretty good meals there and a nice, room and bunk to sleep in. They returned at noon Tuesday, the 20th, to the battery and found the battery getting deloused and new equipment issued. It was just dark enough in the evening when Battery F's turn came to take its shower bath of twenty drops of cold water to enable those who had stood in line naked and shivering in the open to duck back in the woods and don their new underclothes without enjoying the *mock* shower bath.

Wednesday, the 23rd, after reveille, we had close order drill, gas drill, inspections and other things that make a soldier "having his rest" wish so hard he was back again at the front.

The Liberty Players gave two shows at the big stone church Wednesday afternoon and evening. The night performance was interrupted by one of Jerry's air raids. While the anti-craft were popping away the lights were doused in the church. In about fifteen minutes the hum of Jerry's engines had ceased, lights were put on again and the show continued.

Thursday, the 24th, we were notified we are going to move. Not for our expected rest—but back to the line. The order was cancelled at dark and we had to unroll our packs and sleep in our old holes. The canteen sold lots of stuff today, and we laid in a stock of cheese, sardines and honest-to-God real candy.

Reveille Friday, the 25th, and same pleasant routine in the morning, and turned in our saddle bags. At noon mess we were notified to move out immediately for the front. Orders issued for everybody to carry packs. We hiked till an hour after dark and then echeloned in a brambly wood just as it started to rain. Pitched our shelter halves and got a bite of cold corned willy, bread and no coffee.

At 4 a.m. Saturday, October 26th, the four section chiefs and three men of each gun crew along with the camouflage detail were awakened to go forward to our new firing position. It was cold and dark, still raining, and with a little coffee and bacon as a starter we hiked all day until 2 p.m., the main battery following close behind the advance detail and echeloning at Chatel-Chehèry. The firing battery went into position late in the afternoon in a weeded, muddy hollow, halfway between Connay and Marcq—a perfect gas trap. The gun crews bummed some good mess from the 60th C. A. kitchen, about five hundred yards from our position. Work was started at digging our gun-pits and trail logs gathered in. Corporals Kehoe, Labreque and others of the camouflage squad worked laboriously getting our covering up, as secrecy of our position was the one big thing. The drive was planned to start in four or five days and our safety and the success of the undertaking lay mainly in our keeping the enemy unaware of the arrival of new forces.

Late at night we knocked off work and scattered around, blankets in arms, to find a spot that was dry enough to lay down on. Captain Derby and Lieutenant Hill arrived early next morning (about 4.30 a.m. Sunday. October 27th) and couldn't find a soul. The sleepers were well camouflaged, a bit higher up on the slope of the hill back of us, and got hell because they didn't sleep on the wet mud alongside of the gun pits as directed. Ammunition pits and gun pits were completed during the day, and our well camouflaged shelter tents were put up over our shallow safety trenches dug slightly up the side of the hill. We fired 35 shots in registering the battery.

Monday, the 28th, we were up at daybreak, and at it again. Sandbags arrived and we began building our protection around the gun-pits as the ground is so water-soaked that we can't dig in. We strike water at 18 to 20 inches down. This is a fine mud-hole. Jerry threw quite a few shells over today bursting all around us and getting a bunch of *frog* horses.

Tuesday, the 29th, the detail was busy changing our P. C. about five times, and finally settled the matter by getting a *fourgon* wagon sunk into the ground about 200 yards directly to the rear of No. 4 piece. Our forward O. P. is just over the edge of the crest in front of us overlooking the German front lines, and we can get a good view of the coming battle ground. Wednesday, the 30th, the battery fired 153 shots between 4 and 6 a.m. on some trench system for which the data was received shortly after midnight. We took turns during the day was received shortly after midnight. We took turns during the day going over to the 78th delousing station and taking a hot shower bath that was the nearest thing to home in some time. The Salvation Army kitchen at Chatel-Chehèry celebrated Halloween this evening, one night before time, as they expected the big drive to start any minute, and the boys wouldn't have the opportunity to stop and take a bite. Hot chocolate and crackers and home-made fudge made the evening a tempting one to the boys of our echelon and they were all present, swapping rumours with a battalion of infantry which the Salvation Army had stopped on its way to the trenches and was loading up with crackers, nuts and fudge. This happy spot became a regular hang-out for the echelon and whenever the first sergeant wanted a detail to carry ammunition to the gun position it was necessary to send down to the Salvation Army for them.

Thursday, the 31st, we repeated our fire of yesterday between 4 and 6 a.m. There was an aeroplane bombardment with American propaganda on the German lines telling the Huns that their fight was useless. Some of the circulars fell among us and we had a hot time trying to read the German print.

Our aiming stake light gave us particular trouble at this stage of the game on account of the poor batteries. Carl Schaeffer, the Thomas Edison of the telephone detail, put his perpetual-motion energy to work and his new contrivance kept things right.

Our liaison officer was ordered to report to the infantry at once. Lieutenant Hill, sick for the last few days, was all in, but he refused to let Lieutenant Taylor take his place, and finally succeeded in getting Captain Derby to consent to his going in the condition he was in. The runner detail Lieutenant Hill took with him consisted of Privates Brody, Frances, Gottlieb and Forund.

November 1st, Friday, at 3.30 a.m., the last big drive began with sixty gas shells per gun. French and American guns were massed together for the final assault and the sky was ablaze with artillery fire. We pitched in with H. E. at 3.50 a.m. and kept at it all morning and afternoon, our battery getting off 1,444 rounds before firing was suspended in the late p.m. During the night Jerry shelled the top of the crests surrounding us with gas and H. E. and dropped several big ones into the basin where we were without getting any of us.

Saturday, the 2nd, we began firing at 5.50 a.m. Repeated the data of the day before on the "L" shaped trench system of the Germans. Our infantry then went forward in a gallop, the left flank of the Germans now falling back. Our limbers came up shortly after noon, and at 4 p.m. we pulled out in a pouring rain. The roads were terribly blocked and it took us all night, cold and wet, to go about twelve kilometres. We passed through Marcq, St. Juvin and Champignuelle, crossing the Aire on a pontoon hastily constructed by the engineers. Big fires were burning along the roads, barns, stores and supplies set on fire by the retreating Germans, and at our frequent halts we tried to dry our wringing wet shoes and clothes. We pulled off the road at 3.30 a.m. (Sunday) and rested up the horses. We lay down in the mud and slept until 5.30 a.m., daylight, and then had a little cold coffee and hardtack. At 6 a.m. Lieutenant Nissley and twenty-five drivers with their teams left the battery to be attached temporarily to the 1st Battalion. The regiment was so seriously short of horses and the Germans retreating so rapidly that the only hope of our catching them was by the means of leaving one battalion behind and using the good horses of both battalions to get at least some of the guns going after them.

We hiked two kilometres more taking about five hours to make it along the congested roads. We were hungry as wolves and in passing some wonderfully cultivated fields the Germans had left behind untouched, we gathered and ate raw turnips and carrots. We pulled into Verpel about noon and had the same rations for dinner and super as we had for breakfast. Pitched tents and we were in our couches at 6 p.m.

We woke up Monday morning to find it pouring rain again. The echelon moved up today and there was quite a commotion in the battery over our being turned into an ammunition train because of the lack of horses. Cleaned material all afternoon and also some filthy billets the Germans had left behind, spotted here and there with their dead.

The next day, Tuesday, the 5th, we moved into the billets, as it is continually raining and cold. Another bunch of our boys left to go forward as ammunition carriers.

The rain was violent during the night and early Wednesday morning, and through the shell holes in our roof, water poured in on our sleeping quarters. Everything was soaking wet. Time hung heavy. These were the anxious days at the S. O. S., awaiting news from the front. Mysteriously several decks of cards made their appearance in our midst and we began a series of high-powered, *beaucoup franc*, black-jack games that would have made many a Wall Street banker sit up and take notice.

Thursday, the 7th, we were up at 4.30, breakfasted 5.15. Made our packs, put 'em on our backs and moved forward at 9 a.m. All the horses in the 2nd Battalion were used to pull the guns alone. We hiked all day without a rest or any food, passing through Thenorgues, Buzancy, Harricourt, Sommanthe and at 5 p.m. pulled to the very-top of a steep hill at St. Pierremont. All along our march the roads were littered with dead horses, German guns and ammunition dumps, left behind in their retreat. We pitched tent in the rain, had a bite, and pulled under the covers.

The next day we moved into billets in the town and began cleaning out stables, barns, etc. We had only corned willy and coffee to eat, and to help matters it was still pouring rain.

Saturday, November 9th, was the same, cleaning out some more stables and raining all day. Rumours of an armistice with Germany expected within two weeks.

Sunday, the 10th, still raining and still the same poor meals. No rations in sight and we are limited to a quarter loaf of bread per man for all day. No coffee and only corned willy served with a ration of water. More rumours of cessation of hostilities, but the guns still firing to our right flank.

During the morning of Monday, the 11th, it was officially rumoured that the armistice is signed. Nobody believed it. During the afternoon we heard that the wireless station was receiving the different paragraphs of the signed documents, but still we would not believe it.

Tuesday, November 12th, we received official notice of the armistice. The surprising thing was how easily we all took the news, due, no doubt, to the fact that it was hard to believe, hard to realize that it was all over. We immediately began betting as to when we would get home. It was rumoured in the afternoon that Major General Alexander promised the 77th Division to be on board ship December 2nd and home for Christmas. Quite a riot over the good news, in spite of everybody doubting it. Beastly cold today and we had to move out of our billets into the open field in shelter tents as the town had been given over to the 305th Infantry. After dark we made a systematic search of the town for lumber to make a big bonfire on the top of the hill. We sat around the glowing fire and as our wood gave out we proceeded to burn up all the chairs in St. Pierremont, wooden, plush and otherwise.

Wednesday and Thursday we were up at 6.15 in the coldest weather we've hit in France. Heard that the 1st, 2nd, 3rd, 4th, 32nd and 42nd Divisions remain as the American army of occupation and that the 77th sails for the U. S. A. about December 4th. Captain Derby went down to the divisional ration dump. He procured a 50-pound sack of coffee and between a balky horse and a leaky sack he had to get off, hold the leaking bag with one hand and walk or half drag his mount all the way back to St. Pierremont. We had check roll call at night at which the captain had to identify every man personally and account for all the missing.

Friday, the 15th, we were up at 4.30 a.m. and after a nice bite of breakfast, harnessed up our pieces. Pulled out of St. Pierremont. Hiked through Sommanthe to a little group of farmhouses called Warniforet, about three kilometres from Beaumont. We were billeted in the houses, stables and barns, and after having nothing to eat all day had a really good meal for supper. Our men who had gone up as the 1st Battalion ammunition train and the runners with Lieutenant Hill met us here.

Saturday, the 16th, we began close order drill. Major Wamvig made quite a speech to us on the road about parading. He intimated our being in New York soon, and lots of money changed hands on bets of our being home for Christmas. We had to send eleven men away to the 2nd Division going to Germany. The captain did the square thing of drawing lots among the men who had no allotees, and the ones to get stuck were Bill Cheney, Red Hinds, Benny Polack, Mottig, Rees, Joseph Williams, Lane, Quigley, Chapa, Hewitt, Wendolowski. Everybody felt badly over the breaking up of the old bunch, and some of the boys shook hands with tears in their eyes.

Sunday was a real day—no formation. The rumour now is that we hike to Grand Prè, entrain for Chaumont, parade in Paris and then go to our seaport. We were pulled out of bed at 9.30 p.m. to be paid off.

Monday and Tuesday we had plenty of close order drill. Turned in all our horses, sent away all our guns, limbers, caissons and carriages to Grand Prè, drawn by motor truck. A loading detail went along and Sergeant Meagher turned in some fire control instruments to the division salvage agent for which he was almost court-martialled.

Wednesday, the 20th, the battery was up at 4.30, breakfasted at 5.15 and moved out at 7.30 a.m. Everybody carried their full packs. Hiked through Sommanthe, Harricourt, Buzancy, stopping for lunch, consisting of one hardtack and a cup of coffee. Our packs were put in trucks at Buzancy and we raced the rest of the way on foot, through Verpel and on to Beffu. Lieutenant Nissley set a terrific pace and as cold as it was, our cooties got a Turkish bath. It was just 6 p.m. when we reached Beffu and we had covered 32 kilometres since morning. After a piece of bread and a cup of coffee, we made our bunks in the few buildings left standing but which were well ventilated by shell holes.

Had terrible feed Thursday, nothing but corned willy and no bread. We moved out at 1.30 p.m. going about two kilometres to Le Mort Homme. We got pretty nice billets and anchored in them eagerly.

Friday, the 22nd, we held a race among the batteries of the 2nd Battalion for a case of oatmeal. Eddie Lynch fell down when Battery F had the race won, and we ate corned willy the next morning.

Saturday, the 23rd, we went out on a hike and were shown how thoroughly our battery alone had shot up and demolished several farmhouses and special targets around Grand Prè. Held retreat with the battalion and a review by the major.

Sunday morning after breakfast we hiked the four kilometres to Grand Prè to get a bath. Nothing doing—the boilers not working. Got soap and pyjamas at the Red Cross. What the hell are we going to do with pyjamas? Everybody sent cablegrams home from the Red Cross, sending Thanksgiving greetings and saying we would be home for Christmas. There was a big flapjack game in the evening and McHenry was caught in the wreck.

Monday the drizzle of yesterday turned into regular rain, and Lieutenant Taylor took us out for a hike in the mud for a couple of hours. When we got back the room where the firing sergeants slept was a picture. The rain had come through the shell-torn roof, through the telephone detail's room upstairs and down into their quarter. Whenever anyone walked around upstairs a load of dirt would come down from the ceiling above the sergeants and bunks, blankets, floors looked like a trail pit in frog-hollow.

It was still raining Tuesday, the 26th, so we naturally took another hike. Had some physical exercises in the p.m. At night there was a "klu-klux klan" meeting in the sergeants' room with Jake Goodman, Jimmie Ecock and Sergeant Dooley. It broke up in a riot.

Wednesday, the 27th, more rain. All sorts of colonels, lieutenant-colonels and majors visited us in three autos. There was an inspection of billets and now we know we are going home. Sergeant Schwitchenberg chopped his foot pretty severely with an axe. A dizzy night of entertainment with "Whizz-bang" Garry.

Thursday, the 28th, was Thanksgiving Day. Pouring rain. No formations. We had a peach of a dinner. Lamb fricassee, mashed potatoes, dumplings, rice pudding extraordinaire with real nuts and raisins in it, apricot pie, coffee, bread, a piece of cheese, chocolate and a cigar for each one. Thanksgiving was celebrated till a late hour at night in all billets. The rain poured in on top of us on our bunks all night, and many of us slept in our raincoats.

Lieutenant Nissley, at the officers' mess, was informed at Thanksgiving breakfast by the cook that a bountiful supply of eggs had been received. "Niss" ordered some for himself. *Toot-de-sweet!* The major immediately after this entered the room and joined the officer at the table.

"Good morning, major," said Lieutenant Nissley, getting up and gleefully rubbing his hands. "You're just in time. I just ordered some eggs for myself. Shall I order some for you?"

"There'll be no eggs this morning, Nissley. Just cancel that order for yourself," the major gruffly responded.

"Bring me another plate of hash, Fox," said the Lieutenant hungrily.

Friday and Saturday it was still raining. It cleared up a bit Saturday p.m. and Lieutenant Taylor had the battery out in the field playing such games as "Whip," "Bounce 'em up," and the race with three hop-straddle jumps. At night we tied up our section blanket-rolls and put them outdoors expecting an order to move.

Sunday, December 1st, we were called at 4 a.m. Had breakfast in the dark, rolled our packs by candle light, and at 5.40 a.m. were on the march to Grand Prè. It was freezing cold. We built huge bonfires at Grand Prè. Hung around without mess until 1 p.m. Were then carried by motor trucks to an old German camp called Saalburg at Autrey. Brought our guns and carriages down to the station at Autry, tied behind trucks. Had a feed at 6.30 p.m., and lay down in crummy straw bunks in the prison camp.

It was a restless and cold night. We were pulled out of our bunks at 4 a.m., but did not begin loading material until 10 a.m. Finished in quick order. We left Autry at 1 p.m. in U. S. A. box cars. Seventy men to the car with packs and rations, yet we were all in good spirits. Not a wink of sleep all night for anyone. We were piled on top of one another, cramped and freezing cold. We were stiff in every limb by morning.

We detrained at Latrecy 6 a.m. (Tuesday, the 3rd). Had breakfast on the station in a pouring rain. Somebody discovered the Cafe de la Gare had Hennesy Triple Star Cognac in bottles, and it was flowing like water in short order. Nearly 200 bottles were sold to the regiment before the colonel of the M. Ps got wise and closed the cafe up. We hiked about 13 kilometres to Arc-en-Barrois, without packs, thank the Lord, and what members of the battery did survive the march, pulled into Arc-en-Barrois pickled, canned or stewed. It was a banner day for alcoholics in the history of Battery F. We were assigned to bunks in wooden barracks placed neatly in a thick, boggy mud basin. It was a small but inviting town and we sailed out again in search of elixirs to ease the stiffness of our joints and smooth out the wrinkles in our frozen stomachs. There followed two days of unrestricted drinking, so long as the joy rider could pilot himself to port—and the orders to the Provost Guard were to let joy be unconfined these first three days after our arrival. It was our first chance to get something to drink since we hit the front, and the excitement of being among civilization again had its share in the panic.

There were, however, a few arrests for failure to report ship in dock after the hike from Latrecy and for some of the more troublesome warriors who wanted to start a republic of their own in Arc-en-Barrois. The battery enjoyed some wonderful meals in town. We could buy anything our hearts desired for *francs*. Roast veal, pork chops, fried rabbits, chicken, and beefsteaks were in order with *beaucoup pommes de terre* and *vin blanc*.

Friday, the 6th, formations began and Lieutenant Nissley took the battery out in the p.m. snipe hunting for rabbits. There was a ferociously wild inspection of quarters, equipment and side-arms Saturday, and quite a rumpus was raised over a few rusty pistols or the slightest infraction of regulation equipment. The sergeants were granted permission to sleep in billets in town and Rue du Marche, otherwise known to Captain Derby as Sergeants' Row, was totally captured by Battery F. The officers of our battery obtained a nice home at 66 Rue Anatole Gabelle and in short order had everything coming their way from music to cognac.

The boys promenaded through the town Sunday afternoon and Duckworth afforded us and the French civilians lots of amusement by innocently marching at the head of the line with a rabbit foot tied to the back of his collar, unknown to him.

The week of Monday, the 9th, we began close order again. Corporal Gabarino was assigned a squad and was told by the captain to march his squad off. The command Gabby gave has never been deciphered, and the squad members had the presence of mind to march off in a direction as far away from the officers and battery as was possible.

About the 10th of the month Bob Clugston stopped blowing mess calls for us and joined the Argonne Players.

The next few days were all rainy and we were put through such hot stuff as cannoneers' drill, firing imitation barrages, doing gun drill and cannoneers' post.

Thursday afternoon we had a dummy review. It was the first time a good many of the boys had ever gone through the thing, and at the command *eyes right* a few of the drivers snapped into it, doing a hand salute at the same time, seeing Captain Derby do it that way. The sergeants were conspicuous at this dummy review by their absence and they got hell after retreat. Seven men left for Aix les Bain on furlough. Sergeants Anderson, Garry, McKenna; Corporal Jackson, Cook Malatesta; Privates Duffy and George Johnson.

Skillman deserted the sergeants' mess the next day to eat at Cognac Maggies.

We got all dolled up for the inspection Saturday, the 14th, but Lieutenant Nissley did the act and everything went on smoothly. At night Corporal "Duckie" borrowed some of Mag's equipment and masqueraded as a young *demoiselle* through Rue du Marche. He captivated one by one, Manwarren, McDaniels and Swada, and took them in turn promenading in the woods. He collected from each respectively ten *francs*, twelve *francs* and fifteen *francs* with a box of cigarettes and a button off Swada's blouse as a souvenir.

Sunday the "Montrot Trio" made their usual nightly dinner calls. They were evidently dined and wined too well, for when they blew in around midnight, it was mighty dizzy sailing.

Monday, the 16th, we had reveille at 5.30 a.m. and hiked in a pouring rain for seven kilometres with the mud and water oozing in and out of our torn and worn only pair of shoes. After a two-hour wait in a large soggy field, where it rained some more, the entire brigade was reviewed by General McCloskey. Hiked back to our mud-hole at Arc-en-Barrois. In addition it was our battery's turn to do guard mount, followed by guard duty all through that rainy night.

There followed two days of perpetual rain, and in spite of the stone walks already in construction, the mud in and around our barracks was indescribable. Hauk cleverly pictured the scene to us one night, by stepping into the barracks door in a downpour, turning around, saying politely and seriously to the person he imagined behind him: "Never mind the oars, George, leave 'em in the boat."

We received new shoes Thursday—English ones, little better than nothing. Captain Derby was the battalion commander today and Lieutenant Taylor our battery commander. Captain Derby on his battalion inspection tour found something to make comment upon. He sent the following order as battalion commander to Battery F (amounting, in reality, to writing himself the note):

To C. O. Battery F
During his inspection this morning the battalion commander found oats sprouting in one of the *fourgon* wagons belonging to Battery F, as well as an empty champagne bottle in another wagon. He directs that immediate steps be taken to remedy this condition and that you explain by endorsement hereon the action taken.
By order of Captain Derby,
Warren W. Nissley
1st Lieut. 305th F. A.
Acting Adjutant

Lieutenant Taylor bustled around for a while, note in hand, and responded to the battalion commander to the effect that he had sent out a detail of reapers who gathered in the oats and that that he had issued instructions that in the future whenever the battery left champagne bottles around where the inspectors could find 'em, that they should be sure and leave one drink in the bottle for the inspector.

Saturday, the 21st, instead of our customary morning inspection, the regiment marched out to a nice soft, muddy field, and played soldiers. The colonel gave us two rehearsals on receiving regimental colours. As soon as we got back to barracks with mud all over our shoes and leggings there was a battalion inspection at 11 a.m.

Sunday the guard forgot to waken the tireless, unrelenting, punctual Si Kingston, so none of the sergeants were out to reveille. Oh, happy day! Every little bunch had their own little home in town, where their obliging and conscientious little French *madame* would prepare their evening meals so as to recall our own home-made dinner that mother used to make. We could never discover all of these palaces, homes, dives, where the different cliques and elements of our battery went wont to frequent. Yet, the one home that surpassed all others was that where Marshank, Gallagher, Brody, Lynch, Kehr, Gross and Fried dined each evening at 6 sharp. La Belle Madeleine was always there at 5 p.m. to buy milk and Eddie Lynch spent an hour with her trying frantically to demonstrate the English language. Whenever words were necessary to enlighten the mystified miss, Gross did the interpreting into French. Our clever young *demoiselle* would womanly believe only the contrary of his statements. It is a miracle that between the wiles of Gross and the wooing of the amusing, demonstrative Lynch, the poor young thing did not go crazy. And, if it were not for the fact that she had a fiancé in the French army, someone in that crowd would have stayed behind in France when our outfit pulled out, and hooked up with her. Well, even *we* have to admit she was nice—the nearest thing to an American girl yet discovered in France.

Monday, the 23rd, and the next day, Tuesday, we had some real sport, in spite of the perpetual rain. We had mounted drill with the guns and caissons, the first two sections doing the mounted drill with Captain Derby Monday, while the third and fourth sections played war with Lieutenant Nissley, using drivers for gun crews. Tuesday the sections were changed, the limbers only being used in the mounted drill. We laughed and yelled like kids while the horses galloped around dashing into position after the captain with his legs swinging wildly and his whistle a-blowing. We were soaking wet, but we enjoyed it and took pleasure also in viewing a keen horse-race between the Captain, Lieutenant Nissley and Lieutenant Taylor on the way home from the field.

Tuesday night, the 24th, the battalion show gave its first performance under the management and directorship of our Lieutenant Hill at the Arc-en-Barrois opera house, otherwise known as the "Y" hut. It was a howling success. The battery members who contributed to the success of the event were Bill Marshak, Max Brody, "Benedictine" Duckworth, Bill Benjamin, Babe McLoughlin, Kehr, Rosenzweig and Dupree. Brown entertained on the piano. This was Christmas Eve and Chief Labrode was caught returning to his quarters at 1 a.m. The Provost Guard halted him in the rain, but the chief got away with it by answering in French and in the dark the guard thought it was a *frog*.

Christmas Day there were no formations. Most of us stayed in bed until about 10 a.m. and then began celebrating. Benedictine and Triple Sec made a sure and quick ending to a great many of us, who thought we were in for a wild time. One in particular was out in the woods on his back and quite a few were carried to their beds. The furlough boys arrived in the afternoon. The battalion show was repeated in the evening and went stronger, than the previous night.

Gun drill was resumed the 26th with Lieutenant Hill in charge, he seeming to be the only officer who had weathered the Christmas storm. The ground was covered with a slight fall of snow. The official rumour now is that we leave here December 29th, embark for the States January 6th. So McHenry made a couple of more bets on his *sure thing* that we would be in New York by January 18th.

Friday we had the same old drill in the rain and Saturday an inspection by Captain Derby, followed by an equipment check of all sections.

Sunday, the 29th, First Sergeant Dooley received official notice to leave at once for the States to be discharged. Monday, the 30th, we had a review in the big field with "Watch-me-Dolly" at the head. Then some gun drill. At retreat the captain made a brief but touching speech on Dooley's departure for the States. He left Tuesday morning on the 8 o'clock bus for Chaumont.

During the day came the glad tidings of nine more men to leave on furloughs and with it the sad certainty that we would be another month in France. The four officers of our battery must have had some inside dope on the situation, because last night they held a dinner for four of the English nurses from the hospital. It was an up-to-date society event with wine, dancing and everything. Brownie played the piano and drank what the officers couldn't, or, rather, what Lieutenant Hill didn't see, and Capello and Steiner jazzed with their violin and guitar. We wouldn't dare hint that this wasn't the only party that our officers pulled off in Arc, for the reason that we do not like to accuse anybody without being able to prove it, and we can not prove it. They must have been too clever for us at camouflaging, or, perhaps, no more parties were staged owing to our supposition that Lieutenants Hill and Taylor didn't fancy their debut into high society. For one thing, we know that Doc would rather drink where nobody could watch him or where his drinking would not be interfered with by mere dancing.

January 1, 1919. The nine lucky devils to go on furlough were aroused by faithful Si Kingston at the wonderfully romantic hour of 3 a.m. The *permissionaires* consisted of Sergeants Ecock, Greenlee, Jacobson; Corporals Kehoe and Teator; Bugler Millon; Privates Sheppard, Frashour and Christollerson. Chambery and Challe des Eaux was the destination of these nine, with the privilege of visiting Aix-les-Bains. But the lucky break this gang had was that there was no transportation at the expiration of their seven days to bring 'em back to Arc and the poor lonesome boys had such a good time celebrating their sixteen-day stay in Chambery that Ecock, Frashour and Sheppard had to be taken to the hospital.

The first week in January there was a thin covering of snow on the ground and our drills were not so boresome. But from the 7th to the 21st we had practically an unbroken spell of rain. Occasionally we had a little sleet to make the road hikes dangerous, but most of the time it was mud, mud, mud, and drill, drill, drill. Through it all our good American grit and sense of humour carried us with a smile. The work and troubles of one day were forgotten the next when some amusing incident occurred among our men or officers and everything that brought a smile helped drive away the germ of homesickness. Lieutenant Taylor pulled a funny one while drilling the battery on January 20. The battery was marching in column of squads and was then brought into platoon fronts. Lieutenant Hill was in charge of the second platoon and the command was executed admirably. Lieutenant Taylor did not see Lieutenant Hill and absent-mindedly forgetting his presence, complimented the platoon sergeant on the success of the movement. Lieutenant Hill stepped forward at the close of the address, saluting with a snappy "Thank you very much, Lieutenant Taylor." Blondie came back to earth with a sudden jerk at this stage and reddening up, replied in an undertone that was audible to the entire battery: "Damn you, if I had any ammunition I would put some in you."

There's an awful funny one that Barty doesn't want us to tell about him. He claims that the following story is fictitious, and to say the truth, the source of our information was rather unreliable, but here goes, even if we do have to fight Bart a "dool."

Bart had a habit of hanging around in the town *boulangerie*, where Mlle. Louise distributed circular loaves of that wonderful French bread along with her smiles. Barty couldn't *parlez* very much and in order to enlarge his French vocabulary and his acquaintance with the young lady he spent his many off hours sitting on the counter alongside of the Mlle., his trusty little dictionary in one hand and his free arm around the young lady. The bashful *mademoiselle* had the teasing habit of asking Barty something difficult in French which would necessitate his unhitching his free right arm from its, comfortable location to stir the pages of his little French dictionary held in his left hand. After the troublesome word had been found and her sentence understood, Barty would *"Oui, Oui,"* a few times and back went his right arm to its snug quarters. This was repeated many times during each session, when, one day in the heat of conversation and exasperation, Barty finally flung the embarrassing little book on the floor and continued the séance without interruption.

Oh, varied were the methods, means and wherewithals to beguile ourselves into believing we were happy and to fight away our discontentment. Even the venerable and arduous John Quinn, one cold, cold night in the last part of January once quit work by his candle light long enough to drink a good helping of *triple sec* and he wanted to kiss every old woman on the block. The following Sunday it must have still had its effect on him, because we are told he was seen even talking to Dick's housekeeper, Mme. Louise.

Wild boar and venison dinners cooked in several hangouts in the town with that wonderful French flavour helped make many an evening enjoyable that would have been lonesome and dreary. The entire battery to a man was eating at least one meal a day somewhere in town. We spent our money lavishly on good food and it was the best way we could possibly spend it. We were all getting stout and rosy-cheeked and just waiting for General Pershing to send us home in a hurry so mother could see how much weight we had put on from good eats.

We turned in our revolvers January 25th on Saturday and at noon sent our caissons and limbers up to Latrecy with a detail to clean and paint them up when the tractor finished pulling them through the mud and snow. The caissons were stored in a steel hangar in the large aviation field near Latrecy. The guns and limbers arrived at the same hangar January 28th.

The next day the battery was quarantined owing to the epidemic of flu which had broken out. In two days we had fifty cases taken to the hospital and all others were confined to barracks. It was forbidden to eat meals outside barracks. Mess kits had to be left in the kitchen and boiled for fifteen minutes. Every precaution was taken, even the laughable one of having the well men eat in one bunch in the mess hall, followed by the quarantined bunch. Flu masks had to be worn—whenever the officers were around—and we had to gargle before each meal with a preparation of iodine and water. By the last day of the month the hospital list had increased to sixty, the fifty suspect cases confined to barracks were removed to the hospice, and the entire 2nd Battalion quarantined. Tolte, at evening mess in the kitchen, gave out to each of the well men hard macaroni sticks to sip our coffee through saying it was the doctor's orders as a means of sterilization and he caught lots of suckers and sippers.

February

The first day of the month we received official orders that we leave for Latrecy February 7th and everything must be packed. Sunday the 2nd, we issued our haversacks and pack carriers to drivers and non-coms and the unfortunate members of the battery who had been shipped to the hospital lost all or most of their personal belongings in a clean-out of all barrack's. The next day the captain made an inspection of all billets in town to find excess junk in our rooms, but owing to our landladies' cooperation, he had no luck.

Tuesday, the 4th, we had a practice hike in the morning with our packs. Word was received of Klink's death in the hospital at Chaumont. It was the first in the battery and all of us took the news hard. The captain and six men left immediately for Chaumont to attend his funeral and a cloak of despondency settled over everybody which took a long time to shake off, for soon after we lost five more men from the same flu, Turner, Englekeis, Youni, George Smith and Corporal Siegel.

February 5th Bill Marshank received his regimental citation for valorous conduct and bravery as a runner.

We were assigned a new top-sergeant February 6th—Fred A. Wallace, an O.T.S. man and formerly of Battery A, this regiment. Sergeant Tingle was transferred to Battery B and that evening when he dropped in to see his old gang at Cognac Mag's, he was tendered a rousing farewell and a wet one.

The day of our departure from Arc-en-Barrais was changed from the 7th to the 9th and it was a lucky break. The rain we had been having for a week turned into a severe snow storm late Thursday, the 6th, and the weather became bitterly cold Friday and Saturday.

We were called Sunday morning at 4.45 and after breakfast loaded our packs on the four wagons that Captain Derby had generously hired from the French to carry our heavily laden packs to Latrecy. We bade a hasty farewell to Arc and set out at 9.30. It was a stiff walk of 13 kilometres to the station and we are quite sure Monsieur Reechard would never have survived the trip if he had had his pack to carry. The entire regiment was served hot chocolate and sandwiches by the Y. M. in a big tent near the railroad station, and we put in quite a supply of cigarettes and chocolate. The train pulled out at 3.30 p.m. and for the first time in army life we were comfortable in our forty *hommes* in spite of the cold. There was plenty of hay in each car and an average of only 20 men to the car.

We awoke Monday morning to find ourselves passing through beautiful open country and not a sign of snow. Tuesday, the 11th, shortly after noon, we passed through Sable, the new headquarters of our division, and at 4 p.m. reached Noyen and began unloading our train. The battery hiked seven kilometres with full packs and three blankets to Malicorne and it nearly killed 'em. We were assigned billets at the furthest end of the town and trucks were going back and forth from Noyen to Malicorne throughout the night. Sergeant Jacobson, Corporal Quinn, Privates Marshank, McLoughlin, Schaeffer, Forund, Finch and Kiernan were left behind in Noyen at the station on an all night baggage detail; but, thanks to a little knowledge of French and a kind-hearted French blacksmith, home on a twenty-day furlough from his outfit, they had a pleasant restful night sleeping on the floor of his blacksmith shop with a bottle of cognac for company and a couple of wild-eyed French *permissionaires*. Bill Marshank was a sick boy before the festivities began but came out of his daze when the fun started.

The first few days at Malicorne were busy ones, getting our kitchens going, our billets and bunks arranged, salvaging straw for our mattresses and a hundred other things. There were good meals to be had in town, however, and plenty of *vin blanc*, so, what the hell, a little work didn't bother us.

The orderly room was a good ways from regimental headquarters, the officers' quarters and the officers' mess, so bicycle riding rapidly resumed popularity. Captain Derby was "Johnny on the spot," and the second day in Malicorne came up the main street towards our billets riding a well-battered bicycle rolling and swaying from side to side. Nugent was the first to encounter him and noticing the difficulty the skipper was having in navigating was afraid to salute for fear the captain would take a spill returning it.

The 14th, St. Valentine's Day in the civilized world, was market day in Malicorne, being as it was Friday, and it was a circus. The big square was a frantic, howling mob of country women with their wares, and eager bargaining townsfolk anxious to complete their purchases before the more liberal American soldiers could slip away from a formation and arrive on the scene. Rabbits, chickens, eggs—all in little baskets, changed ownership for *beaucoup francs*, and the sideshow peddlers, their canvas tents hastily thrown up, called attention to their bargains by ringing bells and blowing funny horns.

Saturday the colonel had us out for a regimental review and inspection of packs. He must have bawled somebody out, 'cause the major gave us a little speech to the effect: "You have proved yourselves soldiers, now let's look it."

In the afternoon the regimental team trimmed the officers at baseball.

Lieutenant McNevins joined the battery on the 16th after enjoying a "Class C" leave to Paris, and the first thing he did was to make a speech to us about sanitation.

Drills in the rain continued regularly and on the 18th, by way of diversion, we hiked eighteen kilometres to let B. P. Glassford, our new brigadier-general, look us over. The whole brigade was received in a large field the other side of Noyen and after the affair the general held a friendly little *tete-a-tete* with the officers.

The next day we had a regimental review and inspection by the colonel in a pouring rain, and a speech about our review tomorrow at Sable by General Pershing.

We were up at 5.30 Thursday morning, but the review by General Pershing was called off. But as it was still raining the colonel thought it would be a good idea to hold another regimental review, and out to the field we went.

Friday we had encore rain, so we marched out to the drill field and had a battalion review. When we got back the market had sold out and we had to do without eggs.

Saturday was George Washington's Birthday and in celebration of it we had no reveille and breakfast was served about 8.30. The Provost Guard had a wild night keeping order in town, and Sunday there was many a "big" head.

Monday, the 24th, Corporal Quinn left on his well-earned pass to Paris. The battery left in trucks at 8.45 a.m. for our divisional review at Sable by General Pershing. We were standing in ranks for five hours with aching backs and legs. When things did start, however, the sight was impressive. General Pershing and staff with Major General Alexander inspected personally every organization in the field while the divisional band of 226 pieces filled the air with wonderful music. Medals were presented to the heroes of the division and then began the review. Our brigade led off with General Glassford at the head. About fifty yards past the reviewing stand the entire column passed at double time through a mud hole. We sank to our shoe tops in the soft splashing soil and struggled to free one foot at a time. Everybody laughed over it—the general, the troops and the French spectators.

We had our usual reveille the following morning, but the day was declared a holiday on account of the high praise the division received from General Pershing at the review yesterday.

Things went along smoothly enough with the officers studying infantry drill regulations and all of us wondering when, oh, when, would we get those rifles that were now rumoured we are certain of receiving before we leave Malicorne.

On Friday, the 28th, Captain Derby and Captain Dana, figuring that carp fishing would be a little more interesting than infantry regulations and hearing that they were biting good at the lake six kilometres away, borrowed a neat looking high-perched French carriage in which to make the trip. They arrived with two fishing poles and potatoes and carrots for bait. The two set out with a frisky horse, borrowed from the town blacksmith. The spirited young nag tried to make a runaway down the main street and they almost lost a wheel off the carriage. The two captains had no luck at the lake, however, and we believe they can blame it on the bait.

March

Saturday, the 1st, another regimental inspection on the drill field. Our belts and haversacks had been washed so often for our many inspections that by this time they were a ghastly white. At a meeting of the officers and non-coms of the battalion in the afternoon, we were told that we could expect to leave this area about April 1st.

Close order drill and road hikes became less tedious to us the entire first week of March, and we enjoyed real sunny springtime. Even the captain came out for hikes and then one morning he was so full of "pep" he gave us setting up exercises in his original Camp Upton style. The little French kids who used to follow us around at drills and count "one—two" for us were highly amused by the captain's antics leading the battery in physical exercises. They imitated him at every count and had us and the captain laughing wildly at their freakish efforts.

Thursday, the 6th, the captain held an examination of non-coms in drilling squads and explaining squad movements as the book said it should be done. In the evening the 152nd F. A. Brigade dance was held at the Château de Courcilles. Nine men of our battery made the trip there and back in the army taxi-cab, and had the extreme pleasure of climbing over half a dozen soldiers' backs to get a chance to dance two and a quarter minutes with a real live American "Y" girl or Red Cross nurse. The Comte de Murat was present with his daughter, the *comtess*. Sergeant Jacobson and Corporal Jackson got stuck with her— the former for three dances.

Saturday, the 8th, we had our inspection of all equipment on our drill field. Another batch of *permissionaires* left on furlough for the Pyrenees.

Bill Marshak got back Sunday from Paris and told such wonderful stories of the Pantheon de la Guerre and Boulevard des Italiens that all battery members possessing sufficient funds determined to make instant application for "class C" leaves.

Rifles arrived about this time for everybody, sergeants included. The thought of infantry rifle and bayonet drill was another incentive to get a furlough and the competition became keen among the applicants for Paris leave; for an original and forcible excuse to have their "permissions" granted immediately. One's commercial house in the U. S. desired the sudden opening of a branch at Paris; another's concern desired samples of Parisian embroideries and hosiery; uncles, fathers, grandmothers, brothers, were conveniently moved from all parts of the globe to Paris with a street address that might have been the *gendarmerie*; telegrams from imaginary relatives or concerns demanding instant presentation of some battery member at Monsieurs So-and-So's law office in Paris; these were the means and wiles employed to persuade our sceptical but liberal division boss to let us have a peep at gay Paree!

Messrs. Dupree, Liebler and lots of others had their passes come through and on March 14th Captain Derby left for Paris, theoretically as an official delegate from the division to the American Legation, but maybe he wanted to see Paris, too. He brought back a nobby new raincoat which was a long time coming to take the place of his other one that Lieutenant Hill left up in the Argonne. The captain spent quite some time with Lieutenant Burden at Paris, who was acting as the secretary for the American Delegation at the Peace Conference.

Brody, Lynch, Gottlieb and Jacobson left Sunday morning, the 16th, just in time to miss the distribution and cleaning of our well cosmoleyned rifles, to accompany the 77th Division football team to Paris. We take this opportunity of thanking the general or whatever bloke was responsible for the granting of Paris passes through this ruse.

Sergeants Jacobson, Gottlieb and Lynch were picked up in Paris for looking at the styles in the window of the Gallerie Lafayette, instead of saluting some tow-headed M. P. lieutenant. Lynch had the good fortune of not having name taken, but the next night matters were more than evened when Eddie had his pocketbook taken instead of his name. Max landed the cream of Paris and the gang recuperated from the strain of their visit by staying two days at Sable on the way back.

Lieutenant Nissley's order for immediate discharge in the U. S. came through and he left for Le Mans, the 20th. The same day came the news of the postponement of the 77th Division's sailing date to April 24th. We were sick enough of this useless hanging around France. The battery went down to the cafes in unison and steeped their sorrow and disappointment in *vin blanc*.

On the morning of Monday, the 24th, Sergeants Wallace, Greenlee and Jacobson left for Paris. Sergeant Anderson became the acting mess sergeant for six days and we are certain his little gang must have enjoyed some epicurean dinners in high style.

Society notes: Captains Derby and Pike spent the last Sunday of the month in La Fleche. Captain Mitchell saw them off at the railroad station. Sergeants Garry and McHenry were guests at a social tea at Marshak's and Will Hundt's wash-house.

April

Tuesday was the first day of the month and soaped candy was served to all sweet-toothed individuals, the entire orderly room force taking the bait.

The Provost Guard was disbanded Wednesday, the 2nd, and our battery was moved out of its present quarters to a cluster of small farmhouses about two kilometres the other side of town. This move was necessary in order to accommodate and make room for the great number of casuals assigned to our regiment, and naturally, it was Battery F that was picked on.

We received our paratyphoid injection April 3, and were a pretty sick bunch for a few days following the shot. Inspections, however, went on just the same. April 4th rifle inspection, after impatiently awaiting the inspector about four hours on the cold, wet field. April 5th equipment inspection by the lieutenant-colonel. The big inspection by the A. E. C. was held on April 7th on our drill field. It was sweet music to our ears to learn that the inspectors complimented the regiment for our neatness and uniformity.

Marshak and Brody broke into the limelight again in our regimental show which was successfully staged at the "Y" hut the evenings of April 7th and 9th.

The Battle of Malicorne was being fought during this period with Sergeants McHenry and Garry as corps commanders. The battle lasted four days. The field operations were suspended on the last day after Mac and Whizz went *beecyelette* riding. Both were well loaded, Mac with a bag under his arm containing a dozen eggs. At the bottom of the steep hill coming down the bridge at Malicorne, Whizz went over the top—of his handlebars—and Mac followed his partner. Both landed in a heap on the hard gravel road and received grave wounds putting them out of action. Mac got up with his right hand cut in slivers, but miraculously managed to keep his entire dozen eggs unbroken in the fall.

We had an *abandon camp drill* Saturday, the 12th, and Monday a regimental medical inspection.

Tuesday, the 15th, the A. E. C. physical inspection was held in Malicorne and we walked to the town and back in a pouring rain.

Blondie Taylor did not show up in the orderly room till a late hour Wednesday, the 16th. He and Si Kingston had had a wild night. Some drunken *frog* ex-soldier locked out by his loving wife occupying the building next to Blondie tried to gain entrance into his home at 3 a.m. by ladder through Lieutenant Taylor's quarters. Nobody in the neighbourhood got any sleep after that and Si had to call a *gendarme* to end the trouble.

The morning of the 17th we were up at 5.30, made and loaded our packs on the wagons hired to carry 'em to Noyen. Foray showed up at the last minute minus his overseas cap. He had spent a wild night celebrating our departure from Malicorne—and donned one of the captain's head-pieces. Hiked to the station at Noyen where the "Y" served us lunch. Jackson, Spencer and Quinn carried Doc Hill's raincoat for him to Noyen on their truck. In one pocket they discovered a bottle and the three slipped away to a deserted spot to help themselves to a long drink of good cognac. Their disappointment was unspeakable, however, when Doc's hidden treasure turned out to be a bottle of plain ordinary *vin rouge*. We were loaded into our box cars and most of us forgot to put water in our canteens. The train pulled out at 2.20 p.m.

We arrived at Brest about noon without breakfasting. We could see the harbour of Brest and a fleet of transports at anchor. The sight set us all cheering wildly. Rushed through the A. E. C. kitchen for mess and with our packs and overcoats hiked about six kilometres to our squad tents at Camp Pontanezan. Had a battery equipment check and a good meal at the Embarkation kitchen, with a wonderful system of quick, tasteful mess.

We turned in our French money for exchange into American, early Saturday morning, the 19th. We had a medical inspection and a bath, by the numbers. The soap furnished reeked of mustard gas or something worse. No casualties were reported. In the afternoon, wearing our packs and overcoats, we hiked down for an equipment inspection that looked weak and foolish to us.

Sunday, the 20th, we were ordered to make packs for another inspection. Then the order was changed to leave immediately for embarkation on the *Agamemnon*. Left camp at 12.20 p.m. without dinner. We hiked for six kilometres under a boiling sun with packs and overcoats. No one can appreciate the comfort and delight of such a hike without making it personally. Bachman and Hage were out visiting and narrowly missed going along with us to the States, catching the battery before we left camp by only two minutes to spare.

We lined up on Pier No. 5 and as the embarkation officer called each name for loading on the lighters, each member of ten batteries responded more eagerly than his predecessor, all but Lampley. He, in his quaint slothful way, sauntered carelessly up to the booth answering "Frederick M.," as if it never mattered whether he got on board or not. At 3 p.m. we were aboard the *Agamemnon*, assigned to our bunks and began waiting for chow. We stood in line four and a half hours, hungry, tired and wet through and through from our hike to the dock. It was nearly 9 p.m. when the last of our men received their mess consisting of two hot dogs, a piece of bread and a cup of tea.

Gradually the system of feeding the 5,687 army passengers on board from one kitchen was bettered, and by the middle of our voyage things weren't so bad. We were ordered to wear at all times our life jackets and mess kits.

For the first time we appreciated the song *Homeward Bound* by our regimental band, as the *Aggie* started off at 12.40 p.m.

The entire voyage was exceptionally delightful. At all times the sea was calm and the weather perfect. Tuesday night, the 22nd, a show and dance was given on board for the officers and nurses, but 1st and 2nd lieutenants were not permitted to attend.

The different regimental shows performed for the benefit of the enlisted men and officers and beginning Wednesday we had ice cream for several days on sale at the canteen.

Thursday brought a medical and bug inspection on deck.

The next day Lusian, Hair, Williams and seven others were stretched out on "A" deck carelessly talking about what they wouldn't do with a dollar if they had it. The first mentioned won unanimously by suggesting the purchase of 20 packages of Cracker-Jack, two packages to be given each member of the party. But the crowd was bankrupt. Suddenly an envelope flopped down in the centre of the gathering. There was a mad scramble and upon opening the envelope it was found to contain a half dollar and two quarters. One of the ninety-nine Red Cross nurses who were on board had unsuspectingly been the audience to their wish for a dollar. Her stateroom window was just above their heads and in two minutes the boys were smilingly offering their benefactress to join them in munching twenty packages of Cracker-Jack.

Captains Derby and Mitchell took a nightly constitutional around the deck of the boat, fighting the war all over again as they walked along with rapid gait.

Most of us spent all day Monday trying to sew our newly issued double service stripes on blouse and O. C. before we landed.

Land was sighted about 8.30 a.m. The view of New York harbour, with the "Welcome" boats steaming up the bay to meet the *Agamemnon* and the Statue of Liberty in the distance, brought tears of joy to men who never before had felt the pangs of separation from home and dear ones. The crowded ferries and tugs came alongside with banners proclaiming the names of the returning boys whose families were bent on getting the first glimpse of his tanned, smiling face. Jimmie Houlihan's family beat the Mayor's Welcome Boat to it by having a special tug of their own, and for nearly half an hour they held conversation with Jim, till the *Agamemnon* put on speed and raced into dock leaving the puffing little tug hopelessly ploughing through the water far in the rear. We docked at Pier No. 2, Hoboken, and landed on U. S. soil at 10.30 a.m. We were formed in batteries near the railroad yards while our relatives and friends sought to evade the vigilance of the M. P. guards and tried to break through the lines to greet the boys. The guards were incapable of handling the vast crowd. After a short furious stampede the mob burst through the gate in the wire fence and surged around the delighted soldiers. Many a mother, sister and sweetheart slipped through and grabbed a sun-browned soldier in a happy squeeze of welcome. It was the first time this had occurred at the debarkation point. In twenty minutes order was restored and the breathless, elusive civilians were once more barred behind the high wire fence to throw the boys oranges and cigarettes. Eddie Lynch's father, eager to see his boy, resorted to a happy ruse that worked. His hat pulled down far over his head and broom in hand, pretending to be one of the railroad yard workers, he walked along the tracks brushing and sweeping. He quietly inquired of the soldiers in rank where Battery F was. The unsuspecting guards let him pass, and Ed and his pop met in a wild catch-as-catch-can match before the presence of the outsider was discovered. We took the ferry to Long Island and the trains to Camp Mills, where we were quickly lodged in tents and fed. Visitors swamped the camp all this day and the next, and many a fellow took a flyer and beat it to New York City for the night.

Thursday, May 1st, we were up at 4 a.m. to be deloused and re-equipped. All city boys received their 48-hour passes good from noon today until noon Saturday, and it was "Home, Sweet Home" for us by the quickest route. Quite a few of the boys overstayed their passes and did not show up by 7 p.m. Sunday night, when we had to sign the pay-roll sheets, discharge papers, insurance blanks and other things. An order was received that all men not having reported by that time to sign their papers would be transferred to the Depot Brigade—and twelve men in our outfit were out of luck, not being discharged until a week after the battery had been mustered out.

Monday, May 5th, we were roused at 5 a.m., made our packs and boarded the electric train at 8.15. Reached New York and marched to the 9th Coast Artillery Armoury on 14th Street. We left our packs and equipment and were dismissed until tomorrow, the day of the 77th Division parade.

We assembled 7.30 a.m. Tuesday at the armoury carrying our light haversack packs and helmets and formed near Washington Arch. Paraded up Fifth Avenue in great style and with break-neck speed past the great tiers of grandstands filled to overflowing with friends and loved ones. At 110th Street we passed in review before General Alexander and continued on to 125th Street, taking the subway down to the armoury, where we were dismissed for the day.

The next morning we were down to the armoury again at 7.30 and hiked to 34th Street. At 1 p.m. arrived in Camp Upton—the same Camp Upton that we had spent seven months in training before going across. These barracks certainly looked good to us. We felt at home in them and settled into our iron bunks comfortably.

Among the souvenirs Captain Derby brought back with him from France was a German automatic pistol. While in New York he exhibited his trophies to his wife. In demonstrating the action of the revolver, the weapon unexpectedly went off. A tragedy was narrowly averted, as Captain Derby was holding the gun muzzle down. The shot fortunately missed Mrs. Derby and striking the floor bored its way through for more than a foot into the heavy apartment flooring.

Thursday, May 8th, we turned in such of our equipment that was no longer needed. Then we were marched down to the Y. M. C. A. at 8th Street for a series of lectures on re-enlistment, compensation, etc. Corporals Jackson and Quinn and Dick Spenser, the "Office Force Trio," worked till long after midnight getting our service records into completion for the coming discharge.

Friday, the 9th, we were aroused at 2.15 a.m. and walked to 8th Street for our physical examination in the middle of the night. Got back to our bunks about 4.30 a.m. and slept till 7 a.m. At 9.30 we were down again to the "Y" hut for a lecture on insurance and prophylaxis. Turned in our blankets and all other Government property we are not allowed to keep. We slept at night in our overcoats on the iron bunks as we had no blankets.

Up at 4 a.m. Saturday, May 10th. Breakfast served at 4.30 and we cleaned up our barracks. Turned in our mess kits and hiked down to the paymaster's office in a pouring rain. We waited three hours in the incessant cold drizzle before our turn came to receive our final pay with the $60.00 bonus.

It was a happy, singing bunch that walked through the mud and water down to the railroad station, with dripping wet faces and clothes. Captain Derby stood at the gate entrance to the cars, and, as each man of his old loved battery received his honourable discharge and passed through the gate, the captain grasped his hand in a farewell grip of good luck and good-fellowship—and Battery F, 305, ceased to be—in the annals of American History. But in the minds of every member we are still, and will remain forever, the same outfit, the same happy comrades, with our bonds of friendship strengthening with the years. On Tuesday night, May 13th, the 305th F. A. Regimental Association held a dance and entertainment at the 9th C. A. Armoury. It was our farewell night. Mr. and Mrs. Derby were there, Lieutenants Nissley and Taylor, and almost all of the boys. Some of us were already in civilian clothes and before the party broke up the battery presented Captain Derby with a silver smoking service as a token of the eternal esteem and love we hold for him.

(To be continued in the next war)

Appendix A

P. C.
77th Division
3 October, 1918
General Order No. 29
1. The following is published for the information of all concerned. The Division Commander desires that this communication be brought to the attention of every member of the command at the earliest practicable moment: 729/G3.

Advanced Headquarters
First Army Corps,
October 2, 1918.
From Commanding General
1st Army Corps, U. S.
To: Commanding General
77th Division, U. S.
Subject: Commendation
1. The Corps Commander has directed me to extend to you and to the entire 77th Division a most cordial expression of his gratification at the steady, solid progress made since the beginning of the operation now under way. **2.** The difficulties of terrain are fully understood and the amount of ground gained is notable, while your supplies and communications are thoroughly satisfactory. **3.** Individual cases of special merit should be brought promptly to the attention of these headquarters for suitable recognition without waiting for a complete list after the operations are completed.
By Command of Major General Liggett
Malin Craig
Chief of Staff
By Command of Major General Alexander
J. R. R. Hannay
Chief of Staff

Appendix B

Regtl. P. C. (ne aux Charmes, 58.18)
Headquarters 305 F. A.
American Ex. Forces
3rd Oct., 1918
General Orders No. 39
1. The Regtl. C. O. desires the command to be fully informed that on two occasions in the last few days the effective and prompt artillery support rendered by this regiment has been a matter of most favourable report by Infantry Officers, and has made possible the infantry advance, on such occasions, with but small loss, while inflicting heavy losses on the Germans. On the second occasion the mission was over difficult terrain from an artillery standpoint; it had been impossible to see where our shots were falling; no circumstances permitted even any rough registration; yet our very first shots fell squarely in a barbed wire entanglement that marked our initial barrage that did such material damage to same; rolled on and caught the Germans in their trench system, compelling some surrenders, and putting two machine gun nests out of action. The range on both occasions was about 3¼ miles, and very little time had been given the officers to figure the data.
2. The officers and men are equally congratulated, and entitled to complimentary notice for their accurate and prompt work. The accurate computation of the officers would have been useless, unless backed up by the magnificent gun discipline displayed by the gun crews.
3. The above will be read to the command.
F. C. Doyle
Colonel 305 F. A.

Roster

Anderson, Carl, Eaton, Colo.
Anderson, Nils E., 211 West 107th St., New York City.
Anderson, Otto, Wanki, Minn.
Anderson, Victor E., R. F. D. No. 2, Monticello, Minn.
Autrey, Alxie E., Coppell, Texas.
Backman, John M., 208 Lexington Ave., Brooklyn, N.Y.
Barale, Vincent, 989 Enterprise St., McKeesport, Pa.
Barbatsuly, George, P., 312 West 27th St., New York Ctiy.
Bartalini, Omero.
Bartleson, Jesse, 1313 Washington Boulevard, Chicago, 111.
Benjamin, William, 243 Marcy Ave., Brooklyn, N.Y.
Beszpoisnick, Leibe, 713 North Main St., Charles City, la.
Birmingham, Robert.
Blome, Albert R., 311 East 70th St., New York City.
Boernsen, John August, R. F. D. No. 1, Hartley, la.
Bohannan, John A., Wheller, 111.
Boyle, Richard.
Brady, George, 581 East 136th St., New York City.
Brewer, Earl, Orland, Cal.
Brody, Max, 14SS Washington Ave., New York City.
Brouillette, Harry J., 310 River St., North Adams, Mass.
Brown, Charles E., 461 West 155th St., New York City.
Brunk, Jacob G., 179th St. and Webster Ave., New York City.
Burden, Chester G.
Cairns, Hugh, 198 Colyer St., Brooklyn, N.Y.
Carlisle, Willis, Livingston, Texas.
Carroll, Daniel E., 31 Manhattan St., New York City.
Carson, John W., Deposit, N.Y.
Cederburg, Gust.
Christofferson, Christoffer, Lcngly, la.
Clark, Daniel.

Clark, Harry, 1425 Geary St., Harrisburg, Pa.
Clugston, Robert, 139 West 47th St., New York City.
Collins, John.
Connors, Frank J., 162 Lebanon Ave., Pittsfield, Mass.
Cooperstein, Abraham, 352 East 119th St., New York City.
Cordes, Ernest H., Henning, Minn.
Crane, Garnett, 6217 East 14th St., Kansas City, Mo.
Cushman, John, 20 North "A" St., Irvington, N.Y.
Davis, Miles E., 19 Pleasant St., Wellsville, N.Y.
DeBert, Frank, 714 West Grant Ave., Chicago, 111.
Derby, James Lloyd, 48 East 61st St., New York City.
Dooley, John J., 212 East 70th St., New York City.
Doyle, James.
Duckworth, William J., 214 West 16th St., New York City.
Duellmann, Robert, 345 South 4th St., Hamilton, Ohio.
Duffy, John J., 590 East 138th St, New York City.
Dupree, Bernard E., 107 Warburton Ave., Yonkers, N.Y.
Easson, Chester.
Ecock, James, 4th St., Sheepshead Bay, N.Y.
Eidson, James, Enterprise, Ala.
Elkin, Gabe F., Easton, Wash.
Ervin, Roy F., Lawton, Okla.
Ellis, James, Paris, Ky.
Erickson, Severt, Sioux Falls, S. D.
Farina, Gaetano. 169 East 23rd St., Brooklyn, N.Y.
Finch, Charles H., Halcyon Park, New Rochelle, N.Y.
Fomund, Lawrence, 770 Jackson Ave., New York City.
Foray, John M., 15 West 67th St., New York City.
Francis, John Logan, Box No. 82, Tuttle, Okla.
Frasher, Earl J., 412 East 160th St., New York City.
Freed, Oscar A., 1606 11th Ave., S. E., St. Cloud, Minn.
Freshour, Alfred E., Corning, la.
Fried, Philip, 109 Belmont Ave., Brooklyn, N.Y.
Fuglestad, Thorwald, Cooperstown, N. D.
Gallagher, Peter, 2332 Andrews Ave., New York City.
Galliford, Samuel, 215 West Main St., Batavia, N.Y.
Garbarino, Andrew H., R. F. D. No. 1, Huntington, N.Y.
Garry, William A., 421 West 141st St., New York City.
George, Raymond, Livermore, Cal.
Glode, Arthur, 49 Emmett St., Marlboro, Mass.
Goodwin, Walter, 919 East 232nd St., New York City.
Gormley, Martin A., 524 West 159th St., New York City.

Gottlieb, Morris, 8-10 West 117th St., New York City.
Graves, William A., 124th and Yocust Sts., Valley Junction, Iowa.
Greenlee, Gordon B., 543 Prospect Ave., Newark, N. J.
Gross, Emanuel, 1027 East 167th St., New York City.
Gusa, Eddie, R. F. D. No. 1, Plainview, Minn.
Hagan, Peter, 1267 S'. Buckwell St., Philadelphia, Pa.
Hage, Frank J., 1216 Thrall Ave., Woodhaven, L. I.
Hair, Edwin Andrew, Brownell, Kan.
Haller, Albert, 208 Fifth Ave., Virginia, Minn.
Hanley, James W., jr., Wachusett St., Holden, Mass.
Jianlnn, Edison, 22 Orlando St., Sj^rirgfield, Mass.
Hanney, Frank, 108 S. California Ave., Chicago, 111.
Hatfield. Earl.
Hauk, Arthur J., 5511 Hirsch St., Chicago, 111.
Hecker, Arthur J., Sumatra, Mont.
Helgeson, Gilbert, Roslyn, N.Y.
Henderson, William B., 126 Fulton St., Youngstown, Ohio.
Hennessey, Joseph, 837 Main St., Springfield, Mass.
Henricksen, Hans C, Charter Oak, Iowa.
Hensley, Arthur.
Herman, Albert Samuel, 453 West South St., Akron, Ohio.
Hernbon, John F., R. F. D. No. 2, Pecan Gap, Texas.
Herrmann, August, 2442 Myrtle Ave., Evergreen, N.Y.
Hertz, Joseph, 984 Simpson St., New York City.
Hilbold, Carl, Lima, Ohio.
Hill, Albert B., 164 Harrison St., Clarksburg, W.Va.
Hock, William, 383 Berrman St., Brooklyn, N.Y.
Hoerber, John H., 310 Maryland St., Buffalo, N.Y.
Hogan, Arthur, 3222 Washington Ave. N., Minneapolis.
Holmer, William S., 2920 Bryant Ave., N. Minneapolis, Minn.
Hopkins, John J., 101 Rodgers Ave., Brooklyn, N.Y.
Horton, George R., 2187 7th Ave., New York City.
Houlihan, James A., 2867 Bainbridge Ave., New York City.
Hovey, Myron, 305 West 97th St., New York City.
Howard. Patrick, 99 Fort Washington Ave., New York City.
Hundt, William H., 330 East 139th St., New York City.
Hurst, Edward James, 1408 Pleasant St., Cincinnati, Ohio.
Huscher, Robert W., Lincoln Ave. and Baltic St., Jamaica, N.Y.
Ives, Ray, New Underwood, S. D.
Jackson, Douglas N., 345 Fifth Ave., New York City.
Jacobson, Benjamin, 966 St. Nicholas Ave., New York City.
Johnson, Arthur J., Swea City, Iowa.

Johnson, George W., Lester Prairie, Minn.
Kadlec, Frank, 355 East 74th St.. New York City.
Kaplan, Samuel, 331 East 56th St., New York City.
Kaufmann, Samuel.
Kehoe, William, 330 East 34th St., New York City.
Kehr, Albert W., 410 East 155th St., New York City.
Kiernan, Patrick J., Box 41, East Northport, L. I.
Kingston, Cyrus G, 1414 Massachusetts Ave., North Adams, Mass.
Kingston, George R.. Brasher Falls, N.Y.
Kruchell, Fred O, 7403 S. Sangamon St., Chicago, 111.
McClenaghan, Andrew.
McCormack, Joseph, 2084 Anthony Ave., New York City.
McDaniel, Hubert, Gidson, Mo.
McDermott, James.
McElheny, Leo H., Rushford, N.Y.
McHenry, George R., 1010 McGovern St., Little Rock, Ark.
McHugh, Leo Joseph, 496 Linwood St., Brooklyn, N.Y.
McKenna, Bartholomew P, 320 East 140th St., New York City.
McLaughlin, James P., 423 Wrights Court, Scranton, Pa.
McNevin, Alfred C. B., 924 President St., Brooklyn, N.Y.
Labrecque, Alfredo Romeo, 49 Roseland St., Springfield, Mass.
LaBrode, Henry C, 22 Lincoln St., Pittsfield, Mass.
LaManna, John, 3312 Georgia Ave., N.W., Washington, D. C.
Lampley, Frederick M., Hickman, Cal.
Larkin, Eugene L., 2 Marble Hill Ave., New York City.
LaRue, William H., 409 Eldert St., Brooklyn, N.Y.
Lashansky, Hugo, 168 East 90th St., New York City.
Lasher, Mordecai J., 98 Second Ave.. New York City.
Liebler, George, Jr., 246 West 230th St., New York City.
Lingren, Samuel, Tuduck, Iowa.
Lomberg, Benny, 1212 Washburn Ave., Chicago, 111.
Lusian, Isador W., 407 Roberts St., Crookston, Minn.
Luther, Loren Robert, Minden Mines, Mo.
Lynch, Edward A., 2454 DeVoe Terrace, New York City.
Macken, Michael F., 148 First St., Pittsfield, Mass.
Maclis, Juan, Phoenix, Ariz.
Malotista, Adolph, 475 Pearl St., New York City.
Mandelblatt, Nathan, 874 Longwood Ave., New York City.
Manwarren, Will O., Bigelow, Minn.
Marshak, William, 907 East 173rd St., New York Citv.
Martin, Propof, 9 Canal St., New York City.
Masterson, Andrew J., 631 First Ave., New York City.

Meagher, William H., 2671 Bainbridge Ave., New York City.
Michels, John.
Miller, Kenneth L., R. F. D. No. 1, Nashua, N. H.
Miller, Edward W\, 5 Corinth Ave., Elmhurst. L. I.
Millon, Noel, Delmonico Hotel, 44th St. and Fifth Ave., New York
Minkler, James, 31 Powell Ave., Newport, R. I.
Mitchell, C'Von E.
Musgrave, Arthur.
Nagleschmidt, William.
Nelson, Harry, Sibley, Mich.
Neptune, Harold B., Colabar, Mont.
Neuwerth, Charles, 381 East 153rd St., New York City.
Nielsen, Niels Peter. 362 43rd St., Brooklyn, N.Y.
Nikolai, Steve, 308 Tillamook St., Portland, Ore.
Nilson, John.
Nissley, Warren W., 382 Fulton Ave.. Hempstead, L. I.
Nugent, Joseph, 2660 8th Ave., New York City.
Obregon, Jose.
O'Connor, Arthur W., 622 West Belden Ave., Syracuse, N.Y.
Parlee, Arthur, Rockford, 111.
Patterson, Cody F., Kimball, Neb.
Payne, John II., 274 Poultenay St., Geneva, N.Y.
Peasley, Arthur M., Arson, Towa.
Peters, Francis B.
Pohlmann, Robert W., 269 Carmelia St., Brooklyn, N.Y.
Quinn, Tohn A., 2043 North 11th St., Philadelphia, Pa.
Ranck, Roy, 2827 East 64th St., Kansas City, Mo.
Rarrick, Toseph W., 91-2 Moosac St., Adams, Mass.
Riley, William.
Roberson, Arch, R. F. D. No. 1, Lyles, Tenn.
Rodgers, Jerome R., 443 East 165th St., New York City.
Rolke, William.
Roache, Thomas F., 1362 Bergen St., Brooklyn, N.Y.
Romito, Francesco. 78 Skillman St., Brooklyn. N.Y.
Rosenzweig, Max, 707 Cauldwell Ave., New York City.
Roshovsky, Meyer. 1381 Washington Ave., New York City.
Russell, James, 208 Blatchley Ave.. New Haven, Conn.
Russell, Linwood L., Mechanic Falls, Maine.
Salatino, Antonio, 33 Circular Ave., Pittsfield, Mass.
Sammler, Charles, 414 East 138th St., New York City.
Sarver, Grover C, Wexford, Pa.
Sarzen, Frederick R., Westfield, Mass.

Schaeffer, Carl H., 2114 Caton Ave., Brooklyn, N.Y.
Schroeder, William, Box No. 35, Mercer, Wis.
Schultz, Philip, 403 Goethe St., Buffalo, N.Y.
Schwichtenberg, Henry C, 148 West 27th St., Bayonne, N.J.
Searle, Howard.
Shay, Daniel, College Hill, Ohio.
Shepard, John R, 42 Guilds Place, Pittsfield, Mass.
Shepherd, Thornton.
Skillman, Irving S., 414 Convent Ave., New York City.
Smith, Albert Field, 31 Van Dam St., New York City.
Spaulding, Harry.
Spencer, Richard A., 2231 Valentine Ave., New York City.
Spenzola, Angelo, IS Bay 14th St., Brooklyn, N.Y.
Spiegel, Marvin, 909 West End Ave., New York City.
Stanfield, John A., Tulare, Cal.
Stanton Ivan Lee, Enosburg Falls, Vt.
Starkie Henry M., 392 Webster Ave., New Rochelle, N.Y.
Steis, Edmond G.
Stengren, Bernard, 136 Dikeman St., Brooklyn, N.Y.
Strong, Louis P., Jr., 12 Balsam St., Saranac Lake, N.Y.
Sullwold, Friedrich, R. F. D. No. 1, Stillwater, Minn.
Swada, Walter, Blooming Prairie, Minn.
Tagliaferri, Joseph.
Talty, Peter J. 234 East 33rd St., New York City.
Tarulo, Michele, 677 Morris Ave., New York City.
Taylor, Reuben T., Frankfort, Ky.
Teator, Foster, Tivoli, N.Y.
Thomas, Leonard L., Olin, Iowa.
Tingle, John K., Connorsville, Ind.
Tung, Gee, 715 7th Ave., New York City.
Urso, Tony, 347 East 24th St., New York City.
Vallandingham, Oscar, Ward, Ark.
Van Riper, Charles, Holly, Mich.
Vaughan, John J., 217 East 47th St., New York City.
Verdin, Grady.
Waldbillig. Edward, Drummond, Mont.
Wallace, Fred L., 30 Church St., New York City.
Walsh, Thomas P., 773 St. Ann's Ave., New York City.
Ware, Roger, Phoenix, Ariz.
Warmers, Robert.
Watkins, Harry.
Wells, Charles R., 517 North Alastic St., Haddfield, N.J.

Wells, William A., R. F. D. No. 3, Fillmore, N.Y.
Whitman, Francis.
Williams, Daniel F., 68 Ranney St., Springfield, Mass.
Wittenberg, Samuel, 186 Covert St., Brooklyn, N.Y.
Wright, George, Severance, N.Y.
Wubbe, William, 7505 17th Ave., Brooklyn, N.Y.
Younger, Edwin.
Zeliff, Shirlev, Almond, N.Y.

ALSO FROM LEONAUR
AVAILABLE IN SOFTCOVER OR HARDCOVER WITH DUST JACKET

AT THEM WITH THE BAYONET by *Donald F. Featherstone*—The first Anglo-Sikh War 1845-1846.

STEPHEN CRANE'S BATTLES by *Stephen Crane*—Nine Decisive Battles Recounted by the Author of 'The Red Badge of Courage'.

THE GURKHA WAR by *H. T. Prinsep*—The Anglo-Nepalese Conflict in North East India 1814-1816.

FIRE & BLOOD by *G. R. Gleig*—The burning of Washington & the battle of New Orleans, 1814, through the eyes of a young British soldier.

SOUND ADVANCE! by *Joseph Anderson*—Experiences of an officer of HM 50th regiment in Australia, Burma & the Gwalior war.

THE CAMPAIGN OF THE INDUS by *Thomas Holdsworth*—Experiences of a British Officer of the 2nd (Queen's Royal) Regiment in the Campaign to Place Shah Shuja on the Throne of Afghanistan 1838 - 1840.

WITH THE MADRAS EUROPEAN REGIMENT IN BURMA by *John Butler*—The Experiences of an Officer of the Honourable East India Company's Army During the First Anglo-Burmese War 1824 - 1826.

IN ZULULAND WITH THE BRITISH ARMY by *Charles L. Norris-Newman*—The Anglo-Zulu war of 1879 through the first-hand experiences of a special correspondent.

BESIEGED IN LUCKNOW by *Martin Richard Gubbins*—The first Anglo-Sikh War 1845-1846.

A TIGER ON HORSEBACK by *L. March Phillips*—The Experiences of a Trooper & Officer of Rimington's Guides - The Tigers - during the Anglo-Boer war 1899 - 1902.

SEPOYS, SIEGE & STORM by *Charles John Griffiths*—The Experiences of a young officer of H.M.'s 61st Regiment at Ferozepore, Delhi ridge and at the fall of Delhi during the Indian mutiny 1857.

CAMPAIGNING IN ZULULAND by *W. E. Montague*—Experiences on campaign during the Zulu war of 1879 with the 94th Regiment.

THE STORY OF THE GUIDES by *G.J. Younghusband*—The Exploits of the Soldiers of the famous Indian Army Regiment from the northwest frontier 1847 - 1900.

AVAILABLE ONLINE AT **www.leonaur.com**
AND FROM ALL GOOD BOOK STORES

ALSO FROM LEONAUR
AVAILABLE IN SOFTCOVER OR HARDCOVER WITH DUST JACKET

ZULU:1879 *by D.C.F. Moodie & the Leonaur Editors*—The Anglo-Zulu War of 1879 from contemporary sources: First Hand Accounts, Interviews, Dispatches, Official Documents & Newspaper Reports.

THE RED DRAGOON *by W.J. Adams*—With the 7th Dragoon Guards in the Cape of Good Hope against the Boers & the Kaffir tribes during the 'war of the axe' 1843-48'.

THE RECOLLECTIONS OF SKINNER OF SKINNER'S HORSE *by James Skinner*—James Skinner and his 'Yellow Boys' Irregular cavalry in the wars of India between the British, Mahratta, Rajput, Mogul, Sikh & Pindarree Forces.

A CAVALRY OFFICER DURING THE SEPOY REVOLT *by A. R. D. Mackenzie*—Experiences with the 3rd Bengal Light Cavalry, the Guides and Sikh Irregular Cavalry from the outbreak to Delhi and Lucknow.

A NORFOLK SOLDIER IN THE FIRST SIKH WAR *by J W Baldwin*—Experiences of a private of H.M. 9th Regiment of Foot in the battles for the Punjab, India 1845-6.

TOMMY ATKINS' WAR STORIES: 14 FIRST HAND ACCOUNTS—Fourteen first hand accounts from the ranks of the British Army during Queen Victoria's Empire.

THE WATERLOO LETTERS *by H. T. Siborne*—Accounts of the Battle by British Officers for its Foremost Historian.

NEY: GENERAL OF CAVALRY VOLUME 1—1769-1799 *by Antoine Bulos*—The Early Career of a Marshal of the First Empire.

NEY: MARSHAL OF FRANCE VOLUME 2—1799-1805 *by Antoine Bulos*—The Early Career of a Marshal of the First Empire.

AIDE-DE-CAMP TO NAPOLEON *by Philippe-Paul de Ségur*—For anyone interested in the Napoleonic Wars this book, written by one who was intimate with the strategies and machinations of the Emperor, will be essential reading.

TWILIGHT OF EMPIRE *by Sir Thomas Ussher & Sir George Cockburn*—Two accounts of Napoleon's Journeys in Exile to Elba and St. Helena: Narrative of Events by Sir Thomas Ussher & Napoleon's Last Voyage: Extract of a diary by Sir George Cockburn.

PRIVATE WHEELER *by William Wheeler*—The letters of a soldier of the 51st Light Infantry during the Peninsular War & at Waterloo.

AVAILABLE ONLINE AT **www.leonaur.com**
AND FROM ALL GOOD BOOK STORES

ALSO FROM LEONAUR
AVAILABLE IN SOFTCOVER OR HARDCOVER WITH DUST JACKET

OFFICERS & GENTLEMEN *by Peter Hawker & William Graham*—Two Accounts of British Officers During the Peninsula War: Officer of Light Dragoons by Peter Hawker & Campaign in Portugal and Spain by William Graham.

THE WALCHEREN EXPEDITION *by Anonymous*—The Experiences of a British Officer of the 81st Regt. During the Campaign in the Low Countries of 1809.

LADIES OF WATERLOO *by Charlotte A. Eaton, Magdalene de Lancey & Juana Smith*—The Experiences of Three Women During the Campaign of 1815: Waterloo Days by Charlotte A. Eaton, A Week at Waterloo by Magdalene de Lancey & Juana's Story by Juana Smith.

JOURNAL OF AN OFFICER IN THE KING'S GERMAN LEGION *by John Frederick Hering*—Recollections of Campaigning During the Napoleonic Wars.

JOURNAL OF AN ARMY SURGEON IN THE PENINSULAR WAR *by Charles Boutflower*—The Recollections of a British Army Medical Man on Campaign During the Napoleonic Wars.

ON CAMPAIGN WITH MOORE AND WELLINGTON *by Anthony Hamilton*—The Experiences of a Soldier of the 43rd Regiment During the Peninsular War.

THE ROAD TO AUSTERLITZ *by R. G. Burton*—Napoleon's Campaign of 1805.

SOLDIERS OF NAPOLEON *by A. J. Doisy De Villargennes & Arthur Chuquet*—The Experiences of the Men of the French First Empire: Under the Eagles by A. J. Doisy De Villargennes & Voices of 1812 by Arthur Chuquet.

INVASION OF FRANCE, 1814 *by F. W. O. Maycock*—The Final Battles of the Napoleonic First Empire.

LEIPZIG—A CONFLICT OF TITANS *by Frederic Shoberl*—A Personal Experience of the 'Battle of the Nations' During the Napoleonic Wars, October 14th-19th, 1813.

SLASHERS *by Charles Cadell*—The Campaigns of the 28th Regiment of Foot During the Napoleonic Wars by a Serving Officer.

BATTLE IMPERIAL *by Charles William Vane*—The Campaigns in Germany & France for the Defeat of Napoleon 1813-1814.

SWIFT & BOLD *by Gibbes Rigaud*—The 60th Rifles During the Peninsula War.

AVAILABLE ONLINE AT **www.leonaur.com**
AND FROM ALL GOOD BOOK STORES

ALSO FROM LEONAUR
AVAILABLE IN SOFTCOVER OR HARDCOVER WITH DUST JACKET

ADVENTURES OF A YOUNG RIFLEMAN by *Johann Christian Maempel*—The Experiences of a Saxon in the French & British Armies During the Napoleonic Wars.

THE HUSSAR by *Norbert Landsheit & G. R. Gleig*—A German Cavalryman in British Service Throughout the Napoleonic Wars.

RECOLLECTIONS OF THE PENINSULA by *Moyle Sherer*—An Officer of the 34th Regiment of Foot—'The Cumberland Gentlemen'—on Campaign Against Napoleon's French Army in Spain.

MARINE OF REVOLUTION & CONSULATE by *Moreau de Jonnès*—The Recollections of a French Soldier of the Revolutionary Wars 1791-1804.

GENTLEMEN IN RED by *John Dobbs & Robert Knowles*—Two Accounts of British Infantry Officers During the Peninsular War Recollections of an Old 52nd Man by John Dobbs An Officer of Fusiliers by Robert Knowles.

CORPORAL BROWN'S CAMPAIGNS IN THE LOW COUNTRIES by *Robert Brown*—Recollections of a Coldstream Guard in the Early Campaigns Against Revolutionary France 1793-1795.

THE 7TH (QUEENS OWN) HUSSARS: Volume 2—1793-1815 by *C. R. B. Barrett*—During the Campaigns in the Low Countries & the Peninsula and Waterloo Campaigns of the Napoleonic Wars. Volume 2: 1793-1815.

THE MARENGO CAMPAIGN 1800 by *Herbert H. Sargent*—The Victory that Completed the Austrian Defeat in Italy.

DONALDSON OF THE 94TH—SCOTS BRIGADE by *Joseph Donaldson*—The Recollections of a Soldier During the Peninsula & South of France Campaigns of the Napoleonic Wars.

A CONSCRIPT FOR EMPIRE by *Philippe as told to Johann Christian Maempel*—The Experiences of a Young German Conscript During the Napoleonic Wars.

JOURNAL OF THE CAMPAIGN OF 1815 by *Alexander Cavalié Mercer*—The Experiences of an Officer of the Royal Horse Artillery During the Waterloo Campaign.

NAPOLEON'S CAMPAIGNS IN POLAND 1806-7 by *Robert Wilson*—The campaign in Poland from the Russian side of the conflict.

AVAILABLE ONLINE AT **www.leonaur.com**
AND FROM ALL GOOD BOOK STORES

ALSO FROM LEONAUR
AVAILABLE IN SOFTCOVER OR HARDCOVER WITH DUST JACKET

OMPTEDA OF THE KING'S GERMAN LEGION by *Christian von Ompteda*—A Hanoverian Officer on Campaign Against Napoleon.

LIEUTENANT SIMMONS OF THE 95TH (RIFLES) by *George Simmons*—Recollections of the Peninsula, South of France & Waterloo Campaigns of the Napoleonic Wars.

A HORSEMAN FOR THE EMPEROR by *Jean Baptiste Gazzola*—A Cavalryman of Napoleon's Army on Campaign Throughout the Napoleonic Wars.

SERGEANT LAWRENCE by *William Lawrence*—With the 40th Regt. of Foot in South America, the Peninsular War & at Waterloo.

CAMPAIGNS WITH THE FIELD TRAIN by *Richard D. Henegan*—Experiences of a British Officer During the Peninsula and Waterloo Campaigns of the Napoleonic Wars.

CAVALRY SURGEON by *S. D. Broughton*—On Campaign Against Napoleon in the Peninsula & South of France During the Napoleonic Wars 1812-1814.

MEN OF THE RIFLES by *Thomas Knight, Henry Curling & Jonathan Leach*—The Reminiscences of Thomas Knight of the 95th (Rifles) by Thomas Knight, Henry Curling's Anecdotes by Henry Curling & The Field Services of the Rifle Brigade from its Formation to Waterloo by Jonathan Leach.

THE ULM CAMPAIGN 1805 by *F. N. Maude*—Napoleon and the Defeat of the Austrian Army During the 'War of the Third Coalition'.

SOLDIERING WITH THE 'DIVISION' by *Thomas Garrety*—The Military Experiences of an Infantryman of the 43rd Regiment During the Napoleonic Wars.

SERGEANT MORRIS OF THE 73RD FOOT by *Thomas Morris*—The Experiences of a British Infantryman During the Napoleonic Wars-Including Campaigns in Germany and at Waterloo.

A VOICE FROM WATERLOO by *Edward Cotton*—The Personal Experiences of a British Cavalryman Who Became a Battlefield Guide and Authority on the Campaign of 1815.

NAPOLEON AND HIS MARSHALS by *J. T. Headley*—The Men of the First Empire.

ALSO FROM LEONAUR
AVAILABLE IN SOFTCOVER OR HARDCOVER WITH DUST JACKET

COLBORNE: A SINGULAR TALENT FOR WAR by John Colborne—The Napoleonic Wars Career of One of Wellington's Most Highly Valued Officers in Egypt, Holland, Italy, the Peninsula and at Waterloo.

NAPOLEON'S RUSSIAN CAMPAIGN by Philippe Henri de Segur—The Invasion, Battles and Retreat by an Aide-de-Camp on the Emperor's Staff.

WITH THE LIGHT DIVISION by John H. Cooke—The Experiences of an Officer of the 43rd Light Infantry in the Peninsula and South of France During the Napoleonic Wars.

WELLINGTON AND THE PYRENEES CAMPAIGN VOLUME I: FROM VITORIA TO THE BIDASSOA by F. C. Beatson—The final phase of the campaign in the Iberian Peninsula.

WELLINGTON AND THE INVASION OF FRANCE VOLUME II: THE BIDASSOA TO THE BATTLE OF THE NIVELLE by F. C. Beatson—The final phase of the campaign in the Iberian Peninsula.

WELLINGTON AND THE FALL OF FRANCE VOLUME III: THE GAVES AND THE BATTLE OF ORTHEZ by F. C. Beatson—The final phase of the campaign in the Iberian Peninsula.

NAPOLEON'S IMPERIAL GUARD: FROM MARENGO TO WATERLOO by J. T. Headley—The story of Napoleon's Imperial Guard and the men who commanded them.

BATTLES & SIEGES OF THE PENINSULAR WAR by W. H. Fitchett—Corunna, Busaco, Albuera, Ciudad Rodrigo, Badajos, Salamanca, San Sebastian & Others.

SERGEANT GUILLEMARD: THE MAN WHO SHOT NELSON? by Robert Guillemard—A Soldier of the Infantry of the French Army of Napoleon on Campaign Throughout Europe.

WITH THE GUARDS ACROSS THE PYRENEES by Robert Batty—The Experiences of a British Officer of Wellington's Army During the Battles for the Fall of Napoleonic France, 1813.

A STAFF OFFICER IN THE PENINSULA by E. W. Buckham—An Officer of the British Staff Corps Cavalry During the Peninsula Campaign of the Napoleonic Wars.

THE LEIPZIG CAMPAIGN: 1813—NAPOLEON AND THE "BATTLE OF THE NATIONS" by F. N. Maude—Colonel Maude's analysis of Napoleon's campaign of 1813 around Leipzig.

AVAILABLE ONLINE AT **www.leonaur.com**
AND FROM ALL GOOD BOOK STORES

ALSO FROM LEONAUR
AVAILABLE IN SOFTCOVER OR HARDCOVER WITH DUST JACKET

BUGEAUD: A PACK WITH A BATON by *Thomas Robert Bugeaud*—The Early Campaigns of a Soldier of Napoleon's Army Who Would Become a Marshal of France.

WATERLOO RECOLLECTIONS by *Frederick Llewellyn*—Rare First Hand Accounts, Letters, Reports and Retellings from the Campaign of 1815.

SERGEANT NICOL by *Daniel Nicol*—The Experiences of a Gordon Highlander During the Napoleonic Wars in Egypt, the Peninsula and France.

THE JENA CAMPAIGN: 1806 by *F. N. Maude*—The Twin Battles of Jena & Auerstadt Between Napoleon's French and the Prussian Army.

PRIVATE O'NEIL by *Charles O'Neil*—The recollections of an Irish Rogue of H. M. 28th Regt.—The Slashers—during the Peninsula & Waterloo campaigns of the Napoleonic war.

ROYAL HIGHLANDER by *James Anton*—A soldier of H.M 42nd (Royal) Highlanders during the Peninsular, South of France & Waterloo Campaigns of the Napoleonic Wars.

CAPTAIN BLAZE by *Elzéar Blaze*—Life in Napoleons Army.

LEJEUNE VOLUME 1 by *Louis-François Lejeune*—The Napoleonic Wars through the Experiences of an Officer on Berthier's Staff.

LEJEUNE VOLUME 2 by *Louis-François Lejeune*—The Napoleonic Wars through the Experiences of an Officer on Berthier's Staff.

CAPTAIN COIGNET by *Jean-Roch Coignet*—A Soldier of Napoleon's Imperial Guard from the Italian Campaign to Russia and Waterloo.

FUSILIER COOPER by *John S. Cooper*—Experiences in the 7th (Royal) Fusiliers During the Peninsular Campaign of the Napoleonic Wars and the American Campaign to New Orleans.

FIGHTING NAPOLEON'S EMPIRE by *Joseph Anderson*—The Campaigns of a British Infantryman in Italy, Egypt, the Peninsular & the West Indies During the Napoleonic Wars.

CHASSEUR BARRES by *Jean-Baptiste Barres*—The experiences of a French Infantryman of the Imperial Guard at Austerlitz, Jena, Eylau, Friedland, in the Peninsular, Lutzen, Bautzen, Zinnwald and Hanau during the Napoleonic Wars.

AVAILABLE ONLINE AT **www.leonaur.com**
AND FROM ALL GOOD BOOK STORES

ALSO FROM LEONAUR
AVAILABLE IN SOFTCOVER OR HARDCOVER WITH DUST JACKET

CAPTAIN COIGNET by *Jean-Roch Coignet*—A Soldier of Napoleon's Imperial Guard from the Italian Campaign to Russia and Waterloo.

HUSSAR ROCCA by *Albert Jean Michel de Rocca*—A French cavalry officer's experiences of the Napoleonic Wars and his views on the Peninsular Campaigns against the Spanish, British And Guerilla Armies.

MARINES TO 95TH (RIFLES) by *Thomas Fernyhough*—The military experiences of Robert Fernyhough during the Napoleonic Wars.

LIGHT BOB by *Robert Blakeney*—The experiences of a young officer in H.M 28th & 36th regiments of the British Infantry during the Peninsular Campaign of the Napoleonic Wars 1804 - 1814.

WITH WELLINGTON'S LIGHT CAVALRY by *William Tomkinson*—The Experiences of an officer of the 16th Light Dragoons in the Peninsular and Waterloo campaigns of the Napoleonic Wars.

SERGEANT BOURGOGNE by *Adrien Bourgogne*—With Napoleon's Imperial Guard in the Russian Campaign and on the Retreat from Moscow 1812 - 13.

SURTEES OF THE 95TH (RIFLES) by *William Surtees*—A Soldier of the 95th (Rifles) in the Peninsular campaign of the Napoleonic Wars.

SWORDS OF HONOUR by *Henry Newbolt & Stanley L. Wood*—The Careers of Six Outstanding Officers from the Napoleonic Wars, the Wars for India and the American Civil War.

ENSIGN BELL IN THE PENINSULAR WAR by *George Bell*—The Experiences of a young British Soldier of the 34th Regiment 'The Cumberland Gentlemen' in the Napoleonic wars.

HUSSAR IN WINTER by *Alexander Gordon*—A British Cavalry Officer during the retreat to Corunna in the Peninsular campaign of the Napoleonic Wars.

THE COMPLEAT RIFLEMAN HARRIS by *Benjamin Harris as told to and transcribed by Captain Henry Curling, 52nd Regt. of Foot*—The adventures of a soldier of the 95th (Rifles) during the Peninsular Campaign of the Napoleonic Wars.

THE ADVENTURES OF A LIGHT DRAGOON by *George Farmer & G.R. Gleig*—A cavalryman during the Peninsular & Waterloo Campaigns, in captivity & at the siege of Bhurtpore, India.

AVAILABLE ONLINE AT **www.leonaur.com**
AND FROM ALL GOOD BOOK STORES

ALSO FROM LEONAUR
AVAILABLE IN SOFTCOVER OR HARDCOVER WITH DUST JACKET

THE LIFE OF THE REAL BRIGADIER GERARD VOLUME 1—THE YOUNG HUSSAR 1782-1807 by *Jean-Baptiste De Marbot*—A French Cavalryman Of the Napoleonic Wars at Marengo, Austerlitz, Jena, Eylau & Friedland.

THE LIFE OF THE REAL BRIGADIER GERARD VOLUME 2—IMPERIAL AIDE-DE-CAMP 1807-1811 by *Jean-Baptiste De Marbot*—A French Cavalryman of the Napoleonic Wars at Saragossa, Landshut, Eckmuhl, Ratisbon, Aspern-Essling, Wagram, Busaco & Torres Vedras.

THE LIFE OF THE REAL BRIGADIER GERARD VOLUME 3—COLONEL OF CHASSEURS 1811-1815 by *Jean-Baptiste De Marbot*—A French Cavalryman in the retreat from Moscow, Lutzen, Bautzen, Katzbach, Leipzig, Hanau & Waterloo.

THE INDIAN WAR OF 1864 by *Eugene Ware*—The Experiences of a Young Officer of the 7th Iowa Cavalry on the Western Frontier During the Civil War.

THE MARCH OF DESTINY by *Charles E. Young & V. Devinny*—Dangers of the Trail in 1865 by Charles E. Young & The Story of a Pioneer by V. Devinny, two Accounts of Early Emigrants to Colorado.

CROSSING THE PLAINS by *William Audley Maxwell*—A First Hand Narrative of the Early Pioneer Trail to California in 1857.

CHIEF OF SCOUTS by *William F. Drannan*—A Pilot to Emigrant and Government Trains, Across the Plains of the Western Frontier.

THIRTY-ONE YEARS ON THE PLAINS AND IN THE MOUNTAINS by *William F. Drannan*—William Drannan was born to be a pioneer, hunter, trapper and wagon train guide during the momentous days of the Great American West.

THE INDIAN WARS VOLUNTEER by *William Thompson*—Recollections of the Conflict Against the Snakes, Shoshone, Bannocks, Modocs and Other Native Tribes of the American North West.

THE 4TH TENNESSEE CAVALRY by *George B. Guild*—The Services of Smith's Regiment of Confederate Cavalry by One of its Officers.

COLONEL WORTHINGTON'S SHILOH by *T. Worthington*—The Tennessee Campaign, 1862, by an Officer of the Ohio Volunteers.

FOUR YEARS IN THE SADDLE by *W. L. Curry*—The History of the First Regiment Ohio Volunteer Cavalry in the American Civil War.

AVAILABLE ONLINE AT **www.leonaur.com**
AND FROM ALL GOOD BOOK STORES

ALSO FROM LEONAUR
AVAILABLE IN SOFTCOVER OR HARDCOVER WITH DUST JACKET

LIFE IN THE ARMY OF NORTHERN VIRGINIA *by Carlton McCarthy*—The Observations of a Confederate Artilleryman of Cutshaw's Battalion During the American Civil War 1861-1865.

HISTORY OF THE CAVALRY OF THE ARMY OF THE POTOMAC *by Charles D. Rhodes*—Including Pope's Army of Virginia and the Cavalry Operations in West Virginia During the American Civil War.

CAMP-FIRE AND COTTON-FIELD *by Thomas W. Knox*—A New York Herald Correspondent's View of the American Civil War.

SERGEANT STILLWELL *by Leander Stillwell*—The Experiences of a Union Army Soldier of the 61st Illinois Infantry During the American Civil War.

STONEWALL'S CANNONEER *by Edward A. Moore*—Experiences with the Rockbridge Artillery, Confederate Army of Northern Virginia, During the American Civil War.

THE SIXTH CORPS *by George Stevens*—The Army of the Potomac, Union Army, During the American Civil War.

THE RAILROAD RAIDERS *by William Pittenger*—An Ohio Volunteers Recollections of the Andrews Raid to Disrupt the Confederate Railroad in Georgia During the American Civil War.

CITIZEN SOLDIER *by John Beatty*—An Account of the American Civil War by a Union Infantry Officer of Ohio Volunteers Who Became a Brigadier General.

COX: PERSONAL RECOLLECTIONS OF THE CIVIL WAR--VOLUME 1 *by Jacob Dolson Cox*—West Virginia, Kanawha Valley, Gauley Bridge, Cotton Mountain, South Mountain, Antietam, the Morgan Raid & the East Tennessee Campaign.

COX: PERSONAL RECOLLECTIONS OF THE CIVIL WAR--VOLUME 2 *by Jacob Dolson Cox*—Siege of Knoxville, East Tennessee, Atlanta Campaign, the Nashville Campaign & the North Carolina Campaign.

KERSHAW'S BRIGADE VOLUME 1 *by D. Augustus Dickert*—Manassas, Seven Pines, Sharpsburg (Antietam), Fredricksburg, Chancellorsville, Gettysburg, Chickamauga, Chattanooga, Fort Sanders & Bean Station.

KERSHAW'S BRIGADE VOLUME 2 *by D. Augustus Dickert*—At the wilderness, Cold Harbour, Petersburg, The Shenandoah Valley and Cedar Creek..

AVAILABLE ONLINE AT www.leonaur.com
AND FROM ALL GOOD BOOK STORES

ALSO FROM LEONAUR
AVAILABLE IN SOFTCOVER OR HARDCOVER WITH DUST JACKET

THE RELUCTANT REBEL by *William G. Stevenson*—A young Kentuckian's experiences in the Confederate Infantry & Cavalry during the American Civil War..

BOOTS AND SADDLES by *Elizabeth B. Custer*—The experiences of General Custer's Wife on the Western Plains.

FANNIE BEERS' CIVIL WAR by *Fannie A. Beers*—A Confederate Lady's Experiences of Nursing During the Campaigns & Battles of the American Civil War.

LADY SALE'S AFGHANISTAN by *Florentia Sale*—An Indomitable Victorian Lady's Account of the Retreat from Kabul During the First Afghan War.

THE TWO WARS OF MRS DUBERLY by *Frances Isabella Duberly*—An Intrepid Victorian Lady's Experience of the Crimea and Indian Mutiny.

THE REBELLIOUS DUCHESS by *Paul F. S. Dermoncourt*—The Adventures of the Duchess of Berri and Her Attempt to Overthrow French Monarchy.

LADIES OF WATERLOO by *Charlotte A. Eaton, Magdalene de Lancey & Juana Smith*—The Experiences of Three Women During the Campaign of 1815: Waterloo Days by Charlotte A. Eaton, A Week at Waterloo by Magdalene de Lancey & Juana's Story by Juana Smith.

TWO YEARS BEFORE THE MAST by *Richard Henry Dana. Jr.*—The account of one young man's experiences serving on board a sailing brig—the Penelope—bound for California, between the years 1834-36.

A SAILOR OF KING GEORGE by *Frederick Hoffman*—From Midshipman to Captain—Recollections of War at Sea in the Napoleonic Age 1793-1815.

LORDS OF THE SEA by *A. T. Mahan*—Great Captains of the Royal Navy During the Age of Sail.

COGGESHALL'S VOYAGES: VOLUME 1 by *George Coggeshall*—The Recollections of an American Schooner Captain.

COGGESHALL'S VOYAGES: VOLUME 2 by *George Coggeshall*—The Recollections of an American Schooner Captain.

TWILIGHT OF EMPIRE by *Sir Thomas Ussher & Sir George Cockburn*—Two accounts of Napoleon's Journeys in Exile to Elba and St. Helena: Narrative of Events by Sir Thomas Ussher & Napoleon's Last Voyage: Extract of a diary by Sir George Cockburn.

AVAILABLE ONLINE AT www.leonaur.com
AND FROM ALL GOOD BOOK STORES

ALSO FROM LEONAUR
AVAILABLE IN SOFTCOVER OR HARDCOVER WITH DUST JACKET

ESCAPE FROM THE FRENCH by *Edward Boys*—A Young Royal Navy Midshipman's Adventures During the Napoleonic War.

THE VOYAGE OF H.M.S. PANDORA by *Edward Edwards R. N. & George Hamilton, edited by Basil Thomson*—In Pursuit of the Mutineers of the Bounty in the South Seas—1790-1791.

MEDUSA by *J. B. Henry Savigny and Alexander Correard and Charlotte-Adélaïde Dard*—Narrative of a Voyage to Senegal in 1816 & The Sufferings of the Picard Family After the Shipwreck of the Medusa.

THE SEA WAR OF 1812 VOLUME 1 by *A. T. Mahan*—A History of the Maritime Conflict.

THE SEA WAR OF 1812 VOLUME 2 by *A. T. Mahan*—A History of the Maritime Conflict.

WETHERELL OF H. M. S. HUSSAR by *John Wetherell*—The Recollections of an Ordinary Seaman of the Royal Navy During the Napoleonic Wars.

THE NAVAL BRIGADE IN NATAL by *C. R. N. Burne*—With the Guns of H. M. S. Terrible & H. M. S. Tartar during the Boer War 1899-1900.

THE VOYAGE OF H. M. S. BOUNTY by *William Bligh*—The True Story of an 18th Century Voyage of Exploration and Mutiny.

SHIPWRECK! by *William Gilly*—The Royal Navy's Disasters at Sea 1793-1849.

KING'S CUTTERS AND SMUGGLERS: 1700-1855 by *E. Keble Chatterton*—A unique period of maritime history-from the beginning of the eighteenth to the middle of the nineteenth century when British seamen risked all to smuggle valuable goods from wool to tea and spirits from and to the Continent.

CONFEDERATE BLOCKADE RUNNER by *John Wilkinson*—The Personal Recollections of an Officer of the Confederate Navy.

NAVAL BATTLES OF THE NAPOLEONIC WARS by *W. H. Fitchett*—Cape St. Vincent, the Nile, Cadiz, Copenhagen, Trafalgar & Others.

PRISONERS OF THE RED DESERT by *R. S. Gwatkin-Williams*—The Adventures of the Crew of the Tara During the First World War.

U-BOAT WAR 1914-1918 by *James B. Connolly/Karl von Schenk*—Two Contrasting Accounts from Both Sides of the Conflict at Sea During the Great War.

AVAILABLE ONLINE AT **www.leonaur.com**
AND FROM ALL GOOD BOOK STORES

ALSO FROM LEONAUR
AVAILABLE IN SOFTCOVER OR HARDCOVER WITH DUST JACKET

IRON TIMES WITH THE GUARDS *by An O. E. (G. P. A. Fildes)*—The Experiences of an Officer of the Coldstream Guards on the Western Front During the First World War.

THE GREAT WAR IN THE MIDDLE EAST: 1 *by W. T. Massey*—The Desert Campaigns & How Jerusalem Was Won---two classic accounts in one volume.

THE GREAT WAR IN THE MIDDLE EAST: 2 *by W. T. Massey*—Allenby's Final Triumph.

SMITH-DORRIEN *by Horace Smith-Dorrien*—Isandlwhana to the Great War.

1914 *by Sir John French*—The Early Campaigns of the Great War by the British Commander.

GRENADIER *by E. R. M. Fryer*—The Recollections of an Officer of the Grenadier Guards throughout the Great War on the Western Front.

BATTLE, CAPTURE & ESCAPE *by George Pearson*—The Experiences of a Canadian Light Infantryman During the Great War.

DIGGERS AT WAR *by R. Hugh Knyvett & G. P. Cuttriss*—"Over There" With the Australians by R. Hugh Knyvett and Over the Top With the Third Australian Division by G. P. Cuttriss. Accounts of Australians During the Great War in the Middle East, at Gallipoli and on the Western Front.

HEAVY FIGHTING BEFORE US *by George Brenton Laurie*—The Letters of an Officer of the Royal Irish Rifles on the Western Front During the Great War.

THE CAMELIERS *by Oliver Hogue*—A Classic Account of the Australians of the Imperial Camel Corps During the First World War in the Middle East.

RED DUST *by Donald Black*—A Classic Account of Australian Light Horsemen in Palestine During the First World War.

THE LEAN, BROWN MEN *by Angus Buchanan*—Experiences in East Africa During the Great War with the 25th Royal Fusiliers—the Legion of Frontiersmen.

THE NIGERIAN REGIMENT IN EAST AFRICA *by W. D. Downes*—On Campaign During the Great War 1916-1918.

THE 'DIE-HARDS' IN SIBERIA *by John Ward*—With the Middlesex Regiment Against the Bolsheviks 1918-19.

AVAILABLE ONLINE AT www.leonaur.com
AND FROM ALL GOOD BOOK STORES

ALSO FROM LEONAUR
AVAILABLE IN SOFTCOVER OR HARDCOVER WITH DUST JACKET

FARAWAY CAMPAIGN by F. James—Experiences of an Indian Army Cavalry Officer in Persia & Russia During the Great War.

REVOLT IN THE DESERT by T. E. Lawrence—An account of the experiences of one remarkable British officer's war from his own perspective.

MACHINE-GUN SQUADRON by A. M. G.—The 20th Machine Gunners from British Yeomanry Regiments in the Middle East Campaign of the First World War.

A GUNNER'S CRUSADE by Antony Bluett—The Campaign in the Desert, Palestine & Syria as Experienced by the Honourable Artillery Company During the Great War.

DESPATCH RIDER by W. H. L. Watson—The Experiences of a British Army Motorcycle Despatch Rider During the Opening Battles of the Great War in Europe.

TIGERS ALONG THE TIGRIS by E. J. Thompson—The Leicestershire Regiment in Mesopotamia During the First World War.

HEARTS & DRAGONS by Charles R. M. F. Crutwell—The 4th Royal Berkshire Regiment in France and Italy During the Great War, 1914-1918.

INFANTRY BRIGADE: 1914 by John Ward—The Diary of a Commander of the 15th Infantry Brigade, 5th Division, British Army, During the Retreat from Mons.

DOING OUR 'BIT' by Ian Hay—Two Classic Accounts of the Men of Kitchener's 'New Army' During the Great War including *The First 100,000* & *All In It*.

AN EYE IN THE STORM by Arthur Ruhl—An American War Correspondent's Experiences of the First World War from the Western Front to Gallipoli-and Beyond.

STAND & FALL by Joe Cassells—With the Middlesex Regiment Against the Bolsheviks 1918-19.

RIFLEMAN MACGILL'S WAR by Patrick MacGill—A Soldier of the London Irish During the Great War in Europe including *The Amateur Army*, *The Red Horizon* & *The Great Push*.

WITH THE GUNS by C. A. Rose & Hugh Dalton—Two First Hand Accounts of British Gunners at War in Europe During World War 1- Three Years in France with the Guns and With the British Guns in Italy.

THE BUSH WAR DOCTOR by Robert V. Dolbey—The Experiences of a British Army Doctor During the East African Campaign of the First World War.

AVAILABLE ONLINE AT **www.leonaur.com**
AND FROM ALL GOOD BOOK STORES

ALSO FROM LEONAUR
AVAILABLE IN SOFTCOVER OR HARDCOVER WITH DUST JACKET

THE 9TH—THE KING'S (LIVERPOOL REGIMENT) IN THE GREAT WAR 1914 - 1918 by *Enos H. G. Roberts*—Mersey to mud—war and Liverpool men.

THE GAMBARDIER by *Mark Severn*—The experiences of a battery of Heavy artillery on the Western Front during the First World War.

FROM MESSINES TO THIRD YPRES by *Thomas Floyd*—A personal account of the First World War on the Western front by a 2/5th Lancashire Fusilier.

THE IRISH GUARDS IN THE GREAT WAR - VOLUME 1 by *Rudyard Kipling*—Edited and Compiled from Their Diaries and Papers—The First Battalion.

THE IRISH GUARDS IN THE GREAT WAR - VOLUME 1 by *Rudyard Kipling*—Edited and Compiled from Their Diaries and Papers—The Second Battalion.

ARMOURED CARS IN EDEN by *K. Roosevelt*—An American President's son serving in Rolls Royce armoured cars with the British in Mesopotamia & with the American Artillery in France during the First World War.

CHASSEUR OF 1914 by *Marcel Dupont*—Experiences of the twilight of the French Light Cavalry by a young officer during the early battles of the great war in Europe.

TROOP HORSE & TRENCH by *R.A. Lloyd*—The experiences of a British Lifeguardsman of the household cavalry fighting on the western front during the First World War 1914-18.

THE EAST AFRICAN MOUNTED RIFLES by *C.J. Wilson*—Experiences of the campaign in the East African bush during the First World War.

THE LONG PATROL by *George Berrie*—A Novel of Light Horsemen from Gallipoli to the Palestine campaign of the First World War.

THE FIGHTING CAMELIERS by *Frank Reid*—The exploits of the Imperial Camel Corps in the desert and Palestine campaigns of the First World War.

STEEL CHARIOTS IN THE DESERT by *S. C. Rolls*—The first world war experiences of a Rolls Royce armoured car driver with the Duke of Westminster in Libya and in Arabia with T.E. Lawrence.

WITH THE IMPERIAL CAMEL CORPS IN THE GREAT WAR by *Geoffrey Inchbald*—The story of a serving officer with the British 2nd battalion against the Senussi and during the Palestine campaign.

AVAILABLE ONLINE AT **www.leonaur.com**
AND FROM ALL GOOD BOOK STORES

www.ingramcontent.com/pod-product-compliance
Lightning Source LLC
Chambersburg PA
CBHW030216170426
43201CB00006B/110